THE TRANSNATIONAL IN ENGLISH LITERATURE

The Transnational in English Literature surveys English literary history through its transnational engagements and argues that every period of English literature can be examined through its global relations. English identity and nationhood is therefore defined through its negotiation with other regions and cultures.

In the first book to look at the entirety of English literature through a transnational lens, Pramod Nayar:

- Maps the discourses that constitute the global in every age, from the Early Modern to the twentieth century.
- Offers readings of representative texts in poetry, fiction, essay and drama, covering a variety of genres such as Early Modern tragedy, the adventure novel, the narrative poem, Gothic and utopian fiction.
- Examines major authors including Shakespeare, Defoe, Behn, Swift, Coleridge, Wordsworth, Austen, Mary Shelley, the Brontës, Doyle, Ballantyne, Orwell, Conrad, Kipling and Forster.
- Looks at themes such as travel and discovery, exoticism, mercantilism, commodities, the civilizational mission and the multiculturalization of England.

Useful for students and academics alike, this book offers a comprehensive survey of the English canon questioning and analyzing the transnational and global engagements of English literature.

Pramod K. Nayar teaches English at the University of Hyderabad, India.

THE TRANSNATIONAL IN ENGLISH LITERATURE

Shakespeare to the Modern

Pramod K. Nayar

LONDON AND NEW YORK

First published 2015
by Routledge
2 Park Square, Milton Park, Abingdon, Oxon OX14 4RN

and by Routledge
711 Third Avenue, New York, NY 10017

Routledge is an imprint of the Taylor & Francis Group, an informa business

© 2015 Pramod K. Nayar

The right of Pramod K. Nayar to be identified as author of this work has been asserted by him in accordance with sections 77 and 78 of the Copyright, Designs and Patents Act 1988.

All rights reserved. No part of this book may be reprinted or reproduced or utilised in any form or by any electronic, mechanical, or other means, now known or hereafter invented, including photocopying and recording, or in any information storage or retrieval system, without permission in writing from the publishers.

Trademark notice: Product or corporate names may be trademarks or registered trademarks, and are used only for identification and explanation without intent to infringe.

British Library Cataloguing-in-Publication Data
A catalogue record for this book is available from the British Library

Library of Congress Cataloging in Publication Data
Nayar, Pramod K.
The transnational in English literature : Shakespeare to the modern / Pramod K. Nayar.
pages cm
Includes bibliographical references and index.
1. English literature–History and criticism. 2. Transnationalism in literature.
3. National characteristics, English, in literature. I. Title.
PR125.N39 2015
820.9–dc23
2015001816

ISBN: 978-0-415-84001-9 (hbk)
ISBN: 978-0-415-84002-6 (pbk)
ISBN: 978-1-315-74921-1 (ebk)

Typeset in Bembo
by Taylor & Francis Books

CONTENTS

Preface	vii
Acknowledgements	ix

1 Introduction: globality and Englishness · 1

2 Worlds and voyages: English itinerancy and the spaces of
Otherness · 10
England travels 13
The ethnography of the Other 39
Triumphalist geography 62

3 Difference and desire: the exoticized Other · 74
The savage exotic 78
The Noble Savage 87
The erotic exotic 91

4 Consume and commodify: the objectified Other · 130
The vocabulary of things 132
The rhetoric of objectification 154

5 Disease and degeneration: the pathologized Other · 175
Foreign matter/s 180
Foreign bodies 188
Cultural invasion 205

vi Contents

Transnational networks of vice *218*
The 'Parliament of Monsters' and the degeneration of
London/England *225*

6 Civilize and collapse: improveable Others, disintegrating English   238
The global project of moral imperialism *241*
Amelioration and improvement *246*
Discrepant geographies *272*

Bibliography   293
Index   313

PREFACE

England's literary history is a legacy of its transnational linkages, as this book sets out to demonstrate. It argues that, right from the 1550s, the racial-cultural Other was not simply 'out there': it was very much constitutive of English domestic, social and cultural imaginary, life and discourse. Dan Vitkus, Lisa Jardine, Jonathan Gil Harris and others have demonstrated the transnational connections of Early Modern England. Works by Catherine Hall and Antoinette Burton have underscored the centrality of the Empire and its peripheries to the making of imperial Victorian England. In similar fashion, this book makes a case for seeing the peripheries of the known world central to England's cultural landscape from even *before* the age of Empire. English literature's discursive field embodies what I am terming a 'globality', the construction in fictional texts of the space of inter-cultural, interracial encounter of England and Englishness made possible through the journey, by men and women, into various diverse and distant places on earth and those places arriving in some form in England's homes, streets and intellectual spaces.

The examples are indicative and illustrative and not exhaustive. They are necessarily selective but wide-ranging enough to show how discourses of Otherness and Othering operate across centuries. The book makes use of select texts for this purpose, and is more interested in pointing out continuities in literary fictions of Otherness than in tracing each fiction's historical location and specificity. It does not propose a 'one age–one discourse' kind of scheme, opting instead for clusters or constellations of dominant discourses across the ages. As such, the book does *not* locate every age or period's specific historical contexts for forms, themes and tropes. It does not seek to contextualize every trope, theme and motif. Thus, the different traditions of the Gothic or variants in Early Modern/Elizabethan drama are ignored, along with their historical formations, in favour of *continuities* of themes and tropes. These continuities, the book demonstrates, are England's

viii Preface

concerns with and consumption of racial-cultural Others in various forms, as people, ideas, spaces and commodities.

PKN

Hyderabad

December 2014

Note

All references from Shakespeare's plays are taken from *The Norton Shakespeare*, edited by S. Greenblatt, J.E. Howard and K.E. Maus. New York and London: W.W. Norton, 2008.

References from Gutenberg and other online editions of texts are unpaginated. All online sources were last accessed in July 2014.

ACKNOWLEDGEMENTS

To Polly Dodson at Routledge for the enthusiasm with which she greeted the early, admittedly sketchy, ideas for this book – a special thank you right away.

This book took a while to write, unusually. And a part of the pleasure of this sometimes interminable-looking project was a revisit to old haunts: it caused me to return to texts I had forgotten – *Captain Singleton*, *The Masque of Blackness*, *The Giaour*, *Melmoth the Wanderer*, among others. In the process I also discovered another pleasure derived from the reading I was doing: discussing supposedly forgotten texts with people like Narayana Chandran and Anna Kurian.

I would like to acknowledge the sustained help from Saradindu Bhattacharya for sourcing essays, and to V. Premlata for sending me materials she thought I would find useful for the project.

Nandana Dutta loaned me her copy of the Norton *Utopia*, and through the project encouraged ('I am *really* looking forward to this book') me with her special brand of friendship and the SMSs about some literary text, genre or theme.

To K. Narayana Chandran (KNC) for his spectacular memory of both canonical and obscure texts and incisive insights into them, from which I continue to learn, I owe a debt that these lines cannot even begin to capture. The passing textual references and obtuse connections that he sprinkles conversations with have made me aware that scholarship amplified with generosity is as rare as it is valuable.

To my parents, parents-in-law, Nandini and Pranav for their prayers, support and miraculous good cheer under the usual pressures of having me around, working away: the usual unquantifiable gratitude.

To my friends who make sure the conversations are *not* (always) about books, many thanks: Ibrahim, Ajeet, Molly, Saraswathy Rajagopalan, Premlata, Debjani Majumdar, Rita Kothari, Josy Joseph and Panikkar.

To the inimitable Neelu (whose store of jokes forwarded on WhatsApp would require a few gigabytes of space) with her solicitous enquiry daily and the incredible cheeriness (dating back to the MA days): thank you, much.

x Acknowledgements

To Soma Ghosh, for her smiling courage these last two years, and her friendship, much admiration and appreciation.

The chapter on material culture appeared first in abbreviated form in the *Indian Journal of English Studies*. Parts of this chapter were also delivered as a talk, 'The Transnational Turn in English Literature', at the Dept. of Liberal Arts, Indian Institute of Technology, Hyderabad, October 2013.

Sections of Chapters 2, 3 and 4 were delivered as the Inaugural Professorial Lecture at the University of Hyderabad, 3 March 2014.

The section on Alice Perrin's empire fiction in Chapter 2 first appeared in *Brno Studies in English* 38.1 (2012): 123–38.

Parts of the arguments on Dacre's *Zofloya* appeared in the essay, 'The Interracial Sublime: Gender and Race in Charlotte Dacre's *Zofloya*', *Géneros* 2.3 (2013): 233–54.

I should acknowledge my debt to the early builders of the English collections of the Indira Gandhi Memorial Library, The University of Hyderabad, Professor S. Nagarajan and Professor S. Vishwanathan, for the foresight with which they acquired the standard editions of the texts from the English canon, whether it was the Oxford Wordsworth, the Yale Ben Jonson or the Spedding edition of Francis Bacon. This kind of book would not have been possible without such a collection.

Anna Kurian, in the midst of her own writing, found the time (no surprises there, though, sterling First Reader and loyal friend) to read and comment on chapters. For her fund of Shakespeareana (Shakespeare*anna*?) – 'there is *this* theme in Shakespeare *too*' – and the Early Modern, I should add a separate 'thank you'. Like its predecessors, this book could not have happened without her.

At Routledge I would also like to acknowledge Ruth Moody.

1

INTRODUCTION

Globality and Englishness

In Edmund Spenser's *Faerie Queene* (1590, 1596), towards the end of Book I, Spenser predicts a battle between the Queen of England and a Saracen king:

> Faire Goddesse lay that furious fit aside,
> Till I of warres and bloudy Mars do sing,
> And Briton fields with Sarazin bloud bedyde,
> Twixt that great faery Queene and Paynim king.
>
> (1. 11.7. Spenser 1984: 144)

The fields of Britain, predicts Spenser, would be dyed with Saracen blood. Spenser's gory image actually serves the useful purpose, as far as this book is concerned, of demonstrating how Englishness, embodied in the very materiality of English soil, is imbued ('dyed', in Spenser's term) through and through with a foreign 'contaminant', addition and excess. Englishness seems to mark itself through, first, a conflict with a racial-cultural Other and, second, through its ability to absorb this Other. English identity, it would appear from Spenser's formulation, right from the Early Modern and Elizabethan age, characterized as the age of the first wave of globalization, was always already imbricated with the racial-cultural Other as a visible or invisible but always palpable presence. As such, the image of English fields soaked with the blood of the racial-cultural Other seems a gross but appropriately 'incorporative' or assimilative metaphor with which to start thinking of the interracial, multicultural and cosmopolitan transactions and exchanges that enabled the fashioning of English identity across ages. Later Byron would be full of admiration for a cosmopolitan Englishman/European in *Don Juan* (1819):

> The man who has stood on the Acropolis,
> And look'd down over Attica; or he

2 Introduction

> Who has sail'd where picturesque Constantinople is,
> Or seen Timbuctoo, or hath taken tea
> In small-eyed China's crockery-ware metropolis,
> Or sat amidst the bricks of Nineveh.
>
> (Byron 1975: 789)

The present work is informed by the assumption that the exchange, movement, assimilation and appropriation of goods, ideas, people, money across vast distances, dating back to the Early Modern world and continuing through many pathways to date, has influenced the cultural identities of European nations, and more specifically for purposes of this book, England. A related assumption is that Englishness is not a prior condition, but something that is lived and experienced across multiple sites – symbolic, affective and material – and one such site of this *performance* of Englishness is its literary text.

Recent studies, inaugurated by Abu-Lughod (1989), among others, push the 'era' and 'origin' of globalization further back in time, and enable us to see how cultural and national identities were by no means self-contained, coherent and autochthonous. In fact cultural identities were forged through constant, often frictional, encounters with commodities, people and products originating well outside the geopolitical borders. England, like much of Europe, was being continually transformed through these encounters with spice, tea, chintz, chinaware, arithmetic, jugglers, rhinoceros, women, scriptural texts, literary works, opium, elephants, tobacco, among others, from all over the world – America and the 'New World', Africa and Asia – from the sixteenth century. If Dennis Flynn and Arturo Giraldez (cited in McCants 2007: 436) date globalization to 1571 – when direct and permanent linkages were set up between the Americas and East Asia via Manila – others argue that forces of globalization also came out of the Middle East (McCants 2007: 437) in the Early Modern period. This book examines a particular site – English literary texts – where the impact of these cultural forces and influences might be made visible.

It was not Romanticism alone that was, in Saree Makdisi's phrase, 'worldly, but also global' (1998: xii), but practically all of England's literary movements and moments. The book makes a case for treating England's literary history, from the Renaissance and Early Modern period to the modern, as a *history of its transnational engagements*. While I am perhaps using the term 'transnational' anachronistically to work with periods when the nation-state as we now know it didn't exist, it serves the useful purpose of focusing on connections and interactions rather than boundedness and containment. The 'transnational' therefore is a way to think about England's varied connections through the 400 years starting with the early voyages in quest of trade routes and colonies to the twentieth century when its Empire began to break up. This book suggests that in every period of English literature we can locate major movements, authors and texts who/that define English identity and nationhood via a dialectic, a negotiation with Arab, Indian, Chinese and other Asian regions and cultures. Literature is a site where the engagement with difference marks a discourse of Englishness within a discourse of 'globality'.

I use 'globality' in opposition to the 'tropicality' that Nancy Stepan (2001) and David Arnold (2005b) discern in nineteenth-century English discourses about African and Asian regions. It also resonates with Mary Louise Pratt's influential argument about a Eurocentric 'planetary consciousness' that she traces to eighteenth-century natural history (2003). The construction of globality is an ideological move that enables the textual colonization of the distant parts of the world to be produced under the sign of the literary. These texts effect an act of discursive globalization and colonization. The literary is the domain within which science, navigation, trade, conquest, profit, humanitarianism and development might be subsumed. 'Globality' is the discursive construction in fictional texts of *a space of intercultural, interracial encounter of England and Englishness made possible through the Englishman's journey into various diverse and distant places on earth and those places arriving in some form in England's homes, streets and intellectual spaces*. The Englishman's idea of the globe, or the world, was a particular kind of space represented through a repertoire of images that is immediately identifiable in its difference from England, and is also a space of the Englishman's *engagement* with this difference. This cultural space of difference offers a vision of intercultural encounters and the understanding of difference and Otherness in ways that are appealing and accessible.

The 'world' therefore is more than just a geographical concept. It signifies a space of irreducible Otherness of many kinds, but an Otherness with which English identity engages. 'World' here is not to be taken as the entire entity of the earth, but as a set of places far away from 'home'.[1] Hence this book's abiding concern is with spaces in English writings: spaces of Africa, Asia, the poles, Australia and even Europe. Such an idea of globality draws, obviously, from material practices of globalization. Globalization has been underway in the form of economic and cultural networks at least since the fifteenth century according to numerous commentators (Abu-Lughod 1989, Nussbaum 2003). The European Renaissance, for instance, was definitively a product of global exchanges and interactions (Jardine 1996). Every age of course had its specific modes of exchanges and interactions. But what has emerged in critical studies of globalization since the 1990s is the decisive interpretation of European cultures and imaginations as always having grappled with the global. This process of imagining the globe is what I am calling here globality, or the discursive construction of the globe. Literature is one of the cultural practices in which this construction has been achieved.

Globality, manifest as the theme of transnational Otherness, this book proposes, is itself a national project: of English identity-building. *The idea of the English nation is implicitly, but often explicitly, the discourse of the racial-cultural Other*. The loci of English identity, therefore, lie not in England but are constructed across *multiple* sites and spaces. The group of islands might offer a geographical specificity to this construction. However, as will be seen, it is this island's engagements with diverse and dispersed sites over the globe that produces its identity as 'England' and as 'Great Britain'. 'England' or 'Great Britain' is the conceptualization of the islands *in* the world, and Englishness is the Englishness *within* the world made of many races and cultures.

4 Introduction

Every age in England's literary history, from the Early Modern to the Modernists, demonstrates instantiations of these transnational concerns, interests and anxieties. The racial-cultural Other is not merely the backdrop to England's national identity: it is central to the process of England's identity-building. While writers from the 1550s seem, at first reading of the discursive field of English literature, to be concerned only with English culture and identity, this book argues that the Asian, African, Arab and Chinese were constituents of this field. Whether it is English domesticity (as we shall see in Chapter 4) or English travel (Chapter 2), the racial-cultural Other is a part of the English social imaginary. Asia, Arabia, China shape England's imaginary from the *inside*, by being a part of its homes, consumption, world of ideas, and lives (of soldiers, merchants, travellers). This is the globality of English literature the present book hopes to map.

England or Great Britain did not merely 'imagine' a national identity, as Benedict Anderson's influential argument about nationalism (1991) has proposed, or 'forge a nation', as Linda Colley argued (1992) – it did both imagining and forging through an active, consistent engagement with a racial-cultural Other. An English identity was crafted when Britain faced and negotiated 'otherness' in the very real *material* processes of travel, trade, war, conquest, interpersonal relationships, and commodities. Britain/England, to adapt Mary Louise Pratt's words, 'construct[ed] itself from the outside in, out of materials infiltrated, donated, absorbed, appropriated, and imposed' (2003: 137). Britain's imagining itself as a nation was almost always grounded in Otherness. England's cultural identity, as this book treats it, from the period of proto-colonial explorations of the early sixteenth century to the age of decolonization in the twentieth, was constantly negotiated through cultural referents both within and outside the geopolitical territory of the island. Othering is the process of negotiating with such external cultural referents in order for England to develop a sense of self, society and the world. This of course assumes, in Benedict Robinson's formulation (2007: 11) that literary texts and genres imagined, engaged and formed the *world*, especially the world's conflicts, contests and tensions in which England's multiple identities were formed. This book thus treats English literature as a cultural formation constituted out of a constant circulation of material goods, people and ideas between Britain and other cultures (including but not restricted to her colonies). If, as Kevin Grant, Philippa Levine and Frank Trentmann point out, 'the significance of transnationalism reaches beyond spatial movements and physical connections, involving distinct multilocal sets of identities and memories, fluid and hybrid forms of cultural reproduction, and transnational flows of money and expertise' (2007: 1–2), then this book examines the multilocal nature of English identity as a result of its international linkages. That is, the circulation of goods, people and ideas created not only shared economic and administrative realms (imperial Britain) but also a cultural space – that of literature – that brought together Englishness and its racial-cultural Other, Chinese, Asian, African, Arabic and also, on occasion, Europe's internal Others such as the Romany (gypsies) and East Europeans (notably from Transylvania, in *Dracula*, 1897).[2] English literature was inextricably bound up with the globe.

This shift in focus to the globality of English literature is *not* to reject local histories and social contexts that produced English literature and its concerns. Regicide, food riots, industrialization, social mobilities, literacy and other local factors did of course play a crucial role in shaping the nation's literature. Rather, a study of England's transnational and global connections offers us a more nuanced local and national contextualization of the canon. It shows us exactly how local literary themes and concerns were constituted within a transnational and global world 'system' or set of processes.

This transnational turn to studies of English national identity is visible in collections such as *The Global Renaissance* that treat the discourse of identity, manifest in literary and other texts, as instantiating a globalism. This book situates itself in this transnational turn, and sets out to examine the 'provisional instances' (Aravamudan's term, 2005, to which I shall return below) where English literary texts, even as they showcased a national, racial and cultural identity, did so with considerable awareness and narrative cognition of the world and racial-cultural Others.

The 'transnational' in its adjectival form describes 'processes between or beyond national boundaries involving several nations or nationalities'. As a noun, it describes 'someone operating in several countries' (*American Heritage Dictionary*). As Donald Pease notes in his introduction to a volume on transnationalism and American studies, when used as a noun, 'transnational' refers to a condition of 'in-betweenness ... flexibility, non-identification, hybridity, and mobility' (2011: 4). Since it lacks a 'thematic unity', it refers at once to 'factual states of affairs' as well as to 'the interpretive framework through which to make sense of them' (4). Pease further notes that the term frequently 'bears the traces of the violent sociohistorical processes to which it alludes' (4).

I employ the term 'transnational' in this dual sense of a state of affairs as well as an interpretive frame. The state of affairs the term invokes in this book is England's national-cultural imaginary, in every age, of hybridity, mobility, diffuse spatial coordinates – from England to Europe and the world beyond – that explicitly or implicitly reference its racial-cultural Other. As an interpretive framework it re-evaluates social and cultural formations within England's national imaginaries by showing/tracing how identities, people, objects and ideas were never bound within national borders, or even national identifications. That is, my dual sense of the term 'transnational' refers to (1) England's very *real* ideational, material and political engagements with a world (or perhaps that should be 'worlds') outside its national borders and identity through travel, expansion, colonial dominance, trade, tourism, literary-cultural assimilation, labour, etc. and (2) a *reframing* of England's *national* literary past in the light of new coordinates – of the cultural encounter with Otherness.

The book proposes a move from an area (the transnational, with all its flows, convergences, boundary-breaking and remaking) to a number of *sites* where the internal and external of 'England' encounter each other. These sites in the present book are *localized* domains of analysis in which this merging and flows of the transnational might be discerned. It reinterprets England's literary themes in terms of these flows but, for purposes of focus and clarity, does so within specific themes and domains. These sites include the 'fact' of mobility and travel, the ideology of exoticism (and a sub-genre, of erotic exoticism), the culture of commodities and materiality, the politics of pathologization and medicalization, the 'project' of England's virtuous labour on behalf of the Other, and finally the technologies of aesthetic understanding and assimilation.

Literary examples in the chapters that follow illustrate the arguments but are not intended to convey any *genealogy* of a discourse. The chapters are interested in examining a cluster of tropes, themes and images in literary text that convey the ur-discourse of transnational English identity. It therefore studies clusters of sub-discourses, such as travel or objectification, in order to map *continuities* in England's multiple, multi-layered engagements with Otherness.

Like all discourses the discourse of transnational English identity was of a diffuse, unsystematic and uneven nature, appearing in very different ways and modes, subtle or amplified, in literary texts. The transnational often manifests, in other words, in an unevenness and heterogeneity of engagements with other cultural referents rather than in any systematically articulated ideology in English literature. This book maps the heterogeneous, uneven and fragmented discourse of globality (which I take to be a synonym for the transnational throughout this book).

Studies of genres like the English novel have pointed to its multicultural, multiregional, multilingual and multiracial origins (Hunter 1990, Doody 1998). English subjectivity in the genre, the critics tell us, was formed within the crucible of such comparative, mobile and multiple racial interactions, transactions and locations, whether these are Irish, Scottish, African or Asian. Writing about the iconic *English* literary genre, the eighteenth-century novel, Srinivas Aravamudan argues that 'various fictions, including oriental tales and surveillance chronicles, are provisional instances of the translational and transnational aspects of the multitudinous outside excluded by acts of enclosure around the novel' (2005: 50. Also see Dow 2014).

Admittedly, every age has a few *dominant* discourses of Otherness. In the Early Modern it was the discourse of exploration, voyage and discovery. In the Romantic age, Orientalism and its attendant forms of exoticism were in the ascendant. In the Victorian era with its obsession with disease and pathology, the diseased Other (in the form of vampires as well) was the dominant discourse about non-Europeans. The book follows this broad organization of dominant discourses.

It does not seek to situate every literary theme within its historical context. Discourses, admittedly, are context-specific, and as such need to be studied both synchronically and diachronically, especially in the case of colonialism. However, this book sets out to do something else altogether: it maps literary discourses as self-contained and tracks their themes within the literary alone. Echoes and allusions that suggest continuities of thematic concerns of the nineteenth century with the eighteenth are mapped, but without showing the embeddedness of either within their specific contexts. The aim is to show a continuing literary preoccupation with the theme of Otherness.

**

The book begins by framing the transnational theme within the theme of mobility. Travel and voyage, exploration and discovery, resettlement and displacement are all framed under 'mobility' where, as John Urry theorizes, cultural artefacts and practices are 'mobilized' (Urry 2007: 7). Chapter 2 demonstrates how an engagement with the racial, cultural Other in English literature from the Early Modern period to the twentieth century might be profitably read within a discourse of travel and space. The cosmographic and geographical imagination in fictions of travel was articulated through specific rhetorical modes. The fantasy of travel and its related themes of discovery or profit becomes a way of imagining the world but also of imagining England's *place* within this world that was opening up. The chapter then moves on to discuss the discourse of itinerancy as it was organized around three principal axes, spatial distancing, antiquarianism or temporal distancing and somatic geography. This discourse, I argue, conveys significant geopolitical connotations, for it suggested a right of way through Other spaces for the Westerner. In the process of this itinerancy, I argue in the next section of this chapter, an entire ethnography of the Other was instituted to provide detailed information about the exotic, distanced and unknowable Other. This ethnography also captured, I show, the variety of the world. In the final section of the chapter I propose that a triumphalist geography emerges in English writings about distant places. This geographical discourse documents the expansion of the Englishman's agency into new territory, focusing on the dangers faced by the Englishman in new climes and areas and eventual success through sheer 'Brit grit', endurance and physical labour.

I explore the discourses of exoticism in Chapter 3, principally the literary representations of the savage/barbarian and the racially different woman. The savage serves as the exotic backdrop to English adventure, exploration and the colonial project itself. Exoticism here serves the important purpose of marking particular cultural, military and culinary practices against which England defines itself. In certain cases, the chapter shows, the savage exists in and appeals to the British as well. The Noble Savage in such accounts symptomizes the English attempt to come to terms with not only racial-cultural difference but also its ideas of moral universals. For the English and Europeans in general the civil savage epitomizes the civilizational mission itself: that these are humans who can be 'improved'. Reading representations of the Arab harem and the English/European woman's own presence in the Oriental world, I argue that an eroticization of the exotic space of the Other is achieved not only through extensive descriptions of native sexuality and sensuality but through the relocation or transposition of a European femininity into a 'native' context. It is the presence of the European man or woman in exotic settings that also contributes to the erotic charge of the Other place. Despite the cultural difference, or perhaps because of it, there is a sense of

8 Introduction

the English negotiating with the intimate spaces of the racially different feminine. I thus argue that the representation of the possibilities of interracial intimacies in English literature render the harem the space of the Englishman's or woman's intimate cosmopolitanism. Particular discourses of femininity and masculinity – European – emerge in the presence of and engagement with the Other's intimate spaces, I argue.

The globality of English literature might be found, Chapter 4 demonstrates, in its negotiations with objects and commodities. That is, we can think of a *globality of objects*, of various kinds, values, significations and symbolisms, that signal English literature's transnational engagements. It examines English literature's literal and metaphoric commodification of the Other within a vocabulary of objects. The assimilation of tea, chinaware, coffee, Kashmiri shawls into the daily lives of English, as portrayed in numerous texts, the chapter argues, suggests an English identity built around a cosmopolitan and transnational domesticity and taste. The arrival and circulation of exotic objects were instrumental in forming English cosmopolitan tastes in art or gardening or décor but also ensured that English homes, museums and gardens were spaces of assimilation of these accidental or intentional by-products of English imperial processes. In the last section of the chapter I look at the representation of blacks and slaves as emotional objects in what I call the rhetoric of objectification. I argue that the emotional responses to the condition of slaves enable a construction of the sentimental-but-political British subject when s/he encounters and engages with the purely sentimental indigenous object.

In Chapter 5 I turn to a very different form of transnational engagement in English literature. The arrival of the migrant, in the form of commodities, people or pathogens, from the Other space frequently induced panic and anxiety. Difference was the subject of a pathogenic discourse, especially when this difference *entered* the British home, family, street and public space, very often in the form of the inhuman, the monstrous, the addictive or the corrupted, dehumanized Englishman himself. Thus stigmatizing the foreign body in literature as a biological, moral or cultural pathogen might be read as an expression of the anxieties over England's transnational identity-making processes. Material threats, as seen in many texts, while cautioning against the undermining of English economy, production and consumption, also warned about the decadence, corruption and degradation of English character. Invasive and unnameable 'things' that entered England – whether as disease or as vampires – produced alterations within England. Literary texts also focused on cultural invasions where hybridization and multiculturalization led to the degeneration of Englishness. England, in this discourse of the pathogenic Other, *fashions itself an identity under threat of dissolution*.

In the final chapter I turn to another common dimension of England's transnational engagements: its civilizing mission in the colonies. The racial-cultural Other was now, besides being discovered, exoticized, commodified and pathologized, an improveable Other, just as the imperialist was the heroic Englishman/woman seeking to improve the suffering Other. Thus central to England's transnational engagements was a discursive binary constructed around the figures of the to-be-improved native and the improving Englishman or woman. However, concomitant with the literature's discourse of improvement England's literature also demonstrates a certain discrepant geography where the English were the cause of native ruin *and* themselves experienced disintegration, dehumanization and death. After examining the moral imperialism of English literature (which proposed a unification of the world under England's moral leadership), the chapter explores the discourse of the improveable Other, which is often initiated as a discourse of cultural defects. Having until then mapped the cultural defects of the racial-cultural Other, English literary texts from the 1820s are seen to foreground the ameliorative role to be played by Englishmen and women. This includes, as the chapter shows, a deculturation of the native, and by extension an assimilation of English ways. In the last section of the chapter I point to numerous texts where, not only has the civilizational mission of colonial rule failed, but colonization has produced monsters of both English and natives. English literature redraws, the chapter argues, the geography of the world in the form of a discrepant geography.

Notes

1 I also follow Mary Baine Campbell's definition of the world as a space that is habitable or inhabited (1999: 10).
2 For England's Chinese influences see Min (2010), Chang (2010) and the work of David Porter (1999, 2002). For Islam's impact, especially in the Early Modern period, see Benedict Robinson (2007) and Vitkus (1997, 2006, 2007). On gypsies and the Romany in English writing see Behlmer (1985) and Bardi (2006).

2

WORLDS AND VOYAGES

English itinerancy and the spaces of Otherness

This chapter frames the transnational theme in English literature within the theme of itinerancy. It demonstrates how an engagement with the Other in English literature, right from the Early Modern period to the twentieth century, might be profitably read within a *discourse of travel and space*. It is in the persistent and repetitive tropes of travel, distance, discovery and the pursuit of knowledge about the stranger-foreigner, all of which I group under 'itinerancy', that we see manifest England's transnational concerns, interests and anxieties. In order to read this discourse of itinerancy in English literature, the chapter focuses on literary representations of English travels into Africa, Asia and other regions.

The foundational assumption of this chapter is that a key site of the English engagement with the Other, manifest in its literature, is *mobility*, of (1) Englishmen and women out into the wider world or (2) the mobility of the world, in the form of commodities, people, ideas, into and through England. My focus in this chapter is on the former, the English travels into the world, represented in the form of fictions of travel. Concomitant with this discourse of itinerancy is a deep engagement with foreign spaces, territories and terrain. As literary texts map journeys of the Englishmen and women, they also map embodied engagements with other, new spaces and cultures. Fictional journeys therefore deploy, in addition to the thematic of itinerancy, a *spatial* imagination or a *geographic* sensibility. Together, *the journey and the experience of a space outside and beyond one's national-geopolitical borders constitutes an engagement with the Other*. England finds itself at the site of the Other – what we can think of as an out-site – beyond its borders, when it journeys out. But before I turn to the study of this discourse of itinerancy, let me foreground the centrality of mobility to the transnational nature of English literature.

The chapter takes its cue from Rüdiger Kunow who, examining the mobile foundations of the contemporary transnational, argues that since mobilities constitute cultural relations, then mobility must become 'part of ... the critical lexicon wherein a field of study defines itself as cross-cultural, comparatist, and transnational' (2011: 245). From a different critical perspective, theorists of the genre of travel literature treat travel as a mode of exploration of the Self even as it is an exploration of the Other. In their 'discourse on the encounter with foreign Otherness, we witness the travellers' uncertainty of their own religious and cultural Selves, but we also face the discursive construction of an "I" which struggles for new stability', writes Helga Quadfleig (2004: 27). English literature, from the Early Modern period to the twentieth century, foregrounds mobility not only as individual journeys but, very frequently, as *national* projects. Therefore it is possible to see the journeys of a Crusoe, the (unnamed) eyewitness of Aphra Behn's Oroonoko (1688), a Quatermain or a Marlow as embodying a national project wherein the English Self encounters a cultural-racial Other and thus formulates a sense of the Self, whether in the age of exploration or the age of Empire. I treat individual mobility as metonymic of a national mobility itself, and therefore travel as effecting changes in a nation's sense of itself and its identity. But this metonymy is not my focus here. I am interested in the discourse of itinerancy that constructs a cultural space, in an Other *geographical* location or terrain, within which England's engagement with diversity and difference is possible. The imaginative construction of this cultural space founded on itinerancy and spatial difference I have termed 'globality'. Globality in English literature is constructed within a cluster of mutually enabling, supplementing discourses, all of which have to do with journeys and spaces as the English attempted to provide compendious and comprehensive information about the Other. The discourse of itinerancy's representations of the geography of difference offers the facility for the 'apprehension of political systems, social hierarchies, kinship systems, gender relations, sexual practices and terms of being and happiness different from the manners and institutions of the developing national-imperial culture of Britain' (Kaul 2009: 127). But such a geography of difference also enables the construction of an English character in confrontation, conflict, tension and collaboration with its spatially and culturally distant Others.[1] A nation travelling, in real-material terms and in the imaginative-discursive mode, engages with difference and through several such engagements constructs a map of the world, of home and abroad. Globality is predicated upon, and in turn influences, a system of representations of itinerancy into the spaces of the Other.

The Englishman's understanding of the globe across historical periods reflects, to adapt Nancy Stepan's phrasing, aesthetic, political and other projects that expand or limit the Englishman's engagement with the world (2001). My thesis in this chapter is that globality is the *cumulative set of imaginative constructions of (other) places to which the Englishman materially or imaginatively travels.*

Forms of literature that were concerned with discovery, journeys and voyages, explorations, cultural exchanges and encounters with new people are key constituents in the process of globalization, and the imagining of the globe. Literary texts that dealt with travel were instrumental in envisioning even utopias, where utopias might be treated as 'global' texts due to their interest in travel and spaces beyond the national borders (Houston 2009: 84). Globality in literary texts

12 Worlds and voyages

employs a geoaesthetics, an aesthetics of distance, journey, relocation, adaptation and return 'home'. It involves an engagement with sights, sounds, ideas and objects transmitted across distances, and a transformation in the very imagining of space and time as a consequence. Geoaesthetics contributes to the simultaneous process of the shrinking of the world and the expansion of the home. The telescope ensured this dual process of shrinking and expansion in the Early Modern period, just as the Hubble telescope, the *Pioneer* and space travel in the twentieth century have shrunk the universe for us. The circulation of commodities (tea, coffee, chocolate, spices, cotton, animal-heads, precious stones) and people (slaves, Asian sailors and African travellers, and people brought back as exhibits) and narratives of Englishmen's journeys into various parts of the world had the same effect in the eighteenth and nineteenth centuries. Mobility – travel – was the dominant mode of this globalizing geoaesthetic.[2] However, this study of English geoaesthetics does not develop a taxonomy of travellers or even forms of travel – exploration, soldiering campaigns, evangelical-missionary, tourism – choosing instead to collapse different forms of travel and travellers into one literary theme, of itinerancy.

This collapse of categories of travel and travellers in my analysis has a specific discursive teleology in English literary texts about the Other itself. Racial categories blur in several texts from the Early Modern period. Images of Anne Bracegirdle (the mezzotint engraving by W. Vincent) playing the Indian queen Semerina in Aphra Behn's posthumously produced *The Widow Ranter* (1690) showed her being attended to by children wearing plumes and who seem to combine the racial characteristics of American Indians and Africans. Thus a white English woman plays an American Indian and black African children play her attendants. While this theatrical space, as Margaret Ferguson rightly points out (1996: 250), offers up problems of objectification and subjectivity it also conflates racial and ethnic categories. Felicity Nussbaum has persuasively argued that the category of 'black' or 'brown' during the seventeenth and eighteenth century was not entirely rigid, nor even well demarcated in English or European writings. Nussbaum proposes that the history of racial thinking demonstrates a more messy categorization. Nussbaum writes:

> representations of people of colour in the eighteenth century mutate through the spectrum of tawny, sallow, olive, mulatto, sooty, and ebony of East Indian, West Indian, American Indian, Pacific Islander, and North and sub Saharan African, all of whom are at times designated in British (if not American) parlance as 'black'. In some cases we can assign the muddles to historical accident, and in others to geographical confusion … In the imaginative geography of the eighteenth century, Ethiopia (often a synonym for Africa) seems to migrate from Africa to Arabia and back again. It is sometimes contiguous to Egypt and sometimes depicted on the western side of the continent, though Ethiopia eventually comes to represent a lost and unrecoverable premodern glory in the later Ethiopianism movement.
>
> (2009: 143–9)[3]

This 'portability' (as Nussbaum calls it) of the category 'black' through continents and cultures means that we can treat English literature's representation of numerous racial and ethnic Others as resulting from a category confusion, but also as an immanent feature of the concept of 'race'. My conflation of readings of texts that look at African, Turkish, Asian or South American races and spaces is founded on this assumption that numerous races constituted Britain's racial-cultural Other with little to distinguish *among* these races, at least from/in the British perspective. While this does confound the historical specificity of English representations of the South Seas and, say, India, it indicates the broad brushstrokes of a racializing imaginary that itself was not concerned with these specificities, drawing, instead, from a cultural unconscious that simply consigned shades of blackness, physiognomies and cultural practices to one category: the Other. Globality and itinerancy, therefore, was a mixed-up discourse of the Other that, even as it accounted for the heterogeneity and alterity of Africans or Asians from the English, homogenized several kinds of Asians or Africans into one category: the Other. It can of course be pointed out that every age had its own social attitudes, often conflicted, towards travel. Thus if Thomas Nashe (*The Unfortunate Traveller*, 1594), Joseph Hall (*Mundus Alter et Idem* [*Another World and Yet the Same*], 1605) and others expressed anxiety about travel in Early Modern England, others of the same period, such as Francis Bacon ('Of Travel', 1625), prepared extensive templates for the travellers to fill in information about Other cultures, thus signalling the key role of travel for English culture and identity.[4] For the Victorians, since the age of discovery was behind them, travel enabled the quest for extreme exotic spaces, such as interior Africa or the wilds of the Himalayan foothills. The fiction of the age would of course reflect these tensions and attitudes vis-à-vis travel. However, this chapter sacrifices historical specificity regarding the nature of, attitude towards, tensions within and stylistic modes of representing travel for the sake of unravelling patterns within clusters of discourses around mobility.

This chapter is interested in the *persistence* of the discourse of itinerancy, tropes of travel, and the interrelated spatial themes of wandering, exploration and resettlement across English literary history. The persistence of such a discourse of itinerancy over the centuries, mostly in canonical texts of English literature, offers us a way of perceiving how the English engaged with the world. The chapter thus attempts to map this cluster of discourses of itinerancy and geography, many overlapping, some conflictual, across England's literary history. These discourses, as the chapter treats them, are to be seen as *localized* instances, moments and domains of the larger narrative of the transnational.

England travels

The discourse of English itinerancy across centuries is manifest in specific *spatial* tropes and themes in fictions of travel about Other places. What must be kept in mind is the interplay of fact and fiction in the representation of Other spaces. Thus, the fictional accounts of utopias somewhere off America, paradisal islands (with

14 Worlds and voyages

some cannibals) in the Caribbean, or Solomon's mines in Africa are not always at the opposite end from, or in discursive conflict with, geographical discoveries of the poles, sea routes and passages to new worlds. Literary articulations of different spaces might be read as the essential *supplements* that are both excessive and essential to the completion of any 'real' geographical narratives. Two key discourses that constitute the larger discourse of itinerancy can now be mapped: (1) the imagining of new geographies of the world in fictions of travel and (2) the theme of actual movement and English engagement with new spaces.

Cosmography and the geographical imagination

Mary Baine Campbell proposes that 'harmless' travel fictions such as Thomas More's were rhetorical strategies in and through which 'the desire for a better (or different) world can be expressed and satisfied without corrupting the sources of practical geographical knowledge' (1988: 212–13). Before actual travel to strange, new or familiar places, there was the *imagining* of and *desire* for Other places, of the world itself. England in the Early Modern period, for instance, began to imagine the place of the Other, or the Other in its place. The cosmographic and geographical imagination in fictions of travel was articulated, this section demonstrates, through specific rhetorical modes. The fantasy of travel and its related themes of discovery or profit become a way of imagining the world but also, and this is my key point, of imagining England's place within this world that was opening up.

The *Theatrum Orbis terrarum*, the Western world's first atlas prepared by Abraham Ortelius and published in 1570, offered not only a map of the known world but also a metaphor for literary imaginations to work with: the *theatre* of the world. Fuelling the geographical imagination, atlases and maps produced an entire range of accounts of the worlds beyond England and Europe, ready for conquest or mercantile purposes. Martin Behaim, the Nuremberg cartographer, published a globe in 1492 (Magellan was one of the explorers who used this globe), in which he not only annotated the known world but also carefully inventoried the customs duties to be paid at each port in the course of the spice trade (Jardine 1996: 296).[5]

Therefore the 'theatre of the world' was at once a cartographic project as it was a literary theme and trope. Encoded within the cosmographic theme and the imagining of a new geography of the world were the themes of discovery, variety, the unknown and the mysterious along with the hopeful themes of conquest, knowledge and profit.[6]

Very often this theatre of the world was played out on the site of the human body in the Early Modern where the 'introduction of the body is simultaneous with the discovery and fledgling colonization of new worlds' (Sell 2006: 181). The theatre of the world mapped on to the geography of the human form inscribed globality on to the closest terrain a human possesses or is familiar with: the body. This conflation of anatomy and geography is most clearly visible in the Early Modern period.

When John Donne declared 'all the world grows transparent, and I see/through all' ('Obsequies to the Lord Harrington', 1975: 257) he was not only working with extant images of visual explorations of the world and the heavens (made possible by devices such as the microscope and the telescope) but also encoding a fantasy of visual conquest and epistemological understanding of the known and available worlds (like all Donne poems, this one too is loaded with geographical imagery). It is this kind of anatamo-geographical imagination that, I propose, prepares for the discourse of itinerancy in English writings. Others before and after Donne would also map bodies and worlds into one seamless unity. Henry Peacham in Emblem 28 in his *Minerva Brittania* described the human this way:

> Hear what's the reason why a man we call
> A little world? And what the wiser meant
> By this new name? Two lights celestial
> Are in his head, as in the element;
> Eke as the wearied sun at night is spent,
>> So seemeth but the life of man a day,
>> At morn he's borne, at night he flits away.
> Of heat and cold as is the air composed,
> So likewise man we see breath's whot and cold,
> His body's earthy: in lungs enclosed,
> Remains the air, his brain doth moisture hold,
> His heart and liver, do the heat enfold:
>> Of earth, fire, water, man thus framed is,
>> Of elements the threefold qualities.

(1612: 190)

In the human body Peacham finds the world itself. The variety of the world is unified/united within the human form. Shakespeare was also reconstituting the map of the known world in the human form. In *Antony and Cleopatra*, for instance, Cleopatra describes Antony thus:

> His legs bestrid the ocean; his reared arm
> Crested the world; his voice was propertied
> As all the tuned spheres, and that to friends;
> But when he meant to quail and shake the orb,
> He was rattling thunder. For his bounty,
> There was no winter in't an autumn it was
> That grew the more by reaping. His delights
> Were dolphin-like; they showed his back above
> The element they lived in. In his livery
> Walked and crowns and crownets; realms and islands were
> As plates dropped from his pocket.

(V.2, ll. 81–90)

16 Worlds and voyages

In *The Comedy of Errors* the kitchen wench is fantasized by Dromio as 'spherical, like a globe' in which/whom he 'could find out countries' (III.2, ll. 113–14). Later, this somatic geography would assert itself in a slightly different way where fictional representations of English itinerancy foregrounded the corporeal experience of Other places, as we shall see.

Somatic geography of this kind also found expression in eroticized images of the world and the Other places. Offering a fantasy narrative of discovery, exploration and conquest representations of the human form conflated with geography appear regularly in John Donne. In his 'Love's Progress' Donne mapped fantasy spaces of various kinds:

> the straight Hellespont between
> The Sestos and Abydos of her breasts,
> (Not of two lovers, but two loves the nests)
> Succeeds a boundless sea, but yet thine eye
> Some island moles may scattered there descry;
> And sailing towards her India, in that way
> Shall at her fair Atlantic navel stay.

(1975: 123)

Elsewhere in 'The Second Anniversarie' Donne would write:

> The Western treasure, Eastern spicerie,
> Europe, and Afrique, and the unknown rest
> Were easily found, or what in them was best;
> And when w'have made this large discoverie
> Of all, in her some one part then will bee
> Twenty such parts, whose plenty and riches is
> Enough to make twenty such worlds as this.

(1975: 293)

Working with the vocabulary of discovery, appropriation and property, Donne not only eroticizes distant worlds but also sees these worlds (like the woman's body) as possessing the potential for England's rejuvenation (Sawday 1996: 26). These are fantasies of possession and promise. From such a view of the woman/land, a fantasy of conquest follows almost naturally in Donne's (notoriously sexist) verse in 'To his Mistress Going to Bed':

> Licence my roving hands, and let them go,
> Before, behind, between, above, below.
> O my America! My new-found-land,
> My kingdome, safeliest when with one man man'd,
> My myne of precious stones, My Emperie,
> How blest am I in this discovering thee!

To enter in these bonds, is to be free;
Then where my hand is set, my seal shall be.

(1975: 125)

A century and half later, in Maturin's *Melmoth the Wanderer* (1820), Immalee/Isidora lives away from all eligible males, on an uninhabited island in the Indian sea, somewhere off Calcutta, a place unknown to Europeans. Melmoth then sets out to seduce her, thus reiterating an erotic geography. Like the island, Immalee is the desirable Other for the European.

But geography was not only the geography of the human form in fantasy narratives. Fantasises of discovery, exploration and control of Other places have figured in English literature from the Early Modern period. Very often these fantasies appear in the form of massive catalogues of places. The *index locorum* (the indexing of places) unifies these distant places within the narrative – thus proposing a fantastic editorial and textual control over these Other places – but also offering the readers an itinerary of the English nation itself. Note, for example, Spenser's geographical fantasy of England's 'reach' in *The Faerie Queene* (Book 2, proem) where he maps Ireland, Europe, the East Indies and the West Indies:

And dayly how through hardy enterprize,
Many great Regions are discouered,
Which to late age were neuer mentioned.
Who euer heard of th'Indian *Peru*?
Or who in venturous vessell measured
The *Amazon* huge riuer now found trew?
Or fruitfullest *Virginia* who did euer vew?

(Spenser 1984: 169)

Spenser is speaking of the mercantile dimension ('hardy investment') of voyages and travels to distant places but he is also underscoring the theme of *discovery*, and therefore of the expansion of the epistemological empire of England. (It must be noted that Spenser dedicated the book to 'Elizabeth … Queen of England … and Virginia'.) In *Epithalamion* and *Colin Clouts Come Home Againe*, Louis Montrose argues, the Irish allusions enable Spenser to 'create a locus of meaning and value that is defined in part by its otherness from London, the court, and the Queen' (1996: 109).

This geographical imagining of the known world positions England as possessing the potential to discover, conquer, explore and profit from new places and regions that the voyages were revealing. England would bring these distant places closer, unite them, under her banner. Spenser also cleverly positions his discourse of globality within the discourse of epistemology, understanding and measurement. Hearing, seeing and measuring the world constitute Spenser's engagement with regions beyond the national borders as he imagines the globe.

18 Worlds and voyages

We see this ambitious and fantastic geography reflected in Christopher Marlowe's *Tamburlaine*, Part One – set in the period before 1492 and Columbus – which offers a map of the world as was then known:

> I will confuse those blind geographers
> That make a triple region in the world.
> Excluding regions that I mean to trace,
> And with this pen reduce them to a map,
> Calling the provinces, cities, and towns
> After my name and thine, Zenocrate.
>
> (IV.4, ll. 81–6. 1975: 160)[7]

Marlowe's hero hopes to not only alter the world map but plans to rename portions of it after himself. Significantly, the ambition that the English Marlowe displaces on to the Oriental king is of this unification of the earth's distant corners under one name/body/person. Globality is the conjunction of bodies and technologies of mapping and naming.

In Shakespeare's *Antony and Cleopatra* we find a repetition of this cosmographic imagination in the catalogue of places and kings that Octavious Caesar pronounces:

> he hath assembled
> Bocchus, the king of Libya; Archelaus,
> Of Cappadocia; Philadelphos, king
> Of Paphlagonia; the Thracian king, Adallas;
> King Malchus of Arabia; King of Pont;
> Herod of Jewry; Mithridates, king
> Of Comagene; Polemon and Amyntas,
> The kings of Mede and Lycaonia,
> With a more larger list of sceptres.
>
> (III.6, ll. 68–76)

In *The Merchant of Venice* Shakespeare would list Antonio's mercantile world:

> From Tripolis, from Mexico and England,
> From Lisbon, Barbary and India?
>
> (III.3, ll. 265–6)

Portia, says Shakespeare in this same play, is renowned worldwide: 'nor is the wide world ignorant of her worth/for the four winds blow in from every coast' (1.1.167–8). That Shakespeare's plays were performed at The Globe should also tell us something about the Early Modern interest in the theatres of humanity itself.

Shakespeare's Hamlet spoke of the 'undiscovered country from whose bourn/no traveller returns' (II.1, l. 81. 2008: 1734). Central to the geographical imagination was the imagination of the empty spaces and the unknown. But also crucial was that the map represented spaces where the Englishman, or even boy, could see a future unfolding. Thus, paradoxically, English dreams consisted in several cases of being *elsewhere*, away from England and home.

In the Early Modern period this elsewhere could very well be utopia. Travel writing and utopia both 'imagine', as Chloe Houston notes, a 'different society' (2010: 4). Utopian literature is a 'form of fictional travel writing which engages both with the desire for information and the concern with the spiritual, exotic or rewarding journey' (6). Raphael Hythloday, the hero of Thomas More's *Utopia*, on his return, is able to enlighten the listeners (More and Peter Giles) about the politics, social structure and culture of the island. Such texts offered visions of new worlds, new peoples and new cultures. When Amerigo Vespucci, after whom the continent would be named, announced 'surely if the terrestrial paradise be in any part of this earth, I esteem that it is not far distant from those parts' (cited in Houston 2010: 8), he was indicating the fantasy but also the *reality* of newly discovered worlds. Further, science fictional texts such as those by Frances Godwin (*The Man in the Moon*), Johannes Kepler (*Somnium*), Margaret Cavendish (*The Blazing World*) and others often offered up possible worlds, although not always ideal ones. What is certain is that right from the Early Modern period Europe was interested in Other worlds, and Other peoples in those worlds.[8]

Maps, globes and the theatre of the world also helped produce fantasies of war, conquest, profit and expansion. Empty and distant lands could also become spaces of adventure wherein the Englishman could encounter difficulties and become a full-fledged man.[9]

In Ben Jonson's *The Alchemist* (1610) Sir Epicure Mammon, who is seeking the philosopher's stone, tells the gamester Surly:

> Come on sir. Now you set your foot on shore
> In *novo orbe*; here's the rich Peru:
> Great Solomon's Ophir! He was sailing to't
> Three years, but we have reached it in ten months.
>
> (2.1: 1–6. Jonson 1979: 44)

The reference here is to the fabled voyage to Ophir, the Biblical land famed for its wealth, to which Solomon is believed to have travelled. Ophir had been variously identified with parts of Africa, with Columbus believing it was somewhere in China, and others in Peru. Jonson, as David Harris Sacks notes, is sarcastic about Mammon's reasons for travelling (2010: 18–19).

Even pirates and buccaneers like William Dampier and their travel writings were inserted into this English cosmographic imagining of the world, as Anna Neill (2000) and Claire Jowitt (2010) have demonstrated. Such pirate voyages were treated not only as travel for 'business practice' (Jowitt 2010: 116) but as adding to the information-base of a nation seeking imperial pastures. The quest for fantastic lands with wealth that would, therefore, further England's profits and imperial

20 Worlds and voyages

ambitions underwrites the discourse of itinerancy and geography of plenty in several texts from the sixteenth and seventeenth centuries.

In John Dryden's *Annus Mirabilis* (1667), wherein he begins by referring to the obstruction of flows of trade and concludes with the British triumph over Holland (historically referencing the Anglo-Dutch war of 1665), he writes:

> Trade, which, like blood, should circularly flow,
> Stopp'd in their channels, found its freedom lost:
> Thither the wealth of all the world did go,
> And seem'd but shipwreck'd on so base a coast.
> For them alone the heavens had kindly heat;
> In eastern quarries ripening precious dew:
> For them the Idumæan balm did sweat,
> And in hot Ceylon spicy forests grew.
> The sun but seem'd the labourer of the year;
> Each waxing moon supplied her watery store,
> To swell those tides, which from the line did bear
> Their brimful vessels to the Belgian shore.
> Thus mighty in her ships, stood Carthage long,
> And swept the riches of the world from far;
> Yet stoop'd to Rome, less wealthy, but more strong:
> And this may prove our second Punick war.
>
> (Dryden 1956: 59–60)

Writing about the competition and the ruins of English trade, Dryden says:

> Some English wool, vex'd in a Belgian loom,
> And into cloth of spungy softness made:
> Did into France or colder Denmark doom,
> To ruin with worse ware our staple trade.
>
> (1956: 90–1)

Dryden is describing the geography of numerous places where Britain has triumphed, but also proposing a unification of diverse lands under the British banner.[10] Itinerancy here is the focused journeys for trade and profit that not only financially benefit England but also give her a sense of national identity, suggests Dryden.

If Dryden saw profits in a nation's travels, the eighteenth and nineteenth centuries saw conquest, settlement and domination. Note here Gulliver's ambitions:

> My design was, if possible, to discover some small island uninhabited, yet sufficient, by my labour, to furnish me with the necessaries of life, which I would have thought a greater happiness, than to be first minister in the politest court of Europe; so horrible was the idea I conceived of returning to

live in the society, and under the government of *Yahoos*. For in such a solitude as I desired, I could at least enjoy my own thoughts, and reflect with delight on the virtues of those inimitable *Houyhnhnms*, without an opportunity of degenerating into the vices and corruptions of my own species.

(Swift 1960a: 228)

Gulliver's ambition, or fantasy, is really of possible alternative worlds for the Englishman bored of England. It is a fantasy of resettlement, of a self-contained world (which of course is satirized by Swift when Gulliver is shot at and he despondently swims away!). Swift would satirize this English desire for empty spaces elsewhere too in 'Poetry: A Rhapsody' (1733):

So geographers in Afric – maps
With savage – pictures fill their gaps;
And o'er uninhabitable Downs
Place elephants for want of towns.

(Swift 1967: 574)

Australia, in particular, was consistently portrayed as the *terra nullius*, an empty space – ignoring, of course, the aboriginal inhabitants – by Europeans. As late as the twentieth century, D.H. Lawrence spoke of the 'soft, blue, humanless sky of Australia, the pale, white, unwritten atmosphere of Australia' (cited in Ryan 1994: 129).

In *Roderick Random* (1748), Tobias Smollett's Crab encourages Random to go to sea:

Before I was your age, I was broiling on the coast of Guinea. – Damne! What's to hinder you from profiting by the war, which will certainly be declared in a short time against Spain? – You may easily get on board of a king's ship in quality of a surgeon's mate, where you will certainly see a great deal of practice, and stand a good chance of getting prize money.

(Smollett 1979: 30)

For Colonel Brandon in Jane Austen's *Sense and Sensibility* (1811) the 'much encumbered' Englishman has to opt for military service in the East Indies where, Austen suggests, he might even get corrupted amongst the 'nabobs, gold mohrs and palanquins' (unpaginated, http://ebooks.adelaide.edu.au/a/austen/jane/a93s/). Gillian Russell points out that in Austen the militia offers 'opportunities for geographical and class mobility' (2009: 262). What Russell is pointing to is motility, the structures that enable movement. In this case the military and oppressive family finances are the structural conditions that cause the Englishman to travel. For Random and Brandon, the military offers the opportunity to travel.

Steerforth in *David Copperfield* (1850) is a man with wanderlust:

> Afloat, wrapped in fisherman's clothes, whole moonlight nights, and coming back when the morning tide was at flood. By this time, however, I knew his restless nature and bold spirits delighted to find a vent in rough toil and hard weather, as in any other means of excitement that presented itself freshly to him.
>
> (Dickens 1992: 302)

Like Crusoe and Gulliver before him and Marlow after, Steerforth is not simply adrift on open seas: he is *in his mind* a free-floating wanderer. The discourse of itinerancy in such fiction fixes wanderlust as a psychological trait of particular Englishmen (many of whom are 'ruined' as Defoe admits – Steerforth, of course, dies in Dickens' novel – due to the wandering impulse). Itinerancy is a cultural phenomenon, in this reading.

Dickens would declare in *Dombey and Son* (1846–8): 'the earth was made for Dombey and Son to trade in, and the sun and moon were made to give them light … stars and planets circled in their orbits, to preserve inviolate a system of which they were the centre' (unpaginated, http://ebooks.adelaide.edu.au/d/dickens/charles/d54ds). London becomes, as in Dryden's poem quoted above, the centre from which English itinerancy would originate and map, conquer, explore, dominate and profit from the globe:

> Pictures of ships speeding away full sail to all parts of the world; outfitting warehouses ready to pack off anybody anywhere, fully equipped in half an hour; and little timber midshipmen in obsolete naval uniforms, eternally employed outside the shop doors of nautical instrument-makers.
>
> (unpaginated, http://ebooks.adelaide.edu.au/d/dickens/charles/d54ds)[11]

Dickens, like Dryden nearly two centuries before him, paints London, and by extension, England, as a mercantile culture but also a culture that inspires itinerancy. Fully aware of the possibilities of the world, London is constantly ready to embark on its many journeys. Such representations of course encode English ambitions. But they also capture the powerful sense of the culture of *focused* itinerancy that unravels the world, makes itinerancy and the engagement (military, mercantile, evangelical) with the world a marker of English identity. In other words, what we see in these fictional accounts of travel is the fantasy *of an English identity around the twin themes of itinerancy and the Other*.

R.M. Ballantyne, opening his *The Young Fur Traders* (1856) with an account of Northern America in the Lake Winnipeg region, offers us a Crusoe-like island paradise: 'Although far removed from the civilised world, and containing within its precincts much that is savage and very little that is refined, Red River [settlement] is quite a populous paradise' (unpaginated, http://www.gutenberg.org/files/21712/21712-h/21712-h.htm).

Maps, says Marlow of Conrad's *Heart of Darkness*, produced a wanderlust for places and spaces unknown:

> when I was a little chap I had a passion for maps. I would look for hours at South America, or Africa, or Australia, and lose myself in all the glories of exploration. At that time there were many blank spaces on the earth, and when I saw one that looked particularly inviting on a map (but they all look that) I would put my finger on it and say, When I grow up I will go there.
>
> (Conrad 1974: 52)

But he then confesses that these new worlds had 'ceased to be a blank space of delightful mystery – a white patch for a boy to dream gloriously over. It [has] become a place of darkness' (52).[12] In this Marlow echoes Jim Hawkins in R.L. Stevenson's classic tale of boyhood adventure, *Treasure Island* (1883):

> I brooded … over the map [of Treasure Island], all the details of which I well remembered. Sitting by the fire in the house-keeper's room, I approached that island in my fancy, from every possible direction; I explored every acre of its surface; I climbd a thousand times to that tall hill they call the Spy-glass … Sometimes the isle was thick with savages, with whom we fought; sometimes full of dangerous animals that hunted us; but in all my fancies nothing occurred to me so strange and tragic as our actual adventures.
>
> (unpaginated, http://ebooks.adelaide.edu.au/s/stevenson/
> robert_louis/s848tr/)

When Martin Green termed such tales 'dreams of adventure, deeds of empire' in his work of the same title (1980), he was aligning the dreaming of Other spaces with metaphoric but also real conquest over these spaces.[13] The Victorian poet W.E. Henley (1849–1903) would describe this dream of London's supremacy and role in the world order:

> They call you proud and hard,
> > England, my England;
> You with worlds to watch and ward,
> > England, my own!
> You whose mailed hand keeps the keys
> Of such teeming destinies.
>
> ('England, My England', 1892, cited in
> Brantlinger 2009: 2)

So, 'to watch and ward' the world and the Other was Britain's destiny, and therefore its identity as a nation and culture. In controlling the 'teeming destinies' of the Others, England can find its own destiny and identity.

24 Worlds and voyages

In all these cases we see a fascination with the world's imaginary vastness, with the ability (in the Early Modern period made possible with the invention of the telescope) to see great distances. After imagining, of course, there needs to be travel to these places, a dream captured in Ralph Rover's ecstatic prayer in Ballantyne's *The Coral Island* (1858): 'God bless and prosper the missionaries till they get a footing in every island of the sea' (http://ebooks.adelaide.edu.au/b/ballantyne/rm/coral-island/), and echoed by Tennyson's narrator in 'Locksley Hall' (1835):

> Or to burst all links of habit – there to wander far away,
> On from island unto island at the gateways of the day.
> Larger constellations burning, mellow moons and happy skies,
> Breadths of tropic shade and palms in cluster, knots of Paradise.
> Never comes the trader, never floats an European flag,
> Slides the bird o'er lustrous woodland, swings the trailer from the crag;
> Droops the heavy-blossom'd bower, hangs the heavy-fruited tree –
> Summer isles of Eden lying in dark-purple spheres of sea.
> There methinks would be enjoyment more than in this march of mind,
> In the steamship, in the railway, in the thoughts that shake mankind.
> There the passions cramp'd no longer shall have scope and breathing space;
> I will take some savage woman, she shall rear my dusky race.
> Iron-jointed, supple-sinew'd, they shall dive, and they shall run,
> Catch the wild goat by the hair, and hurl their lances in the sun;
> Whistle back the parrot's call, and leap the rainbows of the brooks,
> Not with blinded eyesight poring over miserable books.
>
> (Tennyson 1969: 697–8)

The ambition, or dream, is to 'burst all links of habit' and to 'wander far away'.[14] Tennyson's other famous poems, 'Ulysses' (written 1833, published 1842), and 'The Lotus Eaters' (republished in 1842 with the additions of the choric song), also showcased the travels of Europeans into distant places.

Clearly distances were always meant to be dissolved, if English literature's foregrounding of travel is any indication. One can safely then conclude that the representations of distant worlds in English literature supplemented real-time discoveries of new worlds. They embody, as Mary Baine Campbell has proposed in an argument I cited early in this chapter, a desire for alternate worlds. More importantly, these representations influenced a cultural imaginary of conquest, exploration, self-development (embodied, as always, in the prototype: Robinson Crusoe), control, profits, adventure and labour in the Other space. The persistence of spatial tropes invites the reading that English literary history is as much about English geographical, topographical and cultural spaces as it has been about Other spaces, even if the specific kind of interest in these spaces, or the teleology of travel and settlement, have been varied across the centuries.

What we have seen so far is the construction of Other worlds and spaces in fictions of travel. Running alongside this discursive construction of Other spaces is the discourse that underwrites this chapter, of itinerancy, to which I now turn.

Itinerancy, distance, embodied geography

> Let sea-discoverers to new worlds have gone,
> Let maps to others, worlds on worlds have showne,
> Let us possesse one world, each hath one, and is one.
>
> (John Donne, 'The Good-Morrow', 1975: 60)

Donne, like several others we noted in the preceding section, offers a somatic geography of the world, treating bodies and places as conflated. In these lines the possession of the richly endowed beloved Other demands, Donne suggests, a voyage of discovery.

Having imagined the world's extent and variety in multiple ways, the theme of actual travel might be seen as a natural narrative outcome of the cosmographic imagination discussed in the preceding section. The discourse of wandering and travel into new spaces was often organized around three axes: spatial distancing, antiquarianism or temporal distancing and somatic geography.

For strangeness to be 'reached', the known shores of land, culture and knowledge have to be abandoned, either voluntarily or by error.[15] Crusoe and Gulliver declare their need to travel for their own reasons. Crusoe says – and we recall Dickens' description of Steerforth, cited above – of himself: 'Being the third son of the family and not bred to any trade, my head began to be filled very early with rambling thoughts'. It was a 'propension of nature', says Crusoe, that he wished to go to sea: 'I would be satisfied with nothing but going to sea' (Defoe 1975: 5). In the nineteenth century Ballantyne's *The Young Fur Traders* (1856) gives as its first full character-sketch, Frank Kennedy:

> Frank Kennedy, who, sixty years before the date of our story, ran away from school in Scotland; got a severe thrashing from his father for so doing; and having no mother in whose sympathising bosom he could weep out his sorrow, ran away from home, went to sea, ran away from his ship while she lay at anchor in the harbour of New York, and after leading a wandering, unsettled life for several years, during which he had been alternately a clerk, a day-labourer, a storekeeper, and a village schoolmaster, he wound up by entering the service of the Hudson's Bay Company, in which he obtained an insight into savage life, a comfortable fortune, besides a half-breed wife and a large family.
>
> (unpaginated, http://www.gutenberg.org/files/21712
> /21712-h/21712-h.htm)

Not only is itinerancy a mental condition and personal motif, it also offers the potential, in Ballantyne's hagiography of the wanderer, to assume any/all identities. It is in distant worlds that opportunities present themselves.

26 Worlds and voyages

Spatial distancing

Defoe wrote in *The Compleat English Gentleman* (1730) of the urge to travel:

> [He may] make a tour of the world in books, he may make himself master of the geography of the universe in the maps, atlasses and measurements of our mathematicians. He may travell by land with the historians, by sea with the navigators. He may go round the globe with Dampier and Rogers, and kno' a thousand times more doing it than all those illiterate sailors.
>
> (1975: 255)

Spatial distancing, wandering, errant voyages and travels along unplanned routes are central to the trope of itinerancy. Take four of the most famous early literary expressions of Other spaces: Thomas More's *Utopia* (1516), Francis Bacon's *The New Atlantis* (1626), Daniel Defoe's *Robinson Crusoe* (1719) and Jonathan Swift's *Gulliver's Travels* (1726).

Bacon's *New Atlantis* opens thus:

> We sailed from Peru, where we had continued by the space of one whole year, for China and Japan, by the South Sea … finding ourselves, in the midst of the greatest wilderness of waters in the world.
>
> (1862: 359)

Drifting along, they then believe they might make land: 'knowing how that part of the South Sea was utterly unknown, and might have islands or continents that hitherto were not come to light' (Bacon 1862: 360). Defoe's Crusoe describes himself as possessing a 'rambling' mind (1975: 5). Later he refers to his 'rambling designs' (34). On the disastrous voyage out from Brazil, Crusoe's ship is somewhere off the coast of the 'Caribbee Islands' when it strikes land: 'we knew nothing where we were, or upon what land it was we were driven—whether an island or the main, whether inhabited or not inhabited' (36).[16] When the surviving boats are hit by waves, the men scatter and Crusoe says 'Nothing can describe the confusion of thought which I felt when I sank into the water' (37). Swift's Gulliver takes his last accurate location 'north west of Van Diemen Island' and then loses all sense of direction and distance. Assaulted by stormy weather the men take to smaller boats: 'we therefore trusted ourselves to the mercy of the waves, and in about half an hour the boat was overset by a sudden flurry from the north' (1960a: 16). And before all these drifting and lost characters there is Shakespeare's description of Othello as an 'extravagant and wheeling stranger' (I.1, l. 138), where 'extravagant', etymologically, is linked to *extravagiri*, a 'wanderer beyond bounds' (Gillies 1994: 3). And later there is Coleridge's famous Ancient Mariner who wanders, minus any sense of direction, the oceans from the tropics to the doldrums and the frozen wastes of the north. Mary Shelley's Frankenstein, in pursuit of the monster, plods across the icy wastes of Greenland, again with no sense of direction.

Confused senses and locations constitute a central trope here: the disorientation of the traveller is the relocation into unidentifiable and unmapped spaces. This absence of certainty, of direction and distance, underscores the relatively unknown spaces of the world. That is, to suggest disorientation in a new place is to spatially *and* epistemologically distance the place from home and country. Images of nautical measurement, mapping and location underscore this spatial distancing we see in literary texts about travel.

Ben Jonson would use the compass image in his 'An Epistle to Master John Selden', and Donne would more famously deploy it in 'A Valediction: Forbidding Mourning':

> Though I must goe, endure not yet
> A breach, but an expansion,
> Like gold to ayery thinnesse beate.
> If they be two, they are two so
> As stiffe twin compasses are two,
> Thy soule the fixt foot, makes no show
> To move, but doth, if the' other doe.
>
> (1975: 84)

To think of Other spaces is to think of, simultaneously, journeys to and from them, and home, as seen in Donne's (eroticized) image of the fixed foot of the compass being attached to the other, moving foot. The confusion of spaces that Donne's speaker records is the disorientation of wandering: whither is he bound when he heads for home? Where *is* his home? Phineas Fletcher in a verse that anticipates this thematics of roaming and return, home and abroad in *The Purple Island* (1633) would therefore focus on the humble but *English* home as the place of rest:

> Let others trust the seas, dare death and hell,
> Search either Inde, vaunt of their scarres and wounds;
> Let others their dear breath (nay silence) sell
> To fools, and (swoln, not rich) stretch out their bounds
> By spoiling those that live, and wronging dead;
> That they may drink in pearl, and couch their head
> In soft, but sleeplesse down; in rich, but restlesse bed.
>
> (cited in Mack 1969: 102)

Maynard Mack reads these lines as emblematic of the *secretum iter*, the poetry of retirement that glorifies rural England (1969: 102). However, what needs to be noted in the case of both Donne and Fletcher is the binary being drawn between the home/hearth and abroad/distant, between a poor but safe domesticity and the dangerous but ultimately profitable mobility that, in Fletcher's verse, some Englishmen adopt. Thus a clergyman father in W.H.G. Kingston's *Peter the Whaler*

28 Worlds and voyages

(1851) warns his son, Peter, before the latter sets out on a voyage: 'wherever you wander, my son, remember you are a Briton, and cease not to love your native land' (cited in Brantlinger 2009: 32). The warning suggests that 'home' is still the best place, especially after having wandered the world.[17] The dual theme of travel and home/abroad continues in Victorian and twentieth century literature from England, with one particular trajectory.

Mobility and the geography of distant lands informed debates on emigration and settlements. Thomas Carlyle, for instance, saw the mobility of entire populations into new colonies as essential to the problem of overcrowding. In *Past and Present* (1843) Carlyle would therefore argue the case for an 'Emigration Service' through which 'every honest willing workman who found England too strait, and the "organization of labour" not yet sufficiently advanced, might find likewise a ridge built to carry him into new Western lands' (Book IV, chapter 3, unpaginated, http://www. gutenberg.org/files/26159/26159-h/26159-h.htm). In *David Copperfield* (1849–50) Dickens solves the 'problem' of 'unwanted' and 'fallen' women characters – Martha Endell and Little Em'ly – by sending them to Australia. In Elizabeth Gaskell's *Mary Barton* (1848), Mary and her lover, who is a suspect in a murder case, emigrate to Canada. Novels by Henry Kingsley (*The Recollections of Geoffrey Hamlyn*, 1859, *The Hillyars and the Burtons*, 1865) also thematized emigration to new colonies.

Spatial distancing here works as a mode of cultural purging and purification. Forced itinerancy such as the ones mentioned above essentially distanced the unwanted, the threatening and the unhappy from England's spaces. If William Blake spoke of the 'chartered streets' of London (1973: 216–17) where the many unhappy mourned their lot, the Victorian age solved the problem by utilizing the knowledge of distant places to transport the unwanted away.

Temporal distancing

The discourse of distancing is not cast only within the rhetoric of physical separation and distance: the Other world was also removed from England in terms of its internal time. This spatial distancing is what I am referring to as the discourse of antiquarianism within the discourse of wandering. It situates the racial and cultural Other at a far remove from England and European time.

Antiquity, associated with the new world, contributed to its distance from England's present. Spenser's *The Faerie Queene*, Book 2, opens with a reference to antiquities and the unknowable spaces of 'the happy land of Faery':

> right well I wote most mighty Soueraine,
> That all this famous antique history,
> Of some th'aboundance of an idle braine
> Will iudged be, and painted forgery,
> Rather then matter of iust memory,
> Sith none, that breatheth liuing aire, does know,
> Where is that happy land of Faery,

Which I so much do vaunt, yet no where show,
But vouch antiquities, which no body can know.

(Spenser 1984: 169)

We see this Early Modern theme of antiquity best illustrated in Francis Bacon's important text *The New Atlantis*:

> The great Atlantis was utterly lost and destroyed, not by a great earthquake … but by a particular deluge or inundation … But it is true that the same inundation was not deep; not past forty foot, in most places from the ground: so that although it destroyed man and beast generally, yet some few wild inhabitants of the wood escaped … So as marvel you not at the thin population of America, nor at the rudeness and ignorance of the people; for you must account your inhabitants of America as a young people; younger a thousand years, at the least, than the rest of the world … For the poor remnant of human seed which remained in their mountains peopled the country again slowly, by little and little; and being simple and savage people, (not like Noah and his sons, which was the chief family of the earth), they were not able to leave letters, arts, and civility to their posterity.
>
> (1862: 378–9)

Atlantis, or America, is peopled by an ancient race, remnants from the 'lost' civilization of Atlantis. Aphra Behn in *Oroonoko* presents the 'Indians' of the Caribbean colony as pre-Lapsarian: 'people represented to me an absolute idea of the first state of innocence, before man knew how to sin' (1994: 7–8), and reminds the eyewitness narrator of her 'first Parents before the Fall' (7) thus effectively rendering them distant in time. In both these seventeenth-century texts we see the aesthetics of wonder operating through a distanciation in time. When we reach the nineteenth century this distanciation is tied in with the (colonial, imperial) ideology of primitivism, where the distancing in time becomes a marker of the differential evolutionary scale of civilizations and enables exoticization. (In philosophical terms, Denis Cosgrove notes, the questions of human difference, diversity and unity were 'reformulated' within debates over universal reason and human rights (2001: 195).)

Thus in Rider Haggard's *King Solomon's Mines* (1885) the caves are treated by Quatermain and his men as remnants of the *ancient* empire of the Jewish King Solomon.[18] At least one interpretation of the text situates the interracial contest of the novel as *between Europeans* rather than Europeans and Africans. In this interpretation the novel embodies an imperial anxiety where the Jews were beginning to acquire control over the diamond trade. Haggard's text, in its 'fictionalization of a fabulous lost empire stands in the shadow of his insecurity about an emerging new one' (Kaufman 2005: 519). For Kaufman, then, Haggard's Africa becomes the space of wondrous plenitude and potential profit, but also a space where the English need to confront multiple Others – Europe's internal Others, the Jews and the African Other. Haggard's *She* (1887) opens with Vince appearing at the doors of

30 Worlds and voyages

Holly and entrusting him with the guardianship of his son, Leo. Vince's story situates himself and Leo in a lineage dating back to ancient Egypt:

'Listen; the boy will be the only representative of one of the most ancient families in the world, that is, so far as families can be traced. You will laugh at me when I say it, but one day it will be proved to you beyond a doubt, that my sixty-fifth or sixty-sixth lineal ancestor was an Egyptian priest of Isis, though he was himself of Grecian extraction, and was called Kallikrates. His father was one of the Greek mercenaries raised by Hak-Hor, a Mendesian Pharaoh of the twenty-ninth dynasty, and his grandfather or great-grand-father, I believe, was that very Kallikrates mentioned by Herodotus. In or about the year 339 before Christ, just at the time of the final fall of the Pharaohs, this Kallikrates (the priest) broke his vows of celibacy and fled from Egypt with a Princess of Royal blood who had fallen in love with him, and was finally wrecked upon the coast of Africa, somewhere, as I believe, in the neighbourhood of where Delagoa Bay now is, or rather to the north of it, he and his wife being saved, and all the remainder of their company destroyed in one way or another. Here they endured great hardships, but were at last entertained by the mighty Queen of a savage people, a white woman of peculiar loveliness, who, under circumstances which I cannot enter into, but which you will one day learn, if you live, from the contents of the box, finally murdered my ancestor Kallikrates. His wife, however, escaped, how, I know not, to Athens, bearing a child with her, whom she named Tisisthenes, or the Mighty Avenger. Five hundred years or more afterwards, the family migrated to Rome under circumstances of which no trace remains, and here, probably with the idea of preserving the idea of vengeance which we find set out in the name of Tisisthenes, they appear to have pretty regularly assumed the cognomen of Vindex, or Avenger. Here, too, they remained for another five centuries or more, till about 770 A.D., when Charlemagne invaded Lombardy, where they were then settled, whereon the head of the family seems to have attached himself to the great Emperor, and to have returned with him across the Alps, and finally to have settled in Brittany. Eight generations later his lineal representative crossed to England in the reign of Edward the Confessor, and in the time of William the Conqueror was advanced to great honour and power. From that time to the present day I can trace my descent without a break. Not that the Vinceys—for that was the final corruption of the name after its bearers took root in English soil—have been particularly distinguished—they never came much to the fore ... From the time of Charles II till the beginning of the present century they were merchants. About 1790 my grandfather made a considerable fortune out of brewing, and retired. In 1821 he died, and my father succeeded him, and dissipated most of the money. Ten years ago he died also, leaving me a net income of about two thousand a year. Then it was that I undertook an expedition in connection with *that*,' and he pointed to the iron chest, 'which ended disastrously enough. On my way back I travelled in the South of Europe, and finally reached Athens. There I met my beloved wife, who might well also have been called the "Beautiful," like my old Greek ancestor. There I married her, and there, a year afterwards, when my boy was born, she died.'

(2008: 18–19)

The biography here points to a large geographical spread but also a distancing in time. Antiquarianism and mythic geography come together in Vince's life and family story. The entire family wanders, seeking safety and refuge in various countries, until eventually Vince comes to England. The genealogy of the mysterious box bequeathed to Leo, who is himself special because of the 'antiquity of [his] race', as Vince's letter to him puts it, is ancient, primitive and culturally different. Horace Holly also declares: 'A country like Africa … is sure to be full of the relics of long dead and forgotten civilisations'.

Wilkie Collins's *The Moonstone* (1868) starts the story of the stone with the 'adventures of the Yellow Diamond' from 'the eleventh century of the Christian era' (1982: 2). The story then chronicles the passing of the ages, with the changing fortunes of the stone: 'One age followed another – and still, generation after generation, the successors of the three Brahmins watched'. Then, 'one age followed another – until the first years of the eighteenth Christian … century. … [H]avoc and rapine were let loose once more' (2–3). And: 'time rolled on from the first to the last years of the eighteenth Christian century' (3), where it finally reaches Tipu Sultan and passes on during the Anglo-Mysore wars of 1799, into British hands. Tracing the genealogy of the gem enables Collins to invent a marketable antiquarianism for it.

When Holmes and Watson journey across the country to Baskerville Hall the journey is one in time as well, for as Watson reports to Holmes of his own first impressions of the desolate moor:

The longer one stays here the more does the spirit of the moor sink into one's soul, its vastness, and also its grim charm. When you are once out upon its bosom you have left all traces of modern England behind you, but, on the other hand, you are conscious everywhere of the homes and the work of the prehistoric people. On all sides of you as you walk are the houses of these forgotten folk, with their graves and the huge monoliths which are supposed to have marked their temples. As you look at their gray stone huts against the scarred hillsides you leave your own age behind you, and if you were to see a skin-clad, hairy man crawl out from the low door fitting a flint-tipped arrow on to the string of his bow, you would feel that his presence there was more natural than your own. The strange thing is that they should have lived so thickly on what must always have been most unfruitful soil. I am no antiquarian, but I could imagine that they were some unwarlike and harried race who were forced to accept that which none other would occupy.

(Doyle 1988b: 192–3)

32 Worlds and voyages

The moor is a place of forgotten people, that is, of a time past. Bram Stoker's *Dracula* also showcases the Carpathian–Transylvanian region as antiquarian:

> Sometimes we saw little towns or castles on the top of steep hills such as we see in *old* missals ...
> [The] Slovaks, who were more barbarian than the rest, with their big cow-boy hats, great baggy dirty-white trousers, white linen shirts, and enormous heavy leather belts, nearly a foot wide, all studded over with brass nails. They wore high boots, with their trousers tucked into them, and had long black hair and heavy black moustaches. They are very picturesque, but do not look prepossessing. On the stage they would be set down at once as some *old* Oriental band of brigands.
>
> (1997: 11)

In *Heart of Darkness* Marlow describes his journey through Africa as akin to 'travelling back to the earliest beginnings of the world' (Conrad 1974: 92). His first sight of the settlements in the African landscape reminds him of antiquity: 'Settlements some centuries old, and still no bigger than pin-heads on the untouched expanse of their background' (60). And later, about the forest itself: 'The smell of mud, of primeval mud, by Jove! was in my nostrils, the high stillness of primeval forest was before my eyes' (81). In the twentieth century E.M Forster in *A Passage to India* (1924) would describe Chandrapur as a town made of mud, thereby suggesting a temporal primitivism in its architecture.

What is significant in such representations of the antiquity of the Other (writing, one must note, in the wake of Darwinian theories of evolution of races, species, life forms, an evolution across *time*) is that they generate a *temporal* geography of other spaces. By 'temporal geography' I mean the situating of the Other not only in space but also in time, where the space of the Other is set, or trapped, in the ancient past. In each of the examples cited above we see precisely this: the temporalization of Atlantis, Africa, the Caribbean and the Indian subcontinent, all situated in a remote past.

Somatic geography

Somatic geography involved the documentation of physical-corporeal experience, of sensory experience, in the Other place. The dangers to and trials of the *body* might be read as the point of departure in accounts of distant lands. If Othello claims that Desdemona loves him for the dangers he has passed – or, more accurately, for his ability to *narrate* the dangers he has faced – others like Crusoe, the Ancient Mariner, Gulliver, Marlow, Kim and other famous travellers in English literature invariably begin their account of new places in terms of their corporeal experience. The body is the first site of encounter with the Other's geography and topography.

Thus in *The Tempest* Gonzalo complains 'by'r lakin, I can go no further, sir/my old bones ache: here's a maze trod, indeed,/Through forth-rights and meanders' (III.3, ll. 1–3). Shakespeare's Lavinia (*Titus Andronicus*), after her rape and mutilation, is described as a 'map of woe' (III.2, l. 12). John Donne wonders in 'Hymn to God My God in My Sicknesse':

> Is the Pacific Sea my home? Or are
> The eastern riches? Is Jerusalem?
> Anyan, and Magellan, and Gibraltar,
> All straits, and none but straits are ways to them.
>
> (1975: 348)

And further in the same poem: 'Whilst my physicians by their love are grown/cosmographers, and I their map, who lie/flat on this bed'. And in his Holy Sonnet VII Donne would write:

> At the round earth's imagined corners blow
> Your trumpets, angels, and arise, arise
> From death, you numberless infinities
> Of souls, and to your scattered bodies go.
>
> (1975: 311)

The body and the world are mapped in such images as Donne's, producing a somatic geography, where microcosm and macrocosm are united in navigation and anatomy. In chapter III of *Robinson Crusoe*, he records the terror of being buried in the waves, his aching arms and his laboured breathing. The chapter ends with the following description: 'I walked about a furlong from the shore, to see if I could find any fresh water to drink, which I did, to my great joy; and having drank, and put a little tobacco into my mouth to prevent hunger' (1975: 17). This is Gulliver's first account of Lilliput:

> I attempted to rise, but was not able to stir: for, as I happened to lie on my back, I found my arms and legs were strongly fastened on each side to the ground; and my hair, which was long and thick, tied down in the same manner. I likewise felt several slender ligatures across my body, from my arm-pits to my thighs. I could only look upwards; the sun began to grow hot, and the light offended my eyes. I heard a confused noise about me; but in the posture I lay, could see nothing except the sky. In a little time I felt something alive moving on my left leg, which advancing gently forward over my breast, came almost up to my chin; when, bending my eyes downwards as much as I could, I perceived it to be a human creature not six inches high … In the mean time, I felt at least forty more of the same kind (as I conjectured) following the first. I was in the utmost astonishment, and roared so loud, that they all ran back in a fright; and some of them, as I was

34 Worlds and voyages

afterwards told, were hurt with the falls they got by leaping from my sides upon the ground.

(Swift 1960a: 17)

The focus is on the sensations produced in his body – the word that repeats in this description is 'felt' – and this is the inaugural moment of his somatic geography of the new country. In *Roderick Random* the ship is the site of suffering and torture, and the entire atmosphere is characterized by a foul stench of decaying and diseased bodies. Random, taking a look at the ship's hospital, is appalled:

Here I saw about fifty miserable distempered wretches, suspended in rows, so huddled upon one another, that no more than fourteen inches of space was allotted for each with his bed and bedding; and deprived of the light of the day, as well as of fresh air; breathing nothing but a noisome atmosphere of the morbid streams exhaling from the own excrements and diseased bodies, devoured with vermin hatched in the filth that surrounded them, and destitute of every convenience necessary for people in that helpless condition.

(Smollett 1979: 149)

On another occasion he refers to the hospital ship filled with injured men, 'their wounds and stumps being neglected, contracted filth and putrefaction, and millions of maggots were hatched amid the corruption of their sores' (187).

The harbour too is full of human filth: 'numbers of human carcasses floated in the harbour, until they were devoured by sharks and carrion crows' (189). Smollett is actually mapping what I shall term a discrepant geography where the Englishman's encounter with the space of the Other is not profitable, benevolent or pleasurable but horrific and dehumanizing. Distant spaces here become the spaces of the Englishman's corporeal decay and destruction. The Ancient Mariner in Coleridge's famous poem of that title is 'lank, and brown' (1973: 196) after his voyages, suggesting a deep tan due to sustained exposure to the sun (he sails into the tropics). In the poem we also have references to the blackening of his lips – due to thirst – in the course of the horrific voyage. Rider Haggard's *She* in its first accounts of the African continent documents the sheer embodied terror of the storm and the shipwreck (chapter V). Their journey up the river offers another instance of this somatic geography, and the body-as-eyewitness theme:

About midday the sun grew intensely hot, and the stench drawn up by it from the marshes which the river drains was something too awful, and caused us instantly to swallow precautionary doses of quinine. Shortly afterwards the breeze died away altogether, and as rowing our heavy boat against the stream in the heat was out of the question, we were thankful enough to get under the shade of a group of trees—a species of willow—that grew by

Worlds and voyages **35**

the edge of the river, and lie there and gasp till at length the approach of sunset put a period to our miseries.

(2008: 65)

In each of these cases the distance of the Other world is embodied in the extent of suffering inscribed upon the body of the English/Englishman traveller. It is the body that travels and experiences the full measure of the distance from home, comfort and safety. The land enters the body and the traveller's corporeality, in the form of the strange and new sensations, becomes the index of an-Other geography (such as we see in Haggard's description above).

The first experience of the jungle in Africa is described thus in *Heart of Darkness*:

A great silence around and above. Perhaps on some quiet night the tremor of far-off drums, sinking, swelling, a tremor vast, faint; a sound weird, appealing, suggestive, and wild—and perhaps with as profound a meaning as the sound of bells in a Christian country.

(71)

In a later passage Conrad maps the geography of Africa entirely in terms of Marlow's sensations:

The *living* trees, lashed together by the creepers and every *living* bush of the undergrowth, might have been changed into stone, even to the slenderest twig, to the *lightest* leaf. It was not sleep—it seemed unnatural, like a state of trance. Not the *faintest* sound of any kind could be *heard*. You *looked* on amazed, and began to suspect yourself of being *deaf*—then the night came suddenly, and struck you *blind* as well. About three in the morning some large fish leaped, and the *loud* splash made me jump as though a gun had been fired. When the sun rose there was a white fog, very *warm* and *clammy*, and more *blinding* than the night. It did not shift or drive; it was just there, standing all round you like something *solid*. At eight or nine, perhaps, it lifted as a shutter lifts. We had a *glimpse* of the towering multitude of trees, of the immense matted jungle, with the *blazing* little ball of the sun hanging over it—all perfectly *still*—and then the white shutter came down again, smoothly, as if sliding in greased grooves. I ordered the chain, which we had begun to heave in, to be paid out again. Before it stopped running with a muffled *rattle*, a *cry*, a very *loud cry*, as of infinite desolation, soared slowly in the opaque air. It ceased. A complaining *clamor*, modulated in savage *discords*, filled our ears. The sheer unexpectedness of it made my hair stir under my cap. I don't know how it struck the others: to me it seemed as though the mist itself had *screamed*, so suddenly, and apparently from all sides at once, did this tumultuous and mournful *uproar* arise. It culminated in a hurried outbreak of almost intolerably excessive *shrieking*, which stopped short, leaving us stiffened in a variety of silly attitudes, and obstinately *listening* to the nearly as appalling and excessive silence. 'Good God! What is the meaning—?' stammered at my elbow one of the pilgrims.

(1974: 101–2, emphasis added)

The jungle in this description is alive, seems to sing, mourn, wail, is warm and clammy, blazing and dark, is at once (or alternately) still and mobile. As Wilson Harris quite rightly points out, the enormous quantum and depth of sensations that Conrad bestows on Marlow in the heart of Africa, leads to 'bewilderment at the heart of the original forest he uneasily penetrated' (1999 [1981]: 231–2). This is the somatic geography of the land the Englishman set out to conquer and dominate. It leads to the discovery of 'unfinished senses within him and without him' (1999 [1981]: 232), implying that Africa enables the discovery, recovery and making of the Englishman.

Somatic geography of this kind corporealizes the distant space. The Englishman's body becomes the first site of encounter with the Other. From the eighteenth century through the Victorian and the early decades of the twentieth this somatic 'site' of the encounter would be literalized: cannibals, vampires and aliens threaten the bodily integrity and even survival of the Englishman. The travel out is the scene of the encounter with the Other but also a journey into the self. However, for the encounter to assume really horrific (and Gothic) proportions, it requires a face-off with the truly non-human Other. Judith Wilt writing about *Dracula* and *The War of the Worlds* and mapping the shift from the Gothic to the sci-fi genre in the Victorian era argues, therefore, that the 'real going out' would emphasize the 'un-humanness of the encountered monster' (1981: 621). Bewilderment, disorientation, pleasure, suffering and all such corporeal experiences somatize the distant Other into something immediate, even intimate. The wanderer, therefore, is the signifier that links the distant space of the Other with England in a chain of signification. When the Englishman encounters the space of the Other, he functions as a metonym for the culture he comes from.

The importance of being itinerant

The discourse of itinerancy also generates a new theme: the freedom of mobility the Westerner has in the Asian or African space. Like all themes of itinerancy this too has significant geopolitical connotations, for it suggests a right of way through Other spaces for the Westerner, signifying spatial control and dominance.

The theme of unobstructed (but not always easy) mobility across the Other space is conjoined, especially in the Victorian era, with what M.L. Pratt (2003 [1992]) identifies as a classic trope in explorer writing: the promontory view. The sense of visual mastery that is integral to the 'monarch-of-all-I-survey scene', as Pratt calls it (201–8), is seen in Haggard's *King Solomon's Mines*:

To the right was a scattered native settlement with a few stone cattle kraals and some cultivated lands down by the water, where these savages grew their scanty supply of grain, and beyond it stretched great tracts of waving 'veld' covered with tall grass, over which herds of the smaller game were wandering. To the left lay the vast desert. This spot appears to be the outpost of the fertile country, and it would be difficult to say to what natural causes such an abrupt change in the character of the soil is due. But so it is.

Just below our encampment flowed a little stream, on the farther side of which is a stony slope, the same down which, twenty years before, I had seen poor Silvestre creeping back after his attempt to reach Solomon's Mines, and beyond that slope begins the waterless desert, covered with a species of karoo shrub.

It was evening when we pitched our camp, and the great ball of the sun was sinking into the desert, sending glorious rays of many-coloured light flying all over its vast expanse. Leaving Good to superintend the arrangement of our little camp, I took Sir Henry with me, and walking to the top of the slope opposite, we gazed across the desert. The air was very clear, and far, far away I could distinguish the faint blue outlines, here and there capped with white, of the Suliman Berg.

(unpaginated, http://ebooks.adelaide.edu.au/h/haggard/
h_rider/king/index.html)

To be able to see far into the space of the Other here becomes an anterior moment to a visual empire.

In Sherlock Holmes' 'return' story, 'The Adventure of the Empty House', he recounts his adventures (during the time he went missing after the battle with Moriarty at the Reichenbach Falls) to Watson:

I travelled for two years in Tibet, therefore, and amused myself by visiting Lhassa, and spending some days with the head lama. You may have read of the remarkable explorations of a Norwegian named Sigerson, but I am sure that it never occurred to you that you were receiving news of your friend. I then passed through Persia, looked in at Mecca, and paid a short but interesting visit to the Khalifa at Khartoum the results of which I have communicated to the Foreign Office. Returning to France, I spent some months in research into the coal-tar derivatives, which I conducted in a laboratory at Montpellier, in the south of France.

(Doyle 1986b: 328)

Holmes' (supposedly) easy transit through these varied cultures and lands is a theme visible in colonial fictions about Englishmen's travels. As commentators have pointed out (Roy 1998), mobility comes to be associated with the Westerner and his unhindered passage through the African continent or the Indian subcontinent suggests a (racialized) dominance over the land and its people.

Thus Richard Burton masquerades as an Arab and visits Mecca (*Personal Narrative of a Pilgrimage to Al-Madinah and Meccah*, 1855) and Rudyard Kipling's eponymous

38 Worlds and voyages

hero, Kim, can be any character he chooses to be – a Hindu beggar, a Muslim beggar, a spy – in the streets of Lahore. This is Kipling's description of the Irish boy in India in *Kim* (1901):

> What he loved was the game for its own sake – the stealthy prowl through the dark gullies, the crawl up a water-pipe, the sights and sounds of the women's world on flat roofs, and the headlong flight from housetop to housetop under cover of the hot dark.
>
> (Kipling 1965: 9)

Later, Kim's escapades in the Himalayas as part of the 'Great Game' once again suggest his ease of mobility through the territory of the subcontinent and a mastery over its varied landscapes, from the dusty streets of Lahore to the peaks and valleys of the Himalayas. He moves, says Kipling at one point, 'like a tall ghost' (273), shadowy, immaterial and fluid.

Parama Roy has proposed that it is mimicry and the ability to pass off as a native that characterizes the semiotics of Burton's escapades through India and the Arab world. Further, she proposes, it suggests a 'stable and coherent colonial self that can resist the potential pollutions of this trafficking in native identity' even as the native's identity is presented as imitable (1998: 197–8). Englishness itself, in such a reading, is something that the Englishman can rely upon for purposes of acquiring multiple identities in the colonial space. This argument could apply to Kim as well. Further, geography here is again somatized: the Englishman's body is what liminally connects all parts of the land, as Kim's mobility demonstrates.

If Parama Roy's focus is on the mimetic aspect of the Englishman's identity, my own emphasis is on the linkage between landscape, geography and the *embodied* self of the Englishman that results in the somatization of the land. The colonial space is the space of opportunity. While mimicry and disguise do construct the Englishman as a temporary native it also demonstrates how the native landscape offers the Englishman the opportunity to move out of his so-called 'stable and coherent' identity. The colony is the space where the Englishman can experiment with any/ all possible roles and identities. It is not the innate qualities of the Englishman's body, as Parama Roy seems to suggest, that allow for mimicry. Rather it is the malleable and adaptable quality of the geographical space of the colony that offers the Englishman the *opportunity* of disguise and multiple identities, to maybe even escape, at least temporarily, his English identity. This might also be read as the colony's indifference to the nature of the Englishman's identity as well as the colonial's desire not necessarily for masquerade but for creolization. In other words, I see the disguise and the mobility not as a sign of colonial dominance but as a symbolic marker of a shift away from any stable or pure English identity.

Itinerancy offers an individual and a culture, an 'exemplary autonomy' (as Katie Trumpener termed the idealization of gypsy itinerancy in English writings, 1992). This autonomy is aligned not only with the agency to move but also with the necessity of mobility away from a claustrophobic, inadequate setting towards a different, alternate one. For instance, Gulliver's declaration 'I was weary of being confined to an island where I received so little countenance, and resolved to leave it with the first opportunity', according to some critics, serves as a 'parable' of Gulliver's life. Writes Michael Seidel: 'his travels which then provide an imagined antidote for his insignificance as modern man within his own culture' (1998: 86–7).

From imagined and fantastic geographies to embodied geographies, the discourse of itinerancy has come a long way. But the literary history of England offers us much more than just questions of fantasy and experiential geography. It also offers us specifically political themes that link travel with the space of the Other.

Wandering and random drifting towards the distant was the physical and metaphoric movement away from the certainty of knowledge towards shores of ignorance and absences of certainty. The discourse of itinerancy, therefore, might be read as England's discourse of the search for knowledge about new places. We shall look at this theme in the next section, on the ethnography of the Other.

The ethnography of the Other

> How can the mind take hold of such a country? Generations of invaders have tried, but they remain in exile. The important towns they build are only retreats, their quarrels the malaise of men who cannot find their way home.
>
> (Forster 1970: 135)

This is E.M. Forster in *A Passage to India*, where he notes the sublime incomprehensibility of the subcontinent. There is also a definite gesture at the impossibility of any 'foreigner' finding himself or herself at home in India: they remain travellers, temporary sojourners, in the country. Travel in this case does not lead to knowledge, only a sense of permanent displacement ('men who cannot find their way home'). We shall have reasons to return to the above portrait for entirely different reasons later (see Chapter 3).

The wonders of imagined spaces and the difficulties of voyaging there were not adequate enough to capture the world in writing. An entire ethnography of the Other was instituted to provide detailed information about the exotic, distanced and ostensibly unknowable Other.

Fantastic ethnography

> The cannibals that each other eat
> The anthropophagi, and men whose heads
> Do grow beneath their shoulders.
>
> (Shakespeare, *Othello* I.3, ll. 142–4)[19]

Other lands, situated across the seas, are sites of several dreams. One might think of the Early Modern period in English writings as embodying an aspirational

40 Worlds and voyages

geography of the world in which wonder was the dominant mode of engaging with the strange and the new.

> Will thou know what wonders strange
> be in the land that late was found?
>
> (http://nationalhumanitiescenter.org/pds/amerbegin/
contact/text2/utopia.pdf)

Thus wrote Cornelius Graphey in a poem prefixed to Thomas More's *Utopia* (published originally in Latin in 1516, first English translation by Ralph Robinson in 1551). 'Fantastic geography' is the making of exotic landscapes and spaces peopled with strange creatures and events. With little attention to specifics of location and topography, fantastic geography was the space of difference because it constructed an alternative world as far removed – in distance, time as well as culture – from England as possible.

Fantastic geographies and mythic geographies relied, in addition to such a discourse of wandering and knowledge, on the detailing of monstrosities and grotesqueries. If monsters, as Jeffrey Jerome Cohen has demonstrated, occupy the wastes and outlying areas of the known world (1996), then the discourse of travel and knowledge in fantastic geographies modulate quite naturally into the *discourse of monstrosity*: monsters are Other places. Inaugurated by texts such as John Mandeville's fourteenth-century travel narrative (*The Travels of John Mandeville*, first circulated between 1357 and 1371), this discourse marks numerous texts about England's encounter with the Other. The ugly, the mysterious and the foreign were consigned to the wastes outlying the civilized world. The discourse of itinerancy merges into a discourse of geographical monstrosity in many texts, right from the Early Modern times.

The first moment of the discourse of monstrosity, as Mary Baine Campbell (1999) notes, is to be found in descriptions of anatomical and physiological strangeness and was central to the project of mapping other worlds. Initiated into the cult of the distant monstrous by Mandeville, accounts of monstrous races abound in so-called discovery narratives such as Walter Raleigh's *The Discovery of the Large, Rich, and Beautiful Empire of Guiana* (1596). Raleigh wrote:

> Next unto Arui ... are a nation of people whose heads appear not above their shoulders; which though it may be thought a mere fable, yet for mine own part I am resolved it is true, because every child in the provinces of Aromaia and Canuri affirm the same. They are called Ewaipanoma; they are reported to have their eyes in their shoulders, and their mouths in the middle of their breasts, and that a long train of hair groweth backward between their shoulders ... Such a nation was written of by Mandeville, whose reports were holden for fables many years; and yet since the East Indies were discovered, we find his relations true of such things as heretofore were held incredible (Mandeville, or the author who assumed this name, placed his headless men in the East Indian Archipelago, the fable is borrowed from

older writers, Herodotus & c). Whether it be true or no, the matter is not great, neither can there be any profit in the imagination; for mine own part I saw them not, but I am resolved that so many people did not all combine or forethink to make the report.

(http://archive.org/stream/thediscoveryofgu02272gut/
old/guian10.txt)

This is echoed almost verbatim in Shakespeare's *The Tempest* where Gonzalo tells his fellow castaways:

Faith, sir, you need not fear. When we were boys,
Who would have believed that there were mountaineers
Dewlapped like bulls, whose throats had hanging at 'em
Wallets of flesh? Or that there were such men
whose heads stood in their breasts?

(III.3, ll. 43–7)

Amazonian women, like African women, were rendered monstrous in numerous texts, thereby complicating the Other's sexuality itself as mysterious and monstrous. Translating Juvenal's sixth satire (which, as Laura Brown points out, was an influential model for representing women in the eighteenth century, 1993: 138) Dryden would frame the Amazon woman thus:

Behold the strutting Amazonian Whore,
She stands in Guard with her right foot before:
Her coats tuck'd up; and all her motions just,
She stamps, and then cries hah at every thrust,
But laugh to see her tyr'd with many a bout,
Call for the man, and like a man piss out.

(cited in Brown 1993: 138)

The war-like Amazon woman is at once fascinating as she is revolting in Dryden's description.

Victor Frankenstein, the eponymous hero of Mary Shelley's novel, seeking revenge for the murder of his family and friends, pursues the unnamed monster across Russia. Recalling, as Fred Randel argues (2003: 467–8), Napoleon's disastrous Russian campaign of 1818, Shelley's novel undertakes a geography of horror and nightmare across Russia and later the Arctic wastes of the north. When the novel ends, despite the monster's promise to commit suicide, Shelley leaves the options open: the monster is 'lost in darkness and distance' (1996: 156). Randel sees this ending in political terms, as symbolic of the possible return of the revolution that Napoleon had once embodied. However, I suggest that Shelley offers us a geography of monstrosity that, while originating in Europe (Frankenstein creates the monster in a European city: Ingolstadt, Bavaria), is forced out of Europe towards the peripheries of the known world. Admittedly, Frankenstein is pursuing

42 Worlds and voyages

the monster to exact revenge. But what the novel achieves is a *spatializing* effect, of relocating the monster to the utmost spaces *away* from European civilization. This distancing retains the distant space of the Arctic Circle as the space of monstrosity. Reading the novel's construction of the monster, Karen Piper has argued (2007) that the monster represents the Inuit of Greenland. My own interpretation suggests that while the monster is not really the ethnic Other – the Inuit – of the European, any European creation that does not fit the taxonomy of European races becomes Europe's internal Other, so to speak. The phrase 'lost in darkness and distance' might therefore be read as a consigning (and confining) of the unacceptable European monster to its 'true' location: among the savage and primitive Other of Europeans, the Inuit. The travels of Victor Frankenstein are not suggestive only of the European's quest for revenge but for the more appropriate location for his monstrous creation even though the novel wants us to see the monster as leading the scientist to his death in frozen wastes of the North. It is the strategy of distancing and travelling in order to consign the monster to the wastes as an outcast. When European culture – embodied in the people the creature tries to befriend and Frankenstein himself – fails him, he abandons it in favour of the harshest landscape possible: the polar regions. In his return to nature – to which, of course, he leads Frankenstein as well – the creature suggests a rejection of Europe itself.

In Haggard's *She* Horace Holly initially deems the members of the Amahagger tribe 'exceedingly handsome' with 'aquiline' features. But, says Holly, 'not withstanding their beauty, it struck me that, on the whole, I had never seen a more evil-looking set of faces' (2008: 75). If Behn's Oroonoko had the grandeur and noble bearing of a European, Haggard's blacks, while 'beautiful', cannot be loved.

Having mapped physical strangeness the fantastic geographies of Otherness also move into a fantastic ethnography. This second component of the discourse of monstrosity included detailed accounts of *cultural monstrosities* and the *social monstrous*. Gulliver offers detailed accounts of the 'diversions' at the Lilliput court. These 'arts' are to be performed, notes Gulliver, by those persons who seek any employment at the court:

> When a great office is vacant, either by death or disgrace (which often happens,) five or six of those candidates petition the emperor to entertain his majesty and the court with a dance on the rope; and whoever jumps the highest, without falling, succeeds in the office. Very often the chief ministers themselves are commanded to show their skill, and to convince the emperor that they have not lost their faculty. Flimnap, the treasurer, is allowed to cut a caper on the straight rope, at least an inch higher than any other lord in the whole empire.
> (Swift 1960a: 31)

And:

> The emperor lays on the table three fine silken threads of six inches long; one is blue, the other red, and the third green. These threads are proposed as prizes for those persons whom the emperor has a mind to distinguish by a peculiar

mark of his favour. The ceremony is performed in his majesty's great chamber of state, where the candidates are to undergo a trial of dexterity very different from the former, and such as I have not observed the least resemblance of in any other country of the new or old world. The emperor holds a stick in his hands, both ends parallel to the horizon, while the candidates advancing, one by one, sometimes leap over the stick, sometimes creep under it, backward and forward, several times, according as the stick is advanced or depressed. Sometimes the emperor holds one end of the stick, and his first minister the other; sometimes the minister has it entirely to himself. Whoever performs his part with most agility, and holds out the longest in leaping and creeping, is rewarded with the blue-coloured silk; the red is given to the next, and the green to the third, which they all wear girt twice round about the middle; and you see few great persons about this court who are not adorned with one of these girdles.

(1960a: 32)

The cultural monstrous was itself the effect of an entire raft of messily merged elements making up the fantastic ethnographic narrative of the Other: the moral, the religious-theological, the social-civic and the epistemological.

The moral component of the fantastic ethnography treated, very simply, the space of the Other as one where evil flourishes unchecked. It examined the cultural practices of the Other and categorized them as savage, evil and immoral. Here is a description from Behn's *Oroonoko*, where Behn suggests that the Europeans lived in some fear of these natives having witnessed their [natives'] cruelties:

About this time we were in many mortal fears about some disputes the English had with the Indians ... they [Indians] used them [Dutch] not so civilly as the English: so that they cut in pieces all they could take, getting into houses, and hanging up the mother and all her children about her; and cut a footman, I left behind me, all in joints, and nailed him to trees.

(1994: 52)

Crusoe, when he discovers he is near the Caribbean, thinks:

I had heard that the people of the Caribbean coast were cannibals or man-eaters, and I knew by the latitude that I could not be far from that shore. Then, supposing they were not cannibals, yet they might kill me, as many Europeans who had fallen into their hands had been served, even when they had been ten or twenty together.

(Defoe 1975: 98)

And soon enough he encounters the remains of a cannibal feast:

When I was come down the hill to the shore, as I said above, being the SW. point of the island, I was perfectly confounded and amazed; nor is it possible

44 Worlds and voyages

> for me to express the horror of my mind at seeing the shore spread with skulls, hands, feet, and other bones of human bodies; and particularly I observed a place where there had been a fire made, and a circle dug in the earth, like a cockpit, where I supposed the savage wretches had sat down to their human feastings upon the bodies of their fellow-creatures.
>
> (1975: 129)

As Peter Hulme has demonstrated, it is the 'paradigmatic manifestation of cannibalism [that] finally allows Crusoe to clearly distinguish himself from others' (1992: 198).[20] Crusoe becomes self-aware (that he is not a cannibal) and a 'full-fledged colonial' (198). A fantastic ethnography of the Caribbean islands, as Hulme puts it, 'conjures up the "reality" of cannibalism' (198).

The social-civic component found the manners and civic behaviour of the Other degenerate and immoral. Again, we have a typical example in Behn:

> I took 'em for hobgoblins, or fiends, rather than men: but however their shapes appeared, their souls were very humane and noble; but some wanted their noses, some their lips, some both noses and lips, some their ears, and others cut through each cheek, with long slashes, through which their teeth appeared: they had several other formidable wounds and scars, or rather dismemberings. They had comitias, or little aprons before 'em; and girdles of cotton, with their knives naked stuck in it; a bow at their back, and a quiver of arrows on their thighs; and most had feathers on their heads of divers colors.
>
> (1994: 55)

The violence of this description of dismemberment marks the irreducible geography of horror that such literary texts map when speaking of the space of the Other. Unorganized, chaotic, fragmented and dismembered the body-space of the Other is, implicitly, in sharp contrast to the well-put-together body-space of the European in Behn.

The discourse of monstrosity, specifically of the cultural monstrous, relied on an ideology of antiquarianism that distanced the Other into the past. Antiquarianism was an important component of the fantastic ethnography in English literary texts because it erased contemporary histories of the Other. Instead it located them in a past that was seen as surviving into the present. That is, in the fantastic ethnography of the Other, antiquarianism invented a past that was persistent, and cultural practices seen as remnants of a decaying/decadent past, irrelevant and ridiculous in the present, especially in the eyes of the English traveller.

Yet, it was not just the monstrous. The Englishman traversing the vast spaces of the newly discovered, or efficiently controlled, world of the Other, was often struck by the plenitude and variety of crops, people, animal and plant life, minerals and commodities. The fictional travels, one must reiterate, offered up alternate and desirable worlds. Central to this discursive construction of the desirable Other world was the rhetoric of plenty.

Plenitude and variety

> We have of revolted Grecians, Albanese
> Sicilians, Jews, Arabians, Turks, and Moors,
> Natolians, Sorians, black Egyptians,
> Illyrians, Thracians, and Bithynians,
> Enough to swallow forceless Sigismond,
> Yet scarce enough t'encounter Tamburlaine:
> He brings a world of people to the field.
>
> (Marlowe, *Tamburlaine*, Part Two, I.2, ll. 61–8. 1975: 185)

This survey – 'a world of people' – proposes a demographic sublime where variety and plenty are of near-limitless proportions. The discourse of globality is essentially a discourse of variety.

Several texts represented the space of the Other within a *discourse of desirable plenitude*, whether of nature, demography or even mineral wealth. Bountiful nature, prosperity and excess were characteristic of the space of the distant Other in numerous texts. The seventeenth-century buccaneer William Dampier in the preface to his *A New Voyage to Holland* (the narrative of his 1699–1702 expedition to *Terra Australia Incognita*) argued that the voyage was to examine the 'various and wonderful Works of God in different Parts of the World' (cited in Barnes 2006: 32). This emphasis on variety and multiplicity is common to all fictions of travel, right from the Early Modern period. The geoaesthetics in terms of these fantasies of exploration often enable the literary text to demonstrate the irreducible variety of the world. Plenitude marks the account of several such Other places.

Spenser's account of Mammon's cave with gold in it (*Faerie Queene*, Book 2) has been read as a metaphor for El Dorado and the mines of gold in the new world (Vitkus 2009: 40–2). Aphra Behn's *Oroonoko* very early establishes Surinam – the setting of her tale – as a place of 'rarities':

> marmosets, a sort of monkey, as big as a rat or weasel, but of marvelous and delicate shape … cousheries, a little beast in the form and fashion of a lion, as big as a kitten, but so exactly made in all parts like that noble beast that it is it in miniature. Then for little paraketoes, great parrots, mackaws, and a thousand other birds and beasts of wonderful and surprising forms, shapes, and colors. For skins of prodigious snakes, of which there are some threescore yards in length; as is the skin of one that may be seen at his Majesty's Antiquary's; where are also some rare flies, of amazing forms and colors.
>
> (1994: 6–7)

Oroonoko, as a young prince, himself represents the variety of not only the human race as a whole but also within the Other's race by virtue of his obvious difference from his fellow countrymen. Behn writes: 'he was adorned with a native beauty, so transcending all those of his gloomy race that he struck an awe and reverence even

46 Worlds and voyages

into those that knew not his quality' (1994: 10). Behn complicates this Othering further when she informs us that Oroonoko had acquired several European languages and consequently 'had nothing of barbarity in his nature, but in all points addressed himself as if his education had been in some European court' (1994: 11). Thus the 'black' African in this case is presented as a variant on the black theme, and thus offers the discourse of plenitude in the racial domain as well. (In Felicity Nussbaum's reading African and Oriental cultures and races merge in Behn's description, 2009: 156–7.) In Ben Jonson's *The Masque of Blackness* (1605), he merges geographies and races where the river Niger is described as an Oriental river:

> Sound, sound aloud
> The welcome of the orient flood
> Into the west.

> (Jonson 1975a: 50)

The nymphs wear both Egyptian gowns and Persian mitres, so that Africa metaphorically merges with Asia (Barbour 2003: 83).

Variety and multiplicity is also troped very often as plenitude and bounty. Fictions of travel therefore frequently present paradisal spaces of nature's plenty. Andrew Marvell would say this of the Bermudas in a poem of the same title:

> He gave us this eternal spring
> Which here enamels everything
> And sends the fowls to us in care
> On daily visits through the air.
> –
> He makes the figs our mouths to meet
> And throws the melons at our feet.

> (1971: 18)

Nature itself seems to furnish the travellers with everything they might possibly need. Having established that paradisal spaces might lie beyond the English national borders – established in the very structure of the book: a piece of travel writing – Thomas More treats this space as one of bounty. Thus More's Raphael Hythlodaeus describes the inhabitants of Utopia as possessing 'an abundance of everything' (2003: 40). He reports: 'I have never seen any gardens more productive and elegant' than those on Utopia (35). Crusoe admits that, after the initial shock of finding himself a castaway, he had been fortunate enough to have landed in a place that was nature's bounty:

> I found in the low grounds hares (as I thought them to be) and foxes; but they differed greatly from all the other kinds I had met with, nor could I satisfy myself to eat them, though I killed several. But I had no need to be

venturous, for I had no want of food, and of that which was very good too, especially these three sorts, viz. goats, pigeons, and turtle, or tortoise, which added to my grapes, Leadenhall market could not have furnished a table better than I, in proportion to the company; and though my case was deplorable enough, yet I had great cause for thankfulness that I was not driven to any extremities for food, but had rather plenty, even to dainties.

(Defoe 1975: 87)

In John Dryden's 'To His Sacred Majesty, A Panegyric on his Coronation' (1661) there is the geography of plenty:

Both Indies, rivals in your bed, provide
With gold or jewels to adorn your bride.

(1956: 36)

In Dryden's play *Amboyna* (1673), which was written in the context of the 1623 massacre of a dozen Englishmen by the Dutch near the island of Amboyna (Indonesia), the Indian woman Ysabinda is betrothed to Gabriel Towerson, the East India Company representative. In the play she is also therefore a form of the prize the East offers, and the object of contention *between* Europeans (Dryden 1808b).[21] In another play *The Indian Queen* (performed 1663–4), Dryden would do something more: link commercial profit in artistic representations of the East with voyages into the East. Using the imagery of travel, profit and art in his account of the 'Indies' in the play, Dryden writes:

You see what Shifts we are inforc'd to try,
To help out Wit with some Variety;
Shows may be found that never yet were seen,
'Tis hard to find such Wit as ne'er has been:
You have seen all that this old World cou'd do,
We therefore try the Fortune of the new,
And hope it is below your Aim to bit
At untaught Nature with your practis'd Wit:
Our naked Indians then, when Wits appear,
Wou'd as soon chuse to have the Spaniards here.
'Tis true, y'have Marks enough, the Plot, the Show,
The Poet's Scenes, nay, more, the Painter's too;
If all this fail, considering the Cost,
'Tis a true Voyage to the Indies lost:
But if you smile on all, then those Designs,
Like the imperfect Treasure of our Minds,
Will pass for current wheresoe'er they go,
When to your bounteous Hands their Stamps they owe.

(Dryden 1965: 231)

48 Worlds and voyages

In Andrew Marvell's 'On the Victory Obtained by Blake' he weighs this image of profit down:

> Now does Spain's fleet her spacious wings unfold,
> Leaves the New World and hastens for the old:
> But though the wind was fair, they slowly swum
> Freighted with acted guilt, and guilt to come:
> For this rich load …
> The New World's wounded entrails they had tore,
> For wealth wherewith to wound the Old once more.
>
> (1971: 119)

In an early voyage, says Crusoe, 'I brought home five pounds nine ounces of gold-dust for my adventure, which yielded me in London, at my return, almost £300' (Defoe 1975: 16). It is this profit, many times over his investment, that tempts him to go back to the sea. Alexander Pope in *Windsor Forest* (1713) would write of the possible benefits of the Peace of Utrecht almost entirely in terms of jewellery:

> The coral redden, and the ruby glow,
> The pearly shel its lucid globe infold,
> And Phoebus warm the ripening ore to gold.
>
> (Pope 1963: 209)

In William Cowper's 'Charity' he would underscore the need for a *global* sensibility and mobility driven by the recognition of a geography of plenty that encompasses distant nations:

> God opens fruitful nature's various scenes,
> Each climate needs what other climes produce,
> And offers something to the gen'ral use;
> No land but listens to the common call,
> And in return receives supply from all;
> This genial intercourse and mutual aid,
> Cheers what were else an universal shade,
> Calls nature from her ivy mantled den,
> And softens human rockwork into men.
>
> (http://quod.lib.umich.edu/e/ecco/004792651.0001.000/
1:8?rgn=div1;view=fulltext)

Cowper modulates nature's bounty into commercial transactions – what he calls 'genial intercourse', implying friendly, non-exploitative interactions – in global networking. We shall return to the discourse of commodification and the Other in Chapter 4.

This discourse of variety extended to include multiple models of the human is a mapping of the diversity of the earth itself. Thus the simplistic and easy binary of the White European/Black-rest-of-the-world was never quite the hegemonic model of European literary representations of the Other. Take for example Defoe's description of Friday. Defoe's Crusoe, often assumed to be the paradigmatic white colonial male, carefully calibrates Friday's colour and therefore racial roots and affinities. Crusoe informs us of the physiognomy and the complexion of his Friday:

> He was a comely, handsome fellow, perfectly well made, with straight, strong limbs, not too large; tall, and well-shaped; and, as I reckon, about twenty-six years of age. He had a very good countenance, not a fierce and surly aspect, but seemed to have something very manly in his face; and yet he had all the sweetness and softness of a European in his countenance, too, especially when he smiled. His hair was long and black, not curled like wool; his forehead very high and large; and a great vivacity and sparkling sharpness in his eyes. The colour of his skin was not quite black, but very tawny; and yet not an ugly, yellow, nauseous tawny, as the Brazilians and Virginians, and other natives of America are, but of a bright kind of a dun olive-colour, that had in it something very agreeable, though not very easy to describe. His face was round and plump; his nose small, not flat, like the negroes; a very good mouth, thin lips, and his fine teeth well set, and as white as ivory.
>
> (Defoe 1975: 160)

That Crusoe draws attention to the variants of blackness is an important point, for it indicates Defoe's awareness of the multiplicity of races and therefore of the diversity of the world.[22] Later Conrad's Marlow in *Heart of Darkness* would discover a strange geography of the Congo where he and the other Africans on the ship are all equally strangers/foreigners to the place:

> It was very curious to see the contrast of expressions of the white men and of the black fellows of our crew, who were as much strangers to that part of the river as we, though their homes were only eight hundred miles away. The whites, of course greatly discomposed, had besides a curious look of being painfully shocked by such an outrageous row.
>
> (1974: 102)

This staging of the strangeness of *both* black and white gestures at the theme of racial variety rather than a racial binary. Conrad points out implicitly that not all blacks are the same and the geography of racial identity is diffuse and dispersed and several kinds of blackness exist even within Africa.

The discourse of plenitude often generates a *discourse of possibilities and alternatives*, where the English imaginative geography of the world dreams of spaces where then Other represents something ideal. In More's *Utopia*, we see the discourse of

50 Worlds and voyages

utopianism posit an ideal land. In Swift's *Gulliver's Travels* Gulliver encounters several ways of living, including the extreme rationality that governs all aspects of life in the land of the Houyhnhnms. Alexander Pope's *Temple of Fame* (1715) idolizes Eastern spirituality when he surveys a multiplicity of faiths and beliefs (thus, again, underscoring a geography of plenitude and variety but also of alternative possibilities of ways of thinking). Pope writes:

> The Eastern front was glorious to behold,
> With diamond flaming, and Barbaric gold.
> There Ninus shone, who spread th' Assyrian fame,
> And the great founder of the Persian name:
> There in long robes the royal Magi stand,
> Grave Zoroaster waves the circling wand,
> The sage Chaldaeans rob'd in white appear'd,
> And Brahmans, deep in desert woods rever'd.
> These stop'd the moon, and call'd th' unbody'd shades
> To midnight banquets in the glimm'ring glades;
> Made visionary fabrics round them rise,
> And airy spectres skim before their eyes;
> Of Talismans and Sigils knew the pow'r,
> And careful watch'd the Planetary hour.
> Superior, and alone, Confucius stood,
> Who taught that useful science, to be good.
>
> (Pope 1963: 176)

Pope goes on to describe Egyptian priests, Nordic gods and others as well in the poem.

Both More's *Utopia* and Swift's *Gulliver's Travels*, as studies have documented, are essentially about the impossibility of utopia on earth (Houston 2007). Thus Swift, directly responding to Bacon's famous academy of sciences in *The New Atlantis*, describes the Academy of Lagado where all sorts of projects are underway. There are experiments to turn human excrement into food, and ice into gunpowder, to soften marble into pillows and pin-cushions, to extract sun-beams from cucumbers and a scheme for breeding naked sheep, among others. Knowledge and science, praised by Bacon as the utopian answer to earthly problems, in More and Swift is 'inverted' by the discovery that they are absurd and impractical. Even the Houyhnhnms' emphasis on rationality, Swift demonstrates, is absurd for it leads to both oppressive social conditions and irrational behaviour. It is a land, Gulliver admits, where there are no

> Gibers, Censurers, Backbiters, Pickpockets, Highwaymen, House-breakers, Attorneys, Bawds, Buffoons, Gamesters, Politicians, Wits, Spleneticks, tedious Talkers, Controvertists, Ravishers, Murderers, Robbers, Virtuoso's; no Leaders or Followers of Party and Faction; no Encouragers to Vice, by Seducement or Examples: No Dungeon, Axes, Gibbets, Whipping-posts, or

Pillories; No cheating Shopkeepers or Mechanicks: No Pride, Vanity or Affectation: No Fops, Bullies, Drunkards, strolling Whores, or Poxes: No ranting, lewd, expensive Wives: No stupid, proud Pedants: No importunate, over-bearing, quarrelsome, noisy, roaring, empty, conceited, swearing Companions: No Scoundrels raised from the Dust upon the Merit of their Vices; No Lords, Fidlers, Judges or Dancing-masters.

(1960a: 223)

Such a world, Swift implies satirically, lacks all variety and therefore is hardly organic or dynamic.

As late as Kipling, the East remains a place of plenitude. Writes Kipling in 'Mandalay':

'If you've 'eard the East a-calling', you won't never 'eed aught else.'
No! you won't 'eed nothin' else
But them spicy garlic smells,
An' the sunshine an' the palm-trees an' the tinkly temple-bells;
On the road to Mandalay.

(1977: 174)

Kipling's catalogue of attractions seems to offer the reasons why the Westerner is drawn to the East.

Although these texts do explore the possibilities of other ways of dealing with the world, they conclude that an earthly country, no matter how advanced, was prone to the same conditions of failure, exaggeration and absurdity. The Other, far from being an ideal Other, becomes in Swift in particular, an inverted version of the civilization Gulliver has left behind. The discourse of utopian possibilities demonstrates how in distant worlds what is lost is the variety that marks human-kind. To not have advocates, liars, politicians and scoundrels is to lose the very multiplicity that constitutes the race and the globe. The excessive rationality of the Houyhnhnms, ironically, has continued slavery (as Swift notes) and resulted in a social order that is sanitized so drastically that it seems inorganic. If Crusoe becomes the unchallenged sovereign of the island, he also replicates the conditions of slavery that he has carried with him to the Other place. Thus the fantastic geographies and mythic spaces of these texts invent alternative lifeworlds and possibilities only to discover that the Other space is 'connected' to the present England at least in the form of England's inverted double. This too becomes a vision of globality where one visualizes the Other space as something knowable, recognizable even if in its many absences.

English inquiries

The things to be seen and observed are: the courts of princes, especially when they give audience to ambassadors; the courts of justice, while they sit

52 Worlds and voyages

and hear causes; and so of consistories ecclesiastic; the churches and monasteries, with the monuments which are therein extant; the walls and fortifications of cities, and towns, and so the heavens and harbors; antiquities and ruins; libraries; colleges, disputations, and lectures, where any are; shipping and navies; houses and gardens of state and pleasure, near great cities; armories; arsenals; magazines; exchanges; burses; warehouses; exercises of horsemanship, fencing, training of soldiers, and the like; comedies, such whereunto the better sort of persons do resort; treasuries of jewels and robes; cabinets and rarities; and, to conclude, whatsoever is memorable, in the places where they go.

(Bacon 1860: 138)

This was Francis Bacon in 'Of Travel' (1625), preparing a set of instructions as to what the traveller should observe and record. Geographies of new worlds in English literature when they were not merely fantastic were often detailed written and visual maps of the new worlds. Elsewhere, in *The Advancement of Learning*, Book II, he would write of the centrality of travel to knowledge acquisition:

Proficiency in Navigation, and discoveries ... [would] plant also an expectation of the further proficiency, and augmentation of all Sciences, because it may seem they are ordained by God to be Coevalls, that is, to meet in one Age.

(Bacon 1863: 198–9)

The epistemological component treated the Other as unknowable, darkly mysterious and therefore readily classifiable as 'evil'. The rise of the trope of the 'dark continent' in the case of Africa is a good illustration of the geography of evil that such figures of speech drew of the world. The Other is secretive, mysterious and never fully knowable. Salomon House in Bacon's *New Atlantis*, unearthing the secrets of things, is itself secretive in what it reveals to the world. The head of this laboratory informs the European visitors:

We have consultations, which of the inventions and experiences which we have discovered shall be published, and which not; and take all an oath of secrecy for the concealing of those which we think fit to keep secret; though some of those we do reveal sometime to the State, and some not.

(1862: 411)

Continuing this theme of the secret/secrecy of the Other into the nineteenth century Haggard's *She* is full of secret inscriptions that need to be decoded, the secret of life, secret routes to 'Households' through the swamp, secret paths through the mountains, all of which construct Africa as unknowable and mysterious. Conrad's Marlow travelling up-river deep into Africa encounters a foggy terrain in *Heart of Darkness*:

Worlds and voyages **53**

What we could see was just the steamer we were on, her outlines blurred as though she had been on the point of dissolving, and a misty strip of water, perhaps two feet broad, around her – and that was all. The rest of the world was nowhere, as far as our eyes and ears were concerned. Just nowhere. Gone, disappeared; swept off without leaving a whisper or a shadow behind.

(1974: 102)

The symbolic blurring in this passage is mapped on to the confusion and chaos in Marlow's mind. Surrounding the colonial station, writes Conrad in an erotic spatialization, was the African wilderness 'clinging to the skirts of the unknown' (1974: 94). Conrad is mapping an African darkness that is more than just the darkness of terrain, it is an epistemologically impenetrable space. Conrad also eroticizes the African land and the African woman as dark, brooding and mysterious, as in this passage:

in the hush that had fallen suddenly upon the whole sorrowful land, the immense wilderness, the colossal body of the fecund and mysterious life seemed to look at her, pensive, as though it had been looking at the image of its own tenebrous and passionate soul. She came abreast of the steamer, stood still, and faced us. Her long shadow fell to the water's edge. Her face had a tragic and fierce aspect of wild sorrow and dumb pain mingled with the fear of some struggling, half-shaped resolve. She stood looking at us without a stir and like the wilderness itself, with an air of brooding over an inscrutable purpose.

(1974: 136)

'English inquiries' is my shorthand term for the individual heroic purposes and the national project of knowledge-gathering, eyewitnessing and experiential knowledge that fictions of travel thematize. Thus themes of travel, having documented mythic or real spaces, presented the English traveller to these spaces as heroic. Even fantastic geographies, as we shall see in this section, represented an English triumph over the mythic spaces. This triumph, which in the case of writings on Africa or Asia has been treated as an instantiation of a colonial desire by numerous critics and commentators since Edward Said (1978), is cast within a somatic geography of the new worlds.

Somatic geography, I argued, is the mapping in terms of the Englishman's physical traversals, travails, trials and triumphs in the new lands. It is the embodied geography of new worlds for, the body, writes Jonathan Sell, 'served to represent signically the experiences it had undergone' (2006: 155). As we have already noted, Gulliver and Crusoe foreground the physical-corporeal aspect of their encounter with the Other place. In addition there are the discourses of eyewitnessing and of experiential-physical heroism. Both these discourses are linked, I propose, to the project of travel as travel-knowledge. Travel to the place of the Other entailed a responsibility to know the Other. Eyewitnessing and individual

54 Worlds and voyages

enterprise and heroism are at once a response and a responsibility to the space of the Other. We therefore need to see the emphasis on a personal inquiry into the cultural practices of the Other or the documentary eyewitness account as components of what I have termed the quest for an epistemological empire for England.

To phrase it differently, English literary texts showcase the journey and the individual's personal as well as national-collective yearning for *knowledge* of the distant Other. 'We will … make a coasting voyage along the shores of the arts and sciences, not without importing into them some useful things by the way,' wrote Francis Bacon in his 1620 work, *The Great Instauration* (https://ebooks.adelaide. edu.au/b/bacon/francis/instauration/). Later, expanding this image of exploration, he wrote in *The New Atlantis* (1627): 'the end of our foundation is the knowledge of causes, and secret motions of things; and the enlarging of the bounds of human empire' (1862: 398). It is imperative to explore such distant places because, as Bacon put it, 'there are found in the intellectual as in the terrestrial globe waste regions as well as cultivated ones' (*The Great Instauration*, unpaginated, https:// ebooks.adelaide.edu.au/b/bacon/francis/instauration/).

Abraham Cowley's 'To The Royal Society', a poem originally affixed to Thomas Sprat's *The History of the Royal Society of London* (1667), presented Bacon himself as an explorer, albeit an explorer in the domain of knowledge:

> Bacon, like Moses, led us forth at last,
> The barren wilderness he past.
> Did on the very border stand
> Of the blest promis'd land,
> And from the mountain's top of his exalted wit,
> Saw it himself, and shewed us it.
> But life did never to one man allow
> Time to discover worlds, and conquer too.
>
> (http://cowley.lib.virginia.edu/works/RoyalSociety.htm)

Cowley does not present Bacon as an explorer who sets out on his journey for individual reasons/causes alone. He portrays Bacon as somebody who 'leads' – Cowley's term – the English ('us') like a prophet-saviour ('Moses') through new terrains. In this portrait, Bacon is a hero because he embodies the English public's desire for discovery, conquest and knowledge.

Later Alan Ramsay would write his praise of Newton, 'Ode to the Memory of Sir Isaac Newton', in much the same terms as Cowley:

> May from your Learned Band arise,
> Newtons to shine thro' future times,
> And bring down knowledge from the skies,
> To plant on wild Barbarian climes.
> 'Til nations, few degrees from brutes,

Be brought into each proper road,
Which leads to wisdom's happiest fruits,
To know their Saviour and their God.

(cited in O'Brien 2009: 291)

Here Newton and his 'band' are positioned as a colonial civilizational mission catering to the needs of the primitive tribes in 'Barbarian climes', and exemplifying-embodying, therefore, what Alan Lester (2000) has thoughtfully teased out as the 'global humanitarian regime'.

Aphra Behn's *Oroonoko* opens with a similar emphasis on eyewitnessing:

> I was myself an eye-witness to a great part of what you will find here set down; and what I could not be witness of, I received from the mouth of the chief actor in this history, the hero himself, who gave us the whole transactions of his youth: and though I shall omit, for brevity's sake, a thousand little accidents of his life, which, however pleasant to us, where history was scarce and adventures very rare, yet might prove tedious and heavy to my reader, in a world where he finds diversions for every minute, new and strange. But we who were perfectly charmed with the character of this great man were curious to gather every circumstance of his life.
>
> (1994: 6)

Individual heroism is of course best exemplified by Defoe's Crusoe. Virtuous individual labour in Defoe's text becomes the means of engaging with an alien space. Very early in the novel, during his Brazil sojourn, Crusoe tells us how he worked at the plantation, and how everything was the labour of his hands. When on the island for twenty-eight years, Crusoe works to dominate and cultivate the land there as well. (Although it must be noted that Crusoe's early moves in business involved the slave trade – the Xury part of his story – and later it involved slave labour: that of the Carib Friday.)

Investigating the East for the resolution of its mysteries seems to be an Englishman's individual and national-racial responsibility in these texts. 'My object in following the Indian plot, step by step, is to trace results back, by rational means, to natural causes,' says Murthwaite in Wilkie Collins' detective tale, *The Moonstone* (1982: 317). The Englishman, therefore, performs the work of *knowing* the mysterious Other (as we shall see when discussing the stone in Chapter 4).

The rest of the tale is concerned with unravelling the truth behind the stone's disappearance, ownership and symbolic value. Significantly, the stone's awesome contradiction, of knowledge and mystery, is located at the crucial intersection of English domesticity and the wild spaces of the Orient, of the safe and secure English family and the ungovernable and mysterious East.[23] How the stone constitutes a disturbing experience for the people in the English home is manifest in Betteredge's reflections:

56 Worlds and voyages

> here was our quiet English house suddenly invaded by a devilish Indian diamond – bringing after it a conspiracy of living rogues, set loose on us by the vengeance of a dead man. ... Who ever heard of the like of it – in the nineteenth century, mind; in an age of progress, and in a country which rejoices in the blessings of the British constitution? Nobody ever heard the like of it, and, consequently, nobody can be expected to believe it.
>
> (1982: 36–7)

The improbability of the events around the stone, Betteredge's reflections suggest, have to do with its *itinerancy* and its dislocation: from the subcontinent to the progressive and supposedly safer English home. Thus Collins writes of the 'invasion' of English domesticity by the stone. But the stone's peregrinations are themselves initiated by *England's* own travels. The marvellous story of the stone and its 'devilish' influence on English domesticity is rooted in the English experience of the Other. The stone is first stolen by British soldiers – i.e. traveller-soldier-adventurers – during the Mysore battle of 1799 in southern India. This first level of experiential travel and robbery is followed, some time later, by three Hindu priests from India who travel to England to rescue the stone and take it back to its rightful place in India. The moonstone therefore is the embodiment of two very different travel impulses and the novel's detective format presents the quest for knowledge about the stone as the heart of the story.

Murthwaite, described as the 'celebrated Indian traveller' (1982: 73), is the one who seeks to reconcile English and Oriental epistemological systems. If wandering, as already noted, is the meeting of two epistemological systems then Collins sets up the tension between English domesticity, greed, imperial impulses and family drives and Oriental systems. The novel ends with a set of questions: 'So the years pass, and repeat each other; so the same events revolve in the cycles of time. What will be the next adventures of the Moonstone? Who can tell?' (1982: 522). In Roberts' reading, this is 'an evocation of an Eastern view of history and reality', and that 'what happens to it [the Moonstone] in the cycles of time, remains unknown and unknowable' (1997: 181). Over time the events around the stone are likely to bring the West/England into constant conflict or at least interactions with the East, suggests Collins.

The English traveller initiates a process of knowing when he starts collating and comparing information about the new place with known geographies. Of course what did not fit in with the Western imagination and epistemological frame was consigned to the mythic, mystic and the 'devilish' (as Collins describes the India stone). Here is Conrad's Marlow caught up in a mesmeric vision of something he cannot comprehend and therefore described in 'devilish' terms:

> We were within thirty yards from the nearest fire. A black figure stood up, strode on long black legs, waving long black arms, across the glow. It had horns – antelope horns, I think – on its head ... It looked fiend-like enough.
>
> (1974: 143)

A classic instance of the demonization of the Other, Conrad's description represents not simply a case of colonial stereotyping but the failure of the Western epistemological system which had no category, no lineage and no classificatory system for what it encountered in Africa or the colonies. African voices and language are described as a 'tumultuous and mournful uproar', a 'burst of yells', 'angry and warlike yells', a 'tremulous and prolonged wail', and in the passage already quoted above 'complaining *clamor*, modulated in savage discords'. Robert Hampson has proposed that Conrad treats African language as 'pre-verbal, pre-syntactic sound', as 'sound that is utterance without meaning' (1999: 203). But the descriptions could also be read as Conrad's implicit critique of the *failure* of the Western knowledge systems in the new knowledge ecologies of Africa. What we see here is the assertion of a stereotype: of the failure of comprehension of the English traveller rather than an assertion of conscious, deliberate and courageous typification.

Enumeration, accounting and numbering are key modes of managing knowledge about the Other. These modes become ways of enclosing the wonder of the Other into manageable, understandable forms and formats. Cataloguing the Other meant not simply classifying the Other in terms of racial characteristics within ethnographic and ethnographic frameworks. This kind of accounting in detail situated the text, which was about an Other world, in the real world inhabited by the reader and the author (Sell 2006: 72). The book places itself, as de Certeau would put it, by demarcating the place of the encounter with the Other. The text's operations result in the 'determination or displacement of the boundaries delimiting cultural fields (the familiar vs. the strange) … [it is] the text's reworking of space that simultaneously produces the space of the text' (de Certeau 1986: 67–8). Thus Ralph Rover in Ballantyne's *The Coral Island* clarifies the validity of the belief regarding the African's cannibalism:

> I 'spose 'twas yer tender-hearted friends in England that put that notion into your head. There's a set o' soft-hearted folk at home that I knows on who don't like to have their feelin's ruffled; and when you tell them anything they don't like—that shocks them, as they call it—no matter how true it be, they stop their ears and cry out, 'Oh, that is *too* horrible! We can't believe that!' An' they say truth. They can't believe it, 'cause they won't believe it. Now, I believe there's thousands o' the people in England who are sich born drivellin' *won't believers* that they think the black fellows hereaways, at the worst, eat an enemy only now an' then out o' spite; whereas I know for certain, and many captains of the British and American navies know as well as me, that the Feejee Islanders eat not only their enemies but one another—and they do it not for spite, but for pleasure. It's a *fact* that they prefer human flesh to any other. But they don't like white men's flesh so well as black; they say it makes them sick.
>
> (unpaginated, http://ebooks.adelaide.edu.au/b/ballantyne /rm/coral-island/)

58 Worlds and voyages

In addition to such 'definitive' epistemological claims, different ways of organizing knowledge of the Other space are visible in English writings. Three key modalities of comprehending and apprehending the Other in textual forms might be discerned in English writings of new worlds: the indexing of places, of names and of words.

Michael Drayton in his epic about the glories of England smuggles in navigation as a national project when he writes in *Poly-Olbion* (first part, 1612):

> With Fitch, our Eldred next, deserv'dly placed is,
> Both travelling to see the Syrian Tripolis
> The first of which (in whose noble spirit was shown)
> To view those parts, to us that were most unknown,
> On thence to Ormus set, Goa, Cambaya, then,
> To vast Zelabdin, thence to Echubar, again
> Cross'd Ganges' mighty stream, and his large banks did view,
> To Bacola went on, to Bengola, Pegu;
> And for Mallaccan then, Zeitan, and Cochin cast
> Measuring with many a step, the great East–Indian waste.
>
> ('The Nineteenth Song', ll. 237–46, Drayton
> 1953: 638)

By focusing on the individuals who visit these Other places Drayton creates a personal romanticized geography: these are places the English have physically been to. The list here is not of just any elsewhere but an elsewhere that can now be safely indexed and therefore brought within the ambit of the known and the reachable. The language of the Drayton account is interesting. He speaks of the 'steps' taken by the English traveller even as he sees them as organizing knowledge about distance ('measure') in the case of the East Indies. But Drayton also takes care to specify the places, and draws, as a result, an entire geography of England's travels (England being represented, since it is a national project, in its traders-travellers). This extract demonstrates the use of an *index locorum*, the indexing of places. The *index locorum* becomes the verbal equivalent of the map. By the late sixteenth century taking careful 'observations' of latitudes and longitudes was a responsibility of the sailor. Thus Defoe's Crusoe is able to state with simple pride: 'I ... learn'd how to ... take an Observation' (1975: 16).

Aphra Behn – the narrator is a white traveller to the Caribbean – in *Oroonoko* describes how the Africans and the racial Others are given new names by the Europeans:

> Christians never buy any slaves but they give 'em some name of their own, their native ones being likely very barbarous, and hard to pronounce; so that Mr. Trefry gave Oroonoko that of Caesar; which name will live in that country as long as that (scarce more) glorious one of the great Roman.
>
> (1994: 39)

Such indexing of names and places are effective as strategies of familiarization (with the space of the Other) in Defoe's *Robinson Crusoe*. To be able to fashion one's self in a completely alien setting involves an engagement, often conflictual, with distant-new places, people, things and processes. Defoe's text suggests that the English self of Crusoe emerges in such an engagement. Yet, as we note, Crusoe adapts the territory to his way of life even as he struggles with the specifities of a strange place.

While not exactly a king, Crusoe assumes all the forms of kingship over those parts of the island he familiarizes himself with. (It is interesting that Crusoe does not venture too deep or too far into the island.) He sees himself as 'Lord of the Manor', and whenever he surveys his island 'domain' he does so with a 'secret Kind of Pleasure' (Defoe 1975: 80). Such a fantasy, as critics have noted, clearly suggests colonial ambitions and imperialist dreams in Defoe. Defoe offers a fantasy of absolute sovereignty by suggesting that Crusoe has rights over the lives and bodies of creatures on that island. He 'fixes' the names of the life forms around him, classifies them (domestic, feral, subjects, threats). Most famously Crusoe, in an Adamic act, first bestows a name upon the 'savage': Friday. He then affixes 'slave' as the category of 'person' Friday *must* be/become. To be able to describe himself as 'Lord of the Manor' is to initiate the *index nominum* through which Crusoe asserts editorial and textual control over the new world. Maxmilian Novak writes: Crusoe 'transforms his island world through the agency of language, and particularly ... through a creative process of naming' (cited in McInelly 2003: 5). But it is not, as Novak proposes, only Friday's naming that counts. Crusoe *names* his constructions as well: he now has what he calls a 'country-house' (that quintessential English feature), and a 'sea-coast home' (Defoe 1975: 81). He has a 'country-seat' and a 'plantation' (1975: 119). The *index nominum* merges into an *index locorum* – whether of residence, domestication of animals, pastures or the wilds in *Robinson Crusoe*.

Defoe's fantasy in *Robinson Crusoe* is not simply the conquest of another world, but to be able to exercise the powers of a sovereign over the lives in that world. Crusoe's fear is of being swallowed up by other identities and individuals (Armstrong 1992: 218). He alleviates this fear through acts of spacing but also acts of naming and classifying. Having, therefore, affixed the name and category of 'slave' upon Friday, Crusoe says the savage made 'all the Signs of Subjection, Servitude, and Submission imaginable, to let me know, how he would serve me as long as he liv'd' (Defoe 1975: 161). When therefore Friday takes care of *his* father Crusoe is visibly annoyed, terming the savage's acts 'Extravagancies of his Affection' (1975: 185). Friday's filiation with and fealty to his biological father becomes unacceptable to Crusoe-the-master. With these processes of indexing Crusoe organizes the space of this other – his? – world and the inhabitations of his 'subjects'.

What is forgotten in the midst of Crusoe's acts of naming and assertion of sovereignty is that he is not 'pure' English. His father is a 'foreigner of Bremen, who settled first at Hull'. His real name was Robinson Kreutznaer which, says Crusoe, 'by the usual corruption of words in England, we are now called, nay we call our selves, and write our names Crusoe' (1975: 5). Crusoe's concern with

60 Worlds and voyages

naming the things on the island proceeds from his early experience of having no control over his own name. English culture's *index nominum* of which Crusoe and his family become victims – subjects to the English language processes of linguistic 'corruption' – is what he reverses when given the chance to do the same to other life forms. From the lack of control over his family name in England, Crusoe signs himself King, Lord of the Manor and Master, designating others slaves, savages, criminals and cannibals. Globality here is envisioned as the fantasy of finding and bestowing new names and new identities upon the self and others in another space. Crusoe performs actions that make him new, in line with what Defoe in his 1722 novel, *Moll Flanders*, would propose of English migrants to the Americas as 'new people in a new world' (2004: 238). Newness lies in the naming of space where the two indexes – *nominum* and *locorum* – come together.[24]

It is interesting to see how Defoe's indexing of places and names changes from the practices of the earlier era. In Behn's *Oroonoko* she writes of how the African prince Oroonoko, renamed Caesar by the European slave and plantation owners, when he arrives, 'he was received more like a governor than a slave' (1994: 40). He is given a portion of plantation land to work on, she writes, 'but as it was more for form than any design to put him to his task, he endured no more of the slave but the name' (40). Here the slave is placed on lands marked for slave-labour, he is deemed a slave, but is not treated entirely like one. The epithet 'slave', however, is one he has to 'endure'. Here the indexing of the land and the name are aligned in the representation of the prince-turned-slave, but in a new world. Behn's novel smuggles in the conflictual nature of all white indexing when she writes: 'they all cast themselves at his feet, crying out, in their language, "Live, O King! Long live, O King!" and kissing his feet, paid him even divine homage' (40). Oroonoko remains prince, and semi-divine, to the Africans (ironically, these are Africans he had sold into slavery – to Europeans). Behn points also to the ineffectual nature of European indexing, even in spaces where they are ostensibly sovereign and in control. The place of the Other, which the Europeans hope to adjudicate over, is never entirely Europeanized.

It is in the fantasy of placing the Other – whether Friday or animals and plants native to the new space – through the two indices that the *text* of Crusoe places itself. Crusoe's text is the witness to the Others in/of the Caribbean island. I see Crusoe's acts of naming new places, events and lives as his engagement with a new world. My argument therefore is in consonance with Brett McInelly's which suggests that Crusoe's 'expansion' of the 'venturing self' through relations with the alien Others 'hones ... both its own selfhood and the destiny of others' (2003: 1).

If the venturing self, a key colonial trope in the discourse of globality, sought sovereignty in the form we have noted of Crusoe, it was also astute enough to categorize and enumerate the qualities of the Other. A preeminent example of these alternate forms of engagement with the space of the Other might be found in the opening sections of Behn's *Oroonoko*. Here Behn describes the European colonists and the practice of slavery. Behn demonstrates how the Europeans were careful about the 'Indians' in Surinam: 'for those we live with in perfect amity, without daring to command 'em; but, on the contrary, caress 'em with all the brotherly and friendly affection in the world'. That is, the Europeans did not dare make slaves of the Surinam 'Indians':

> So that they being on all occasions very useful to us, we find it absolutely necessary to caress 'em as friends, and not to treat 'em as slaves, nor dare we do other, their numbers so far surpassing ours in that continent.
>
> (1994: 9)

The slaves are 'are negroes, black slaves altogether', i.e. Africans.

Index verborum is the indexing of words and the slow incorporation of the language of the Other into the Englishman's vocabulary. Thus Lemuel Gulliver writing about the various countries he found himself trapped in is able to acquire enough of the local language to communicate minimally. At Brobdingnag, says Gulliver, 'I began to learn their language and make my wants known' (Swift 1960a: 77). From chapter 2 of Part II (dealing with Brobdingnag) Gulliver introduces words from Brobdingnagian into his writing, glossing the words in English for his readers. In the case of Laputa he discovers:

> The knowledge I had in mathematics, gave me great assistance in acquiring their phraseology, which depended much upon that science, and music; and in the latter I was not unskilled. Their ideas are perpetually conversant in lines and figures. If they would, for example, praise the beauty of a woman, or any other animal, they describe it by rhombs, circles, parallelograms, ellipses, and other geometrical terms, or by words of art drawn from music, needless here to repeat.
>
> (1960a: 129)

This incorporation of the speech of the Other marks a crucial mode in familiarizing oneself with the culture of the place. In the case of Crusoe it works differently. Crusoe makes it clear that Friday will be the one who needs Crusoe's (English) language. The first word Friday is made to recognize is 'Master'. In *Melmoth the Wanderer*, Melmoth has to teach Immalee, living on an uninhabited island, the meanings of words. 'Only with difficulty', writes Maturin, 'was she able to comprehend the meanings of these words' (2012: 352). While the absence of language grants her 'impregnable innocence' (353), Melmoth's task is to bring her into the realm of the 'civilized' (it must be noted that Immalee, however, is not of an indigenous ethnic group, she is hybrid: she is of Spanish origin, and is, like Crusoe, the sole survivor of a shipwreck off Calcutta).

In Ballantyne's *The Gorilla Hunters* Peterkin tells their new African servant, Makarooroo: 'Don't you suppose I'm going to stand on ceremony with you. Your name's too long, by half. Too many rooroos about it, so I'm going to call you Mak in future, d'ye understand?' (unpaginated, http://www.gutenberg.org/files/21736/21736-h/21736-h.htm). Ralph's authority over the black man includes the right to take away, deny and modify the latter's family name and history.

62 Worlds and voyages

The discourse of itinerancy, as we have seen thus far, has enabled the production of knowledge about the Other place. One could argue that itinerancy enables a certain epistemological and textual control over the Other space even when this knowledge is codified or cast in the form of fiction. Besides this clearly political theme of an epistemological empire through travel, itinerancy also engenders a crucial theme: that of the Other space as the site of English triumphs. Anticipated in the theme of English epistemological successes at decoding the mysterious Other and in the portrait of the adventurous Englishman, this theme is integral to the discourse of itinerancy.

Triumphalist geography

In Mary Shelley's *The Last Man*, Raymond the Englishman, having led the Greeks in their battles against the Turks, is believed dead on the battlefield and immediately becomes a hero and a martyr for the Greeks:

> No man had ever excited so strong an interest in the public mind; this was apparent even among the phlegmatic English, from whom he had long been absent. The Athenians had expected their hero to return in triumph; the women had taught their children to lisp his name joined to thanksgiving; his manly beauty, his courage, his devotion to their cause, made him appear in their eyes almost as one of the ancient deities of the soil descended from their native Olympus to defend them. When they spoke of his probable death and certain captivity, tears streamed from their eyes; even as the women of Syria sorrowed for Adonis, did the wives and mothers of Greece lament our English Raymond—Athens was a city of mourning.
>
> (2004: 133–4)

This account of course recalls Rupert Brooke's famous image of the 'corner of a foreign field' that would forever be England because an Englishman had died there. But the larger point is the triumphalism of mourning in Shelley where the Greek nation deifies the Englishman, who therefore expands at least symbolically the 'reach' of England into other regions. (When Raymond comes back alive he is greeted by crowds thronging the streets of Athens, 2004: 139–40.)

If several texts such as the ones cited here encoded the fantasy of profits, others treated the geography of difference and of distance as encoding the possibility of English triumphs and success. As early as the mid-seventeenth century William Davenant's play *The History of Sir Francis Drake* (1658–9) offered a new version of the European conquest of Peru. The Symarons and the Peruvian villagers welcome Drake as a liberator from their Spanish oppressors (who nearly made them slaves). In such a play we see, as Suvir Kaul notes, a whole new vision of colonial conquest where England extends its territories and authority with honour, compassion and charity (2009: 37–8).

Defoe's *Robinson Crusoe* is an exploration of the growth of the individual self within the ambit of mercantilism (Novak 1962), but this self is fantasized as possessing authority over other lives and in the space of the Other which then is transformed through Crusoe's efforts into the space of his triumph. In Tennyson's 'To the Queen' (1873) he refers to the 'ever-broadening England' with its 'throne' in the 'vast Orient' (1969: 1755). This *expansion* of the self, of the national project and of the national boundaries, is an entirely new geography of both England and the world that begins to appear from the early eighteenth century but gathers strength in the Victorian period. Triumphalist geography is this cluster of spatial discourses that document the expansion of the Englishman's agency into new territory. It focuses on the dangers faced by the Englishman in new climes and areas and eventual success through sheer 'Brit grit', endurance and physical labour.

Crusoe first establishes sovereign powers over the birds on the island, which he believes ruin his crops. The birds are nominated 'thieves'. Crusoe kills three of them 'and serv'd them, as we serve notorious Thieves in England, (viz.) Hang'd them in Chains for a Terror to others' (Defoe 1975: 92). Next he reinforces his sovereign authority:

> I might *call* my self *King*, or Emperor over the whole Country which I had Possession of. There were no Rivals. I had no Competitor, none to dispute Sovereignty of Command with me.[25]
>
> (101, emphasis added)

Defoe's Crusoe separates his domesticated animals from the feral, 'or else they would always run wild when they grew up'. The tamed flocks are kept on 'some enclosed Piece of Ground, well fenc'd either with Hedge or Pale, to keep them in so effectually, that those within might not break out or those without break in' (115). Crusoe 'senses' his power *as* sovereign *after* pronouncing himself 'King'. He can, after this, demonstrate the validity of his assertion by pronouncing the right to others' lives: 'I had the Lives of all my Subjects at my absolute Command. I could hang, draw, give Liberty, and take it away, and no Rebels among all my Subjects' (116). His parrot, dog and cats sit beside him at the table, to whom he grants permission to talk (the parrot) and offers tidbits as 'a mark of special favour' (116–17). Defoe's hero is the prototype of the English colonial who converts the space of the other into a map of individual, racial and national triumph.

In Charlotte Brontë's *Jane Eyre*, Jane praises St John Rivers for his noble aim of going to India as a missionary:

> As to St. John Rivers, he left England: he went to India. He entered on the path he had marked for himself; he pursues it still. A more resolute, indefatigable pioneer never wrought amidst rocks and dangers. Firm, faithful, and devoted, full of energy, and zeal, and truth, he labours for his race; he clears their painful way to improvement; he hews down like a giant the prejudices of creed and caste that encumber it. He may be stern; he may be exacting; he may be ambitious yet; but his is the sternness of the warrior Greatheart, who guards his pilgrim convoy from the onslaught of Apollyon. His is the

exaction of the apostle, who speaks but for Christ, when he says—'Whosoever will come after me, let him deny himself, and take up his cross and follow me.' His is the ambition of the high master-spirit, which aims to fill a place in the first rank of those who are redeemed from the earth—who stand without fault before the throne of God, who share the last mighty victories of the Lamb, who are called, and chosen, and faithful.

St. John is unmarried: he never will marry now. Himself has hitherto sufficed to the toil, and the toil draws near its close: his glorious sun hastens to its setting.

(2010: 385)

Soldier, saint, priest, physician, but above all else, a patient toiler in new lands. This is a profile of one kind of man who would produce the triumphalist geography of the British Isles, well beyond the isles. Jane too has similar ideals, for work within England, as she tells Rochester:

I'll be preparing myself to go out as a missionary to preach liberty to them that are enslaved ... I'll stir up mutiny; and you, three-tailed bashaw as you are ... shall in a trice find yourself fettered amongst our hands.

(2010: 230)[26]

In the nineteenth-century genre of adventure fiction Africa and Asia become less spaces of the Other than the triumphalist spaces of English individualism and enterprise. Patrick Brantlinger's succinct formulation about the era's explorer writings on Africa gestures at the triumphalist geography of the continent. Such writings, he argues,

are nonfictional quest romances in which the hero-authors struggle through enchanted, bedeviled lands toward an ostensible goal: the discovery of the Nile's sources, the conversion of the cannibals ... The humble but heroic authors move from adventure to adventure against a dark, infernal backdrop where there are no other characters of equal stature, only bewitched or demonic savages ... Center stage is occupied not by Africa or Africans but by a Livingstone or a Stanley, a Baker or a Burton, Victorian St. Georges battling the armies of the night.

(Brantlinger 1988: 180–1)

Brantlinger's argument fits the fiction and several poems of the age. Take, for instance, the triumphalism of Felicia Hemans' 'The Traveller at the Source of the Nile' (1826):

In sunset's light, o'er Afric thrown,
A wanderer proudly stood
Beside the well-spring, deep and lone,
Of Egypt's awful flood;

Worlds and voyages **65**

The cradle of that mighty birth,
So long a hidden thing to earth!
He heard its life's first murmuring sound,
A low mysterious tone;
A music sought, but never found,
By kings and warriors gone;
He listen'd – and his heart beat high –
That was the song of victory!
The rapture of a conqueror's mood
Rush'd burning through his frame, –
The depths of that green solitude
Its torrents could not tame;
There stillness lay, with eve's last smile,
Round those calm fountains of the Nile.
Night came with stars: – across his soul
There swept a sudden change;
E'en at the pilgrim's glorious goal
A shadow dark and strange
Breathed from the thought, so swift to fall
O'er triumph's hour – and is this all?

Then, adds Hemans, as though the triumphalism might be treated as unpatriotic, the conqueror-hero ponders:

No more than this! what seem'd it now
First by that spring to stand?
A thousand streams of lovelier flow
Bathed his own mountain land!
Whence, far o'er waste and ocean track,
Their wild sweet voices call'd him back.
They call'd him back to many a glade,
His childhood's haunt of play,
Where brightly through the beechen shade
Their waters glanced away:
They call'd him, with their sounding waves,
Back to his fathers' hills and graves.

(www.unc.edu/~ottotwo/hemanspoem.html)

His heart, she writes, is full of 'yearnings for his home'.

Places like Spain also offered the opportunity of romances, as Byron demonstrated in *Childe Harold's Pilgrimage* (Canto 1), describing the Iberian Peninsula as a 'fabled' and 'romantic' land. (Thus it would be wrong to see only the Orient as offering the English Romantic poets the space of exoticism and romance. See Sánchez, 2009, on Byron's Iberian romanticism.)

66 Worlds and voyages

In Ballantyne's *The Gorilla Hunters*, the protagonists return to the African continent, but as adults this time. Ballantyne now depicts them in ways that look forward to Conrad's depictions of English/European savagery in Africa.

'It seems to me,' said Jack, breaking silence at the end of a long pause which had succeeded an animated discussion as to whether it were better to spend one's life in the civilised world or among the wilds of Africa, in which discussion Peterkin, who advocated the wild life, was utterly, though not admittedly, beaten—'it seems to me that, notwithstanding the short time we stayed in the gorilla country, we have been pretty successful. Haven't we bagged thirty-three altogether?'

'Thirty-six, if you count the babies in arms,' responded Peterkin.

'Of course we are entitled to count these.'

'I think you are both out in your reckoning,' said I, drawing out my notebook; 'the last baby that I shot was our thirty-seventh.'

'What!' cried Peterkin, 'the one with the desperately black face and the horrible squint, that nearly tore all the hair out of Jack's head before he managed to strangle him? That wasn't a baby; it was a big boy, and I have no doubt a big rascal besides.'

'That may be so,' I rejoined; 'but whatever he was, I have him down as number thirty-seven in my list.'

'Pity we didn't make up the forty,' observed Jack.

'Ah! yes indeed,' said Peterkin. 'But let me see: could we not manage to make it up to that yet?'

'Impossible,' said I. 'We are far away from the gorilla land now, I know; for, in addition to the fact that we have seen no traces of gorillas for a long time, we have, within the last few days, seen several lions, which, you are well aware, do not exist in the gorilla country.'

'True; but you mistake me,' rejoined Peterkin. 'I do not mean to make up the number to forty by killing three more, but by proving, almost to demonstration, that we have already been the death of that number, in addition to those noted down.'

'You'll find that rather difficult,' said Jack, laughing.

'Not at all,' cried Peterkin. 'Let me think a minute. You remember that enormously big, hairy fellow, that looked so like an ugly old man that Ralph refused point-blank to fire at him, whereupon you fired at him point-blank and wounded him in the shoulder as he was running away?'

'We treated several big fellows in that way,' replied Jack; 'which of them do you allude to?—the one that roared so loud and terrified you so much that you nearly ran away?'

. . .

'Well, that fellow flew into such a horrible rage when he was wounded,' continued Peterkin, 'that I am perfectly certain he went straight home and murdered his wife in a passion; which brings up the number to thirty-eight.

Then there was that old woman–gorilla that I brought down when we were descending yon hill that was covered with such splendid vines. You remember? Well, I'm quite certain that the young man–gorilla beside her, who ran off and escaped, was her son, and that he went home straightway and died of grief. That makes thirty-nine. Then—'

'Oh, do be quiet, Peterkin, please,' said I, with a shudder. 'You put things in such a fearfully dark and murderous light that I feel quite as if I were a murderer. I feel quite uneasy, I assure you; and if it were not that we have killed all these creatures in the cause of science, I should be perfectly miserable.'

'In the cause of science!' repeated Peterkin; 'humph! I suspect that a good deal of wickedness is perpetrated under the wing of science.'

(unpaginated, http://www.gutenberg.org/files/21736/21736-h/
21736-h.htm)

Just as Defoe's Crusoe establishes sovereignty over the lives of the animals on the island and Friday, Ballantyne's young men establish, in horrific fashion, their utter and total control over the tribes and the land. Such a control is primarily exercised as violence. This landscape of violence that is drawn in Ballantyne's text becomes the space of national heroism as boys become men and men become conquerors. It renders the Other space passive and abject in the light of the British advance.

Resonating with Ballantyne's imperialist fiction, practically all of G.A. Henty's fiction (*With Clive in India*, 1884, *With Roberts to Pretoria*, 1902, and *With Kitchener in the Soudan*, 1903) maps such a triumphalist British geography around the world, mainly achieved, as Mawuena Logan notes, by English gentlemen (1999: 87–8). In the case of fiction about Africa, more than in the works about India or South America, we discern colonial physical violence upon the bodies of the natives. In Laura Franey's excellent study of African travel writings, she suggests that this is partly due to the fact that Victorian England saw the Africans as subjects rather than as citizens (2003: 16–17). Further, she proposes, British sovereignty was marked on African bodies as a mode of disciplining violence or in the form of indirect violence manifest as mercy (18). Haggard's fiction is full of detailed scenes of violence, mostly culminating in the decapitation and dismemberment of the African body (see Franey 2003: chapter 3) and which was inaugurated by a similar account in Behn's *Oroonoko* where the African prince-slave is finally killed slowly through mutilation and dismemberment. (I shall return to this theme of dismemberment and colonial violence in the last chapter.)

A different kind of triumphalist geography might be seen in authors like Tennyson. Tennyson believed that the expanding British Empire would actually see a unification of the races and cultures. Take, for instance, his 'Opening of the Indian and Colonial Exhibition by the Queen' (1886). Here he first refers to the 'Gifts from every British zone' (1969: 1358), thus already offering up the image of a convergence of spaces where the products and people from various parts of the

68 Worlds and voyages

British Empire are now congregated in the imperial capital. The last stanza of the poem goes thus:

> Sharers of our glorious past,
> Brothers, must we part at last?
> Shall we not thro' good and ill
> Cleave to one another still?
> Britain's myriad voices call,
> 'Sons, be welded each and all
> Into one imperial whole,
> One with Britain, heart and soul!
> One life, one flag, one fleet, one throne!'
> Britons, hold your own.

(1969: 1358)

'One imperial whole', where the colonies with their different races and cultures would be 'one with Britain': this is the triumphalist geography of Victorian England.

Admittedly, such a triumphalist geography often documented fictional (and real) deaths of British 'heroes' like General Gordon (and therefore might be said to overlap with the *discrepant* geography of suffering, trauma and death in alien lands – a theme for my last chapter). A poem eulogizing Gordon went this way:

> Too late! Too late to save him,
> In vain, in vain they tried.
> His life was England's glory
> His death was England's pride.

(qtd. in James Morris 1984: 512)

Tennyson's famous 'The Defence of Lucknow' (1879) describes the brave soldiers 'English in heart and limb', imbued with the 'strength of the race to command,/to obey, to endure' (1969: 1252).

The discourse of triumphalism accounted for such sacrifices but elided the thematic of tragedy (of, say, young men) in favour of the thematic of heroism. Such deaths were not only reminders of violence but also of European settlements in inhospitable places. Graves and burial rituals in these 'foreign' places 'settled' by Europeans, as David Bunn (2002) eloquently argues, acquired symbolic significance both in the colony and the British press. Which is precisely what Brooke's famous lines seem to suggest. We have already noted W.E. Henley's poem about England that showcases England's destiny. Felicia Hemans sees the death of soldiers in strange lands as redeemed by the 'spells of home' in her poem of the same title:

> It hath led the freeman forth to stand
> In the mountain-battles of his land;

It hath brought the wanderer o'er the seas
To die on the hills of his own fresh breeze.
(http://digital.library.upenn.edu/women/hemans/records/
records.html#spells)

The Englishman who travels out – as sailor, soldier, merchant – not only maps the
world on to his body and mind, but also converts, if Rupert Brooke is to be
believed, a corner of the world into England when he dies outside his nation:

If I should die, think only this of me;
That there's some corner of a foreign field,
That is forever England.

This echoes Felicia Hemans' 'England's Dead' (1822) where the world is mapped
in terms of the places in which England's heroic sons lie dead: Egypt, the banks of the
Ganges, Pyrenees, Colombia. We see a similar triumphalist geography constituted
by killings and deaths in Tennyson. In his 'Ode on the Death of the Duke of
Wellington' (1852), Tennyson expands England's influence to the entire European
territory, calling her 'the soul of Europe' (1969: 1013). The Crimean war was the
context of Tennyson's famous 'The Charge of the Light Brigade' (published in
1854 in *The Examiner*) that celebrated what Tricia Lootens calls the 'senseless
sacrifice' (267) in the poem's oft-quoted 'their's not to reason why,/Their's but to
do and die' (1969: 1034–6). Kipling's poetry celebrated the good the English had
wrought among the 'lesser breeds without the law' ('Recessional', 1977: 130). In
'The English Flag' winds from the four corners of the earth affirm the triumph of
the English flag.

As late as 1948 in Graham Greene's *The Heart of the Matter* the map on Scobie's
wall 'was of no more use to him: he carried the whole coastline of the colony in
his mind's eye' (1948: 8). Although Greene eventually maps the African colony as a
space of the collapse of English identity, the novel opens with the imprint of the
land's topography in the Englishman's mind as triumphalist geography. The entire
façade of moral superiority assumed by the English in their relationship with their
colonial subjects helped generate a triumphal rhetoric of benevolence, control and
this in turn helped the making of an English identity. It is this very façade that later
writers like Paul Scott would expose.

Thus, despite death and suffering, the world's geography is mapped in terms of
the Englishing of Other spaces. The English bodies that lie buried in various parts
of the world assert the Englishness of their deaths, and transform the Other land
into sites of not simply mourning but of celebration.

**

England, then, develops a cluster of discourses predicated upon itinerancy and
geography and in the process develops its theme of a transnational English identity.

70 Worlds and voyages

Travel and associated discourses of profit, exploration and discovery with/of the land of the Other contributed to the sense of a national project and therefore of a national identity as early as the Early Modern period. Contiguous and sometimes conflictual discourses of ethnography – including fantastic ethnography – enabled the documentation and 'comprehension' of the Other place and its inhabitants, as we have seen.

Other societies and their lifestyles entering into the English imagination and knowledge banks served, as Edward Test summarizes it, as the alternative lifeworlds that Montaigne and More envisioned in their writings (2009: 257). It must be emphasized that both real discoveries and geographical knowledge about new worlds, as well as mythic-creative imaginings of new worlds contributed equally to the vision of alternative spaces to which Europe could possibly journey and discover things about itself.

Triumphalist geography, with its indexing of the Other place, however, rubbed up against a discrepant geography from the late nineteenth century as Britain's exploration, conquest and dominance of the Other worlds runs alongside the suffering and deaths of its young men, the creolization of others and the recognition that their (English) presence in foreign lands has not always been beneficial to the natives. We shall return to this discrepant geography of England's transnational encounters in Chapter 6.

What this chapter has demonstrated is the recurrent discourse of itinerancy and a spatial imagination in English writings. The examples, from the Early Modern to the twentieth century, are illustrative of the multiple discourses that referenced, studied and constructed the racial and cultural Other through this literary history. Globality is the construction of this distant but reachable Other and, as this chapter has demonstrated, English literature has always been engaged with its outsites, or the globe. Globality demands, as the English literary tradition demonstrates, an itinerancy even as itinerancy constructs England's engagement with the world. English literature's most consistent aesthetic has, therefore, been a geoaesthetic.

Notes

1 In the Early Modern period it was common practice to situate plays elsewhere in Europe. Middleton placed his *The Changeling* in Spain and *The Revenger's Tragedy* in Italy. *The Duchess of Malfi*, *The White Devil* and *Women Beware Women* were set in Italy. Ancient Italy is the setting of *Coriolanus*, *Titus Andronicus* and *Julius Caesar*.

2 Geoaesthetics can also, surely, be about the intrusion of the distant world/globe into the home. Catherine Hall (2002), Hall and Rose (2006) and Antoinette Burton (1998) in the case of the late nineteenth and early twentieth century, for instance, have shown how Victorian ideas of Englishness were under pressure due to the visible presence of the once-distant Empire at the heart of London. But my concern in this chapter is not this intrusion by the Other but the structural condition of the Englishman going away, or out into the world.

3 In the same vein Roxann Wheeler (1995) argues that Defoe's *Robinson Crusoe* does not do a simply white/black racial binary but instead offers a 'racial multiplicity'. Wheeler's

reading teases out 'juxtapositions' of the British with Europeans, Moors, West Africans or Native Caribbeans, but also notes the complications of slavery, European Christians, cannibals and the Caribs in the novel.

4 In other European cultures commentators warned against travel. Antoninus Florentius' *Summula Confessionale*, published in Venice in 1474 and a text Columbus carried on his voyage, claimed that the life of the merchant-adventurer gave ample opportunities for sinning – the sins included bartering worthless objects for precious ones, price-rigging, excessive profit, usury and lying in the making of marriage contracts, although the ones who carried on trade across great oceanic distances were tolerated a lot more, given the risks they undertook (Jardine 1996: 324–5).

5 The inventory ran thus: 'First, the inhabitants of … Java Major buy them [spices] in other islands … and sell them in their own island … Secondly, those from the island Seilan … buy the spices in Java and bring them to their own island … Thirdly, Ceylon … they are once more unloaded, charged with Customs duty and sold to the merchants of the island Aurea Chersonesus … Ninthly, at Frankfurt, Bruges, and other places … Tenthly, in England and France' (Jardine 1996: 296–8). A spice-geography of the world is what this represents.

6 The Early Modern period saw an explosion of publications in geography: Pierre Duval's *A Geographical Dictionary* (1662), George Meriton's *Geographical Description of the World* (1671), Edmund Bohun's *A Geographical Dictionary* (1688), and Laurence Echard's geographical index, *The Gazatteer's: or, Newsman's Interpreter* (1692), among others. Earlier texts such as George Abbot's *Briefe Description of the Whole World* (1599), Peter Heylyn's *Microcosmos* (1621, revised and expanded as *Cosmographie* in 1652) and Bernard Varenius' Latin *Cosmography and Geography* (1650, translated into English in 1680) were reprinted as well.

7 Ethel Seaton's classic essay 'Marlowe's Map' (1924) was an extensive study of Marlowe's geographical imagination. For a contemporary study see Jones (2008).

8 For studies of these early examples of science fiction see among others Poole (2010), Cottegnies (2010).

9 In some cases travel served as the analogy for faith. Thus Jonathan Gil Harris detects in George Herbert's *The Temple* (1633) an analogy between the Jews' lack of geographical progress and the Christians' inability to progress in their devotions (2009: 53). The Herbert lines that draw Harris' attention are:

> For as the Jews of old by Gods command
> Travell'd, and saw no town:
> So now each Christian hath his journeys spann'd:
> Their storie pennes and sets us down.
>
> (Herbert 1972: 128)

10 Such a cosmographic imagination was not, however, always triumphalist or positive in its outlook. Considerable anxiety about what the travels would uncover in the distant places is expressed in several texts. Thus when Adam ponders over the distant spaces of the world in Milton's *Paradise Lost* (1674, Book VII), Raphael tells him:

> the great architect
> Did wisely to conceal and not divulge
> His secrets to be scanned by them who ought
> Rather admire; or, if they list to try
> Conjecture, he his fabric of the heavens
> Hath left to their dispute, perhaps to move
> His laughter at their quaint opinions wide
> …
> Think only what concerns thee and thy being;
> Dream not of other worlds, what creatures there

72 Worlds and voyages

> Live, in what state, condition or degree,
> Contented that thus far hath been revealed
> Not of earth only but of highest Heaven.
> > (unpaginated, http://www.dartmouth.edu/~milton/reading_room/
> > pl/book_1/index.shtml)

11 John Peck proposes that such narratives demonstrate how 'maritime concerns ... permeate every aspect of the nation's life' (2001: 75). But Britain's maritime concerns were only one part of the larger culture of exploration and itinerancy, which is what I focus on here.
12 It must be noted that the one who voyages is also the Other. John Gillies notes that there are three voyaging Others in Shakespeare: Prospero, Othello and Morocco (1994: 3).
13 On the adventure fiction of the colonial period see also Bristow's *Empire Boys* (1991) and Phillips' *Mapping Men and Empire* (1995). Martin Green states unequivocally:

> The adventure tales that formed the light reading of Englishmen for two hundred years and more after Robinson Crusoe were, in fact, the energizing myth of English imperialism. They were, collectively, the story England told itself as it went to sleep at night; and in the form of its dreams, they charged England's will with the energy to go out into the world and explore, conquer, and rule.
> > (1980: 3)

> The English public school, writes Kathryn Tidrick in her study, *Empire and the English Character* (1990) instilled the 'flamboyant cult of manliness' (218) wherein the student 'learned to do as he was told without question; later he learned to take it for granted that he would be obeyed. He learned to punish and encourage. He learned ... to rule' (170).

14 Such images of control, mobility and travel in distant lands in the nineteenth century were linked to questions and debates about the vicissitudes of long-distance governance. Duncan Bell has shown how through the nineteenth century, with new developments in navigation and technologies of travel and communication, debates about a global polity and an integrated political structure over distance were common (2005).
15 'Error' is etymologically 'errare' which means both 'wandering' and 'mistake'. Thus random, mistaken wandering and knowledge seem to be implicitly connected.
16 Denis Cosgrove notes that with development in navigational aids and cartography through the seventeenth century, the ocean and the island became the dominant topographical imagination (2001: 188–9).
17 However, occasionally the distant is what the English recall when they return home. Having described a dismal landscape of an African colony, Graham Greene in *The Heart of the Matter* (1948) presents the landscape as one the Englishmen miss when they return home. Far from seeing their present location (England, home) as a *secretum iter*, they recall at least briefly the dingy landscape of the colony. Greene writes:

> Men who had left the port for ever sometimes remember on a grey wet London evening the bloom and glow that faded almost as soon as it was seen: they would wonder why they had hated the coast and for a space of a drink they would long to return.
> > (1948: 20)

> The profit on mobility, in the form of nostalgia for a lost life, comes to haunt the ones who have left the space of the Other behind.

18 As Patrick Brantlinger has noted, the discovery of the mines in the later decades of the nineteenth century puzzled the Europeans, who had always argued that the Africans were incapable of civilization. Thus was born, according to Brantlinger, the myth of the caves as remainders of Solomon's ancient empire (1988: 195).
19 'The wylde and myscheuous people called *Canibales* or *Caribes*, which were accustomed to eate mannes fl she (and called of the olde writers, *Anthropophagi*) molest them

[meaning the *Arawaks*] excedyngly, inuadynge theyr country, takynge them captiue, kyllyng and eatyng them.' This was Peter Martyr de Anghiera, who compiled the first accounts of the Columbus voyages.

20 Scotland during Shakespeare's time was also believed to have had cannibals in its tribes. There were similarities; Jean Howard notes that the 'barbarous' Picts of Scotland and the tribes of the New World as portrayed by Theodor de Bry share a 'primitivist discourse' (2003: 317–18).

21 The treachery of the Dutch is thematized in Ysabinda's rape by Harman, the Dutchman.

22 Geraldine Heng's work on the Middle Ages and texts such as the Arthurian legends, Geoffrey of Monmouth's *History of the Kings of Britain* and others. Heng writes of Europe's 'colonizing impulse that domesticates all alterity by narcissistically reproducing oneself, and the image of one's culture, even while ostensibly speaking of otherness' (254). Thus, although in Europe's emphasis on similarities, a certain, limited, 'domestication' of otherness is achieved, it was effectively a narcissistic reproduction of oneself by the European.

23 Critics have argued for and against Collins' novel as a critique of imperialism. John Reed in his 1973 essay summarized it thus: 'the Moonstone becomes the sign of England's imperial depredations, the symbol of a national rather than a personal crime' (286).

24 Joseph Bartolomeo argues that although figures like Colonel Jack and Moll Flanders seem to acquire economic success and social status *after* being transported as indentured servants, Defoe's fictions of such success in fact offer more ambivalent stories of emigration because each 'is subject to more subtle forms of coercion' (2011: 457). On the emigration propaganda in these two novels, see Novak (1962) and Richetti (1987), among others.

25 Crusoe of course has moments wherein he recognizes that as God's creature he must accepts that God is a bigger sovereign power: 'I was not to dispute his Sovereignty, who, as I was his Creature, had an undoubted Right by Creation to govern and dispose of me absolutely as he thought fit; and who, as I was a Creature who had offended him, had likewise a judicial Right to condemn me to what Punishment he thought fit' (Defoe 1975: 123). But the fantasy of being the sole sovereign in that space is too powerful for Crusoe to let go. On kingship in *Robinson Crusoe* see Schonhorn (1977).

26 For incisive readings of the tension and dynamics between patriarchy, race, gender and Empire in *Jane Eyre* see, among others, Spivak (1986), Azim (1993), Zonana (1993).

3

DIFFERENCE AND DESIRE

The exoticized Other

He had an extreme good and graceful mien, and all the civility of a well-bred great man. He had nothing of barbarity in his nature, but in all points addressed himself as if his education had been in some European court … He was pretty tall, but of a shape the most exact that can be fancied: the most famous statuary could not form the figure of a man more admirably turned from head to foot. His face was not of that brown rusty black which most of that nation are, but of perfect ebony, or polished jet. His eyes were the most awful that could be seen, and very piercing; the white of 'em being like snow, as were his teeth. His nose was rising and Roman, instead of African and flat. His mouth the finest shaped that could be seen; far from those great turned lips which are so natural to the rest of the negroes. The whole proportion and air of his face was so nobly and exactly formed that, bating his color, there could be nothing in nature more beautiful, agreeable, and handsome. There was no one grace wanting that bears the standard of true beauty. His hair came down to his shoulders, by the aids of art, which was by pulling it out with a quill, and keeping it combed; of which he took particular care. Nor did the perfections of his mind come short of those of his person; for his discourse was admirable upon almost any subject: and whoever had heard him speak would have been convinced of their errors, that all fine wit is confined to the white men, especially to those of Christendom.

Cruel, false, thievish, murderous; addicted more or less to grease, entrails, and beastly customs; a wild animal with the questionable gift of boasting; a conceited, tiresome, bloodthirsty, monotonous humbug.

'Tis very easy to see, they have in reality more liberty than we have. No woman, of what rank soever, is permitted to go into the streets without two *murlins*, one that covers her face all but her eyes, and another, that hides the whole dress of her head, and hangs half way down her back. Their shapes are also wholely [*sic*] concealed, by a thing they call a *serigee*, which no woman of any sort appears without; this has strait sleeves, that reach to their fingers-ends, and it laps all round them, not unlike a riding-hood. In winter, 'tis of cloth; and in summer, of plain stuff or silk. You may guess then, how effectually this disguises them, so that there is no distinguishing the great lady from her slave. 'Tis impossible for the most jealous husband to know his wife, when he meets her; and no man dare touch or follow a woman in the street ... This perpetual masquerade gives them entire liberty of following their inclinations, without danger of discovery. The most usual method of intrigue, is, to send an appointment to the lover to meet the lady at a Jew's shop, which are as notoriously convenient as our Indian-houses; and yet, even those who don't make use of them, do not scruple to go to buy pennyworths, and tumble over rich goods, which are chiefly to be found amongst that sort of people. The great ladies seldom let their gallants know who they are; and 'tis so difficult to find it out, that they can very seldom guess at her name, whom they have corresponded with for above half a year together. You may easily imagine the number of faithful wives very small in a country where they have nothing to fear from a lover's indiscretion, since we see so many have the courage to expose themselves to that in this world, and all the threatened punishment of the next, which is never preached to the Turkish damsels. Neither have they much to apprehend from the resentment of their husbands; those ladies that are rich, having all their money in their own hands. Upon the whole, I look upon the Turkish women, as the only free people in the empire.

Almost naked, and splendidly formed, he sat on a raised platform near the back, in the middle of the central gangway, and he caught her attention as she came in ... He had the strength and beauty that sometimes come to flower in Indians of low birth. When that strange race nears the dust and is condemned as untouchable, then nature remembers the physical perfection that she accomplished elsewhere, and throws out a god ... This man would have been notable anywhere; among the thin-hammed, flat-chested mediocrities of Chandrapore he stood out as divine.

These four extracts come from (1) Aphra Behn's 1688 work *Oroonoko* (1994: 11–12), (2) Charles Dickens' 1853 essay 'The Noble Savage' (http://www.djo.org.uk/media/downloads/articles/2204_The%20Noble%20Savage.pdf), (3) Mary Montagu's (non-fictional) 1725 *Letters* [from Turkey] (also known as the *Turkish Embassy Letters*, http://ebooks.adelaide.edu.au/m/montagu/mary_wortley/letters) and (4) Forster's 1924 novel *A Passage to India* (1970: 212), respectively. The first two exemplify English attitudes towards the so-called savage, barbaric races. The third

76 Difference and desire

transforms the sartorial code of the woman of a different culture into a moral code. The fourth clearly sexualizes the Indian's body – a subaltern's at that – ostensibly viewed by the *Englishwoman*.

What is common to all three is a representational strategy whereby the Other's difference becomes the object of admiration (Behn, because Oroonoko seems to erase his difference from Europeans), derision (Dickens, because the 'noble savage' is not only 'wild' but also aspires to states of greatness through his boasts), envy (Montagu, because the Turkish women's very costume seems to encourage sexual freedom) and desire (Forster, because the half-naked body of the punkah-wallah is what arrests Adela Quested's attention although the context of this 'viewing' is the traumatic setting of her own deposition in court). This representational strategy through which difference is highlighted, sentimentalized and morally adjudicated is *exoticization*. Behn, Dickens, Montagu and Forster by *showcasing the difference of the African, the savage and the Turkish woman draw boundaries of inside (Europe, white) and outside (Africa, Turkey), of civilized and uncivilized even as they engender, in the case of Montagu and Forster, desire.*

English authors sought ways of coping with the difference they heard about, perceived and consumed – whether in terms of people, commodities or cultural practices. As England's engagement with different parts of the world grew through the seventeenth century, the island nation discovered, literally, worlds out there. The national and cultural borders of identity and character now began to mark not just a distinction between, say, England and France (alternately old rivals, friends, allies and enemies) or Protestantism and Catholicism, but a whole raft of *culturally, racially and religiously different* people and places. Arabs, Africans, Asians, Chinese, Russians, Native Americans and indigenous tribes appeared in the English imagination and became a part of its fantasy of a multicultural geography.

Exoticism, technically, is what deals with the outside: 'exo'. It was traditionally associated with imported plants and botanical specimens in the eighteenth century (Knellwolf 2002: 13). The foregrounding of cultural difference and foreignness, with varying intentions and consequences – from pleasure to terror – is now described as 'exoticization'. The discourse of exoticism is clearly, therefore, a discourse of borders and boundaries. It is something outside of everyday experience, beyond the ordinary, maybe even the fantastic (Rousseau and Porter 1990: 15). 'The term exotic', writes Christa Knellwolf, 'defines the implicit borders of society, state, and church' (2002: 10). More importantly in Knellwolf's reading, the exotic described both fantasies and real historical responses to Otherness (11). The exotic is a reminder of an early, primal stage and gestures at the outside, between the home and the world (Eaton 2006). The exotic recalls a boundary, 'inside which familiarity reigns and outside which is wild' (Aravamudan 2012: 227). However, as Eugenia Jenkins reminds us, exoticism was not simply a representation of non-European others. It was also 'a mode of European self-representation, asking how and why it is used to generate diverse models of selfhood in the context of global economic expansion and exchange' (2012: 5). Echoing Jenkins' overall interpretation of the exotic, Laura Rosenthal sees exoticism as serving an important function: it offered 'multiple cosmopolitan possibilities' for the cultural reinvention of the self, society and the nation (2012: 11). Exoticism, as theorized in the writings of Rosenthal, Aravamudan and Jenkins, was a key feature in the self-fashioning of English identity. It is with such constant engagements with strangeness and foreignness that England begins to redefine itself, its national, geopolitical and cultural boundaries, even as difference could be charming, threatening, desirable, repulsive, frightening, in turn, in literary representations.

This book in its entirety, of course, deals with England's discourse of globality and negotiation of Otherness in its literature. In this chapter I explore the discourses of exoticism. It leaves out literary representations of imported foreign commercial commodities – cotton, tea, china – that became incorporated into English *daily lives*, and which will be the subject of the next chapter. Such exotic as became a part of the everyday, as I have proposed elsewhere following Beth Tobin (1999: 27–55), demonstrated to the English that the distant exotic was now a part of the Empire, their home and thus their *routine* lives (Nayar 2012: 60). In a sense, therefore, this commodity culture from about the later seventeenth century *domesticated* the exotic. This present chapter looks at people and objects that were thematized as foreign, not-easily-available or understood, as unusual and even as the marvellous. I focus on forms and discourses of exoticization in English literature – from primitivization to eroticization. While objects do enter the discussion, they are examined from a different perspective here. The aim of this chapter is to demonstrate how English literature has always been engaged with things, places and cultures beyond its borders. It argues that discourses of exoticization, primarily in the aesthetic domain, constitute a key form of England's engagement with the outside, the 'exo', and therefore with itself. Exoticization was not only a form of discussing the racial-culture Other – it was also a means of negotiating radical difference in ways that occasionally thrilled, terrorized, delighted and threatened. Exoticist discourses transformed the Other into a primitive Noble Savage, a vulnerable woman, a seductive woman, a singular scientific event and evoked strong sentiments of terror and pleasure. The exotic savage in the eighteenth century was one, Kate Fullagar notes, who exhibited 'a lack or simplicity of what we might call custom' (2008: 213). Thus cultural practices were markers of civilizational difference and rendered the Other savage and exotic at the same time.[1]

Conversely the seductive Arab woman, the minerals of the Indian subcontinent, the native tribe of the African jungle were exotic *because* they existed outside the boundaries of what the English knew and understood. This I characterize as the imperial exotic, because it emphasized not the acquirable and knowable Other in the routine of English life but the distant Other. If 'colonial' gestures at settlement and proximity to the Other, 'imperial' gestures at the incontrovertible distance between Self and Other.

The discourse of the exotic Other took two principal forms. In one, the Other evoked shock, awe, pity, sympathy and desire. A moral evaluation also, frequently, accompanied this *sentimentalization* of the exotic. Behn's admiration for an African (Oroonoko) who, despite his race, was able to close the distance between himself

78 Difference and desire

and the European by his bearing, Dickens who disputes, with considerable irony, that the savages had any kind of culture and Mary Montagu who envies the Turkish woman's sartorially facilitated licentiousness exemplify the sentimental exotic. In the second, the exotic functioned as the foundation of a whole episte-mological project, where the Other was cast in ways that solicited and elicited inquiries, investigations and particularization in what could be thought of as the *scientific* exotic. The scientific exotic was a particular trait of travelogues and memoirs where the individual, with the target audience of peers in mind, offered explanations for non-European phenomena as diverse as plant life, architecture, physiognomies and cultural practices.

This chapter focuses on the sentimental exotic. The discourse of sentimental exoticism carries within itself strains of both the sentimental and the scientific in particular ways. The sentimental exotic mystifies the Other while within the same text we often find the European witness seeking ways of containing, explaining and demystifying the Other. My key cases for the study of the English exoticization of the racial-culture Other are the literary representations of the savage/barbarian and gender identity. The former includes a wide range of 'savage' Others – from blacks to American Indians. The latter includes Turkish, Indian, American Indian and Arab women but also the sexual dynamics of masculinity and femininity of Europeans in Other lands.

English sentimental discourse mapped sites of difference within an aesthetic-emotional rhetoric. It constructed the non-European as something that evokes horror, revulsion, attraction or sympathy. It perceived and represented difference from an affective and moral standpoint and foregrounded the *individual* observer's subjective and affective reactions to difference.

The savage exotic

The savage and Other was marked by excessive cruelties on the battlefield, the lack of ethics in warfare, the ill-treatment of prisoners. But cruelty, in some English texts, was also measured in terms of greed and financial manipulation. An early instance of the 'barbarity' of the Saracen, for example, occurs in Spenser's *Faerie Queene*, and is imaged in terms of financial exploitation. In Book 5, Canto 2, Artagell hears of the 'cursed, cruell Sarazin' (1984: 535), Pollente, who guards a bridge and whose daughter Munera had accumulated wealth from her father's misdeeds. Artagell eventually decapitates Pollente, thus putting an end to his financial cruelties. Similarly, Souldan the Saracen is described (in Book 5, Canto 8) as one who has neither

> religion nor fay,
> But makes his God of his ungodly pelfe,
> And Idols serves.
>
> (1984: 583)

Greed and the quest for wealth are markers of a barbaric civilization that then the European/English knight must overcome.[2]

The cannibal, however, is the epitome of the savage. 'Cannibals', as Peter Hulme shows in his remarkable 1986 study, 'was a non-European name used to refer to an existing people – a group of Caribs in the Antilles' (1992: 15). The term emerges first in Columbus' narrative of 1492 (1992: 17) and has a direct correlation to the racialized discourses of Orientalism, discovery and savagery.

Shakespeare's Caliban – the name serving as an anagram for 'cannibal' – is described as a wild man, and at one point, a 'strange fish' (Trinculo's first description for Caliban, II.2, l. 27). He is believed to have been 'got by the devil himself' (I.2, l. 321), and is a 'born devil/on whose nature, Nurture can never stick' (IV.1, ll. 188–9. On the genealogy of the 'wild man' in European representations see White 1972). He is 'not honour'd with/a human shape' (I.2, ll. 281–4). Hulme sees these accounts as indicating Caliban's 'distanc[ing] from the social world into the satanic and the bestial' (1992: 114). Inaugurating an entire discourse of non-European savage beings, Shakespeare emphasizes Caliban's animal-devil nature. Cannibalism is the subtext to the animal-devil, and would be a sustaining trope for European writers later.[3]

In Edmund Spenser's *Faerie Queene* (Book 6, Canto 8) he describes an entire tribe or nation of cannibals – and a besieged (European?) woman, Serena, in their midst before the knight saves her:

> a savage nation, which did live
> Of stealth and spoil, and making nightly rode
> Into their neighbours borders; ne did give
> Them selves to any trade, as for to drive
> The painful plough, or cattle for to breed,
> Or by adventurous merchandize to thrive;
> But on the labours of poor men to feed,
> And serve their own necessities with others need.
> Thereto they used one most accursed order,
> To eat the flesh of men, whom they mote find,
> And strangers to devour, which on their border
> Were brought by error or by wreckful wind.
>
> (1984: 678)

The savages 'round about her flock, like many flies' and are about to dine when the knight Calepine arrives to decimate them:

> swarms of damned souls to hell he sends;
> The rest that scape his sword and death eschew,
> Fly like a flock of doves before a Falcons view.
>
> (1984: 680)

Robert O'Brien (2001) traces Spenser's account of the cannibal nation to multiple sources, including Irish and American ones. Arguing that in Elizabethan England

80 Difference and desire

'cannibalism was often used as a conclusive signifier of otherness' (36), O'Brien believes that Serena's would-be 'consumers' 'closely resemble the natives in the European-Native American encounter' (43). Both Shakespeare and Spenser therefore associate cannibalism with the racial and cultural Other, or what I have designated the savage exotic. Always elsewhere, at a distance, the savage exotic becomes a cultural marker of civilization/primitivism.

Thus in Daniel Defoe's *Captain Singleton* (1720), the hero says that all his shipmates were worried, when arriving at a new place, about 'being devoured by wild beasts, murdered, and perhaps eaten by cannibals' (1969a: 12), although, he adds, there was 'no reason for … [the] suggestion [that the inhabitants of the land they had arrived at were cannibals]' (13). Crusoe in Defoe's classic novel is of course constantly worried about the possible existence of cannibals on 'his' island. There seems to be, at least until the eighteenth century, the automatic assumption that distant lands which do not figure on European maps are more than likely to be inhabited by cannibals. The Englishman's (or woman's) journey to a distant land becomes the setting where the literary text can fashion the English as civilized, virtuous, moral and courageous in contrast with the cowardly savages who, in Spenser's description that would echo as a trope through English literature, can only attack as a mindless collective ('swarms' and 'flies').

The savage, epitomizing a premodern life form and culture, serves as the exotic backdrop to English adventure, exploration and the colonial project itself. Standing in sharp contrast to the 'civil' and fair-minded Englishman, ostensibly, the savage Caliban of Shakespeare or the cannibals of Defoe effectively demonstrate an English identity that emerges in conflict with these Others who occupy the distant places where England seeks to establish its territory. The savage is not simply the Other – the savage is the creature who occupies the very space the Englishman seeks to explore, settle in and perhaps dominate.

In *Humphrey Clinker* (1771), Tobias Smollett offers a detailed account of the torture of two Scotsmen at the hands of Native Americans:

> He and ensign Murphy had made their escape from the French hospital at Montreal, and taken to the woods, in hope of reaching some English settlement; but mistaking their route, they fell in with a party of Miamis, who carried them away in captivity. The intention of these Indians was to give one of them as an adopted son to a venerable sachem, who had lost his own in the course of the war, and to sacrifice the other according to the custom of the country. Murphy, as being the younger and handsomer of the two, was designed to fill the place of the deceased, not only as the son of the sachem, but as the spouse of a beautiful squaw, to whom his predecessor had been bethrothed; but in passing through the different whigwhams or villages of the Miamis, poor Murphy was so mangled by the women and the children, who have the privilege of torturing all prisoners in their passage, that, by the time they arrived at the place of the sachem's residence, he was rendered altogether unfit for the purposes of marriage: it was determined therefore, in

the assembly of the warriors, that ensign Murphy should be brought to the stake, and that the lady should be given to lieutenant Lismahago, who had likewise received his share of torments, though they had not produced emasculation.—A joint of one finger had been cut, or rather sawed off with a rusty knife; one of his great toes was crushed into a mash betwixt two stones; some of his teeth were drawn, or dug out with a crooked nail; splintered reeds had been thrust up his nostrils and other tender parts; and the calves of his legs had been blown up with mines of gunpowder dug in the flesh with the sharp points of the tomahawk.

The Indians themselves allowed that Murphy died with great heroism, singing, as his death song, the *Drimmendoo*, in concert with Mr Lismahago, who was present at the solemnity. After the warriors and the matrons had made a hearty meal upon the muscular flesh which they pared from the victim, and had applied a great variety of tortures, which he bore without flinching, an old lady, with a sharp knife, scooped out one of his eyes, and put a burning coal in the socket. The pain of this operation was so exquisite that he could not help bellowing, upon which the audience raised a shout of exultation, and one of the warriors stealing behind him, gave him the *coup de grace* with a hatchet.

> (http://ebooks.adelaide.edu.au/s/smollett/tobias/
> clinker/complete.html)

Tim Fulford offers a prescient reading of the scene:

> Smollett shows that colonial encounters empower the man of few principles rather than the chivalric hero, he for whom morals as well as manufactures are commodities to trade for advantage. In the colonial culture produced by the meeting of Britons and Indians, survival of the fittest turns out to be survival of the fixer.
>
> (2006: 108)

If Behn showed an African dying with dignity in *Oroonoko*, Smollett bestows the European with a similar moral courage and dignity. The point, however, is that Smollett is able to establish the Englishman's courage and moral strength only as contrasted within a context of savagery where the Indians' treatment of prisoners-of-war, climaxing in cannibal feasts, is palpably horrific and unethical.

But Smollett also engenders the non-Europeans' savagery when he writes:

> Lishmahago's bride, the squaw Squinkinacoosta, distinguished herself on this occasion.—She shewed a great superiority of genius in the tortures which she contrived and executed with her own hands.—She vied with the stoutest warrior in eating the flesh of the sacrifice.
>
> (http://ebooks.adelaide.edu.au/s/smollett/tobias/
> clinker/complete.html)

82 Difference and desire

Even when Robert Southey in 'The Dirge of the American Widow' (1799) portrays an Indian woman's anguish and mournful widowhood – which then metamorphoses into revenge as we shall see – he cannot entirely abandon the stereotype of the vicious savage and the history of the Indian scalping of enemies. The widow says:

> The scalps that we number'd in triumph were there,
> And the musket that never was levell'd in vain,
> What a leap has it giv'n to my heart
> To see thee suspend it in peace.
>
> (http://spenserians.cath.vt.edu/TextRecord.php?action
=get&textsid=38644)

Southey folds savagery into anguish, sliding a history of warfare and cruelty into a present of grief and widowhood which does not allow us, however, to forget this history. Another example of this trope of the grieving native woman (mother/ wife) may be found in Felicia Hemans' 'The Indian City', where yet again the bereaved woman seeks vengeance.

This continuity of representation of the Other as barbarian and savage takes an interesting turn in Charlotte Smith's *The Old Manor House*. Dealing with the repercussions of the American Revolution, Smith, in Janina Nordius' reading, shows how the English soldiers in America were as savage as the Native Americans (2005: 43).[4] Smith speaks of the 'natural' predilection the Indians have for savagery:

> Their savage appearance, and the more savage thirst of blood which they avowed—that base avidity for plunder, with an heroic contempt of danger, pain, and death, made them altogether objects of abhorrence, mingled with something like veneration.
>
> (1969: 360)

This appears, at first sight, a stereotyping of the savage exotic. But this account *follows* a particular interesting moment in the novel. A white man, formerly a prisoner with the Native Americans, tells Orlando how: 'he had been met by a party of Indians, whom the British commanders had lately let loose upon the Americans' (1969: 359). Smith elaborates:

> Mr Jamieson informed him, that among all the unfair advantages which the Colonists complained of in the manner of carrying on the war, there was none that seemed so unjustifiable as that of sending forth the Indians against them. And when Orlando saw in the hands of the Bloody Captain eleven scalps, some of them evidently those of women and children, others of very old ... the young unhardened Englishman shuddered with horror, and blushed for his country.
>
> (1969: 360–1)

Another British soldier, Fleming, defends the commissioning of Indians to perform such hideous massacres (1969: 361). While this transformation of the British soldiers when in America suggests the discrepant geography I shall examine in the concluding chapter, it also gestures at *the savage exotic as something to which the British are culturally adaptable*. They command the savages to indulge in savagery thereby indicating that they have stereotyped the Native Americans as savages but also implicitly signalling, I propose, their own fascination with/for the savage exotic. It is not, in other words, about the Native American-as-savage-exotic alone but about the *malleability* of the British character which incorporates this savagery by harnessing it for their purposes. The savage exotic is not, again, out there, it is now a part of the British army's military culture: the savage exotic is 'Englished'.

Orlando, who escapes being killed, is now a witness to the many excesses of the 'savage' race where the Iroquois 'attacked the defenceless villages of the English Americans … and destroyed the women and children, or led them away to captivity infinitely worse than death' (1969: 379–80). The exotic which was out there, marking the border between home and aboard, native and foreign, in such cases gets disturbed when figures like Orlando or Coleridge's Ancient Mariner return home. That is, the exotic is no longer a determining factor of national and cultural boundaries. The *exotic is what arrives with the returning native* whose uncanny resemblance, in Charlotte Smith's account (and as we shall see in the case of Kurtz in *Heart of Darkness*, although Kurtz does not return to England), to the Native American savages renders him a stranger to his fellow countrymen on his return.

The giaour of Beckford's *Vathek* demands children as food as a price for allowing Vathek access to the 'Palace of Subterranean Fire':

> Know that I am parched with thirst, and cannot open this door till my thirst be thoroughly appeased. I require the blood of fifty of the most beautiful sons of thy viziers and great men, or neither can my thirst nor thy curiosity be satisfied. Return to Samarah; procure for me this necessary libation; come back hither; throw it thyself into this chasm; and then shalt thou see!
>
> (1970: 23)

The giaour – who is Indian – is clearly of cannibalistic taste, and his difference from the Mohammedan Vathek is marked, it could be said, with this difference in taste.

Bloody Bill the pirate tries to convince the boys in *The Coral Island* that cannibals do exist:

> I s'pose 'twas yer tender-hearted friends in England that put that notion into your head. There's a set o' soft-hearted folk at home that I knows on, who don't like to have their feelin's ruffled, and when you tell them anything they don't like—that shocks them, as they call it—no matter how true it be, they stop their ears and cry out, 'Oh, that is *too* horrible! We can't believe that!' An' they say truth. They can't believe it 'cause they won't believe it. Now, I believe there's thousands o' the people in England who are sich born

84 Difference and desire

> drivellin' *won't-believers* that they think the black fellows hereaway, at the worst, eat an enemy only now an' then, out o' spite; whereas, I know for certain, and many captains of the British and American navies know as well as me, that the Feejee islanders eat not only their enemies but one another; and they do it not for spite, but for pleasure. It's a *fact* that they prefer human flesh to any other. But they don't like white men's flesh so well as black. They say it makes them sick.
>
> (Unpaginated, http://ebooks.adelaide.edu.au/b/ballantyne/rm/coral-island/)

Interestingly Europe's internal Others were also exoticized as cannibals. As Ahsan Chaudhury puts it:

> Narratives of native cannibalism were an indispensable part of these new discourses and practices ... the cannibalistic other of the New World became a yardstick by which to measure the threat posed by internal enemies, be it the indigenous Irish, the French Catholics, or the Moorish inhabitants of Spain.
>
> (2008: 151)

Most famously depicted as such in Jonathan Swift's 'A Modest Proposal' (1729), Ireland was a cannibal nation to the English. But Swift's proposal – that the Irish eat their children – is really inaugurated by a New World savage:

> I have been assured by a very knowing American of my acquaintance in London, that a young healthy child well nursed is at a year old a most delicious, nourishing, and wholesome food, whether stewed, roasted, baked, or boiled, and I make no doubt that it will equally serve in a fricassee, or a ragout.
>
> (1960b: 441)

That is, the very idea of a cannibal culture comes to the speaker of the tract from an American, who is presented as something of a connoisseur in these culinary habits. Swift, therefore, treats the Americans as the New World savages, and proposes that the Irish can learn something from them. There is one further point. England, supposedly civilized, is presented towards the end of the essay as a cannibal nation:

> But as to myself, having been wearied out for many years with offering vain, idle, visionary thoughts, and at length utterly despairing of success, I fortunately fell upon this proposal, which as it is wholly new, so it hath something solid and real, of no expense and little trouble, full in our own power, and whereby we can incur no danger in disobliging ENGLAND. For this kind of commodity will not bear exportation, the flesh being of too tender a consistence, to admit a long continuance in salt, although perhaps I

could name a country, which would be glad to eat up our whole nation without it.

(1960b: 445)

Thus while Swift shows how the 'man-eating myth could be recuperated for liberatory goals ... as a resistant ploy' (Chaudhury 2008: 155) *it also positions England and America as savage nations*. Cannibalism here is not simply the exotic marker of the cultural and racial difference of the Irish, it is also a marker of the so-called civilized England and the New World, America.

In the classic Gothic tale of the age, Charles Maturin's *Melmoth the Wanderer* (1820), the decaying Irish estate of the Melmoths was obtained, Maturin tells us, in the form of 'the confiscated property of an Irish family' (2012: 24). Two lovers locked up in a convent starve to death. The details of their dying are cannibalistic, and given to us by the monk who has locked them in: as 'the agony of hunger increased ... [t]hey were rapidly becoming objects of hostility to each other,—oh what a feast to me!' (259). And finally: 'It was on the fourth night that I heard the shriek of the wretched female,—her lover, in the agony of hunger, had fastened his teeth in her shoulder' (260). Later in the novel the colony (India, which serves as a code for Ireland, claims at least one critic of the novel, Julia Wright 2001: 94) starves under English rule. Europe in the novel, says Wright, is 'a culture in which figurative cannibalism and predatory violence are, ultimately, the consequences of a social system' that is inherently unequal (96). The Irish family degenerates, just as the colony does, into real and imagined cannibalism and savagery. Wright comments:

At the end of the novel, cannibalism strikes the Wanderer's auditors, the latest heir of the Irish estate and the disinherited Moncada. After the close of the Wanderer's narration, knowing that the Wanderer is soon to be dragged to hell, they 'passed the remainder of that day without even thinking of food, from that intense and burning anxiety that seemed to prey on their very vitals' (701), as eating is once again supplanted by being eaten.

(99)

For Wright, Maturin's representations of cannibalism are 'with particular reference to the disinheritance of indigenous peoples through the imposition of a commercial-imperial economy' (100).

A century later R.M. Ballantyne would also speak of English savages. In *The Coral Island*, Ralph Rover and his friends seeking refuge in caves comment: 'Little did we imagine that the first savages who would drive us into it [the cave] would be white savages, perhaps our own countrymen' (http://ebooks.adelaide.edu.au/b/ballantyne/rm/coral-island/). In an Other place, as we discussed in the chapter on travel, discrepant geographies cause the worst aspects of the English character to emerge.

That is, the savage Other or the cannibal in such texts could either be the non-European Other (Indian, Arab, Native American in Shakespeare, Beckford, Defoe)

86 Difference and desire

or s/he could be the European (Irish) product of a colonial project (Maturin). In both cases English identity is constantly in negotiation with the savage Other, whether internal or external to their race. Exoticism here serves the important purpose of *marking particular cultural, military (as seen in Smollett's criticism of the Native American codes of military conduct) and culinary practices against which England defines itself*. This becomes a means of dealing with not just difference but the possibility of a difference that cannot be pinned down or 'formulated in a phrase'. As Martin Munro puts it in Saidian terms, 'the non-European other is fixed in a conception of timeless essence which would deny the inevitable "corruption" ... of primal innocence brought about by cultural contact' (2003: 56). Primitivism is thus an ideological position where the Other enters the cultural imaginary of the European as a fixed essence, an 'authentic' antiquity, that has been incorruptible over the ages. A prime example of this 'fixing' of the native in antiquarian terms, to which I shall return in the chapter on the assimilable Other, is to be seen in Haggard's *King Solomon's Mines* and his description of Gagool:

> I observed the wizened monkey-like figure creeping from the shadow of the hut. It crept on all fours, but when it reached the place where the king sat it rose upon its feet, and throwing the furry covering from its face, revealed a most extraordinary and weird countenance. Apparently it was that of a woman of great age so shrunken that in size it seemed no larger than the face of a year-old child, although made up of a number of deep and yellow wrinkles. Set in these wrinkles was a sunken slit, that represented the mouth, beneath which the chin curved outwards to a point. There was no nose to speak of; indeed, the visage might have been taken for that of a sun-dried corpse had it not been for a pair of large black eyes, still full of fire and intelligence, which gleamed and played under the snow-white eyebrows, and the projecting parchment-coloured skull, like jewels in a charnel-house. As for the head itself, it was perfectly bare, and yellow in hue, while its wrinkled scalp moved and contracted like the hood of a cobra.
>
> (Unpaginated, http://ebooks.adelaide.edu.au/h/haggard/h_rider/
> king/index.html)

Gagool is here nominally a woman, but compared to a monkey and an ancient one at that. Anne McClintock speaks of this as the representation of a 'racial regression' where the native regresses to childhood and even animal-like behaviour/manner (1995: 245–6). She is barely alive (her visage, says Haggard, is 'corpse-like'). Thus European primitivization here renders the biologically aged native into an animal, akin, almost, to a savage. Compounding this primitivization is the careful blurring of biological categories: Gagool is monkey-like but also compared to a cobra. In the African wilds, according to Haggard's primitivizing discourse, the line between humans, older humans and animals blur. Yet it is important to note that despite the nightmarish quality of the African presence, what Haggard underscores is her sheer physicality (Low 1996: 52–3).

The Noble Savage

If the savage exotic tracked the figure of the inhuman and bestial figure in the peripheries and unknown regions of the world, a different form of savage makes his appearance in English writings from the seventeenth century. Troy Bickham has documented how from the 1770s English life was compared unfavourably with the 'innocent happiness' of the life of Tahitians and other South Pacific islanders (2005: 263).

Alexander Pope's 'An Essay on Man' has this to say about the American Indian:

> Lo, the poor Indian! whose untutored mind
> Sees God in clouds, or hears Him in the wind;
> His soul, proud science never taught to stray
> Far as the solar walk, or milky way;
> Yet simple Nature to his hope has given,
> Behind the cloud-topped hill, an humbler heaven;
> Some safer world in depth of woods embraced,
> Some happier island in the watery waste,
> Where slaves once more their native land behold,
> No fiends torment, no Christians thirst for gold.
> To be, contents his natural desire,
> He asks no angel's wing, no seraph's fire;
> But thinks, admitted to that equal sky,
> His faithful dog shall bear him company.
>
> (1963: 508)

Pope sees the 'untutor'd mind', symbolic of innocence, as a characteristic of the Indian. He is without guile but also without inordinate ambition or greed. An English identity then is forged in these lines in sharp contrast with the character of the 'innocent' Indian: the English 'thirst for gold', writes Pope. Pope undermines the civilizational glamour of the English/Christian world by speaking of the unsullied innocence of the pagan. The pagan's rudimentary science (lacking any knowledge of 'the solar walk/the milky way', which the Englishman does) does not teach him to 'stray far', says Pope. Pope seems to locate in the innocent Indian the apotheosis of a simple virtue. The exoticization of the Other here is a process *through which a clear binary of civilized but unhappy Christian and the pagan but happy Indian is forged*. The innocence of the civil savage was of course a marker of a premodern life/culture and therefore treated as 'pure' and prelapsarian. In the age of Wordsworth, 'innocence', particularly of children, would acquire considerable cultural currency, and the comparison was to the innocence of the Indian, as in Wordsworth's 1805 *Prelude* (Book 1):

> Oh, many a time have I, a five year's child,
> A naked boy, in one delightful rill,

A little mill-race severed from his stream,
Made one long bathing of a summer's day;
Basked in the sun, and plunged and basked again
Alternate, all a summer's day, or coursed
Over the sandy fields, leaping through groves
Of yellow groundsel; or when crag and hill,
The woods, and distant Skiddaw's lofty height,
Were bronzed with a deep radiance, stood alone
Beneath the sky, as if I had been born
On Indian plains, and from my mother's hut
Had run abroad in wantonness, to sport
A naked savage, in the thunder shower.

(Wordsworth 1969: 498)

In Daniel Defoe's *Captain Singleton* (1720) when the Europeans penetrate the African jungles in search of gold they encounter the natives. The encounter is described this way:

We made signs of friendship to them, and found them a very frank, civil, and friendly sort of people ... we made signs to them that we were hungry, and immediately some naked women ran and fetched us great quantities of roots, and of things like pumpkins, which we made no scruple to eat ... Our artificer shewed them some of trinkets that he had made ... They had so much judgment to chuse that of silver before the iron, but when we shewed them some gold, we found they did not value it so much as either of the other ... They were the civilest and the most friendly people that we met at all.

(1969a: 107)

This 'civil savage' also occurs in Robert Southey's narrative poem, *Madoc* (1805). Madoc, who leaves England for the New World, is treated with enormous courtesy, exactly like Singleton and his group, by the natives:

The elders of the land
Came forth, and led us to an ample hut,
Which in the center of their dwellings stood,
The Stranger's House. They eyed us wondering,
Yet not for wonder ceased they to observe
Their hospitable rites; from hut to hut
The tidings ran that strangers were arrived,
Fatigued and hungry and athirst; anon,
Each from his means supplying us, came food
And beverage such as cheers the weary man.

(Southey 1909: 479)

Difference and desire **89**

In Robert Rogers' *Ponteach: Or the Savages of America* (1766), the first English literary text on the American Indians, Ponteach speaks:

> Indians a'n't Fools, if White Men think us so;
> We see, we hear, we think as well as you;
> We know there 're Lies, and Mischiefs in the World;
> We don't know whom to trust, nor when to fear;
> Men are uncertain, changing as the Wind,
> Inconstant as the Waters of the Lakes,
> Some smooth and fair, and pleasant as the Sun,
> Some rough and boist'rous, like the Winter Storm;
> Some are Insidious as the subtle Snake,
> Some innocent, and harmless as the Dove;
> Some like the Tyger raging, cruel, fierce,
> Some like the Lamb, humble, submissive, mild,
> And scarcely one is every Day the same;
> But I call no Man bad, till such he's found,
> Then I condemn and cast him from my Sight;
> And no more trust him as a Friend and Brother.
> I hope to find you honest Men and true.

(cited in Fulford 2006: 21)

The 'Romantic Indian', notes Tim Fulford reading the above speech, 'was, more times than not, a figure of honour, courage, liberty and oratorical authority', and is, in such passages, given considerable 'interiority' suggestive of autonomy and self-conscious agency (2006: 21). If Rogers' Indian is a self-reflexive, cerebral one, in the Defoe account cited above, the African is a 'barbarian', but a civil one. They are naive in terms of evaluative capabilities, according to the Europeans, since they seem to prefer silver to gold. Defoe's romanticization of the African is exemplified in their playing host to the Europeans (an event that recurs elsewhere in the novel, 1969a: 110).

Wolf-hunter, who befriends and protects Orlando in Charlotte Smith's *The Old Manor House*, is 'distinguished from the rest' by his 'more open countenance' and 'more gentle manners' (1969: 361). Thus Wolf-hunter is a savage who does not fit the stereotype – that this portrait follows two pages of accounts of British-sponsored Native American savagery is surely not coincidence. Smith, I believe, draws our attention to the savage exotic but suggests that the savage exists in and appeals to the British as well, just as nobility and compassion exist in the so-called savage Native Americans. Hence her comment 'the secret sympathy between generous minds [that] seems to exist throughout the whole human kind' (1969: 361), thereby proposing a moral universalism.

In Thomas Gray's 'The Progress of Poesy' (1768) the Native American is a bard, and not just a savage warrior:

> In climes beyond the solar road,
> Where shaggy forms o'er ice-built mountains roam,
> The Muse has broke the twilight-gloom
> To chear the shiv'ring Native's dull abode.
> And oft, beneath the od'rous shade
> Of Chili's boundless forests laid,
> She deigns to hear the savage Youth repeat
> In loose numbers wildy sweet
> Their feather-cinctured Chiefs, and dusky Loves.
> Her track, wher'er the Goddess roves,
> Glory pursue, and generous Shame,
> Th'unconquerable Mind, and Freedom's holy flame.
>
> (Gray 1974: 48–9)

While it might lack a rhythm and proper 'rhyme' ('loose numbers'), the Indian's song remains 'wildy sweet', suggesting an uncontaminated if untrained innocence. The very simple eloquence of the savage becomes not only a marker of the innocent primitivism of the non-European – which had a marked exotic appeal – but also of the unsullied, 'natural' native. Laura George has argued that 'for writers from Rousseau to Blair, primitive people demonstrate not simply a kind of proto-eloquence but eloquence itself, unhampered by the increasingly prosaic and proper stages of civilized and rational literacy' (2002: 34).[5] It is not the savage African but the 'civil savage' that we see emerging in Defoe, Southey and Thomas Gray.

I have already cited Behn's very flattering depiction of the black prince, Oroonoko. But in poems such as Wordsworth's 'Her Eyes Are Wild', Felicia Hemans' 'The Indian City' and Robert Southey's 'The Dirge of the American Widow' the Native American woman is a picture of grief, inadequacy and even revenge (Hemans' and Southey's women embark on a saga of revenge). The savage here, in these cases, is not simply a primitive creature but one whose moral values, sentimentality and integrity are almost on par with that of the Englishman/woman. The American Indian, the Arab woman, the East Indian woman, show Southey, Wordsworth and Hemans in their poems about these 'types', are as grief-stricken at the deaths of their loved ones as the European mothers and wives. I shall return to these poems in a later section, for a different reason.

There is in Conrad another version of the savage–Noble Savage dynamic. Marlow hires a band of ostensible 'cannibal' natives for the steamboat. Marlow notes:

> Fine fellows—cannibals—in their place. They were men one could work with, and I am grateful to them. And, after all, they did not eat each other before my face: they had brought along a provision of hippo-meat which went rotten, and made the mystery of the wilderness stink in my nostrils.
>
> (1974: 94)

Yet he also notes that these 'cannibals' seem curiously restrained in their eating habits: 'And I saw that something restraining, one of those human secrets that baffle probability, had come into play there' (104). Marlow's puzzle at their restrained behaviour has less to do with the 'real' character of the 'cannibals' than with European expectations of them within the process of exoticization.[6]

The Noble Savage in such accounts symptomizes the English attempt to come to terms not only with racial–cultural difference but also ideas of moral universals (as Fulford notes, this was the age of humanitarianism and the early stirrings of universalizing cosmopolitan views, 2006). For the English and Europeans in general the civil savage epitomizes the civilizational mission itself: that these are humans who can be 'improved' (I shall turn to the 'improveable Other' theme in Chapter 6). Vestiges of humanity survived in (even) the savages, and this would require European efforts to bring to the surface.

The erotic exotic

Accompanying the territorial conquest was a different form of epistemological conquest: the making of the Orient as an erotic geography – what Felicity Nussbaum aptly termed the 'torrid zones', or 'porno-tropics', referring to European representations of the climatic conditions, the supposed hypersexed nature of the natives and the excessive fecundity of its women (1995). This erotic geography, embodied in numerous sketches of the Oriental woman, the seraglio and the harem, represents what Ali Behdad termed 'the desire for the Orient' (1994: 15).

English femininity's status was a matter of considerable concern in the imperial context. Woman, as Anne McClintock (1995) puts it, was a 'boundary-marker'. The Englishwoman under sexual threat from the African, Arab or Asian male was a common trope (Sharpe 1991) in colonial writings. In this section I am interested in the emergence of an English femininity *abroad*.

My argument here is that the *eroticization of the exotic space of the Other is achieved not only through extensive descriptions of native sexuality and sensuality but through the relocation or transposition of a European femininity into a 'native' context. It is the presence of the European man or woman in exotic settings that also contributes to the erotic charge of the Other place.* If Miranda eroticizes Prospero's island in *The Tempest* it is the English feminine presence, I propose, that crafts a feminized domestic space in the subcontinent-as-colony.

English femininity and the eroticization of geography

When Asambeg in Philip Massinger's *The Renegado* (1630) kidnaps Paulina, English femininity itself is incarcerated. Paulina, however, is protected by a charm, and Asambeg is confounded by it. He exclaims:

> Stout men quake at my frownes and in returne
> I tremble at her softnesse.

> (II.4. n.d.: 144)

92 Difference and desire

Not only does English femininity survive the onslaught of Turkish 'infidels', it becomes the very symbol of the power of Christianity. English femininity under threat from the non-European male and religion is a theme that runs through *The Renegado*, and I shall have reason to return to it.

In Daniel Defoe's *Roxana* (1724), the French-born and English-bred protagonist narrator describes a masque she attended. The events described occur in London, where Roxana settles down after an extended sojourn in Europe. In the masque she arrives 'dress'd in the habit of a Turkish princess', itself bought for her by her 'foreign prince', who also bought her, at the same time, a Turkish slave (1969b: 173). Complete with resplendent turban and a fabric that is described as a 'fine Persian, or India damask' (174), she is the cynosure of all eyes. Later in the programme she is called upon to dance. This is her account:

> I danc'd by myself a figure which I learnt in France … it was indeed, a very fine figure, invented by a famous master at Paris … being perfectly new, it pleas'd the Company exceedingly, and they all thought it had been Turkish, nay, one gentleman had the folly to expose himself so much, as to say, and I think swore too, that he had seen it danc'd at Constantinople.
>
> (175–6)

It is at the end of this dance that she is christened by the ecstatic crowd, 'Roxana'. Soon after at another ball, Roxana is asked to repeat her 'Turkish' dance. Roxana notes a Georgian and an Armenian woman dancing. She writes:

> The novelty pleas'd, truly, but yet there was something wild and bizarre in it, because they really acted to the life the barbarous country whence they came; but as mine had the French behaviour under the Mahometan dress, it was every way as new, and pleas'd much better indeed.
>
> (179)

There are several points of interest here. Felicity Nussbaum's interpretation proposes that 'Turkey … is imaginatively linked to sensual dissipation and male tyranny … Sexuality, which was confusedly incorporated into the nation in the person of Charles [Charles II], metamorphoses into an Other who is a transgressive woman at home and abroad' (1995: 33–4). Nussbaum goes on to argue that Roxana's feminism 'is always realised through an imitation of women of empire rather than an Other with a subjectivity and culture of her own' (35). Thus the impersonation of a Turkish identity makes the English audience prefer, Nussbaum proposes, Roxana's 'imitation of the exotic' (36). Nussbaum gestures presciently, I think, towards the erotically charged exotic. But this is an erotic exotic that emerges in the transposition and mimicry of the non-European woman by a European one. In what could be read as an eroticized geography of the world represented in Roxana's masque, the sensuality of the non-European woman is *in between* her European self and the signifier of Turkish costume.

Difference and desire **93**

What strikes one in this Defoe passage is the layering of the exotic as at once accessible and distant. First, the distant and dissolute Turkish sexuality seems to be accommodated and made available within the English court, for *English* consumption. Second, a French-born, English-bred woman is able to position herself comfortably in France, Holland and England with equal ease primarily as a sexual creature, whose identity is mired in Defoe's tale in a sexual citizenship, itself an eroticizing exotic. Third, Roxana proposes that it is the *hybridity* of European and 'Mahometan' costume, where the French, she says, is partially and *tantalizingly* hidden under the 'Mahometan' one, that pleases the audience more, thus suggesting a dualism of visible and hidden exoticism in her (sexualized) personhood. Difference here is doubly coded in a series: as accessible and distant, desirable and dangerous, assimilable and inviolable. I see Defoe's rhetoric of exoticism as delivering an *imperial exotic where, in the hidden/visible dynamic embodied in Roxana's sexual citizenship, distant difference is also brought under a measure of comprehensible control and a controlling desire* that evokes both terror and thrill. This imperial exotic becomes Defoe's way of engaging with racial and cultural differences that were being increasingly and incrementally made visible as Britain's engagements with the world grew throughout the eighteenth century.

Roxana thus demonstrates an instance of the imperial exotic where, in the hidden/visible dynamic embodied in Roxana's sexual citizenship, distant difference is also brought under a measure of comprehensible control and a controlling desire. The European woman who usurps the costume and appearance of the Arab/Turkish woman even as she performs a French dance evokes desire and thrills among her male audience. Defoe's representation suggests that when a European woman wears a Turkish dress (1) the European male is able to 'see' a *transfer* of the sensual quality of the Turkish woman to the European one and (2) the presumed sexual power of the Other is something the European woman aspires to (Nussbaum 1995: 40). Both suggest the sexualized Other as either an aspirational or a transgressive model for the European woman. Roxana's career up to this moment in the novel has been polygamous. Her promiscuity culminates in a Turkish impersonation which suggests that Roxana was already moving towards some form of sexual citizenship in several places – and her taking on the appearance of the racial Other is one more means of achieving the same. The Turkish costume, in other words, is a signifier of the deeper sensuality of the woman, and Defoe is only echoing a theme discernible in other eighteenth-century texts. Further, the entire episode shows the transformation of the European woman – and the male audience – into what Ben Jonson would call a 'civil savage' in his 1614 play, *Bartholomew Fair* (III.iv. 37–8. Jonson 1968: 79).[7] By primitivizing herself in native costume Roxana moves away from her European identity to a Turkish – but essentially hybrid (since she dances a French dance when in Turkish costume) – one.

However, Roxana's sexual citizenship looks forward to other more complicated forms of citizenship that the European women engaged in vis-à-vis the colony and the non-European Other. Colonial novels such as those by Alice Perrin, B.M. Croker, Elizabeth Hamilton, Flora Annie Steele and Olive Schreiner posit an

94 Difference and desire

English femininity that can emerge only within the inimical context of daily interactions with natives, the social life of the English in 'camp' or the 'station' (as English settlements, temporary and permanent respectively, were called in nineteenth-century India) and domesticity. English femininity is circumscribed not only in the public role the Englishwoman plays in the colony but in the sphere of domesticity. It is in the place of the racial-cultural Other that a certain kind of domesticity demands a certain kind of femininity of the Englishwoman. Studies of these novels have argued that they embody a more complex negotiation of both empire and the Englishwoman's identity (Sainsbury 1996, Bilston 2001). They have been characterized as romances (Stieg 1985). Anglo-Indian domesticity and the household in nineteenth-century India were sites where we can see imperial ideologies inflecting family relations, social ties and attitudes (George 1993–4, Joseph 2004). Rosemary George identifies a 'public domesticity' in Maud Diver and other colonial writers. She writes:

> novel after novel suggests that it is the daily construction of the home country as the location of the colonizer's racial and moral identity and as the legitimization of the colonizer's national subjecthood that made possible the carrying out of the work of Empire.
>
> (107)

India became, notes Elizabeth Buettner, 'a family affair in which "wife and babe" were also core participants' (2004: 4–5). I classify the colonial novel under the head of 'erotic exoticism' because many of these were concerned with *sexual relations of white women with white men but also often articulated anxieties of miscegenation in the Other land*. The erotic exotic, in other words, is not simply the exoticization of the culturally and racially different woman, *it is also the construction and reconstruction of English femininity in an exotic setting*.

Colonial domesticity conveyed imperial authority, efficiency and moral superiority. It was always, thus, a visible and 'public domesticity'. I argue that the political domesticity generates a social sphere – a concept developed by Denise Riley to describe a feminized space that is an extension of the domestic into the public, but often works in antagonism to and in competition with the masculine public space (1988: 51). The social sphere assimilates into itself the features of both the public and the domestic, thus converting the hitherto private space of domesticity into what I am calling political domesticity. Political domesticity is the transplantation of mundane Anglo-Indian domesticity into the social sphere, thereby investing it with greater official and political – imperial – weight. Political domesticity is the domesticity characterized by the participation of the colonial social sphere in the household, and the extension of the household into the social, in the course of which a model of *English* or *imperial* femininity – to be followed by the Englishwomen in the colony – emerges.

Alice Perrin's fiction – *The Anglo-Indians* (1912), *Government House* (1925), *The Woman in the Bazaar* (1926) and *The Charm* (1910) – depicts the erosion of English womanhood in India by mapping the failure of the English woman at this political domesticity. Perrin, I suggest, in her depiction of the 'disorderly Memsahib' (Indrani Sen's term, 2002: 16) implicitly signals the 'true' Memsahib as one who adroitly moves across the domestic and the social spheres.

The colonial social sphere was a space where Englishness had to be defined and reinforced. It had to reflect the glory of both race and Empire. Social events within the 'public' intimacy of an Anglo-Indian household had to, therefore, embody this Englishness. Mrs Taylor and Mrs Rice wore 'garden-party confections recently acquired from England, the other mothers had competed locally to the limit of their purses', writes Perrin (1925: 102). Marion and Isabel in *The Anglo-Indians* 'have such a craze for English life, and for everything English' (1913: 20). Mrs Cardale collects curios which are described as '"a heterogeneous collection of china ornaments, electro-plate graven with storks and bamboos ... so English!," she [Mrs Cardale] said proudly' (1925: 34). Meeting natives at such purely English 'dos', Mrs Cardale informs Annabel, might not be quite acceptable to the English (1925: 62), conveniently eliding the fact that the 'do' was possible because the native servants slaved away. In this emphatically *English* social sphere the English Memsahib had to fit in. Her clothes, dancing skills, social etiquette, ability to organize proper meals, organize festivities for children, behave with a consciousness of rank and hierarchy were all under scrutiny in the social sphere. Whether she would be a good, true Memsahib was determined in the social sphere. Her household itself was drawn into the social sphere, even as the social sphere intruded into her home. The necessity of a 'correct' domestic arrangement that fits the *social sphere* of Anglo-Indian life is hinted at — and this leads us directly into the argument on domesticity — by Mr Banister in *The Charm* when he warningly tells Mark of an Englishman who had married a Eurasian: 'He couldn't accept big stations because of the memsahib — she was totally unfitted for any sort of social or official position — and they just grubbed along in small places eating too much *dal* [lentils] and rice and curry, and taking too little exercise' (n.d.: 75–6). When Teresa complains that she does not quite like the 'semi-official' engagements in the community (209) she is indicating that she does not approximate to the idea of the Memsahib. When Teresa socializes, she attracts opprobrium and Eve validates the Banister comment about class superseding race as a social category when she asks Norah: 'Would you feel anxious to be on intimate terms with English people like that? — there are plenty of them' (216). Everybody at the social gathering notes that Mark, Teresa's husband, was embarrassed and unfortunate in his choice of wife. The domestic arrangements of this 'unfortunate' Englishman, suggests Banister, had disastrous consequences in the public as well as the social sphere. In other words, when in India, one could not, if one were an ambitious Englishman, hope to keep the domestic out of the public because the intervening social sphere would entail a blurring of boundaries, for which the Memsahib had to be suited.

Perrin's fiction portrays the disorderly Memsahib as the Englishwoman who fails in the domestic domain as well as in the social. Thus in the case of Lady Rochford, Mrs Fleetwood, Mrs Cardale, Teresa and Rafella the inability to secure the

96 Difference and desire

domestic economy – emotional stability, financial security and comfort – in the home is mirrored in their failures in the social realms as well. This failure on the domestic front and the social front suggests that all domesticity in colonial India was political domesticity because its disruption introduced debates about the functioning of women in the imperial set-up. Perrin suggests that there can be no 'mere' domesticity in Anglo-India: the Memsahib had to ensure that both the domestic and the social spheres were equally well negotiated.

While other writers presented India as a potential space for the white woman's burden, Perrin's focus is on domesticity as the space where the Englishwoman has a more-than-domestic role. Documenting the failures of the Rochfords, Teresas, Cardales and others, Perrin offers us a different vision of India: a space where Englishwomen fail if they are not of the right temperament. Women who do not quite make the grade in acquiring Memsahib skills are the subjects of Perrin's novels, which therefore implicitly signal the ideal Memsahib as one who is at ease in both domains. Several instances of the socially 'unsuitable' Memsahib figure in Perrin.

Take, as an example, Rafella in *The Woman in the Bazaar*. That Rafella as a new bride in India does not fit into the land or Anglo-Indian society is first brought home to us when Perrin describes the inappropriateness of her clothes: 'Deluded by the perpetual sunshine she had worn summer garments to start with, her husband's advice to the contrary; but now she sat wrapped in a cape that, though useful and warm, was unbecoming both in colour and style' (1925: 48). This is Rafella's first entry into the social sphere of Anglo-India, and it is indicated that she does not quite fit in. Lady Rochford, 'an engaging example of human sophistry' (143), is a disaster in her public/social role as well, and seeks Annabel's help with 'letters and the study of reports in connexion with native women's hospitals, schools, colleges, all the associations of which the Governor's wife had been elected president' (175). She thus fails as a wife and mother, as hostess, as a socialite and as the Governor's wife. She had, before Annabel, simply 'muddled along' (176). Her party is marked by confusion, 'a seething mass of dandies and rickshaws, natives yelling abuse, buffeting, fighting in their efforts to get forward' (109). She cannot, even at social gatherings, remember the names of the people present (142).

Rafella's domestic problems spill over into the social realm and vice versa because she is unable to assimilate the norms of gender roles for a white wife in India. Her friendship with Kennard, which eventually leads to the break-up of her marriage, is a disruption in the domestic arrangements but is mirrored in the conflicts she produces with Mrs Greaves and other Anglo-Indians in the social realm. When she dances endlessly with Kennard at the Club (1925: 93) it becomes symptomatic of the disruption in her household, where this social event becomes the source of disruption. When Mark Rennard dances with Eve Lancaster at a social event, he realizes that his domestic life is fraught, and that his true love 'had slept under the drug of his passion for Teresa' (n.d.: 178). Eve's 'purity' and appropriateness for the Memsahib role become clear to Mark at this social event.

Perrin shows how the Englishwoman who has little or no sense of the significance of domesticity seems to fail in the social sphere as well. The social sphere, as already noted, is a space between the public and the private. Bad domesticity, Perrin's fiction suggests, results in bad social roles as well, and vice versa.

Mrs Fleetwood visits her kitchen, like a 'conscientious mem-sahib' in order to ensure 'cleanliness, regularity, and order throughout her household arrangements', but is otherwise a woman who has little control over the domestic economy (1913: 55). Mrs Cardale in *Government House* is described as 'erratic' and unable to assert any kind of control over her home and children. Even when Annabel works to teach Billie Cardale (the Cardale's son), 'Mrs Cardale constantly undermined it with foolish indulgences' (1925: 36). 'Rosie blows her nose in her frock ... Jim licks his plate ... George and Tiny run about naked after their baths ... Then he [Billie] would agree reluctantly with Annabel that such behavior was unworthy of sahib-people' (1925: 37). Lady Rochford ignores her children too: 'the education of Pamela and Elizabeth was a secondary consideration compared with her own requirements' (1925: 176). Howard Klint mocks his sister Teresa for her lack of social skills: 'Now, Teresa, you a hostess, and not joining the invitation – you did not learn hospitality in Calcutta – whatever else they taught you there!' (n.d.: 45). Mark Rennard in *The Charm* discovers that his Eurasian wife, Teresa, lacks organization, ability or even interest in running an efficient household. Mark, writes Perrin, 'went to endless trouble in his endeavours to help and improve his wife':

> He urged her to exert herself and take more exercise. He subdued her taste in dress and persuaded her always to wear white, he liked her in it best. He tried to inspire her with an emulative spirit in the management of her household, but it was solely that he might be made more comfortable and have things as he wished that she studied cookery books, and asked questions of other ladies, and attended personally to details she had never troubled herself about previously.
>
> (n.d.: 127)

He warns her that 'the people you meet here are not quite like the people you knew in Calcutta' (196). He would feel, he realizes, 'a sense of humiliation' when he had to introduce Teresa to Koranabad society and Eve Lancaster, while Teresa herself finds it 'irksome' (213).

Political domesticity marks the transformation of the Anglo-Indian woman, from just a housewife into an icon of English respectability and authority in *another* place. When the children, as in the case of *Government House*, are badly dressed or ill-mannered, it is not simply a failure of the family, but symbolic of a blot on the imperial escutcheon itself, Perrin suggests. What was at stake in the 'proper' behaviour of the Memsahib was the Empire's dignity and authority itself.

Mrs Cardale in *Government House* has absolutely no control over the native servants, and is overtly racist. The result is that the children are badly behaved (as already noted) and can be controlled only by Annabel. The Rochford home runs

98 Difference and desire

in a 'machine-like order' because of Lady Rochford's 'complete indifference as to the amount spent in purchasing domestic peace' (158). Teresa in *The Charm* has no idea about the way her servants function. Teresa, having no cook to assist her, tries her hand at cooking, but is a complete disaster (128, 136).

Mrs Fleetwood does not regulate her expenses while in India. Her friend Mrs Bullen is worried that the amount the Fleetwoods spend on social events should be used to secure their retirement lives in England:

> 'Why should you give it, Emily? ... You'll want all the money you can scrape together when you have to retire next spring.'

To which the impractical Mrs Fleetwood responds:

> 'It's our last season, and I shouldn't like to go away and say good-bye to all our friends without doing something.'

And Mrs Bullen retorts:

> 'But on an average you've given a large dinner-party every week, as well as an At Home, not to speak of luncheons and picnics and the children's fancy ball.'
>
> (1913: 22)

Here, Mrs Fleetwood's emphasis on the social role of her family ignores the strain it places upon her domestic economy – even though her friend points it out in no uncertain terms. Rafella in *The Woman in the Bazaar* assumes that her social role is innocent and cannot be open to misinterpretation: 'The boys are just like brothers to me. They miss their women relations at home, and I can give them advice, and listen to their troubles, and often help them very much' (1926: 78–9). Here, again, what we see is the over-emphasis on a social role that directly affects the domestic.

The political domesticity of these novels suggest that Perrin, rather than being concerned with the interracial Other (the native), was more concerned with the intra-racial Other – the Englishwoman who could not keep a household properly English or adapt to the life in the Anglo-Indian community. When Banister warns Mark that it is less about colour than class, we see the beginnings of a different kind of Other – one from *within* the racial-national grouping. Perrin seems to make the English household at once a microcosm and an extension of the Empire, but solely the Englishwoman's responsibility. When the Englishwoman fails, the household fails, and as a result the imperial icon is defaced just a little bit. The disorderly Memsahib, argues Sen, was contrasted with the moral ideal of the Englishwoman in England (2002: 17). Perrin, however, presents the teleology of the disorderly Memsahib within the individual rather than the context of colonial India.

Rafella in *The Woman in the Bazaar*, when chastised by Mrs Greaves for her flirtatious behaviour, retorts: 'India is a wicked place! ... full of gossips and scandalmongers and evil-minded people' (1926: 81). Mrs Greaves corrects this impression:

> India is no worse than any other part of the globe that is inhabited by human beings. Out here we are all necessarily thrown a great deal together, and women of our class associate with men much more than is usual or possible for us to do at home. If we are sensible it does the men no manner of harm, rather the reverse. If we are fools, it may turn our heads.
>
> (1926: 81)

The onus, Mrs Greaves suggests here, is on the individual Englishwoman to keep up the imperial grandeur by strengthening her character. Perrin, through Mrs Greaves, emphasizes the nature of the colonial set-up within which English domesticity attains a different valence and therefore places different burdens and responsibilities upon the Memsahib – which she must fulfil. Rafella criticizes the Anglo-Indian society for its narrow-mindedness, but Mrs Greaves suggests that it is every Englishwoman's job to keep her head. This argument is underscored when in a later conversation with another Memsahib Mrs Greaves says:

> She is a typical example of the kind of girl who deteriorates rapidly in India; and then people at home, who won't try to understand, think India is to blame. She would have been the same in England, or anywhere else, if she had been pitchforked into a different kind of lifestyle.
>
> (1926: 95)

In Rafella's case it is a matter of inducing tastes and habits 'in direct opposition to the one in which she had been reared' (1926: 55–6), thus suggesting that Rafella is *inherently* incapable of acquiring the necessary Memsahib-qualities.

What emerges from this reading of an author of Empire fiction is the emphasis on a certain model of English femininity that is constructed *within* an Other space. Just as Roxana's sexual citizenship emerges when she assimilates a signifier of Turkish sensuality, the heroines of Empire fiction seem to acquire, reinforce or subvert their erotic appeal and sexual manners when relocated to the colony. The *eroticization of the exotic space of the colony is embodied in colonial fiction's emphasis on the sexual and gender dynamics, within races but also across races*, at play 'out there'. But this is not the only mode of eroticizing a different place in the colonial encounter. In other cases the English/European focus was on the beauty and erotic appeal of the native woman, whether seductive or vulnerable. It is in the space of domesticity and intimacy that the sexual politics of Otherness plays out.

The houri and the harem

> The loveliest of the Moores
> We can command, and Negroes everywhere.

100 Difference and desire

> Italians, French, and Dutch, choice Turkish Girles
> Must fill our Alkedavy, the great Palace,
> Where Mullisheg now daines to keepe his Court.
>> (Thomas Heywood, *Fair Maid of the West*, cited in Robinson
>> 2007: 101–2)

> Swaying slowly she quits her station.
> All one silken undulation,
> Past the rows of swarthy faces ...
> She winds her snaky wreathings to the droning of the hymns;
> Till the truth is lost in seeming,
> And our spirits fall a-dreaming.
>> (Webb 1984: 36–7)

There, not more than forty or fifty miles from us, glittering like silver in the early rays of the morning sun, soared Sheba's Breasts; and stretching away for hundreds of miles on either side of them ran the great Suliman Berg. Now that, sitting here, I attempt to describe the extraordinary grandeur and beauty of that sight, language seems to fail me. I am impotent even before its memory. Straight before us, rose two enormous mountains, the like of which are not, I believe, to be seen in Africa, if indeed there are any other such in the world, measuring each of them at least fifteen thousand feet in height, standing not more than a dozen miles apart, linked together by a precipitous cliff of rock, and towering in awful white solemnity straight into the sky. These mountains placed thus, like the pillars of a gigantic gateway, are shaped after the fashion of a woman's breasts, and at times the mists and shadows beneath them take the form of a recumbent woman, veiled mysteriously in sleep. Their bases swell gently from the plain, looking at that distance perfectly round and smooth; and upon the top of each is a vast hillock covered with snow, exactly corresponding to the nipple on the female breast. The stretch of cliff that connects them appears to be some thousands of feet in height, and perfectly precipitous, and on each flank of them, so far as the eye can reach, extent similar lines of cliff, broken only here and there by flat table-topped mountains, something like the world-famed one at Cape Town; a formation, by the way, that is very common in Africa.
>> (Haggard, *King Solomon's Mines*, unpaginated, http://ebooks.adelaide.
>> edu.au/h/haggard/h_rider/king/index.html)

Heywood's account of the harem, says Benedict Robinson in a perceptive comment, is not only the representation of Oriental despotism but also the 'scene of a radically cosmopolitan social and political life' (2007: 101). That is, the harem, the domain of the intimate, is a space where multiple identities are in conflict. What we see here is a racialized *spatializing of the Other's sexual relations*, but also a *representation of the possibilities of interracial intimacies*, thereby rendering the harem the erotic-exotic cosmopolitan in scope, a part of what Robinson calls 'an expanding global capitalism['s] strange erotic and commercial entanglements' (143).

In *Jane Eyre*, Rochester tells Jane Eyre, as a supposed paean to her beauty and his love for her, that he would not trade her 'for the Grand Turk's whole seraglio; gazelle-eyes, houri forms and all' (Brontë 2010: 229). If Brontë was positing the seraglio as the densest space of sexuality, Haggard transformed the entire African continent into a woman's body waiting to be discovered, penetrated and conquered in his notorious map affixed to *King Solomon's Mines* with the description quoted above. Both these texts, along with several others from the seventeenth century onwards, treated Africa, Asia and the Orient in general as the space of heightened sexuality.

In *She* Holly speculates on the kind of woman who lies behind the curtains: 'some naked savage queen, a languishing Oriental beauty, or a nineteenth-century young lady, drinking afternoon tea?' (Haggard 2008: 131). This is the sexualized imagination of the European anticipating the erotic thrill of exotic women. Holly, writes Haggard, is trapped in the 'web of her fatal fascinations' (162). The dark continent, Haggard makes clear, is a sexual predator manifest, literally, in the form of Ayesha in what Joseph Bristow terms a 'vengeful, demonic sexuality' (1991: 134). A few decades later, as we shall see, Forster would depict the Indian landscape also as a female predator who 'calls' the Englishman. Trego Webb's poem on the famous/notorious Indian dancing girl ('nautch girl') epitomizes her as a snake, mystical and magical, whose charms bewitch the viewers. She is at once sexual predator and witch.

Arguably in the representations of sexualized geography of the world in the English (and French) literary imagination, the harem and the seraglio are the most dominant images. The imperial exotic produced an erotic or sexual geography of the world in which distant spaces, such as the Turkish bath in Mary Wortley Montagu or the seraglio of sultans in numerous Orientalist texts, became synonymous not only with hypersexed natives but also with the space of sexual liberation/libertarianism. These therefore function as spaces of sexual Otherness where excessive and alternate sexualities were not transgressive. While on the one hand, as Felicity Nussbaum notes (1995: 97), such a sexual geography involves a geographical displacement and a moral distinction – of sexual morality in European men/women and the morality of Arab men/women – it also evoked envy and desire. Thus in this section I study the *imperial exotic as erotic geography where distant lands become desirable lands* due to their supposed freedom in the domain of desiring, spaces that Mary Louise Pratt termed 'feminotopias', 'idealized worlds of female autonomy, empowerment, and pleasure' (2003: 166–7), and in which the European woman could possibly find a measure of sexual citizenship. Arguably, one of the most sustained examinations of erotic-geography-as-feminotopia of the Other was Mary Montagu's Turkish Embassy letters (written in 1717–18, published 1763). By situating sexual 'excesses' in other lands the European/ English author was able to displace anxieties, desires and envy over sexual freedom.[8]

102 Difference and desire

Montagu begins by detailing the cosmetic devices of the women:

> I can assure you with great truth, that the court of England (though I believe it the fairest in Christendom) does not contain so many beauties as are under our protection here. They generally shape their eye-brows, and both Greeks and Turks have the custom of putting round their eyes a black tincture, that, at a distance, or by candle-light, adds very much to the blackness of them. I fancy many of our ladies would be overjoyed to know this secret, but 'tis too visible by day.
>
> (Unpaginated, http://ebooks.adelaide.edu.au/m/montagu/
> mary_wortley/letters)

Montagu has already revealed a supposed secret − of the source of eyeliners that enhance the beauty of the native women's eyes. Soon after this Montagu shifts her focus to how the costumes enhance the beauty but also serve a very different purpose. She writes:

> 'Tis very easy to see, they have in reality more liberty than we have. No woman, of what rank soever, is permitted to go into the streets without two *murlins*, one that covers her face all but her eyes, and another, that hides the whole dress of her head, and hangs half way down her back. Their shapes are also wholely [*sic*] concealed, by a thing they call a *serigee*, which no woman of any sort appears without; this has strait sleeves, that reach to their fingers-ends, and it laps all round them, not unlike a riding-hood. In winter, 'tis of cloth; and in summer, of plain stuff or silk. You may guess then, how effectually this disguises them, so that there is no distinguishing the great lady from her slave. 'Tis impossible for the most jealous husband to know his wife, when he meets her; and no man dare touch or follow a woman in the street.

Montagu now establishes the entire country as a space of licentious women:

> This perpetual masquerade gives them entire liberty of following their inclinations, without danger of discovery. The most usual method of intrigue, is, to send an appointment to the lover to meet the lady at a Jew's shop, which are as notoriously convenient as our Indian-houses; and yet, even those who don't make use of them, do not scruple to go to buy pennyworths, and tumble over rich goods, which are chiefly to be found amongst that sort of people. The great ladies seldom let their gallants know who they are; and 'tis so difficult to find it out, that they can very seldom guess at her name, whom they have corresponded with for above half a year together. You may easily imagine the number of faithful wives very small in a country where they have nothing to fear from a lover's indiscretion, since we see so many have the courage to expose themselves to that in this world, and all the threatened

punishment of the next, which is never preached to the Turkish damsels. Neither have they much to apprehend from the resentment of their husbands; those ladies that are rich, having all their money in their own hands. Upon the whole, I look upon the Turkish women, as the only free people in the empire.
(Unpaginated, http://ebooks.adelaide.edu.au/m/montagu/
mary_wortley/letters)

Critics (Lowe 1991, Yeğenoğlu 1998: 89) note that Montagu treats the veil as symbolic of the freedom – sexual – the Turkish woman possesses, as can be seen in the above extracts where she speaks of the intrigues facilitated by the 'masquerade' of the veil.[9] I suggest that a dynamics of visible/hidden operates in the construction of an erotic geography. Montagu focuses on the concealment of the face and the feminine figure behind the veil and the costume but constantly hints at having *uncovered* intrigues behind the masquerades. Just as in *Roxana* Defoe brought distant difference under a measure of comprehensible control and a controlling desire through the use of a hidden/visible dynamic, Montagu suggests that the masquerade literally masks transgressive sexuality, excessive sexuality and feminine sexual liberty but which she has discovered. Thus what the veil conceals is not only feminine beauty but also feminine sexual intrigues. Montagu converts, I propose, *the exotic object of the veil into a map of erotic desires and sexual pleasure by suggesting that something more lies hidden behind the veil.*[10]

Interestingly, Montagu's text also suggests an envy of the intimacies among women in such spaces. Having left behind some women in the bath – to whom, she records:

The lady, that seemed the most considerable among them, entreated me to sit by her, and would fain have undressed me for the bath. I excused myself with some difficulty. They being however all so earnest in persuading me, I was at last forced to open my shirt, and shew them my stays; which satisfied them very well; for, I saw, they believed I was locked up in that machine, and that it was not in my own power to open it, which contrivance they attributed to my husband,—I was charmed with their civility and beauty, and should have been very glad to pass more time with them; but Mr W – resolving to pursue his journey next morning early, I was in haste to see the ruins of Justinian's church, which did not afford me so agreeable a prospect as I had left, being little more than a heap of stones.
(Unpaginated, http://ebooks.adelaide.edu.au/m/montagu/
mary_wortley/letters)

The 'prospect' of the woman's space she left behind, Montagu admits, was far more interesting for her than the 'heap of stones'.[11]

It is in such an (envying) acknowledgement of the liberated sexual subject that is the Turkish woman that Montagu recognizes 'herself as a subject ... outside national boundaries, in the encounter of a sexually same yet culturally different

104 Difference and desire

other' (Yeğenoğlu 1998: 107). Lisa Lowe (1991) is accurate when she sees a dual rhetoric – of identification with Turkish woman and of differentiation and Othering of the Turkish woman – in Montagu's representation of the Turkish women, although, as Judith Still cautions us (2009), Montagu does suggest that the Turkish women are only relatively free (91). Extending Yeğenoğlu's argument I suggest that Turkish erotic geography becomes for Montagu the space of discovering a sexual citizenship through an unravelling of a deeper meaning of the woman's veil. That is, by proposing that she knows exactly what the masquerades conceal, Montagu positions herself as a *comprehending* subject, one whose awareness of the sexual dynamics at work gives her own self a sense of sexual citizenship – including the lesbian identity – within the space of the Other. Erotic geography here is at once enabling in the sense of comprehending the (sexualized) Other but also constructing the opportunities, at least in the case of Montagu, the 'multiple cosmopolitan possibilities' (11) that Laura Rosenthal associates with exoticism.

Among these possibilities was one of wealth and sexual conquest. In Ben Jonson, George Chapman and John Marston's *Eastward Ho!* (1605) we see the intertwining of commodity and sexuality (III.3, ll. 15–31):

> *Seagull.* Come boys, Virginia longs till we share the rest of her Maiden-head.
>
> *Spendall.* Why is she inhabited already with any English?
>
> *Seagull.* A whole Country of English is there man, bred of those that were left there in '79. They have married with the Indians, and make them bring forth as beautiful faces as any we have in England: and therefore the Indians are so in love with them, that all the treasure they have, they lay at their feet.
>
> *Scapthrift.* But is there such treasure there Captain, as I have heard? I tell thee, Gold is more plentiful there then Copper is with us … Why, man, all their dripping pans and their chamber-pots are pure gold; and all the chains with which they chain up their streets are massy gold; all the prisoners they take are fettered in gold; and for rubies and diamonds, they go forth on holidays and gather 'em by the seashore to hang on their children's coats, and stick on their caps, as commonly as our children wear saffron-gilt brooches, and groats with holes in 'em.
>
> (1973: 60–1)

Seagull and Scapthrift speak of Virginia in terms of acquirable women and acquirable gold/treasure. One, supposedly, leads to the other because the native/Indian women 'lay' all their precious gold at the feet of the Europeans.

In Robert Daborne's *Christian Turn'd Turk* (1612) Governor Ward falls in love with Voad, the Turkish woman. His first articulations of love suggest the erosion of Christian faith in the face of the woman's non-European beauty:

> Or beauty made a conquest of poore man
> I am thy captive by heauen, by my religion.
>
> (Sc. 4, unpaginated)

The conversation proceeds thus:

> Voade: As my belief's in that, my faith gives trust
>   To your protest.
> Ward: Then by thy God, by the great Mahomet.
> Voad: To weak a bond to tie a Christian in.
>
> (Sc. 4, unpaginated)

'Turn Turk and I am yours', Voad tells him (Sc. 4, unpaginated). The suggestion in Daborne's play is that Ward abandons his faith for the sake of the Turkish woman. The erotic appeal of the Other here is so powerful that he, Ward, cannot stay English or Christian any longer.

In Philip Massinger's *The Renegado* (1630) the Venetian Christians barely escape the Turkish influence. In the play Donusa is being tempted by Vitelli with multiple products at his stall. When he claims he can show her the 'rarest beauties of the Christian world' (n.d.: 137), Donusa responds with an unveiling of herself and asks 'can you match me this' (I.iii, n.d.: 138). Benedict Robinson's reading proposes that Donusa, in competition with a market of goods, commodifies herself by 'entering into potentially scandalous transactions with a Christian stranger' (2007: 121). Thus commerce and eroticism go together in the Early Modern, in Robinson's reading. But what is also important is that such transactions gesture at the multiple possibilities in commerce and sexuality that opened up for the English/ European. The *erotic-exotic was a space where such possibilities of 'acquiring' or transacting with the Other began to be available.*

But Vitelli, who is seduced by Donusa, finds enough resolve inside him to convert her to Christianity.[12] If Daborne's play suggests the overwhelming erotic-sexual power of the Turkish woman, Massinger has high hopes for the European strength of character. Daniel Vitkus argues that such 'theatrical spectacle[s] of Mediterranean adventuring introduced English audiences to the possibility of a mobile, adaptive foreign trade, and to the potential power of investment and risk' and 'helped to cultivate a cult of heroic risk-takers' (2007: 92). While Vitkus' focus is on the power of Christianity in the face of Turkish-Islamic aggression (in the context of English mercantile expansion) there is the other, gendered, angle to the two texts. Daborne and Massinger both foreground the seductive power that is the 'face' of Turkish aggression. By suggesting that it is the Turkish woman who draws the European in and causes him to lose his faith, unless he is, like Vitelli, firm in his resolve, the plays foreground the dangerous appeal of the erotic-exotic to not just European masculinity but to its religion and national identity as well. A threat to the English/European *man*, in terms of the immoral, sexualized Turkish woman, is seen in these plays as a threat to national identity itself. The erotic, clearly, has a more-than-sexual charge, embodied in the form of the non-European woman. However, just as Paulina survives Asambeg's (masculine, non-Christian) onslaught, Vitelli survives Donusa's (feminine, non-Christian). Both instances suggest the triumph of, above all, Christian virtue, whether of men or women.

106 Difference and desire

The erotic appeal of the Other need not be embodied, however, in the form of the non-European woman – it could be in the form of imported, exotic materials from abroad that add to the erotic and sensual appeal of the English woman. In the early lines of *The Rape of the Lock*, Alexander Pope explicitly links the European/ English woman with the material products of the Empire:

> A heav'nly image in the glass appears,
> To that she bends, to that her eyes she rears;
> Th' inferior Priestess, at her altar's side,
> Trembling begins the sacred rites of Pride.
> Unnumber'd treasures ope at once, and here
> The various off'rings of the world appear;
> From each she nicely culls with curious toil,
> And decks the Goddess with the glitt'ring spoil.
> This casket India's glowing gems unlocks,
> And all Arabia breathes from yonder box.
> The Tortoise here and Elephant unite,
> Transformed to combs, the speckled, and the white.

> (1963: 222)

Evoking a deep feminine sensuality, Pope aligns the woman's body with several products of the imperial enterprise, each one more exotic than the other. The erotic exoticism here imbricates the woman's body with the commodities so that they are inseparable. In Laura Brown's pithy formulation, the woman puts on the 'commercialist spoils of imperialist expansion' (1993: 146). The fact that Pope chooses to underscore the *uncountable* nature of the product – *Unnumber'd* treasures, *various* off'rings, *all* Arabia – suggests that the exotic escapes comprehension even when, or especially when, adorning the female body. Later, in the very next canto, Pope would refer to 'this Nymph, to the destruction of *mankind*', once again indicating an excessive sensual effect on many men of *one* woman adorned with the exotic products of the empire. The excess of signifiers of mercantile expansion in the above passage implies, I propose, an *unbounded eroticism* that doubles the limitlessness of territorial expansion and capital accumulation of the Empire already underway by the time of Pope's poem.

To take another example of such a cautionary tale warning of possible corruption of English/European women by the East from the same age, Jonathan Swift in his 'A Proposal that All the Ladies and Women of Ireland should Appear Constantly in Irish Manufactures' (1729) offers a very different interpretation of the exotic from that of Defoe. Unlike Pope, who treats the exotic as delectable difference, Swift portrays exotic commodities as a threat to national and cultural identity in this essay. Swift argues that the fascination for foreign commodities and apparel by the women of Ireland leads to excessive imports of these and a consequent ruin of indigenous industries. Swift writes:

It is to gratify the vanity, and pride, and luxury of the women, and of the young fops who admire them, that we owe this insupportable grievance, of bringing in the instruments of our ruin. There is annually brought over to this kingdom near ninety thousand pounds worth of silk, whereof the greater part is manufactured. Thirty thousand pounds more is expended in muslin, holland, cambric, and calico. What the price of lace amounts to, is not easy to be collected from the custom-house book, being a kind of goods that takes up little room, and is easily run; but, considering the prodigious price of a woman's head-dress, at ten, twelve, twenty pounds a yard, must be very great. The tea, rated at seven shillings per pound, comes to near twelve thousand pounds; but, considering it as the common luxury of every chambermaid, sempstress, and tradesman's wife, both in town and country, however they come by it, must needs cost the kingdom double that sum. Coffee is somewhere above seven thousand pounds. I have seen no account of the chocolate, and some other Indian or American goods. The drapery imported is about four-and-twenty thousand pounds. The whole amounts (with one or two other particulars) to one hundred and fifty thousand pounds ... if the ladies, till better times, will not be content to go in their own country shifts, I wish they may go in rags.

Let them vie with each other in the fineness of their native linen: their beauty and gentleness will as well appear, as if they were covered over with diamonds and brocade.

(http://jonathanswiftarchive.org.uk/browse/year/
text_10_9_1.html)

In this diatribe, as Laura Brown rightly points out, 'the pernicious corruptions of an expansionist culture are so intimately and inevitably associated with the figure of the woman' (1993: 180). Swift transforms the desire for the exotic into the danger of the exotic here, suggesting that the national economy and national identity are at stake because of the feminine fascination for difference.

A more direct instantiation of this theme of a corrupt/ing non-European sensuality is visible in texts like William Beckford's Gothic tale, *Vathek* (1786). Having established beyond doubt the utter dissoluteness of Vathek, the Caliph, Beckford suggests through the novel that Vathek's mother Carathis is far more dangerous. Vathek's fifth palace is of course the 'Retreat of Mirth, or the Dangerous'. It was, writes Beckford, 'frequented by troops of young females, beautiful as the Houris, and not less seducing; who never failed to receive with caresses all whom the Caliph allowed to approach them' (1970: 3). The novel's emphasis on Oriental excess revolves around the women, Carathis and later Nouronihar. Carathis, who is Greek (8), is presented as somebody well versed in the dark arts and satanic magic, and a purveyor of exotica:

By secret stairs, known only to herself and her son, she first repaired to the mysterious recesses in which were deposited the mummies that had been

108 Difference and desire

> brought from the catacombs of the ancient Pharaohs. Of these she ordered several to be taken. From thence she resorted to a gallery, where, under the guard of fifty female negroes, mute, and blind of the right eye, were preserved the oil of the most venomous serpents, rhinoceros' horns, and woods of a subtle and penetrating odour, procured from the interior of the Indies, together with a thousand other horrible rarieties. This collection had been formed for a purpose like the present, by Carathis herself, from a presentiment that she might one day enjoy some intercourse with the infernal powers, to whom she had ever been passionately attached, and to whose taste she was no stranger.
>
> (30–1)

She is a 'chameleon, [who] could assume all possible colours' (38). She says of herself: 'there is nothing so pleasing as retiring to caverns; my taste for dead bodies and everything like mummy is decided' (42). Not only is Carathis a knowledgeable woman she is also irreducible to an identity. Compared, unfavourably, to a chameleon she is the epitome of the threatening non-European woman.

When Vathek falls ill, writes Beckford,

> one of his [Vathek's] Ethiopian wives (for he delighted in variety) clasped him in her arms, threw him upon her shoulder like a sack of dates, and finding that the fire was hemming them in, set off with no small expedition, considering the weight of her burden.
>
> (48)

It is significant that the harem, the queen's quarters and the domestic sphere in *Vathek*, becomes not simply the site of (erotic) feminine domesticity but also a space where the home is 'fraught with anxieties related to the masculine world of the outside' (Saglia 1997: 202). Carathis' actions within the domestic sphere are almost entirely determined by her eagerness and anxiety to influence Vathek's actions in the world of the kingdom, whether this be the marriage of Vathek or the attempt to gain for her son something from the giaour. Converting the woman's space into the seat of real power, Beckford seems to echo Mary Montagu's view of the relative autonomy and power of the Turkish and Arab women. Byron's Gulnare (*The Corsair*), likewise, is a strong woman and one who reverses the stereotype of the weak, vulnerable non-European (she is a Turk).

Defoe and Montagu in their discourses of eroticized exotic commodification and erotic geography respectively find alternate (sexual) citizenship and identity even in limited role-playing. Let me now turn to Charlotte Dacre's 1806 Gothic text, *Zofloya*. Set in Venice and its neighbouring towns, this is the story of Victoria who, as mistress of Berenza, finds herself attracted to Zofloya, the Moor servant of Berenza's brother, Henriquez (but is also attracted to Henriquez, and resents his wife, Lilla). Echoing Aphra Behn's account of Oroonoko as noble and majestic, Dacre presents Zofloya as graceful, powerful and majestic. Ironically, Zofloya first appears to Victoria in a dream:

> Clad in a habit of white and gold; on his head he wore a white turban,
> which sparkled with emeralds, and was surmounted by a waving feather of
> green; his arms and legs, which were bare, were encircled with the finest
> oriental pearl; he wore a collar of gold round his throat, and his ears were
> decorated with gold rings of enormous size.
>
> (2008: 136)

This is the eroticization of the Moor, where corporeal form and appearance (the jewels) combine to produce a desirable figure in her dream. Like Behn's Oroonoko it is revealed that Zofloya is also of noble birth (141). Such descriptions move out from the realm of the dream to real life for Victoria who begins to see in Zofloya 'a beauty that delighted and surprised' (145). Victoria, writes Dacre, let her eyes 'wander with admiration over the beauty of his form' (147) as her own body is filled with 'the most agreeable sensations' (151). He 'appeared not only the superior of his race, but of a superior order of beings' (234). Dacre emphasizes Zofloya's great physique and he is described as a 'demi-god' at one point (164). But the eroticization is not complete. The erotic appeal of Zofloya, I propose, is due to the interplay of apparently contradictory and incompatible features: racial slavishness and mastery, magnificent 'countenance'/physique and insidious evil.

Zofloya plays his racial and gender cards well when he asks her in 'silver tones', 'does the Signora believe, then, that the Moor Zofloya hath a heart dark as his countenance?' (151). A Moor who speaks in silver tones is appealing in itself, and Zofloya then tells her he is well accomplished in chemistry and other sciences (153). Zofloya's erotic attraction, in Victoria's eyes, rests in the strange conjunction of his racial identity (Moor), his majestic bearing, his 'silver tones' and his apparent wisdom. That is, Zofloya's attraction lies in his being at once Moor and an accomplished person, in the same way as Behn's Oroonoko. Erotic exoticism here is the effect of *blurred* racial-cultural identities where the Moor who claims to be an 'unworthy slave' (153), 'the humble fool of [her] wishes' (162) demonstrates his superiority, grace, majesty and knowledge. This suitable conflation of racial and cultural categories – slave, wise man, Moor, savant, servant and master – completes the eroticization of Zofloya.

It is also from within such an erotically charged situation – in which the European Victoria is attracted to the majestic Moor – that Victoria herself begins to act out her deepest fantasies – of getting rid of her husband. This shift in the character of Victoria begins when she rejects her European marriage. Her reactions to Zofloya, on the other hand, are classically romantic:

> 'Say you so, enchanting Moor?' exclaimed Victoria, half frantic with
> joy at the meaning contained in his words; and, breathless with contending emotions of hope and doubt, seizing his hand, she pressed it to her
> bosom.
>
> (152–3)

110 Difference and desire

Having drugged Henriquez (and kidnapped Lilla), Victoria ravages Henriquez and stabs Lilla to death, covering the latter's body, writes Dacre, 'with innumerable wounds' (226). But even this powerful woman (Victoria), Dacre shows, becomes subservient to the Moor. After his sexual triumph over the white Victoria Zofloya acquires, also, a moral ascendancy over her. The Moor's seraglio becomes the space where the European woman is fully orientalized and sexualized. But it is also important to note that the independent white woman becomes dependent on the Moor. After promising Victoria that she will have her wishes Zofloya makes it clear that he is in control: 'I direct, Signora, not advise, and at the same time must observe your fullest confidence is to be placed in me ... [I]f you wish my assistance, I must be suffered, without comment, to pursue that line best calculated to render it effectual' (172–3). Victoria recognizes her dependence on the Moor. Dacre writes:

> Never till this moment, had she been so near the person of the Moor—such powerful fascination dwelt around him, that she felt incapable of withdrawing from his arms; yet ashamed, (for Victoria was still proud) and blushing at her feelings, when she remembered that Zofloya, however he appeared was but a menial slave ... she sought but vainly, to repress them; for no sooner ... did she behold that beautiful and majestic visage, that towering and graceful form, than all thought of his inferiority vanished, and the ravished sense, spuming at the calumnious idea, confessed him a being of superior order.
>
> (234)

Victoria cries out: 'O Zofloya! I perceive too clearly, how much, how completely, I am in your power!' (234). The white woman–black man master–slave relationship has been reversed here, and a key factor in this reversal is the eroticism and sexuality the two share.

Carol Davison is correct to speak of 'Victoria's incremental seduction by Satan in the spectacular guise of Zofloya' (2009: 35) and that she is 'subjected to the treachery of love and reduced to the status of a submissive, vulnerable female' (40). He is, in Sara Schotland's words, 'foreign, sexually threatening but also satanic in his color and conduct' (2009: 129). But Dacre, as Kim Ian Michasiw notes, makes Zofloya different from the blacks of the Abolitionist verse of the age (I shall discuss some of these verses in the next chapter) in not having him possessed of compassion or family sentiment (2003: 46). He appears in Victoria's dream and as such, in Davison's reading, 'seems an emanation of a repressed aspect of Victoria, an "other" side of herself' (2009: 42). By showing Victoria's descent into not just sensual 'excesses' but also murderous violence Dacre represents the 'corruption' of the European woman in the presence of the Moor. While Defoe and Dacre both suggest that it is a certain kind of 'transgressive' European woman who would be so corrupted, in both cases this *corruption is associated with the East*. But perhaps the climactic moment in the novel is when we are told that Zofloya is not a Moor but the devil himself, 'a figure, fierce, gigantic and hideous to behold' (267) who, 'under semblance of the Moorish slave' had misled Victoria (267).[13] Having already told us of Zofloya's magnificent physical appeal/appearance, Dacre then proceeds to suggest that this is the visible aspect of the Moor's character. Concealed beneath the magnificence is the devil himself.

Elsewhere Dacre has the banditti admit to his strange influence: 'when he was among them, they felt impelled to deeds which otherwise would have remained unattempted' (2008: 245). Kim Michasiw proposes that Dacre's portrait of Zofloya 'wrests Africans out of the primitive realm where both pro-slavery and abolitionist texts preferred to lodge them' and in 'emphasizing Europe's erased debt to Africa … files a salutary protest against the primitivism and pathos of abolitionism's negro' (2003: 49–50). Further, Michasiw argues that Zofloya 'gains his vengeance through the agency of a corruptible white woman' (51). While Michasiw's argument holds good overall, it does not explain *why* the stereotyping of Zofloya as black and as the devil need to be read separately, as the above reading does. My argument instead is that Zofloya's power proceeds from his appeal – an erotic appeal in the case of Victoria – which is a *mix of the racial, the sophisticated and the Satanic*.[14] In other words, the 'corruptible' white woman cannot resist, Dacre warns, the potent mixture of race, sophistication, glamour and evil embodied in Zofloya. Victoria's transgression is racial, sexual and ethical when she consorts with and then becomes dependent on the Moor-devil. Zofloya is thus also a *cautionary* tale, warning the European woman of alliances with the racial-cultural Other.[15]

We have noted earlier the representation and romanticization of the Noble Savage as an example of the exotic Other in English writings. Zofloya presents a version of this theme where neither the Savage Exotic nor the Noble Savage are mutually exclusive. The erotic-exotic results from the strange *mixture* of the two in one person in Dacre's construction of Zofloya. A racial type who does not conform to the type is a contradiction, a monstrosity and exotic – and this is what attracts and then corrupts the European woman, Victoria. Racialized evil is a general outcome of the collapse of the European home and family. What Dacre foregrounds is not, I have argued elsewhere (Nayar 2013a), the threat of invasion by the racial Other but the erosion, from *within*, of the European 'family values' of fidelity that leads to the invasion. In other words, the blurring of social boundaries, the collapse of familial relations and parenting norms are Dacre's focus. It must be noted that Zofloya – who, incidentally, first appears on page 137 of the novel – does not initiate the collapse of the Berenza home. He does not, in my view, constitute the threat. Rather, he helps an already collapsing structure to its full and total ruin. Zofloya makes use of the opportunity presented by Victoria's temperament and desires in order to wreck the Berenza home. In this, of course, Zofloya reverses the master–slave dialectic, as Diane Hoeveler notes (1997: 188), but this reversal follows (but does not initiate) a process well underway much *before* he arrives at the house of Berenza. The full terror of the collapse of Berenza's home and Victoria's final annihilation is without doubt engineered by Zofloya but this

112 Difference and desire

has nothing to do with the collapse of the ideal European family – a collapse which, in my opinion, is the focus of the tale.

Further, by suggesting that the collapse of the two houses (of the Marchese, and later of Berenza) is entirely due to their women, Dacre is pointing to the woman as place-holder and 'boundary-marker' (Anne McClintock's term, 1994). In this, of course, Dacre's novel continues the theme of English femininity under threat from the African, Arab or Asian male. The novel, ultimately, calls for a reassertion of the gender roles in the upholding of the home and family – race, as far as I can see, is only a threat when the European woman goes 'loose', so to speak. It is when the woman seeks pleasure and agency outside the boundaries of her home, relations and race that true horror begins.

I would go so far as to say that the eroticized Other that we see in Montagu, Beckford, Dacre and other texts represents a certain envy and anxiety over what the Westerner saw as a feminine or feminized civilization, with touches of the magical, the mystical and the erotic (or perhaps the erotic is the effect of the first two). Felicia Hemans describes the feminine spaces of the Moorish palace thus in *England and Spain* (1808):

> Its fairy-palace and enchanted bowers;
> There all Arabian fiction e'er could tell,
> Of potent genii or of wizards spell.
> (http://digital.lib.ucdavis.edu/projects/bwrp/Works/
> HemaFEngla.htm)

Carathis' magic and witchcraft in Beckford's account of the palaces of Vathek seems to illustrate Hemans' description.

Further, the feminine space of the Alhambra, the harem and the home, seems to invert the traditional gender roles of protected-women/protector men.[16] In Beckford's *Vathek*, as we can see, it is the woman, Carathis, who guards the kingdom, ensures that its king is safe and intrigues to make certain that enemies and threats are disposed of. Whether Carathis therefore possesses the erotic charge of a dominatrix is unclear but the empowerment of the women, as Carathis the queen or the veiled Turkish women in Montagu, defies the stereotypical gender roles.

In several cases the harem and the seraglio remain a space of confinement. In *Rasselas*, for instance, Johnson suggests that the imprisoned women possess no knowledge and as such are little more than savage, if pretty, creatures. Pekuah, incarcerated briefly in such a harem, offers Johnson's criticism when she says of the inhabitants:

> 'The diversions of the women,' answered Pekuah, 'were only childish play, by which the mind accustomed to stronger operations could not be kept busy. I could do all which they delighted in doing by powers merely sensitive, while my intellectual faculties were flown to Cairo. They ran from room to room, as a bird hops from wire to wire in his cage. They danced

for the sake of motion, as lambs frisk in a meadow. One sometimes pretended to be hurt that the rest might be alarmed, or hid herself that another might seek her. Part of their time passed in watching the progress of light bodies that floated on the river, and part in marking the various forms into which clouds broke in the sky.

'Their business was only needlework, in which I and my maids sometimes helped them; but you know that the mind will easily straggle from the fingers, nor will you suspect that captivity and absence from Nekayah could receive solace from silken flowers.

'Nor was much satisfaction to be hoped from their conversation: for of what could they be expected to talk? They had seen nothing, for they had lived from early youth in that narrow spot: of what they had not seen they could have no knowledge, for they could not read. They had no idea but of the few things that were within their view, and had hardly names for anything but their clothes and their food. As I bore a superior character, I was often called to terminate their quarrels, which I decided as equitably as I could.'

(1970: 103–4)

Johnson reduces the seraglio to a frivolous space of mindless recreations of the Arab women.

The entry into such a feminized space becomes, therefore, a major theme for authors like Byron. In *The Giaour*, Leila, who lives inside the palace of Hassan, is seduced by the Christian giaour. The Arab's bower, Byron's poem suggests, is a prison for the woman, and this kind of treatment of women is sanctioned by Hassan's creed:

his creed,
Which saith that woman is but dust,
A soulless toy for tyrant's lust.

(1975: 257)

Radically different from Mary Montagu in his evaluation of the feminine space, Byron implicitly endorses the destruction of the Arab home/harem for having imprisoned and tyrannically exploited the women. Thus Byron describes how, in the course of the Christian giaour's revenge upon Hassan, the Arab's bower (where Leila had been incarcerated) is reduced to ruins:

The steed is vanished from the stall;
No serf is seen in Hassan's hall;
The lonely spider's thin grey pall
Waves slowly widening o'er the wall;
The bat builds in his harem bower,
And in the fortress of his power

114 Difference and desire

The owl usurps the beacon-tower;
The wild-dog howls o'er the fountain's brim,
With baffled thirst and famine, grim;
For the stream has shrunk from its marble bed,
Where the weeds and the desolate dust are spread.

(1975: 255)

In *Zofloya* the Moor seduces, over a period of time, Victoria. The feminine space's erotic appeal lies now in the seduction scene, the space where the racial-cultural Other disturbs feminine domesticity. As Byron puts it in *The Giaour*:

The faithless slave that broke her bower,
And − worse than faithless − for a Giaour!

(1975: 257)

This is more than seduction, it becomes akin to cultural invasion and political subversion. Diego Saglia points out that in poems such as Felicia Hemans' *England and Spain* (1808), the 'Moors and their royal palace are turned into the symbols of a historical tyranny that the Spaniards had to defeat in order to regain full territorial possession' (1997: 204).[17] Saglia also cites Thomas Moore's *Lalla Rookh* (1817) where Hafed courts the Emir's daughter Hinda by climbing into her tower. Hinda's home is depicted almost like a prison by Moore:

So, Hinda, have thy face and mind
Like holy mysteries, lain enshrined.
And, O, what transport for a lover
To lift the veil that shades them o'er!

(2002: 219–20)

Her lover takes the 'steeps, through dark and dread' (224) into the bower. Saglia proposes that this kind of account (seen also in Byron's *The Bride of Abydos*) suggests 'protection and enslavement' (210).[18] In Johnson's *Rasselas* (1759), Pekuah is imprisoned in the seraglio, although she is treated deferentially and is careful to avoid attracting the attentions of the Arab chief.

While Saglia is undoubtedly correct in proposing that the heavily guarded bower or harem or women's quarters in the English imagination represents the tyranny and oppression of women by the Arab/native men, it misses the obvious strategy here − the erotic-exotic functions by keeping the object of desire at a distance and to be attained through danger. The exotic is at once that which is desirable and dangerous, and this combination culminates in a spatial trope: the bower/harem.

An erotic geography different from the bower/feminine space is also visible in English texts when speaking of the Other. In Byron's *The Island*, Torquil and his shipmates wed island brides. Byron uses the word 'tamed' to describe the change in the Europeans at the hands of the native women. Byron writes:

The airy joys of social solitudes,
Tamed each rude wanderer to the sympathies
Of those who were more happy, if less wise,
Did more than Europe's discipline had done,
And civilised Civilisation's son!

(1975: 355)

Byron emphasizes this taming as a form of emasculation of the European, seduced by the native woman (the island, Toobonoi, is set somewhere in the South Pacific):

His heart was tamed to that voluptuous state,
At once Elysian and effeminate.[19]

(1975: 356)

In *Don Juan* (Canto IV) Haidee's Arab mother is described thus:

large dark eye show'd deep Passion's force,
Though sleeping like a lion near a source.

(1975: 705)

But Byron was also a poet who associated 'pure' womanliness with Sultana Gulbeyaz in *Don Juan*, because, even though 'imperial, or imperious', she is moved to tears as well. Byron describes Gulbeyez (Canto 5) in the following terms:

Her rage was but a minute's, and 't was well—
A moment's more had slain her; but the while
It lasted 't was like a short glimpse of hell:
Nought 's more sublime than energetic bile,
Though horrible to see yet grand to tell,
Like ocean warring 'gainst a rocky isle;
And the deep passions flashing through her form
Made her a beautiful embodied storm.
A vulgar tempest 't were to a typhoon
To match a common fury with her rage,
And yet she did not want to reach the moon,
Like moderate Hotspur on the immortal page;
Her anger pitch'd into a lower tune,
Perhaps the fault of her soft sex and age—
Her wish was but to 'kill, kill, kill,' like Lear's,
And then her thirst of blood was quench'd in tears.
A storm it raged, and like the storm it pass'd,
Pass'd without words—in fact she could not speak;
And then her sex's shame broke in at last,
A sentiment till then in her but weak,
But now it flow'd in natural and fast,

116 Difference and desire

As water through an unexpected leak;
For she felt humbled—and humiliation
Is sometimes good for people in her station.

(1975: 727)

Starting off as a stormy individual she calms down into a sentimental and 'weak' woman. This is essentially the erotic geography of the Other that does not threaten: the imperious but womanly queen is finally moved to tears, feels humbled, and that, says Byron's narrator, 'is some times good for people in her station'. As in the case of Maimuna and the numerous mourning women in Southey, Wordsworth and Hemans, Byron's racially and culturally different woman is erotic in her imperiousness but becomes truly feminine in her vulnerability.

The imperious woman may be desired, but is also somebody who has to be controlled. Haggard, who created such an imperious native woman, achieves a neutralization of her threat, at least for a time, by focusing on feminine functions such as caring and healing in *King Solomon's Mines*:

> Women are women, all the world over, whatever their colour. Yet somehow it seemed curious to watch this dusky beauty bending night and day over the fevered man's couch, and performing all the merciful errands of a sick-room swiftly, gently, and with as fine an instinct as that of a trained hospital nurse. For the first night or two I tried to help her, and so did Sir Henry as soon as his stiffness allowed him to move, but Foulata bore our interference with impatience, and finally insisted upon our leaving him to her, saying that our movements made him restless, which I think was true. Day and night she watched him and tended him, giving him his only medicine, a native cooling drink made of milk, in which was infused juice from the bulb of a species of tulip, and keeping the flies from settling on him. I can see the whole picture now as it appeared night after night by the light of our primitive lamp; Good tossing to and fro, his features emaciated, his eyes shining large and luminous, and jabbering nonsense by the yard; and seated on the ground by his side, her back resting against the wall of the hut, the soft-eyed, shapely Kukuana beauty, her face, weary as it was with her long vigil, animated by a look of infinite compassion—or was it something more than compassion?
>
> (http://ebooks.adelaide.edu.au/h/haggard/h_rider/king/index.html)

An outstanding example of such a feminized, eroticized and desirable geography of non-European space occurs as late as 1922, in Forster's *A Passage to India*. In the famous account of the country as a whole Forster writes (it is ostensibly Adela speaking in the novel, but the tone and tenor suggests it is a male voice) in a passage I have already cited earlier:

> How can the mind take hold of such a country? Generations of invaders have tried, but they remain in exile. The important towns they build are

only retreats, their quarrels the malaise of men who cannot find their way home. India knows of their trouble ... She calls 'Come' through her hundred mouths, through objects ridiculous and august. But come to what? She has never defined. She is not a promise, only an appeal.

(1970: 135)

Attractive but mysterious, this is the Other country the Englishman has to deal with, and cannot stay away from.

However, erotic geographies are not always about European femininity constructed within the encounter with racial and cultural Otherness. European masculinity too finds its identity, so to speak, in an engagement with Otherness.

One more point needs to be made in connection with the erotic geographies of English literature. Sexual liaisons and miscegenation become modes of engaging with the racial and cultural Other in the intimate sphere. I turn here to Anne Mellor's intriguing proposition that 'enduring international, interfaith and inter-racial marriages [in Romantic women writers] ... become the hallmarks of a truly cosmopolitan subjectivity, what I am calling an "embodied cosmopolitanism"' (2006: 292). Using a variety of texts from the 1780s–1840s period Mellor argues that 'cultural harmony through romance' (Peter Hulme's phrasing, 141, cited in Mellor 2006: 293) might erase gender politics in favour of a 'utopian imperative' (297). From Mariana Starke's play, *The Widow of Malabar* (1791), Mellor quotes the following lines:

Hold, gentle creatures! In these favour'd times,
Mercy prevails, even o'er distant climes,
And makes the human race her fondest care,
Whether their hue be tawny, black or fair.

(296)

The negotiation with the Other is deemed feasible at the personal-intimate level. However, in the twentieth century, in Forster's *A Passage to India*, we see the space of intimacy itself as the possible threat to the status quo of Empire: it is when Adela Quested and Mrs Moore seek friendships with Indians that the crisis of the novel is precipitated.[20]

Mellor proposes that a cosmopolitan subjectivity emerges in such engagements. Thus her arguments resonate with my own argument throughout this book, that English identity emerged through a constant if varied interaction with the racial-cultural Other. From Roxana's sexual citizenship through Zofloya's seduction by the Moor within the space of the European city and finally to the examples of miscegenation in Anne Mellor and the complications of political domesticity, all seem to indicate the intimate sphere as a site of cosmopolitan, interracial and transnational interactions, a form of *multicultural sexual citizenship*. If exoticism is about the opening up of 'multiple cosmopolitan possibilities' for the cultural rein-vention of the self, as Laura Rosenthal argues (cited above), then Miranda/

118 Difference and desire

Desdemona (Shakespeare), Roxana (Defoe), Victoria (Dacre), Rafella (Perrin) might be seen as characters who do examine these possibilities via the intimate and in engagement with the sexualized racial-cultural Other. The erotic Other, it appears, is a crucial figure in the construction of English identity, as threatened, seduced or cosmopolitan.

The vulnerable Other

A standard model for the representation of the Oriental woman, especially the Indian one, was that of the vulnerable, oppressed and exploited but chaste, religious and devoted woman. William Hodges' visual representation of the widows of India portrayed them as docile, heads bowed and vulnerable. The vulnerable Oriental woman provided the justification for the Westerner's rescue mission. Thus the Arab woman as a sexual slave is a theme common to Byron's *The Siege of Corinth*, *The Giaour* and *The Corsair*. Caroline Franklin notes: 'the Byronic adventure of rescuing the Greek slave necessitates the erotic fantasy of entering the harem, and entails a form of vicarious identification with its master' (2005: 229).

An interesting novel about the vulnerable native woman was Sydney Owenson's *The Missionary* (1811). In the portrait of Luxima, the Hindu priestess of the novel, Owenson manages to conflate several gender roles. The Portuguese missionary who is fascinated by Luxima idolizes her:

> When he beheld her receiving the homage of a deity, all lovely as she was, she awakened no other sentiment in his breast than a pious indignation, natural to his religious zeal, at beholding human reason so subdued by human imposition.
>
> (1811: I: 118)

Alert to the sheer physical presence of the Oriental woman, the European man hurriedly shifts focus to her religiosity that he finds irrational. What we see here is an avoidance theme that highlights, ironically, what is being avoided. To alleviate the threat of the sensual Oriental woman, Owenson's European man chooses instead to turn towards her other characteristics. Hillarion (the missionary) therefore engages in extended debates with Luxima about god, religion and rational belief. All the while, Owenson shows how Hillarion's attention is divided between her supposed vulnerability to such irrational religiosity and her powerfully attractive form. What is also significant is that this Hindu woman needs to be converted to 'right-thinking' ways by the European. But, Owenson notes, this conversion is *not* true, for Luxima continues to yearn for her original beliefs and sees her conversion as false:

> Oh! Give me back to my country, my peace, my fame; or suffer me still to remain near thee, and I will rejoice in the loss of all … [I]f it is a virtue in thy religion to stifle the best and purest feelings of the heart, that nature implants, how shall I believe in, or adopt, its tenets?—I whose nature, whose faith

itself, was love—how from thee shall I learn to subdue my feelings, who first taught me to substitute a human, for a heavenly passion?

(III: 111–12. See Freeman 2005 for a reading of this theme of conversion in Owenson)

The discovery of her 'true' identity is what inexorably leads to her death. The vulnerability of the native woman, Owenson suggests, is at once due to her irrational faith and her love for the European. Thus it seems inevitable that such a woman has to die, and Luxima does.

A slightly different version of the vulnerable woman figures in Felicia Hemans' 'The Indian City'. What makes this poem interesting is that Maimuna, the Muslim woman protagonist of the poem, is initially portrayed as an angry, vengeful – her son has been killed by some Brahmins – leader of soldiers. On the death of her son:

> She rose
> Like a prophetess from dark repose!
> —
> And said – 'Not yet – not yet I weep,
> Not yet my spirit shall sink or sleep,
> Not till yon city, in ruins rent,
> Be piled for its victim's monument.
> – Cover his dust! bear it on before!
> It shall visit those temple-gates once more.'

(Wu 1997: 547)

An army gathers around the grief-stricken mother, and an attack is launched upon the Brahmin city:

> And the sword of the Moslem, let loose to slay,
> Like the panther leapt on its flying prey.

(Wu 1997: 549)

But this portrait of the warrior Oriental woman is undermined by Hemans. The war, it seems, is driven not by political concerns but by personal grief. Depoliticizing the woman's role Hemans sentimentalizes the war effort. Further, Maimuna, we are told, 'wither'd faster, from day to day'. Her 'frail dust', writes Hemans, was 'ne'er for such conflicts born'. Maimuna therefore dies. Hemans returns us, briefly, to the quietitude of the early picturesque:

> She spoke, and her voice, in its dying tone
> Had an echo of feelings that long seem'd flown.
> She murmur'd a low sweet cradle song,
> Strange midst the din of a warrior throng.

(Wu 1997: 549)

120 Difference and desire

Hemans retains the 'quiet woman' stereotype, as Maimuna's martial role is quietly erased as she lies dying. Hemans' trope of the grieving mother demonstrates the cultural influence of feminine grief and its limited political utility but ultimately shies away from expanding on this role for Maimuna, retaining her as the vulnerable, emotional Oriental woman.

Robert Southey's 'Dirge of the American Widow' is similar to Hemans' poem in that its protagonist is a (Native) Indian woman who seeks the 'vengeance of anguish'. Part mourning, part furious diatribe, the poem presents an injured Indian woman who refuses to be just a widow. Instead, says Southey's heroine:

> To-morrow thy Widow shall wield
> The knife and the fire.

While the widow recalls the exploits, the courage and the heroism of her dead husband she prepares for the execution of the captives: 'The stake is made ready, the captives shall die'. Her sorrow transformed into anger, Southey's protagonist differs from Hemans' in that the poem does not present her, even at the end, as a maudlin woman (perhaps because her breakdown has occurred after the revenge has been achieved and she now recognizes the futility of it). The poem concludes with:

> To-morrow the victims shall die,
> And I shall have joy in revenge.
>
> (http://spenserians.cath.vt.edu/TextRecord.php?
> action=get&textsid=38644)

Wordsworth's 'The Complaint of a Forsaken Indian Woman', published in the *Lyrical Ballads*, also focuses on the vulnerable Indian woman, abandoned to die while her tribe marches onward. The poem documents the woman's grief at being parted from her son:

> My child! they gave thee to another,
> A woman who was not thy mother.
> When from my arms my babe they took,
> On me how strangely did he look!
> Through his whole body something ran,
> A most strange something did I see;
> —As if he strove to be a man,
> That he might pull the sledge for me.
> And then he stretched his arms, how wild!
> Oh mercy! like a little child.
>
> (1969: 90)

Her food is gone and she recognizes signs of death approaching – she 'cannot lift [her] limbs to know/If they have any life or no'. The poem ends with her wishing she could see her son once more before she dies.

We shall return to the vulnerable Indian woman, especially in the form of the *sati*, in Chapter 6.

Masculinity's trials

Abraham Cowley presented Bacon, in a passage I cited in Chapter 2, as a heroic explorer, discoverer and unraveller of mysteries:

> Bacon, like Moses, led us forth at last,
> The barren wilderness he past.
> Did on the very border stand
> Of the blest promis'd land,
> And from the mountain's top of his exalted wit,
> Saw it himself, and shewed us it.
> But life did never to one man allow
> Time to discover worlds, and conquer too.

While the emphasis remains on discovery and knowledge production in Cowley's portrait, the gender of the person doing the discovering is never in doubt. This 'masculinizing' of imperial knowledge-making has a strong discursive tradition in English writing. Like the erotics of femininity, masculinity was also often articulated along two trajectories: an English masculinity in flux, under test or crisis and a native masculinity that was organized around martialism (for Arabs, Pathans and particular groups of people) and the emasculated Hindu.[21]

Three principal modes of dealing with Other masculinities might be seen in the English literature of the 1750–1900 period. In one mode, we see an exaggerated European masculinity in the adventure fiction of Haggard, Ballantyne and Kipling. In the second the racial-cultural Other was reduced to an effeminate, emasculated creature such as Beckford's Gulchenrouz (in *Vathek*). A third mode is of an English masculinity rendered vulnerable and uncertain in the colonial context.

The dominant model of masculinity in English representations when Englishmen had to deal with the racial male Other was that of the adventurer. Adventure tales in English literature are the genre in which the masculinity ethos of imperial Britain is most visible. English masculinity emerges, as Madhudaya Sinha (2008) notes in connection with Rider Haggard's fiction, in the English boy/man's contest with nature, the body of the African native and Ayesha (the female presence in *She*) herself. In Ballantyne's *The Coral Island* it is the rescue of the Samoan Avatea from the cannibal chief that becomes a key element in the emergent masculinity of Ralph Rover and his group of young men.

But English literature also deals with the question of English masculinity by emasculating and feminizing the non-European male. In the case of India,

122 Difference and desire

especially in the case of the Bengalis, the English representation of their effeminate nature dates back to the seventeenth and eighteenth centuries, in the writings of Robert Orme and others. In Beckford's *Vathek* Gulchenrouz is described thus:

> Gulchenrouz could write in various characters with precision, and paint upon vellum the most elegant arabesques that fancy could devise. His sweet voice accompanied the lute in the most enchanting manner; and when he sung the loves of Megnoun and Leileh, or some unfortunate lovers of ancient days, tears insensibly overflowed the cheeks of his auditors. The verses he composed (for like Megnoun, he too was a poet) inspired that unresisting languor so frequently fatal to the female heart. The women all doated upon him, for though he had passed his thirteenth year, they still detained him in the harem. His dancing was light as thantique gossamer waved by the zephyrs of spring; but his arms which twined so gracefully with those of the young girls in the dance, could neither dart the lance in the chase, nor curb the steeds that pastured his uncle's domains ...
>
> Both had the same tastes and amusements; the same long languishing looks; the same tresses; the same fair complexions; and when Gulchenrouz appeared in the dress of his cousin, he seemed to be more feminine than even herself. If at any time he left the harem to visit Fakreddin, it was with all the bashfulness of a fawn that consciously ventures from the lair of its dam; he was however wanton enough to mock the solemn old grey-beards to whom he was subject, though sure to be rated without mercy in return. Whenever this happened, he would plunge into the recesses of the harem, and sobbing take refuge in the arms of Nouronihar, who loved even his faults beyond the virtues of others.

Beckford's description of Gulchenrouz is an instance of the discourse of 'effeminism' (Krishnaswamy 1998).

But a third mode is also visible in certain writers of the Romantic era – of a troubled, challenged masculinity. This mode is prefigured in Behn's *Oroonoko* where the first descriptions of Imoinda go like this:

> a beauty, that to describe her truly, one need say only, she was female to the noble male; the beautiful black Venus to our young Mars; as charming in her person as he, and of delicate virtues. I have seen a *hundred white men sighing after her, and making a thousand vows at her feet, all in vain, and unsuccessful*. And she was indeed too great for any but a prince of her *own* nation to adore.
>
> (1994: 12, emphasis added)

Behn admits that the black woman is attractive to the white men, but the conclusion of the account seems to offer a caution to these men: that Imoinda is perfect for men 'of her own nation'. Colonial desire here, in Behn's terms, might prove just a bit 'unsuccessful', and this, suggests Behn, might be a good thing too. Imoinda represents, in other words, a threat not only to racial purity but to European masculinity as well.

We have already noted Byron's suggestion of the 'taming' of European masculinity when in Other places, a 'taming' that is akin to the effeminizing of the European male by natives. Byron turned to Sardanapalus the seventh-century Greek ruler (considered by many to be a fictional figure, actually) to speak of masculinity as a façade or a charade. In the play Sardanapalus does not wish to be a soldier, and through much of the play he resists persuasions to fight. Even his slave Myrrha tries to persuade him that for a ruler, his authority (what she calls, in Act I, Sc. 2, 'men kept in awe and law', 1975: 461) depends on an aggressive soldierly masculinity. Byron, however, transforms Sardanapalus' effeminacy less as an autonomous choice than as self-indulgence. Saradanapalus' self-immolation at the end of the play, in Andrew Elfenbein's interpretation (2004), indicates that aggressive masculinity results only in death.

Byron's giaour in the poem of the same title revolves around an assertion of masculine ego. Hassan kills Leila for her infidelity and then the Venetian (Christian) giaour, who was Leila's lover, hunts down the (Muslim) Hassan. The giaour's masculinity is a troubled one:

> He stood – some dread was on his face,
> Soon hatred settled in its place:
> It rose not with the reddening flush
> Of transient anger's hasty blush,
> But pale as marble o'er the tomb,
> Whose ghastly whiteness aids its gloom.
> His brow was bent, his eye was glazed;
> He raised his arm, and fiercely raised,
> And sternly shook his hand on high,
> As doubting to return or fly.
>
> (1975: 254)

The entire tale is in the form of a confession that the giaour makes to a monk in a monastery to which he has now retired after his bloodbath. The savage masculinity of this Other is so frightening to the listener monk that he bursts into prayer:

> Lo! – mark ye, as the harmony
> Peals louder praises to the sky,
> That livid cheek, that stony air
> Of mixed defiance and despair!
> Saint Francis, keep him from the shrine!
> Else may we dread the wrath divine
> Made manifest by awful sign.
> If ever evil angel bore
> The form of mortal, such he wore:

124 Difference and desire

By all my hope of sins forgiven,
Such looks are not of earth nor heaven!

(268)

Nigel Leask notes that in Byron the heroism of epics is reduced to 'a bloody and vengeful pattern of action and reaction which confounds hero and villain' (1993: 30).

It is also in *Don Juan*, notes Susan Wolfson, that we see white masculinity *challenged*, when faced with the Other woman. Gulbeyez's tears, argues Wolfson, with its 'suspicion of calculation' are 'inimical to male independence and power' (1987: 588). Byron writes in Canto V:

A woman's tear-drop melts, a man's half sears,
Like molten lead, as if you thrust a pike in
His heart to force it out, for (to be shorter)
To them't is a relief, to us a torture.

(1975: 725)

The cross-dressing scenes in *Don Juan*, however, complicate the masculinity stereotype. Don Juan, dressed in women's clothes by Julia, Haidee and Zoe, is described several times in feminine terms: as 'a pretty gentleman' with a 'half-girlish face' in Canto 1 (1975: 655, 656), as being 'feminine in feature' in Canto 8 (759) and as 'a most beauteous Boy' in Canto 9 (775).

Rider Haggard in *She* also suggests that what is at threat from the non-European woman is not just English masculinity but England's national identity itself. First, there is Holly's masculinity under stress and threat when he beholds Ayesha's 'unveiling':

She was clothed, as I had seen her when she unveiled, in the kirtle of clinging white, cut low upon her bosom, and bound in at the waist with the barbaric double-headed snake, and, as before, her rippling black hair fell in heavy masses down her back. But her face was what caught my eye, and held me as in a vice, not this time by the force of its beauty, but by the power of fascinated terror. The beauty was still there, indeed, but the agony, the blind passion, and the awful vindictiveness displayed upon those quivering features, and in the tortured look of the upturned eyes, were such as surpass my powers of description.

For a moment she stood still, her hands raised high above her head, and as she did so the white robe slipped from her down to her golden girdle, baring the blinding loveliness of her form. She stood there, her fingers clenched, and the awful look of malevolence gathered and deepened on her face.

(2008: 149–50)

He is transfixed to the spot as much by the sight of her great beauty as by the 'malevolence' on her face. (Later of course Ayesha would consider conquering

England – I shall come to this in Chapter 5.) Elsewhere in *Allan Quatermain* the physicality of the African afflicts the English with its nightmarish quality:

> I turned my eyes to look for the other canoe which should be alongside of us. I could not see it, but instead I saw a lean and clutching black hand lifting itself above the gunwale of the little boat. Surely it was a nightmare! At the same instant a dim but devilish-looking face appeared to rise out of the water, and then came a lurch of the canoe, the quick flash of a knife, and an awful yell from the Wakwafi who was sleeping by my side (the same poor fellow whose odour had been annoying me), and something warm spurted into my face. In an instant the spell was broken; I knew that it was no nightmare, but that we were attacked by swimming Masai.
>
> (https://ebooks.adelaide.edu.au/h/haggard/h_rider/allan/)

In Gail Low's reading the description of the attack has the elements of a 'sexually charged encounter' (1996: 53). More than anything else it is the sheer corporeal presence and effect of an Ayesha or the Masai warrior that produces the sense of being threatened to the Englishman. Such accounts of course reinstate the old stereotype of the African as sheer *matter* (as opposed to the Englishman as 'mind'), and a matter that seems to threaten the bodily as well as mental integrity of the Englishman. Thus the psychosexual dynamics of an Ayesha, the Masai and even the (East European) Dracula constitute the desirable but dangerous exotic for the English.

Debates over concubinage (of Europeans with non-European women) were, as Robert Young documents (1995), extensive during the Victorian age. Some argued that miscegenation weakened the European race while others believed, especially in the context of the United States and the black race, that it might further vitalize the white race. The desire for the black/brown woman that we see encoded in texts from Behn to Haggard is often, therefore, yoked to an anxiety of the dangers of miscegenation. Rafella in Perrin's *Government House* becomes the mistress of an Indian, and eventually perhaps a prostitute. While Kipling does seem to suggest that the Indian woman is treated badly by the English husband/lover (in, say, 'Lispeth'), his overarching theme appears to be the impossibility of a successful miscegenation. Thus Kipling in a strongly worded condemnation of such racial mixing in India would declare in tales like 'Yoked with an Unbeliever'. Miscegenation, it would appear, is a threat to both English masculinity and racial purity.

But masculinity's trials in the context of England's imperial and transnational interests also sometimes meant Englishmen dealing with established gender roles in the colonies. In Kipling's 'Wressley of the Foreign Office' in *Plain Tales from the Hills*, Kipling writes 'In India … you can watch men being driven, by the women who govern them, out of the rank-and-file' (unpaginated, https://ebooks.adelaide.edu.au/k/kipling/rudyard/plain/chapter33.html). A prime example of such a 'trial' for masculinity would be E.M. Forster's *A Passage to India* (1924), a novel that Sara

126 Difference and desire

Suleri (1992) appropriately describes as a 'meticulous revision of a colonialist-as-heterosexual paradigm' (139).[22] Forster's rather unabashedly misogynist novel suggests that women are very often obstacles to the creation of (male) friendships across races. Early in the novel at a bridge party there is socializing between Indians and British officials. Forster then writes that the Englishmen would have made greater efforts to socialize with the Indian guests but are 'prevented from doing so by their womenfolk whom they had to attend, provide with tea, advise about dogs, etc' (1970: 46). At the party, Aziz, writes Forster, 'was disappointed that other guests were coming, for he preferred to be alone with his new friend' (66).

Towards the end of the novel the Collector Turton also suggests that it is the Englishwomen who make the Empire such a difficult process. Indians also recognize this. About Fielding Forster says: 'he had discovered that it is possible to keep in with Indians and Englishmen, but that he who would also keep in with Englishwomen must drop the Indians. The two wouldn't combine' (62). An imperial connection and a cross-cultural friendship was more than possible between men, as long as they kept the women out of the picture, suggests Forster (Forster's engendering of colonial relations draws the ire of Elaine Showalter, who proposes that Forster saw women as 'part of the enemy camp', 1977: 7). In Forster's liberal view of imperialism, masculinity's greatest trial in the context of the colony is the Englishwoman and therefore the novel offers, in Sara Suleri's phrase 'an alternative colonial model: the most urgent cross-cultural invitations occur between male and male' (1992: 133) and this is his 'imperial erotic' (the title of Suleri's chapter itself).

But there is one more dimension to the English-masculinity-under-threat theme. In Forster's novel Indian males like Aziz pose a threat as well because, Forster implies, Englishwomen might be attracted to them rather than to English men. When Aziz is accused of rape (by Adela, although she later withdraws her charge) the policeman testifies in court thus: 'the fact which any scientific observer will confirm ... the darker races are physically attracted by the fairer' (1970: 213). McBryde echoes a sentiment dating back to the eighteenth century when, in Felicity Nussbaum's pithy formulation, 'the domestic enclosure of chaste, stubbornly nonsexual English gentlewomen poses the apparent antithesis to the teeming sexuality of empire and its torrid zones' (1995: 150–1). The Englishwoman who 'goes out' into the Empire thus overturns this trope of 'protected', chaste English femininity and therefore implicitly signals the threat to English masculinity (the 'protector') and domesticity.

This theme of English masculinity threatened by native masculinity acquires its most explicit expression in Paul Scott's *The Raj Quartet* (1966–75), written several decades after Indian independence. Ronald Merrick the homosexual policeman's hatred of the Westernized Hari Kumar/Harry Coomer might be due to the fact that not only does Kumar belong to a better class despite being Merrick's racial inferior, he (Kumar) also seems to have attracted the attentions of an Englishwoman. Merrick's abuse of Kumar when the latter is in custody (which is detailed in *The Day of the Scorpion*, 1979: 237–317) sexualizes the tension between English and native men. This clearly positions the Indian Hari Kumar as a threatening male, one who threatens, due to his possible miscegenation with the English-woman, Daphne Manners. Thus the exotic Indian male is a direct challenge to English masculinity.

**

This chapter has demonstrated how the exotic was never very far from the English imagining of themselves. It has concomitantly suggested that the exotic was a key element and aesthetic in England's engagement with the racial-cultural Other, an engagement that produced a certain set of assumptions of themselves, their race, nation and culture. Savages and seductive women, erotic geographies and threatened masculinities constituted a Möbius strip structure of desire and danger in this engagement. Such an engagement, as this chapter has shown, is visible even within the domestic-intimate sphere. The exotic, as we have seen, far from being 'out there', in many cases was at the heart of English familial and intimate relations, and as a result of identity itself. It offered, as noted, multiple possibilities for the English in terms of role-playing, consumption, relationships and identities. A vision of globality in English literature, in other words, was not simply one of an explored, studied, conquered world. It was a vision in which this world and its constituents, whether in the form of exotic fashion accessories or women, enabled the English to fashion themselves in particular ways.

Notes

1 To render an object, individual or culture 'primitive' was to consign them to an antiquated past, what Mary B. Campbell would term an exoticization in time (1988). Anne McClintock proposes the idea of 'anachronistic space' where Europeans traversing the colony figured the journey 'as a journey backward in time to an anachronistic moment in prehistory' (1995: 40).
2 The entire Early Modern chivalric romance, argues Benedict Robinson, 'enabled new ways of thinking about identity and difference, embodied above all in fictions of encounter with Saracens, Moors, and Turks' (2007: 3). On Saracens in Medieval English writings see Cordery (2002) and Turks in Stuart pageants and masques see Bergeron (2010), among others.
3 For the various shifts in treatment of the cannibal see Avramescu's *An Intellectual History of Cannibalism* (2011).
4 Janina Nordius is right in her assessment that Smith's 'criticism is specifically directed at the English war efforts; and it is the Anglo-American colonists—that is, the white settlers rebelling against British authority—who take on the role of "good guys"' (2005: 43). Hiring Native Americans as soldiers, Troy Bickham notes, also adds to the shame of British soldiery because the Native Americans' cruelties, at least in the British press, were deemed to be far in excess of the acceptable (2005: 255–7).
5 Wordsworth's theory of poetry in the famous 'Preface' to the *Lyrical Ballads*, Laura George notes, seems to embody the same idea of a 'natural' eloquence and language free of 'foreign' embellishments and artifice. George singles out the following passage as evidence:

> for, if the Poet's subject be judiciously chosen, it will naturally and upon fit occasion, lead him to passions in the language of which, if selected truly and judiciously,

128 Difference and desire

must necessarily be dignified and variegated, and alive with metaphors and figures. I forbear to speak of an incongruity which would shock the intelligent Reader, should the Poet interweave any foreign splendor of his own with that which the passion naturally suggests: it is sufficient to say that such addition is unnecessary. And, surely, it is more probable that those passages, which with propriety abound with metaphors and figures, will have their due effect, if, upon other occasions where the passions are of a milder character, the style also be subdued and temperate.

(cited in George 2002: 38)

6 This leads Ahsan Chaudhury to comment:

Marlow ... misses the most likely explanation for the uncharacteristic behaviour of these 'cannibals.' Perhaps they are parodying the European discourse of cannibalism in order to ingratiate themselves to their white employers because they wish to exploit the European expedition to advance their own territorial ambitions against the tribe that has adopted Kurtz as a demi-god.

(2008: 135)

At this point it is also significant to note Kristen Guest's point about the very trope of cannibalism: 'the cannibal, long a figure associated with absolute alterity and used to enforce boundaries between a civilized "us" and savage "them," [which] may in fact be more productively read as a symbol of permeability, or instability, of such boundaries' (2001: 2).

7 Ben Jonson's *The New Inn*, a later version of *Bartholomew Fair*, notes Rebecca Bach, 'posited an equivalence between London's underworld inhabitants and the dangerous presences in the colonies – both Indians and "corrupted" Englishmen' (Bach 1997: 289).

8 For studies of the harem motif in literature, visual arts and travel see, among others, Lewis (2004).

9 In a fascinating reading Ruth Yeazell links the Englishwoman's blush with the Arab woman's veil. Both veil and blush, writes Nussbaum glossing Yeazell, disguise the body. The Englishwoman's blush 'distinguishes her from the immodest woman at home and from the woman of color whose blush may not be seen' (1995: 122).

10 Felicity Nussbaum suggests that Montagu's letters are also suggestive of the Western woman's penetrative gaze: since European males were not allowed access to the native woman, the female functioned in this capacity (1995: 137). The question of masculinity, Turkish/Arab and English, was one that dates back to Early Modern representations, in travel writing, of the Asian, Middle Eastern and other geographical regions and cultures. See Suranyi (2009) for a study.

11 Other critics have noted the hints at lesbian interests in her letters (Nussbaum 1995: 140–2).

12 The tale recalls, also, the 'myth' of the Amerindian princess Pocahontas who marries John Smith, and eventually accepts English culture and even religion (see Hulme 1992: chapter 4, for a reading of this myth).

13 The description of the Moor is close to Beckford's account of the giaour: 'there arrived in his metropolis, a man so hideous that the very guards who arrested him were forced to shut their eyes as they led him along. The Caliph himself appeared startled at so horrible a visage' (1970: 5). He is later described as a 'monster' (6). The giaour is, of course, the racial Other, being from India (14).

14 Shakespeare's Othello, who is also seen in exactly these same three ways, is the predecessor of Zofloya the Moor. I am grateful to Anna Kurian for drawing this connection to my attention.

15 Beatriz Moreno concludes her interpretation of *Zofloya* by claiming that 'by punishing both Victoria and Lilla, Charlotte Dacre condemns ineffectual models of femininity, as well as models of femaleness constructed on false premises of what it is to have masculine

strength' (2007: 432). But such a reading ignores the point that the downfall of both Victoria and Lilla are traceable to Victoria's manipulation (and not just her tyrannical psychology) by the racial Other (Zofloya). I am more inclined towards Sara Schotland's reading where she sees *Zofloya* as embodying a cultural and national anxiety about slave revolts (2009).

16 The Alhambra and the harem are also treated as impenetrable spaces. Thus Byron's *The Bride of Abydos* puts it this way:

> None can pierce that secret bower
> But those who watch the women's tower.
>
> (1975: 265)

Numerous commentators, especially in postcolonial studies, have drawn attention to this anxiety over impenetrability of the Arab or Muslim women's quarters. See Alloula (1986), Lewis (2004), among others.

17 In some cases the erotic space is also romanticized as the site of the death of a beautiful woman. Thus in Hemans' 'Moorish Bridal Song' we have:

> The citron-groves their fruit and flowers were strewing
> Around a Moorish palace, while the sigh
> Of low sweet summer-winds, the branches wooing
> With music through their shadowy bowers went by;
> Music and voices, from the marble halls,
> Through the leaves gleaming, and the fountain-falls.
>
> (http://quod.lib.umich.edu/b/bwrp/HemaFFores/1:6.1?
> rgn=div2;view = fulltext)

18 In Frances Sheridan's *History of Nourjahad* (1767), the prince Nourjahad is the one imprisoned in the harem.

19 Catherine Addison has argued that this 'taming' must be read as the education of the European. She points to Byron's use of the word 'civilization', which Addison reads as an 'equation that ironically deranges the civilized-savage opposition' (1995: 699).

20 Forster's Aziz is one of the few characters in English writing where the Indian commodifies the English woman. In a series of observations, Aziz reduces Englishwomen, specifically Adela Quested, to a sexual object.

21 For studies of early (seventeenth-century) English representations of Hindu 'effeminacy' see Teltscher (2000). Also see Mrinalini Sinha (1995).

22 On homosexuality and colonial encounters see Silverman (1989).

4

CONSUME AND COMMODIFY

The objectified Other

Edmund Spenser was fascinated by New World plants. The wealth and jewellery of Indian and Arab emperors came in for attention in Marlowe, Shakespeare, Drayton and Bacon. House décor with imported goods and objects is described in detail in Maria Edgeworth, Jane Austen and other eighteenth-century authors. Daniel Defoe's *Captain Singleton* (1720) expends a considerable portion of narrative space detailing how its pirate-hero and his gang acquire gold in Africa, with each man, says Singleton, profiting to the tune of 'four pound weight' (1969a: 136). Tea, cotton, china/porcelain, tapestries, coffee, Kashmiri shawls, tobacco and cocoa, accompanied by appurtenances and rituals of consumption such as teapots or china, figure in numerous texts from Pepys and Congreve right up to Samuel Coleridge, Joanna Baillie, William Cowper and Charlotte Brontë. An India 'stone' is the centre of Wilkie Collins' 1868 novel, *The Moonstone*. In Christina Rossetti's *Goblin Market* (1862), the advertisement has an inventory of fruits:

> Pomegranates full and fine,
> Dates and sharp bullaces,
> Rare pears and greengages,
> Damsons and bilberries,
> Taste them and try:
> …
> Figs to fill your mouth,
> Citrons from the South
> Sweet to tongue and sound to eye;
> Come buy, come buy.

(1979: 11)

The inventory, indicating perhaps fruits whose origins are not in England, draws this response from Laura:

> Who knows upon what soil they fed
> Their hungry thirsty roots?[1]

(12)

Besides these everyday commodities, exhibitions and museums from the 'curiosity cabinets' of the seventeenth century, the botanical gardens of the mid-nineteenth century organized by Joseph Hooker and Joseph Banks, to the industrial exhibitions of the late nineteenth century, invariably had plants, flowers, art objects, tapestries and designs from all parts of the world. Upper-class and royal households had rooms filled with artefacts and ornamental objects from the colonies. Add to these varied representations of slave or foreign *bodies* reduced to objects for different ideological reasons and with different emphases – from dismemberment to emancipation to insubstantiality – from the seventeenth-century Aphra Behn to nineteenth-century Bram Stoker and twentieth-century Joseph Conrad and we have an encyclopaedic collection of England's forms of engagement with foreign 'objects'. The globality of English literature that in the earlier chapters I had associated with itinerancy and exoticism, this chapter demonstrates, inheres in objects and commodities. That is, we can think of a *globality of objects*, of various kinds, values, significations and symbolisms, that signal English literature's transnational engagements.

The literary and cultural imagination of England, right from the sixteenth century, documented the encounter with the racial-cultural Other in terms of material objects and goods from outside its geopolitical borders. This chapter examines English literature's literal and metaphoric commodification of the Other within a vocabulary of objects. It studies (1) the vocabulary of material objects and (2) the rhetoric of objectification in English literature.

The vocabulary of material objects is not simply an inventory or description of china or tea or foreign plants. This vocabulary, as I hope to demonstrate, embeds a biography of objects in the biography of characters' lives. In material culture theorist Janet Hoskins' words, we can discern a 'narrative elaboration' of objects in the context of human settings and 'lifestories' (2006: 78–9). Early Modern studies tell us that objects 'can be made to absorb other evanescent cultural realities especially within the institutionalized contexts of ... theatrical display, symbolic representation, and ritual observance' (de Grazia *et al.* 1996: 9). Yet, this is not the only narrativization of objects we can see in English literature's engagements with the Other.

The rhetoric of objectification is a key mode of dealing with a different culture and nation. Objectification, as Chris Tilley argues, is a concrete embodiment of an idea. Objectification shows us how subjects and objects relate to each other, where making, using, exchanging, consuming, interacting and living with things enables people to make themselves (2006: 61). I use the term 'objectification' in a related though variant sense. I see objectification in English literature as a means of engaging with the Other, primarily in the form of an objectification of humans of different races and ethnicities. This objectification is also gendered – although that is not the subject of this chapter – and very often eroticized. The rhetoric of objectification treats the slave or black body as a thing, whether for purposes of commerce or emancipation (quiescent, passive, agency-less) or as an object of desire.

Together, this chapter argues, *the vocabulary of things and the rhetoric of objectification in literary texts demonstrate a history of England's engagement with Other-objects.* 'Other-object' is my portmanteau term for both the foreign 'bodies' – tea, china, coins, jewels, art, apparel, plants – that find narrative elaborations in English characters' lives *and* the rhetoric of objectification in which other bodies are reduced to mere *things* for specific affective, political and cultural values that the English ascribe to them. It is through these two modes in which the Other-object emerges, the chapter proposes, that English identity fashions itself. England's transnational concerns, this chapter claims, manifest in the form of desires for, fascination with and anxieties about Other-objects.

The vocabulary of things

Life stories that partake of objects and object biographies that intertwine with characters' lives in English writing very often involve objects that are *imported* and *non-European*. The act of consumption itself was seen as a sign of national character. As Daniel Defoe put it in his *A Plan of the English Commerce* (1728): 'the trading, middling sort of people … are the life of our whole commerce, it is by their expensive, generous, free way of living, that the home consumption is rais'd to such a bulk, as well of our own, as of foreign production' (99–102). Imports of china and other objects improved, also, the English industry that rushed to imitate these designs, as William Cowper records in 'Charity' (1782):

> These are the gifts of art; and art thrives most
> Where Commerce has enrich'd the busy coast;
> He catches all improvements in his flight,
> Spreads foreign wonders in his country's sight,
> Imports what others have invented well,
> And stirs his own to match them, or excel.
> > (http://quod.lib.umich.edu/e/ecco/004792651.0001.000/
> > 1:8?rgn=div1;view=fulltext)

Matters for consumption

However, the vocabulary of foreign things we see in English writing was not restricted to the simple act of consuming tea or tobacco or cocoa or sugar. Alan Bewell argues that the 'power of an empire has been symbolically conveyed in its rulers' ability to go beyond a local diet by eating, at a single sitting, foods from all the regions that lie within their control' (1999: 144), what he calls an 'imperial geophagy'. Integral to consumption were both the appurtenances of consumption and the ritualized processes of consumption. In terms of consumption I first refer to not artefacts and splendid tokens of indigenous design adorning the Victorian parlour, but rather to *everyday* Other-objects that were key presences in English literature as England engaged with distant cultures and nations. Thus from the mid-seventeenth century tea, coffee, sugar and tobacco were major constituents of England's grocery expenditure (Smith 1996: 183).[2] China and porcelain, by the age of Charles Lamb (to whose essay 'Old China' I shall return later), were no longer luxury products but products of mass consumption that, in Karen Fang's words, 'offer[ed] everyday access to an exotic world' (2003: 823). The Other-objects get absorbed into *English domestic and public spaces*, rituals of dining and display, so that they become 'Englished'. English life stories as reflected in its literature, I propose, were constituted by the foreign objects consumed within domestic as well as public spaces. The 'domestic', the *OED* informs us, means 'of or pertaining to one's own country or nation; not foreign, internal, inland, "home"'. Yet this domesticity, that by definition excludes the foreign, is constituted by something foreign.

The Other-object consumed thus became a part of English culture, and this material Othering in literature is precisely what I plan to trace here. While looking at everyday consumption I focus on Other-objects that become a *habit* with the English.[3]

One of the first Other-objects that made its way into everyday English consumption and which eventually provoked, as early as 1604 (in King James' *A Counter-blaste to Tobacco*, a text to which I shall return in Chapter 5), furious diatribes, was tobacco. Edmund Spenser in *The Faerie Queen* (Book 3, Canto 6, 32. Spenser 1984: 361) has been credited with the first literary/poetical reference to tobacco: Spenser refers to its medicinal properties. Francis Beaumont's brother, John Beaumont in *The Metamorphosis of Tabacco* (1602) had praised the substance as something that inspires with its 'ethereal vapours'. He even claimed that in the age of barbarism, it inspired poetry and religious belief. More significantly Beaumont linked tobacco cultivation with Empire and English fortunes, praising the queen for having:

> uncontroll'd stretcht out her mighty hand
> Over Virginia and the New-found-land,
> And spread the colors of our English Rose
> In the far countries where Tobacco grows,
> And tam'd the savage nations of the West,
> Which of this jewel were in vain possest.
> (unpaginated, http://spenserians.cath.vt.edu/TextRecord.php?
> action=GET&textsid=33000)

To have acquired the territory where tobacco grew, says Beaumont, is truly a magnificent achievement, for anyway the 'savage nations' of the New World (the

134 Consume and commodify

'West' in the above lines) had 'possessed' this jewel in 'vain'. Beaumont concludes his hagiography with:

> For this our praised plant on high doth soar,
> Above the baser dross of earthly ore,
> Like the brave spirit and ambitious mind
> Whose eaglet's eyes the sunbeams cannot blind;
> Nor can the clog of poverty depress
> Such souls in base and native lowliness,
> But proudly scorning to behold the Earth,
> They leap at crowns, and reach above their birth.
>
> (http://spenserians.cath.vt.edu/TextRecord.php?
> action=GET&textsid=33000)

Beaumont here compares gold unfavourably with tobacco. Jonson's Bobadill, a tobacconist, in *Every Man in His Humour* (staged in 1605) claims that for twenty-one days in the Indies they had no 'nutriment' but only the 'fume' of tobacco and declares it to be 'divine'. Bobadill also claims tobacco has medicinal properties: 'an antidote that, had you taken the most deadly poisonous plant in all Italy, it should expel it' (III.5, ll. 77–95. Jonson of course is satirizing these claims, and Bobadill. Jonson 1969: 120–1).

Let us now turn to the preeminent English beverage of habit, tea. 'I did send for a cup of tee (a China drink) of which I never had drank before', wrote Samuel Pepys in his diary entry of 25 September 1660. In an often-ignored exchange in William Congreve's *The Way of the World* (1700), a few decades after Pepys, Mirabel announces that, after their marriage, he would allow Millimant to serve only 'native' drinks to visitors: 'tea, chocolate and coffee' (IV.5. Congreve 1966: 158). Tea, a product of China and India, has, as early as 1700, become a 'native drink'. In *The Eve of St Agnes* Keats would describe a sumptuous table spread:

> A heap
> Of candied apples, quince, and plum, and gourd;
> With jellies soother than the creamy curd,
> And lucent syrops, tinct with cinnamon;
> Manna and dates, in argosy transferred
> From Fez; and spiced dainties, every one,
> From silken Samarcand to cedar'd Lebanon.
>
> (Keats 1973: 203)

If Keats celebrates a 'geophagy' (Alan Bewell's term, 1999, for the 'consumption' of the world) of foods, other modes of consumption also figure in English writings. For instance, the world is also consumed by the Englishwoman in the form of jewellery and fashion accessories, from which act emerges the Englishwoman's globality of objects. Even opium gets absorbed into domesticity when Englishwomen consumed opium for its medicinal effects that 'aided them in their wifely and motherly duties' (Freeman 2012: 1), as presented in numerous poems: Sara Coleridge ('Poppies'), Henrietta O'Neill ('Ode to Poppy'), Anna Seward ('To the Poppy') and others. The Empire's product, in other words, enabled the Englishwoman to escape the drudgery of housework and was thus integral to the very running of an English household.

Pepys marks the event as special, for a foreign product has been imbibed. The second example is more interesting. Tea, chocolate and coffee in Congreve's account function as markers of Englishness, but also of English domesticity. What Mirabel is proposing is tea-serving – which is gendered in the above lines – and tea- or coffee-drinking with visitors is a *habit* they must acquire. English domesticity, as I mentioned above, is now constituted by the foreign so that the foreign has been habituated to and been given a habitation. Socialization within the English home now involves the ritual consumption of tea or coffee.

The consumption of these drinks, in the social space (which might be thought of as located somewhere between the private and the public) of the home such as the parlour, constructs the identity of the household through a repeated set of rituals. Thus we need to pay attention not just to the Other-object here but also to the apparatuses of consumption.

The vocabulary of things that ties object biographies with individual lives, social functions, economy and even national character is exemplified in Alexander Pope's inventory of products of mass consumption and rituals of consumption in *The Rape of the Lock* (1712). Pope links an individual's consumption to patterns and policies of trade and mercantile capitalism in his account. On Belinda's dressing table appear, satirizes Alexander Pope in *The Rape of the Lock*, 'unnumber'd treasures ope at once, and here,/the various off'rings of the world appear':

> Now when, declining from the noon of day,
> The sun obliquely shoots his burning ray;
> When hungry judges soon the sentence sign,
> And wretches hang that jurymen may dine;
> When merchants from th' Exchange return in peace,
> And the long labours of the toilet cease,
>
> ———
>
> The board's with cups and spoons, alternate, crowned,
> The berries crackle, and the mill turns round;
> On shining altars of Japan they raise
> The silver lamp, and fiery spirits blaze:
> From silver spouts the grateful liquors glide,
> While China's earth receives the smoking tide.
> At once they gratify their smell and taste,
> While frequent cups prolong the rich repast.
> Coffee (which makes the politician wise,
> And see through all things with his half-shut eyes)

136 Consume and commodify

> Sent up in vapours to the baron's brain
> New stratagems, the radiant lock to gain.

(1963: 227–30)

Coffee, sugar and lacquer are here signs of the English business class ('merchants from th' Exchange') plotting profits, strategies and politics, according to Pope. These become in a sense appurtenances to the *public* display of English power and authority. Affordable, attractive and invested (even by Pope's time) with considerable symbolic value, these products make the transitions from expensive luxury products to mass consumption products, as their lives are woven into the very processes of business deals, political negotiations and identity-making.

Pope mentions coffee, but there was more literature on tea. Tea-drinking is a good habit, as several texts of the eighteenth century would state. Peter Motteux's *A Poem Upon Tea* (1712) began by listing the medicinal advantages of the drink. But he also lists, for contrast, the deleterious effects of wine and derides coffee as equally dangerous. Motteux treats tea as the drink of English Enlightenment itself (Kowaleski-Wallace 1994: 133). 'It has', writes Motteux in his Preface, 'the balm and comfort of a cordial, without the headiness of our strong spirits'. 'It cheers the heart, without disordering the head', he continues. Motteux also cleverly makes tea the drink that unites classes in England: it is the 'treat of the frugal, yet the regale of the luxurious'. He describes tea as replacing wine because, once people recognize the abusive nature of wines, 'tea, temperance and reason will prevail' (1712: 9). Tea, says Motteux, 'gives light'. Then, addressing tea as a 'liquid blessing', Motteux writes:

> I drink and the kindly streams arise,
> Wine's vapour flags, and soon subsides and dies.
> The friendly spirits brighten me again,
> Repel the brute, and re-enthrone the man ...
> So its parent with presenting light,
> Recalls distinction, and displaces night.

(7)

Now, it is significant that Motteux proposes a national habit of tea-drinking across classes thereby proposing a social function for the Other-object. Tea, Motteux seems to suggest, is a national drink. By identifying this imported object and gesturing at its intimate relationship with the lives of every kind of Englishman and woman, Motteux has demonstrated the incorporation of the Other into English culture.

Advising the English on how to be properly English were Joseph Addison and Richard Steele through the columns of *The Spectator*. Joseph Addison's emphatic statement from *The Spectator* suggests tea is the typical English beverage: 'all well-regulated families ... set apart an hour every morning for tea and bread and butter' (*The Spectator* No. 10). Tea is an integral feature, Addison believes, of 'well-regulated families'. It had become the standard-bearer of English middle-class respectability.[4]

If Motteux presents the lives of Englishmen and women as narratives of tea-drinking and Addison declares tea-drinking as a sign of the moral economy of families, William Cowper treats tea and the ritual of tea-drinking as a marker of quiet English domesticity. In 'The Task' (1785) Cowper would paint a picture of such warm English *domesticity* (in contrast with Pope's depiction of the public ritual of coffee-drinking):

> Now stir the fire, and close the shutters fast,
> Let fall the curtains, wheel the sofa round,
> And while the bubbling and loud-hissing urn
> Throws up a steamy column, and the cups,
> That cheer but not inebriate, wait on each,
> So let us welcome peaceful evening in.
>
> (1994: 142)

Like Motteux, Cowper also sees tea as distinguished from wine in that it does not 'inebriate'. But what is more significant in Cowper's eulogy of tea is that it *centres* the English home. The emphasis on soft sounds (the bubbling and loud hisses) and closure (curtains down, shutters closed) suggests intimacy but also enclosed spaces. Tea-drinking as a ritual in Cowper marks a withdrawal from the world's chaos into the quiet routine of placid consumption. At the heart of a pleasant evening in the English home is tea.

Later writers would, similarly, focus on both the beverage and the appurtenances and social rituals of consumption. S.T. Coleridge in 'Monody on a Tea-kettle' (1790) speaks of his great 'domestic griefs': 'the tea-kettle is spoilt and Coleridge is undone' (1973: 18). Like Motteux and Cowper, Coleridge also evidently sees tea as the centrepiece of quiet English domesticity, and tea as a beverage that is calming:

> Delightful Tea!
> With thee compar'd what yields the madd'ning Vine?
> Sweet power! who know'st to spread the calm delight,
> And the pure joy prolong to midmost night!
>
> (17–18)

In the case of Joanna Baillie's 'Lines to a Teapot' (1840), the teapot is used again as a sign of English identity, but in a different sense. On the walls of the painted teapot, says Baillie, 'a distant nation's manners we behold'. That is, the tea vessel becomes synecdochic of a culture and the means of English culture's acquisition of knowledge. The teapot has journeyed from its place of origin and 'now thou 'rt seen in Britain's polished land'. The teapot becomes the star attraction at tea-time, notes Baillie. It becomes a much-coveted and admired object of aristocratic, upper-class women:

138 Consume and commodify

But O! when beauty's hand thy weight sustained,
The climax of thy glory was attained!
Back from her elevated elbow fell
Its three-tired ruffle, and displayed the swell
And gentle rounding of her lily arm,
The eyes of wistful sage or beau to charm –
A sight at other times but dimly seen
Through veiling folds of point or colberteen.
With pleasing toil, red glowed her dimpled cheek,
Bright glanced her eyes beneath her forehead sleek,
And as she poured the beverage, through the room
Was spread its fleeting, delicate perfume.

(unpaginated, http://digital.lib.ucdavis.edu/projects/bwrp/
Works/BailJFugit.htm#p161)

At this point in Baillie's poem the teapot is a luxury item, affordable by the wealthy. Baillie links the femininity of the woman with the teapot, to the object itself – thus merging object biography with human biography. The teapot is elaborated in the narrative of the woman's life – the courtship, the quiet romance and the imminent domesticity.

But Baillie's paradigmatic poem also gestures at the mass consumption of china and teapot later when she speaks of the working classes also consuming tea:

Although in modern drawing-room, a board
May fragrant tea from menial hands afford,
Which, poured in dull obscurity hath been,
From pot of vulgar ware, in nook unseen,
And pass in hasty rounds our eyes before,
Thou in thy graceful state art seen no more.
And what the changeful fleeting crowd, who sip
The unhonoured beverage with contemptuous lip,
Enjoy amidst the tangled, giddy maze,
Their languid eye – their listless air betrays.

Tea-drinking is no more the ritualized structure of English upper-class domesticity. Eventually of course it has to be shelved because it is too old and faded: 'the honours of thy course are passed away'. But then it quickly gets appropriated by connoisseurs and art collectors:

Sober connoisseurs, with wrinkled brow
And spectacles on nose, thy parts inspect,
And by grave rules approve thee or reject.

What Baillie does here is a fascinating object biography of the teapot. If Motteux suggested tea-drinking as a social habit cutting across classes, Joanna Baillie shows the teapot itself as offering different uses to different segments of English society. She *unites* multiple layers of society through the teapot which therefore takes on the form and content of a changing-yet-unchanging *English* thing: with different meanings to different classes but indispensable, coveted and desired by all. It becomes a serving device, a supplement to English feminine beauty, a marker of English working-class drudgery and finally an aesthetic icon that may or may not satisfy the connoisseur. Therefore the foreign object enables a certain coalescence of English classes around itself.

Decades later we see a reaffirmation of the centrality of tea and tea-drinking to English domesticity and English social life in the Victorian age. Here is a scene from Charlotte Brontë's *Villette* (1853):

> During tea, the minute thing's movements and behaviour gave, as usual, full occupation to the eye. First she directed Warren, as he placed the chairs.
> 'Put papa's chair here, and mine near it, between papa and Mrs. Bretton: *I* must hand his tea.'
> She took her own seat, and beckoned with her hand to her father.
> 'Be near me, as if we were at home, papa.'
>
> (1984: 19, emphasis in original)

The arrangement of the table, the seating order and of course the (gendered) service are a part of the comforting ritual of tea-drinking, together they make the individuals feel 'at home'. Brontë would emphasize the centrality of tea-time throughout the novel:

> How pleasant it was in its air of perfect domestic comfort! How warm in its amber lamp-light and vermilion fire-flush! To render the picture perfect, tea stood ready on the table—an English tea, whereof the whole shining service glanced at me familiarly; from the solid silver urn, of antique pattern, and the massive pot of the same metal, to the thin porcelain cups, dark with purple and gilding. I knew the very seed-cake of peculiar form, baked in a peculiar mould, which always had a place on the tea-table at Bretton. Graham liked it, and there it was as of yore—set before Graham's plate with the silver knife and fork beside it.
>
> (246–7)

It should be noted that the description speaks of rituals, appurtenances and therefore the habit of English domesticity that revolves around tea-drinking. The setting itself suggests comfort and security in the above passage. The serving of tea – a gendered theme as noted already – is a moment in which affections, domestic tensions and individual character are all played out, as seen in this earlier account from the novel:

140 Consume and commodify

> It happened that Graham was not coming to the breakfast-table; he had some exercises to write for that morning's class, and had requested his mother to send a cup of tea into the study. Polly volunteered to carry it: she must be busy about something, look after somebody. The cup was entrusted to her; for, if restless, she was also careful. As the study was opposite the breakfast-room, the doors facing across the passage, my eye followed her.
>   'What are you doing?' she asked, pausing on the threshold.
>   'Writing,' said Graham.
>   'Why don't you come to take breakfast with your mamma?'
>   'Too busy.'
>   'Do you want any breakfast?'
>   'Of course.'
>   'There, then.'
>   And she deposited the cup on the carpet, like a jailor putting a prisoner's pitcher of water through his cell-door, and retreated. Presently she returned.
>   'What will you have besides tea—what to eat?'
>   'Anything good. Bring me something particularly nice; that's a kind little woman.'
>
> (29)

The kindness of the little woman in the novel's typical sexist phrasing is embodied in the careful serving of tea and comfort food for the working gentleman. The act of serving tea, in other words, becomes an embodiment of the kind of character Polly is ('restless but careful', 'kind', etc.). The 'perfect domestic comfort' in the above passage is a vocabulary of things and human lives, showing how each partakes of and constitutes the other so that this perfection is achieved.

When in the twentieth century James Joyce makes a reference to tea-consumption he imbues it with considerable doubt. In a passage in *Ulysses* (1922) Leopold Bloom is meditating on tea:

> Choice blend, made of the finest Ceylonese brands. The far east. Lovely spot it must be: the garden of the world, big lazy leaves to float about on, cactuses, flower meads, snaky lianas they call them. Wonder is it like that.
>
> (1992: 86)

Here Joyce's account undermines itself and Bloom is uncertain as to whether things are really as he believes they are in the 'far east'. Joyce reverses the confident globality we have seen thus far in English texts from Congreve downwards and instead offers a scepticism towards these histories of the exotic east.

This description of an Other-object as 'comfort' rather than as luxury was partly due to the increased circulation of such products in England's homes and tea- and coffee-houses. But it was also due partly to the shifting sense of 'luxury' itself. Objects like china, cotton, muslin and others arrived as luxuries and then percolated downward into the class hierarchies, even as the very notion of luxury changed during the eighteenth century. By the eighteenth century, argue Maxine Berg and Elizabeth Eger, 'luxury gradually lost its former associations with corruption and vice, and came to include production, trade and the civilising impact of superfluous commodities' (Berg and Eger 2003: 7). These commodities included, Berg notes, 'Asian consumer goods – cottons, especially muslins and printed calicoes, silk, porcelain, ornamental brass and ironware, lacquer and paper goods – became imported luxuries in Europe, and were later to become indigenous European consumer goods' (7). This means, simply, people across the class spectrum could afford new habits, whether in beverages or in clothing. And this implies a shift in the narrative elaborations of the Other-objects themselves as they move into the lives of workers, dairy farmers, earls and dukes and tradesmen.

But consumption could also take a very different route: in the form of home décor and the collection. The spectacularization of foreign bodies through apparel, décor, art collections but also the formal rituals around consumption of, say, tea with porcelain ware was a key form of engagement with the Other-object.

Spectacular matter

Just as tea-drinking in Congreve, Pope, Baillie and others represented the beverage as serving a critical social function, other forms of consumption such as clothing or interior décor were useful as social markers of status and individual taste. Texts in which the wealth of other nations was documented produced a cultural imaginary of wealthy lands and a fantasy of profit and conquest. Gentlemen who acquired products and curios from various parts of the world often put together a curiosity cabinet in the Early Modern period or simply displayed it as furnishings and décor in the Victorian. Displaying the Other-object in some form or the other was a prominent mode of appropriating the Other, as we shall see. It must be noted that such displays were not always only private. Larger and officially created spaces such as gardens and museums constitute a vocabulary of things in which the lives of Other-objects begin to permeate English lives and identities. The 'aesthetics of British mercantilism', as James Bunn termed it (1980), involved such displays of assorted Other-objects. While this too involves consumption of a particular kind – the connoisseur examining and evaluating a piece of Aztec pottery or a Mughal miniature – I treat the plants, artefacts and other such objects as a distinct category of material culture here. Such collections of Other-objects shaped English taste, attitudes and even styles of art. That is, *the arrival and circulation of exotic objects was instrumental in forming English cosmopolitan tastes* in art or gardening or décor but also ensured that English homes, museums and gardens were spaces of assimilation of these accidental or intentional by-products of English imperial processes. English domesticity, to phrase it differently, was, if not constructed, partially informed by the passage through and presence of objects in kitchens, dining tables, parlours and bedrooms.

In this process of objectifying Englishness occasionally the imported object is invested with English meanings divergent from or indifferent to the original. Thus

142 Consume and commodify

in Lamb's 'Old China', he writes of the china teacup as: 'those little, lawless, azure-tinctured grotesques, that under the notion of men and women, float about, uncircumscribed by any element, in that world before perspective'. Lamb carefully disconnects the china from its origins, meanings and cultural connections here. As a first step in the indigenization of china, Lamb has successfully emptied the cup of any meaning preliminary to giving it new ones. Lamb's Elia makes a case for the use of china (in the face of opposition by his austere cousin, Bridget) that tells us the new meanings of these Other-objects. One must, says Elia, 'live better, and lie softer'. This includes, Elia points out, 'a well-carpeted fireside, sitting on this luxurious sofa'. Consumption here of imported objects that have since gotten indigenized, says Lamb, is a marker of improved living conditions, and therefore of their social mobility. Other-objects, to phrase it differently, become symbolic of advancement, progress and English modernity itself. (Of course it is evident that circumstances have enabled their acquisition of china: Elia refers to recent 'favourable circumstances' – which, Karen Fang says, refers to imperialism [2003: 819] – and better incomes.)

In Jane Austen's *Mansfield Park* (1814), Lady Bertram wants her nephew, William, at the start of his naval career, to go to the 'East Indies'. Her reason is very simple: 'that I may have a shawl. I think I will have two shawls' (1970: 277). In a brilliant scene of self-fashioning through foreign commodities, in *Villette* a rather desperate and perhaps lower-class working woman acquires a job in a Belgian family. Lucy Snowe tells the story:

> I think myself, she might possibly have been a hanger-on, nurse, fosterer, or washerwoman, in some Irish family: she spoke a smothered tongue, curiously overlaid with mincing cockney inflections. By some means or other she had acquired, and now held in possession, a wardrobe of rather suspicious splendour—gowns of stiff and costly silk, fitting her indifferently, and apparently made for other proportions than those they now adorned; caps with real lace borders, and—the chief item in the inventory, the spell by which she struck a certain awe through the household, quelling the otherwise scornfully disposed teachers and servants, and, so long as her broad shoulders *wore* the folds of that majestic drapery, even influencing Madame herself—*a real Indian shawl*—'un véritable cachemire,' as Madame Beck said, with unmixed reverence and amaze. I feel quite sure that without this 'cachemire' she would not have kept her footing in the pensionnat for two days: by virtue of it, and it only, she maintained the same a month.

> (1984: 96)

Brontë is here demonstrating the power of an Other-object when displayed on the person of an Englishwoman. The object biography of the imported shawl bestows upon its wearer a smattering of dignity, an air of trustworthiness and moral rectitude. *Villette* presents yet another element within the discourse of consumption where Other-objects are not merely conveniences of luxuries, they are markers of taste, moral correctness and social status.

China, tapestries, cotton clothing, Kashmiri shawls constitute as we can see from the above texts, signs of privilege, class and modernity, and are instruments of self-fashioning. In Lamb the china vessels signified social mobility. In Austen and Brontë they symbolized not vulgar luxury but the signs of social respectability. By the mid-eighteenth century an individual's personality, Deborah Cohen argues, was deemed to be intertwined with the domestic interior, and objects were modes of self-expression. Taste became a major concern for the middle and upper classes and led, in Cohen's words, to the 'moralization of possession' (2006: 19). What Cohen does not spell out is that these possessions were now inclusive of objects that were patently *not* English but had been absorbed into English culture so thoroughly that, as the lines from *Villette* demonstrate, without the ownership of some such object, Englishness would remain incomplete or even suspect. As Suzanne Daly puts it in her analysis of the circulation of the Kashmiri shawl in Victorian England, the foreign accessory became 'a marker of respectable English womanhood and as magical and mysterious "oriental" garments' (2002: 238. Also Zutshi 2009). But Daly ignores the point that the magic and mysteriousness of the oriental garment becomes emblematic of an *English* rectitude and pragmatism in *Villette*, just as china becomes in Elia's account a symbol of irreversible *English* progress. There is no magic when the oriental object is Englished in the process of self-fashioning, and English identity itself relies on the consumption of global objects. In a sense the commodification of the foreign object as object biography in the lives of the Englishman and woman *'naturalized' or 'nativized' the foreign*.

The wealth of the Indies was a subject that, judging from the literature of the period, never ceased to fascinate the Early Modern writer. Travel writers brought back stories of the wealth of Arabia and the Indies, and these fed directly into accounts of grandiose, sometimes garish, spectacles of mercantile fantasy in the early eras. Elizabeth I's letter that the merchants carried when they departed for the East Indies called for a more equitable sharing of the world's resources – a request whose ironic import would be witnessed in retrospect by history.

In Geoffrey Chaucer's 'The Knight's Tale', the 'king of Inde', Emetreus, is practically covered in jewellery:

> Upon a steed bay trapped in steel,
> Covered in clooth of goldm dyapred weel,
> Cam riding lyke the god of armes, Mars.
> His cot-armure was of cloth of Tars
> Couched with perles white and round and grete;
> His sadel was of brend gold new ybete;
> A mantelet upon his shulder hangynge,
> Bret-ful of rubyes red as fyr sparklynge.

(Chaucer 1976: 446)

144 Consume and commodify

Marlowe's Faustus plans to send the spirits he would eventually command through necromancy to India:

> I'll have them fly to India for gold,
> ransack ocean for orient pearl,
> and search all corners of the new-found world
> for pleasant fruits and princely delicates.
>
> (Faustus I.1, ll. 81–4. 1975: 268)

Barabas in Marlowe's *The Jew of Malta* says: 'give me the merchants of the Indian mines,/That trade in metal of the purest mould' (I.1, ll. 19–20. 1975: 349). The Persian aristocrats, says Marlowe in *Tamburlaine*, Part One, 'march in coats of gold/ with costly jewels hanging at their ears' (I.1, ll. 143–4. 1975: 109–10).

In Middleton's *Triumphs of Honour and Industry* (1617) he describes India as a 'rich personage', the 'seat of merchandise', holding a 'wedge of gold' in her hand as she rides an 'illustrious chariot'. She is surrounded in Middleton's description by labouring bodies, some 'planting nut-meg' some other 'spice-tree of all kinds' (298–9). These Indian youth also break into a spontaneous dance, writes Middleton. Middleton's India has thus three specific material aspects in terms of spectacle: wealth, labour and entertainment.

Besides the mention of Peru, Virginia and the Amazons in Book 2 of *The Faerie Queene*, Spenser's Garden of Adonis offers interesting insights into a new kind of commodity that brought the Other closer to English sensibilities: plant life. Spenser (Book 3, Canto 6) mentions Amaranthus, a New World flower, in the course of his botanical account:

> And all about grew every sort of flower,
> To which sad lovers were transformed of yore;
> Fresh Hyacinthus, Phoebus paramour,
> And dearest love:
> Foolish Narciss, that likes the watery shore,
> Sad Amaranthus, made a flower but late,
> Sad Amaranthus, in whose purple gore
> Me seems I see Amintas wretched fate,
> To whom sweet poets verse hath given endless date.
>
> (1984: 363)

In a meticulous study Edward Test shows how the amaranthus enters the English imagination through Spenser's account, and carries with it stereotypes of Mexican bloodshed and brutalities. As Test puts it, 'not only did the abundance of Meso-american plants growing in the gardens of Europe lead scientific nomenclature to become more specific ... but their myths were also "transplanted" to European culture' (2009: 257).

Gardens, such as the one in Spenser, were attempts to collect the known universe into a manageable *hortus conclusus*, an enclosed garden (Drayton 2005: 6). Right up to the seventeenth century, gardens were seen as bringing together 'all the tributaries of Creation' (11–12). Eventually, the herbarium and the book began to replace the garden (20–1). Reports about New World and Asian plants appeared regularly from the 1580s in Europe and fed the imagination about the geography and topography of the globe. Travellers brought back specimens of plants, flowers and seeds as Britain slowly compiled the *theatricum botanicum* – incidentally the title of John Parkinson's 1640 work – the theatre of plants. What emerges here is the European insistence on botanical collection, classification and knowledge about plant life from around the world – which reaches its apotheosis in the work of Joseph Hooker, Joseph Banks, Robert Kyd and the botanists of the nineteenth century working in Kew and the other great gardens of metropolitan London – that then dovetails into an imperial project of knowledge of the Other culture/region/nation. The plant-as-object becomes the means of engaging with the Other, in the form of myth, as seen in the Spenser lines above, or in the form of discovering underlying principles of order, as embodied in Francis Bacon's observation in his *Brief Discourse Touching the Happy Union of the Kingdoms of England and Scotland* (1603):

> There is a great affinity and consent between the rules of nature, and the rules of policy: the one being nothing else but an order in the government of the world and the other an order in the government of an estate ... The Persian magic, which was the secret literature of their Kings, was an observation of the contemplations of nature and an application thereof to a sense politic ... making the government of the world a mirror for the government of the state.
>
> (90)

To establish knowledge and control over nature, Bacon suggests, was akin to establishing authority over people and places. The garden was a useful metaphor for such a process of establishing both knowledge and power.

An unusual representation of plant life in the form of a naval-mercantile image occurs in Pope's *Windsor Forest*. For Pope the forest was an integral component of not only English topography but of its culture as well. Gesturing at the English enthusiasm for New World and Asian plants Pope writes:

> Let India boast her plants, nor envy we
> The weeping amber of the balmy tree,
> While by our oaks the precious loads are born,
> And realms commanded which those trees adorn.
>
> (1963: 196)

This is an interesting way of comparing fauna. Pope proposes that England's oaks remain its chief resource. In his note to 'oaks' Pope mentions the fact that ships are

146 Consume and commodify

built of English oak, and these ships bring spices ('loads') to England and also help her travel far and establish her Empire. Thus Pope sees the English oak as a symbol of the culture and nation's stability but also as a symbol of her imperial ambitions, facilitated by the very nature of the oak tree's wood.

In an entirely different key other writers saw the plantations in the colonies as spaces where the benevolent (and profitable) Englishman 'plants' his *culture*. James Grainger's long poem *The Sugar-Cane* (1764) maps the conquest and settlement of the Caribbean, the topography and geology, the kind of soils needed for sugar cane and then focuses on the profits to be had from the crop. The poem was a paean to the crop but also glorified slavery by demonstrating how 'with placid looks' and 'willing ardour' the slaves went to work in the Englishman's plantations. It becomes, in short, a symbol of England's national culture itself. In Maria Edgeworth's short story 'The Grateful Negro' (1804) the slaves of Mr Edwards have little gardens attached to their huts, and they get one day to cultivate them. Unlike other farmers, says Edgeworth, Edwards did not take away their produce. Crops and produce in such representations become integral to the image of the labouring Englishman: where landowners are heroes. In both cases English culture manifests in not simply cultivation of crops or commodities but in the commanding of slaves' loyalty and acts of benevolence in the course of the cultivation.

Elsewhere Pope would present carefully planned English gardens with their collection of antiquarian buildings and exotic plants as wonderful English spectacles. Here the material culture of the distant shores become spectacles for the amusement and enjoyment of the English, but more importantly such gardens become embodiments of the English ability to enclose, encapsulate and comprehend the variety of the world. Pope would write in his 'Epistle IV: To Richard Boyle, Earl of Burlington' of the latter's ability to have in his gardens at Stowe, temples and assorted architectural wonders, as befits royalty with *taste*, and suggests they are 'imperial works' (1963: 586–95, quoted from 595).

Chinese temples or pagodas became common sights in English gardens in the eighteenth century. William Temple introduced the Chinese principle of *sharawadgi* (artful disorder), in an essay on gardening (1692). Later of course the Chinese garden of Kublai Khan (first described by Venetian traveller Marco Polo) would be extolled as a paradisal, even near-utopian, place in Coleridge's 'Kubla Khan' (1797). William Chambers (who lived in China for two years in the mid-eighteenth century) in his *Dissertation on Oriental Gardening* (1772) offered detailed illustrations and examples of the Chinese garden, and was instrumental in making the style an English commonplace.

This fascination for exotic architecture from the Orient was an extension into another domain of a rapidly expanding interest in all things Chinese. 'Chinoiserie' was a major movement from the early eighteenth century, as David Porter demonstrates (1999).[5] As expected, the movement was informed by current trends of thought about China (as in the case of Orientalism). In Wycherley's *The Country Wife* (1675), in the famous 'china scene' Lady Fidget complains: 'I have been toyling and moyling for the prettiest piece of China, my dear' (IV.3, l. 195.

Wycherley 1975: 112). In the scene's series of double entendres, Squeamish offers his 'China', comments on Horner's China, Horner does not think he can 'make enough China' for all the women, and Lady Fidget declares: 'we women of quality never think we have China enough' (l. 210. Wycherley 1975: 112). Wycherley links the Other-object here with English morality when he shows how the upper-class Englishwoman's pursuit of consumer satisfaction in the form of porcelain also makes her an 'immoral' woman in pursuit of sexual gratification, since 'China' is clearly a coded reference to sex. In similar fashion the breaking of china suggests the loss of English feminine innocence (Porter 1999: 48) in Pope's *The Rape of the Lock*:

> Then flash'd the living lightning from her eyes,
> And screams of horror rend th' affrighted skies.
> Not louder shrieks to pitying heav'n are cast,
> When husbands, or when lapdogs breathe their last;
> Or when rich China vessels fall'n from high,
> In glitt'ring dust and painted fragments lie.
>
> (1963: 231)

While in this case it does seem to reveal an underlying anxiety about English society, where the piece of china becomes a useful device with which to speak of the unspeakable: the loss of innocence. Yet it is also about the more public displays of character and individuality in the form of commodities.

Elsewhere, in Charlotte Brontë's *Jane Eyre*, there is, as Elaine Freedgood notes, considerable insistence on the appropriate furniture for English homes. Mahogany, the wood of choice in the novel, is a marker of the imperial violence that enables the import of wood that then constitutes English domesticity. In Freedgood's words:

> Mahogany becomes more than a weak metonym for wealth and taste ... It tells a story of imperial domination—the history of deforestation and slavery from Madeira to Jamaica—that crosshatches the manifest narrative of *Jane Eyre*, in which empire is banished with the (psychologically assisted) suicide of Bertha Mason. After this death, the novel seems to reestablish domesticity both in a habitational and in a national sense. I argue for a return of the imperial repressed in the violence that inheres in the old mahogany furniture that would otherwise seem (if it seemed at all) perfectly at home.
>
> (2006: 3)

What Freedgood points to is not simply imperial violence that contextualizes the arrival of particular commodities for English consumption. The prevalence of particular tropical wood in the novel indicates, in Freedgood's analysis, the incorporation of the Other-object into English households as markers of *English* domesticity. It is this domestication of the Other-object that enables English self-fashioning.

148   Consume and commodify

Jewels and precious ornaments and stones remained of course the most fascinating object-spectacles for the English when viewing Africa, the Arab world or the East. An extended account of the English trade with 'Indians' in Behn's *Oroonoko* is almost entirely in terms of commodities:

> trading with them for their fish, venison, buffalo's skins, and little rarities; as marmosets, a sort of monkey, as big as a rat or weasel, but of marvelous and delicate shape, having face and hands like a human creature; and cousheries, a little beast in the form and fashion of a lion, as big as a kitten, but so exactly made in all parts like that noble beast that it is it in miniature. Then for little paraketoes, great parrots, mackaws, and a thousand other birds and beasts of wonderful and surprising forms, shapes, and colors. For skins of prodigious snakes, of which there are some threescore yards in length; as is the skin of one that may be seen at his Majesty's Antiquary's; where are also some rare flies, of amazing forms and colors, presented to 'em by myself; some as big as my fist, some less; and all of various excellencies, such as art cannot imitate. Then we trade for feathers, which they order into all shapes, make themselves little short habits of 'em and glorious wreaths for their heads, necks, arms, and legs, whose tinctures are unconceivable.
>
> (1994: 6–7)

Then Behn's female narrator immediately shifts focus into ornaments: 'I had a set of these presented to me, and I gave 'em to the King's Theater, and it was the dress of the Indian Queen.' Behn's narrator is also impressed by the natives' skills in making ornaments. We are given a glimpse of the spectacle she herself witnessed:

> knives, axes, pins, and needles; which they used only as tools to drill holes with in their ears, noses, and lips, where they hang a great many little things; as long beads, bits of tin, brass or silver beat thin, and any shining trinket. The beads they weave into aprons about a quarter of an ell long, and of the same breadth; working them very prettily in flowers of several colors; which apron they wear just before 'em, as Adam and Eve did the fig-leaves; the men wearing a long stripe of linen, which they deal with us for. They thread these beads also on long cotton threads, and make girdles to tie their aprons to, which come twenty times, or more, about the waist, and then cross, like a shoulder-belt, both ways, and round their necks, arms, and legs. This adornment, with their long black hair, and the face painted in little specks or flowers here and there, makes 'em a wonderful figure to behold. Some of the beauties, which indeed are finely shaped, as almost all are, and who have pretty features, are charming and novel; for they have all that is called beauty, except the color, which is a reddish yellow; or after a new oiling, which they often use to themselves, they are of the color of a new brick, but smooth, soft, and sleek. They are extreme modest and bashful, very shy, and nice of being touched.
>
> (1994: 7)

The effect of this dizzying description is to transform the native *body* into spectacle: we see from Behn's description that both their nakedness and their ornament-laden bodies are equally attractive as spectacles. In the theatre of early colonial encounters, this spectacularization is, I propose, a significant one, for it offers the native body as something to be seen, as something to be civilized (the bodies are naked), as something to be admired (for their statuesque beauty, as Behn seems to do) and their jewellery. The ornaments on the native bodies, Margaret Ferguson argues in her reading of this scene from *Oroonoko*, instantiates a 'necessary luxury' (1996: 245) in the early stages of capitalism. I extend this argument to propose that what Behn maps is a luxury (of the natives) that is at once a set of objects to be admired (on native bodies) and acquired (through trade). That is, the spectacle of Other-objects here marks a specific kind of encounter: of colonial capitalism. Further, native bodies – slaves, performers, artists – were exhibited in the English institutions (theatres, museums, exhibitions) as curios and spectacles (Ferguson 1996: 247).

There is a further dimension to the commodity fetishism of Behn's novel, and this has to do with the way in which Japan, Picts, Africa and the Caribbean are represented in conjunction with objects. Imoinda is described as 'carved … in fine Flowers and Birds … as if it were Japan'd' (1994: 44). Oroonoko himself has a 'Polished Jet' blackness and possesses a 'statuary' bearing. Asian ornamentalism on African skin that then is involved in trade and social relations in the Caribbean with the British – all this is embodied, literally, in the spectacle of Imoinda and Oroonoko's figures. Oddly, Imoinda is deemed to resemble, according to the narrator, 'our ancient Picts' (44), that is the ancient *British* tribes. As we can see the African woman's body with its aesthetic decorations intersects with multiple sites and discourses of ancestry, trade and consumption. In Chi-ming Yang's words Imoinda's body

> allegorizes the meeting of four continents: Africanized nobility civilizes British primitiveness in America, through the Asiatic technique of japanning. Indeed, the entire globe—and its Asia-centered trade—is condensed in a description of a New World slave.
>
> (2009: 241)

It is a spectacularization of an African woman's body with its markings but *within* the commodity and labour culture of England's transnational interests. Imoinda is the embodiment of these interests, so to speak.

Interestingly, Lady Mary Montagu in her now-famous letters from Turkey presents herself as a (erotic, transcultural) spectacle worthy of admiration. Itemizing her clothing, Montagu foregrounds the Turkish costume that adds to her charm, comfort and value. The entire passage is worth quoting in full:

> THE first part of my dress is a pair of drawers, very full that reach to my shoes, and conceal the legs more modestly than your petticoats. They are of

150 Consume and commodify

a thin rose-coloured damask, brocaded with silver flowers. My shoes are of white kid leather, embroidered with gold. Over this hangs my smock, of a fine white silk gauze, edged with embroidery. This smock has wide sleeves hanging half way down the arm, and is closed at the neck with a diamond button; but the shape and colour of the bosom is very well to be distinguished through it.—The *antery* is a waistcoat, made close to the shape, of white and gold damask, with very long sleeves falling back, and fringed with deep gold fringe, and should have diamond or pearl buttons. My *caftan*, of the same stuff with my drawers, is a robe exactly fitted to my shape, and reaching to my feet, with very long strait falling sleeves. Over this is my girdle, of about four fingers broad, which, all that can afford it, have entirely of diamonds or other precious stones; those who will not be at that expence, have it of exquisite embroidery on sattin [*sic*]; but it must be fastened before with a clasp of diamonds.—The *curdee* is a loose robe they throw off, or put on, according to the weather, being of a rich brocade (mine is green and gold) either lined with ermine or sables; the sleeves reach very little below the shoulders. The head dress is composed of a cap, called *talpock*, which is, in winter, of fine velvet embroidered with pearls or diamonds, and in summer, of a light shining silver stuff. This is fixed on one side of the head, hanging a little way down with a gold tassel, and bound on, either with a circle of diamonds (as I have seen several) or a rich embroidered handkerchief. On the other side of the head, the hair is laid flat; and here the ladies are at liberty to shew their fancies; some putting flowers, others a plume of heron's feathers, and, in short, what they please; but the most general fashion is a large *bouquet* of jewels, made like natural flowers; that is, the buds, of pearl; the roses, of different coloured rubies: the jessamines, of diamonds; the jonquils, of topazes, &c. so well set and enamelled, 'tis hard to imagine any thing of that kind so beautiful.

(unpaginated, http://ebooks.adelaide.edu.au/m/montagu/
mary_wortley/letters)

The spectacularization of the English woman's body relies almost entirely on non-European material products and styling. If Behn gave us a map of the desirable native body Montagu maps the Englishwoman's body in an interesting dual move. She makes the wealth of the Turks desirable because they thrive on the spectacular *English* form: note the number of times she speaks of her form which the Turkish costume *highlights* and *makes visible*. Next she makes the English female form itself even more desirable through the addition of Turkish/foreign costumes and jewellery. The woman's body and the material object enter into a dynamics that generates the erotic charge of the passage in which Montagu is demonstrating an exercise in self-fashioning as an attractive, shapely, fashionable woman *because* she adapts to non-European clothing so easily. In Walter Scott's *The Surgeon's Daughter* (1827) we see an echo of Montagu's costume drama:

Consume and commodify **151**

a Semiramis-looking person, of unusual stature and amplitude, arrayed in a sort of riding-habit, but so formed, and so looped and gallooned with lace, as made it resemble the upper tunic of a native chief. Her robe was composed of crimson silk, rich with flowers of gold. She wore wide trowsers of light blue silk, a fine scarlet shawl around her waist, in which was stuck a creeze with a richly ornamented handle. Her throat and arms were loaded with chains and bracelets, and her turban, formed of a shawl similar to that worn around her waist, was decorated by a magnificent aigrette, from which a blue ostrich plume flowed in one direction, and a red one in another. The brow, of European complexion, on which this tiara rested, was too lofty for beauty, but seemed made for command; the aquiline nose retained its form, but the cheeks were a little sunken, and the complexion so very brilliant, as to give strong evidence that the whole countenance had undergone a thorough repair since the lady had left her couch. A black female slave, richly dressed, stood behind her with a chowry, or cow's tail, having a silver handle, which she used to keep off the flies. From the mode in which she was addressed by those who spoke to her, this lady appeared a person of too much importance to be affronted or neglected, and yet one with whom none desired further communication than the occasion seemed in propriety to demand.

This is Mother Montreville, whose native costume is so rich (and perhaps garish) that she is referred to as the 'Queen of Sheba'. The European body is rendered nativized, and more interesting, in such accounts.[6] When Adam Hartley in Scott's novel is puzzled by her identity, somebody tells him:

'Is it possible you do not know the Queen of Sheba?' said the person of whom he enquired, no way both to communicate the information demanded. 'You must know, then, that she is the daughter of a Scotch emigrant, who lived and died at Pondicherry, a sergeant in Lally's regiment. She managed to marry a partisan officer named Montreville, a Swiss or Frenchman, I cannot tell which ... '.

(http://ebooks.adelaide.edu.au/s/cott/walter/surgeon)

European identities are spectacularly hybridized through the use of native costume.

The spectacularization of native bodies, and their skills, achieves another effect: the native body as a reduced body, their skills as less valuable. A preeminent example of this form of commodification – where the native body is a passive spectacle and the object of an English gaze – is William Hazlitt's essay 'The Indian Jugglers' (1828). Hazlitt begins with an elaborate eulogy to the juggler. He is watching, he says, a brilliant spectacle of the Indian's skill:

It is the utmost stretch of human ingenuity, which nothing but the bending the faculties of body and mind to it from the tenderest infancy with

152 Consume and commodify

incessant, ever-anxious application up to manhood, can accomplish or make even a slight approach to.

He is made aware, he says, of his own inadequacies when he sees what the Indian juggler does:

> It makes me ashamed of myself. I ask what there is that I can do as well as this! Nothing. What have I been doing all my life! Have I been idle, or have I nothing to shew for all my labour and pains! Or have I passed my time in pouring words like water into empty sieves, rolling a stone up a hill and then down again, trying to prove an argument in the teeth of facts, and looking for causes in the dark, and not finding them? Is there no one thing in which I can challenge competition, that I can bring as an instance of exact perfection, in which others cannot find a flaw? The utmost I can pretend to is to write a description of what this fellow can do ... I have always had this feeling of the inefficacy and slow progress of intellectual compared to mechanical excellence, and it has always made me somewhat dissatisfied.

Hazlitt then proceeds to meditate upon the mechanics of this kind of feat:

> I might observe that mechanical dexterity is confined to doing some one particular thing, which you can repeat as often as you please, in which you know whether you succeed or fail, and where the point of perfection consists in succeeding in a given undertaking. – In mechanical efforts, you improve by perpetual practice, and you do so infallibly, because the object to be attained is not a matter of taste or fancy or opinion, but of actual experiment, in which you must either do the thing or not do it ... There is then in this sort of manual dexterity, first a gradual aptitude acquired to a given exertion of muscular power, from constant repetition, and in the next place, an exact knowledge how much is still wanting and necessary to be supplied. The obvious test is to increase the effort or nicety of the operation, and still to find it come true. The muscles ply instinctively to the dictates of habit. Certain movements and impressions of the hand and eye, having been repeated together an infinite number of times are unconsciously but unavoidably cemented into closer and closer union; the limbs require little more than to be put in motion for them to follow a regular track with ease and certainty; so that mere intention of the will acts mathematically, like touching the spring of a machine, and you come with Locksley in *Ivanhoe*, shooting at a mark, 'to allow for the wind'.

Then Hazlitt makes the damning comparison of these mechanical artists with other kinds of artists:

> But the artist undertakes to imitate another, or to do what nature has done, and this it appears is more difficult, *viz.* to copy what she has set before us in

the face of nature or 'human face divine,' entire and without a blemish, than to keep up four brass balls at the same instant; for the one is done by the power of human skill and industry; and the other never was nor will be … there have been more people in the world who could dance on a rope like the one than who could paint like Sir Joshua [Reynolds].

Hazlitt argues that any single instance of manual dexterity – such as that of the Indian jugglers – pales in comparison with art and other intellectual exercises. Mechanical arts acquired through skills, he says, are limited to a performance, and do not leave lasting changes in the world:

No act terminating in itself constitutes greatness. This will apply to all displays of power or trials of skill, which are confined to the momentary, individual effort, and construct no permanent image or trophy of themselves without them.

Spectacularizing Indian bodies in the mechanical arts, as Hazlitt does, is to reinstate a traditional binary. The Eastern skill is entirely through practice and repetition. Further it is limited to a performance or two with no lasting impact. The native body acquires these skills and performs these feats only through years of repeated and rigorous training. Hazlitt here, I propose, reduces the native body to mindless matter, to endless and ultimately futile exercise of mechanical skills. These have nothing to do with latent genius or taste in Hazlitt's indictment. To quote again:

In mechanical efforts, you improve by perpetual practice, and you do so infallibly, because the object to be attained is not a matter of taste or fancy or opinion, but of actual experiment, in which you must either do the thing or not do it.

(http://ebooks.adelaide.edu.au/h/hazlitt/william/
table-talk/v1.9.html)

In contrast with these Hazlitt offers us painting, fine arts and other domains in which taste and genius are visible. Such skills as the juggler's exhibit lack of taste, and of genius, because they simply repeat their performances until they get better at the feat.

Comparing the juggler with Joshua Reynolds Hazlitt exhibits considerable contempt for the mechanical arts. The word 'mechanical' occurs nine times in the short essay. The word itself, from Shakespeare's (in)famous 'rude mechanicals' (*A Midsummer Night's Dream*, III.2, l. 9), as Patricia Parker notes, was used to describe an artisan, 'one who worked with the material, manual labor, or the work of the hand' (1996: 45). It was, she argues, in contrast with both the natural-spontaneous as well as the contemplative. Hazlitt's use of the term repeatedly through his essay captures this contrast nicely: of Eastern mechanical skill and the Western contemplative spontaneous talents or genius, of Reynolds and others. He underscores the contrast in other ways as well in his spectacularization of the

154 Consume and commodify

native body/skill. These skills are repetitive and acquired through repetition (to cite Parker again, the mechanical is also connected with theatrical mimicry and mechanical reproduction, 1996: 47). Great art, Hazlitt proposes, cannot be achieved merely through repetition nor can it be reproduced, unlike the skills of the jugglers. Spectacularization here results in reducing the Eastern skills to matter, to bodies and repetitions, lacking taste, genius or lasting value, while depicting English artistic skills as acts of creative genius.[7]

That Indian artists were curios whose consumption was contingent upon English dominions in India rather than on the artistry of the artists comes home to us in James Green's poem, 'Indian Jugglers' (1820). Green's poem, narrated from the Indian jugglers' point of view, speaks of the shift in perceptions of their art by the English. It opens with:

> We were a curio back then, historical
> now, dark and small, barefoot, in shawls.

The Daniells (Thomas and William) painted them, as they did the Taj Mahal, and when exhibited in London, Green says, 'everyone wanted to havalooksee'. But after 1857 the perceptions of these Indian artists changes:

> we were the rotten curio,
> ungrateful, badly-behaved.

Nobody wants to now immortalize them in art, says Green. Painters like the Daniells who specialized in Indian subjects, notes Green, were sidelined in favour of painters like Gainsborough who did traditional English subjects. The poem ends with:

> The Anglo-Indian school of artists was done for
> as we were (the clever people juggling).

> (Vazirani 1998: 368)

Whether the 'clever people' refers to the Indian jugglers or to the cleverness of the English in changing the market demand for Indian artistry (and British art founded on Indian artistry) is left unclear. In either case, what is made visible is the presence of market forces that determine the value of any Eastern art or artefact. In and of themselves the Eastern juggler has no lasting value (those are restricted, Green's poem seems to suggest, to properly English goods, like Gainsborough paintings of English countryside life), and recalling Hazlitt's formulation, leave no mark on the world of either art or consumption.

The rhetoric of objectification

Beyond the ornaments and the jewellery, however, another category of Other-object makes its appearance in Behn's description, and that is the body of the non-

European. I am proposing here that the slave or the African/Asian native serves as a particular kind of *corporeal* spectacle for visual consumption in these texts. Maureen Quilligan correctly points out that the slave presents a 'boundary case' for the relationship between human subject and reified object (1996: 213). Slaves, since they performed manual labour, were 'things' (219).[8] However, as I shall demonstrate, the slave body also gets resignified as the site of English ethics wherein the discourses of freedom, emancipation and compassion get emplotted.

If 'objectification', in Tilley's terms, is the embodiment of an idea that then shows how subjects and objects *relate* to each other, English literature's treatment of black bodies as things, labour or animals, constitutes the embodiment of two key ideas: of the slave as labouring body deserving nothing more than an animal's status and attention and of the slave as an emotional body that is in reality unthinking *matter* demanding benevolence and protection or *even* emancipation. In the former case the rhetoric of objectification manifests in a discourse of slavery in which the subject (the English landlord, plantation owner, trader) has a master–slave relationship with the object (the black man/woman). In the latter the rhetoric of objectification emerges as the discourse of emancipation in which the subject and object have a benevolent saviour–vulnerable human relationship.

The rhetoric of objectification has two strands. In one the rhetoric emphasizes the black body as a thing (minus agency, voice, feelings), fragments it into parts (as 'hands', indicating labouring hands) or animalizes it. Historically, as Page duBois has mapped, this might be traced to the slave body of ancient Greece where slaves were often rendered into objects, or subjected bodies. DuBois lists various representations of such an objectified slave body: the bound and beaten, whipped, sexually vulnerable, tortured, tattooed, ubiquitous and murdered (2008: 101–13). Here the rhetoric usually focuses on a black body destined and fit only for labour, and nothing more. In the second strand the rhetoric gets the slave body to speak the language of suffering and victimage, offering a nominal agency in terms of voicing. This second strand, seen mainly in anti-abolition literature from the 1760s, is a special case of objectification.

Labouring matter

By the seventeenth century slave labour, mercantilism, profit and Empire were established as an unquestionable continuum in the English mind and discourse, as several scholars have demonstrated.[9] The devaluation and dehumanization of the black man and woman into things and objects was within this context. The slave body is a thing, a machine, a piece of property and possession to be acquired or sold as its owner deems fit. Overdetermined by the manual *labour* it is forced/destined to perform, endlessly, the human is reduced to a thing, a mechanical device.[10] Both land and labourer become commodities in this form of engagement with the Other-object. Curiously the rhetoric of objectification works to either depict the slave body as labouring body (minus anything else, such as intelligence) or as an invisible, ghostly body. We shall look at examples of both variants.[11]

156 Consume and commodify

First a quick look at one of the early instances of the slave body as Object-other, representations that are in line with much of duBois' classification of slave bodies as objects: bound and beaten, whipped, sexually vulnerable, tortured and murdered. This is the representation of Oroonoko and Imoinda in Aphra Behn's novel. This is an account of Oroonoko's killing of his beloved Imoinda:

> All that love could say in such cases being ended, and all the intermitting irresolutions being adjusted, the lovely, young, and adored victim lays herself down before the sacrificer; while he, with a hand resolved, and a heart breaking within, gave the fatal stroke, first cutting her throat, and then severing her yet smiling face from that delicate body, pregnant as it was with the fruits of tenderest love. As soon as he had done, he laid the body decently on leaves and flowers, of which he made a bed, and concealed it under the same cover-lid of Nature; only her face he left yet bare to look on.
>
> (1994: 68)

He then tries to kill himself: 'he ripped up his own belly, and took his bowels and pulled 'em out, with what strength he could' (70). He fails in his attempt and then, arrested, he is executed. The description of his execution goes thus:

> He had learned to take tobacco; and when he was assured he should die, he desired they would give him a pipe in his mouth, ready lighted; which they did. And the executioner came, and first cut off his members, and threw them into the fire; after that, with an ill-favored knife, they cut off his ears and his nose and burned them; he still smoked on, as if nothing had touched him; then they hacked off one of his arms, and still he bore up, and held his pipe; but at the cutting off the other arm, his head sunk, and his pipe dropped, and he gave up the ghost, without a groan or a reproach.
>
> (72)

The black bodies of Imoinda and Oroonoko, it must be remembered, were initially described as beautiful and near-perfect. After his attempt to kill himself Oroonoko is reduced to a mutilated body: 'if before we thought him so beautiful a sight, he was now so altered that his face was like a death's-head blacked over, nothing but teeth and eye-holes' (71). Finally of course he is dismembered. The black body is therefore not retained in its entirety and Alberto Rivero's comment summarizes this well: 'the author, having made their beautiful bodies, must now unmake them, must render them repulsive' (1999: 457).

A text that revolves almost entirely around the subject of the slaves' labouring bodies is James Grainger's extended *The Sugar-Cane* (in four books, 1764). Grainger presents the British plantation owner as heroic, struggling with the land, its inimical climate and pestilential insects. He then in passing mentions the labour force:

> The Negroe-train, with placid looks, survey
> Thy fields, which full perfection have attain'd.

Note that the black slaves who work on the field in these same inimical conditions give only 'placid looks'. Grainger then adds:

Nor thou, my friend, their willing ardour check;
Encourage rather; cheerful toil is light.

Grainger seems to propose that the slaves are yearning to work hard for their master. Their 'willing ardour' must therefore be encouraged. Grainger pre-empts the anxiety about the difficulty of their labour by focusing instead on the attitude and emotional states of the labour, not their physical contexts: they perform, he claims, 'cheerful toil'. All this, Grainger proposes, proceeds from the white man's benevolent handling of the slaves:

In time, a numerous gang of sturdy slaves,
Well-fed, well-cloath'd, all emulous to gain
Their master's smile, who treated them like men,
Blacken'd his Cane-lands: which with vast increase,
Beyond the wish of avarice, paid his toil.
(unpaginated, http://mith.umd.edu/eada/html/display.php?docs
=grainger_sugarcane.xml)

In a tone reminiscent of the country-house poems of the eighteenth century Grainger presents the entire plantation as a space of wonderful hospitality, where even the 'Ethiop' (like the servants in Jonson's 'To Penshurst') are warm and welcoming:

His gate stood wide to all; but chief the poor,
The unfriended stranger, and the sickly, shar'd
His prompt munificence: No surly dog,
Nor surlier Ethiop, their approach debarr'd.[12]

From a different text, a similar scene where the slaves bring food and garden produce to the visitor may be found in Edgeworth's 'The Grateful Negro'. Edgeworth's description goes thus:

He [Mr Edwards, the plantation owner] and his family came out at sunset, when the fresh breeze had sprung up, and seated themselves under a spreading palm-tree, to enjoy the pleasing spectacle of this negro festival. His negroes were all well clad, and in the gayest colours, and their merry coun- tenances suited the gaiety of their dress. While some were dancing, and some playing on the tambourine, others appeared amongst the distant trees, bringing baskets of avocado pears, grapes, and pine-apples, the produce of their own provision-grounds; and others were employed in spreading their

158 Consume and commodify

> clean trenchers, or the calabashes, which served for plates and dishes. The
> negroes continued to dance and divert themselves till late in the evening.[13]
>
> (http://ebooks.adelaide.edu.au/e/edgeworth/maria/grateful-negro/)

The labouring body of the slave is co-opted into the structure of munificence and
generosity of the planter. This kind of a plantation is the place to live for the
Briton, suggests Grainger.

> Say, is pre-eminence your partial aim?–
> Distinction courts you here; the senate calls.
> Here, crouching slaves, attendant wait your nod:
> While there, unnoted, but for folly's garb,
> For folly's jargon; your dull hours ye pass,
> Eclips'd by titles, and superior wealth.
>
> (unpaginated, http://mith.umd.edu/eada/html/display.php?docs
> =grainger_sugarcane.xml.)

The rhetoric here is interesting for it converts the plantation into the space of
labour – not Edenic space but Georgian, certainly – and suggests that the Briton
would be far happier here in the West Indies than in England with its titles and
wealth. A key contributing factor that makes this space so wonderful is the presence of slaves: 'crouching slaves, attendant wait your nod'. Implicitly acknowledging that the Englishman's identity is fashioned partly due to the work of the
slaves, Grainger makes it evident that it is slave labour that *produces* English glory.
(Grainger recommends that the plantation owners treat the slaves with some
kindness so that they would remain faithful to the white man. I shall return to this
theme of benevolence in the next section.)

In Thomas Carlyle's 'Occasional Discourse on the Nigger Question' (1849) he
draws attention to the success of West Indian plantations, but attributes the economic
triumph to European endeavour:

> And now observe, my friends, it was not the Black Quashee, or those he
> represents, that made those West-India Islands what they are, or can, by any
> hypothesis, be considered to have the right of growing pumpkins there. For
> countless ages ... Till the European white man first saw them ... those
> Islands had produced mere jungle savagery, poison-reptiles, and swamp-
> malaria ... they were as if not yet created, – their noble elements of cinnamon,
> sugar, coffee, pepper black and grey, lying all asleep, waiting the white
> enchanter who should say to them, Awake!
>
> (http://www.efm.bris.ac.uk/het/carlyle/occasion.htm)

This is an extraordinary passage. First Carlyle speaks of 'discovery', as though the natives
had never understood the true value of the plants and products of their habitations.
Second, Carlyle converts the islands into spaces of primordial life, premodern and

poisonous, almost in an exact replication of Shakespeare's Prospero. Third, he presents the white man as a magician, an enchanter, who transforms the land with one word, 'Awake!' This last move effectively elides the decades of labour, by the blacks, that produced the transformation of the islands. By attributing the change and prosperity to white magic, as opposed to black labour, Carlyle invisibilizes black labour.

There is a far more insidious mode of invisibilizing the black body, and the apotheosis of the labouring, disintegrating and dematerializing body may be found in Conrad. *Heart of Darkness* first thrives on an imagery of the African land as body. An organicization, so to speak, of Africa as human (and, of course, on several occasions, as female). Marlow notes that he enters the 'mouth of the big river' (1974: 62) and is perhaps headed for 'the bowels of the land' (87). The jungle is anthropomorphized as a living breathing thing, in Conrad's famous metaphor of drums: 'perhaps on some quiet night the tremor of far-off drums, sinking, swelling, a tremor' (71). The novel also ends with the drum-as-metaphor when Conrad refers to the 'throb of drums' (144). The jungle, Marlow says, seems to be the 'colossal body of the fecund and mysterious Life' (136) and affects him deeply. Here 'the contorted mangroves ... seemed to writhe at us in the extremity of an impotent despair' (62). The 'silent wilderness ... was waiting patiently for the passing away of this fantastic invasion' (76). Marlow says: 'I wondered whether the stillness on the face of the immensity looking at us two were meant as an appeal or a menace' (81).

Curiously, as Conrad vivifies the land, the black inhabitants of the land become shadowy, ghostly and immaterial. The Other-object here is a spectral body, only marginally alive, but rarely demonstrably so. A series of images of ghostification occurs in the novel: 'To the left a clump of trees made a shady spot, where dark things seemed to stir feebly.' And in a more sustained account:

> A slight clinking behind me made me turn my head. Six black men advanced in a file, toiling up the path. They walked erect and slow, balancing small baskets full of earth on their heads, and the clink kept time with their footsteps. Black rags were wound round their loins, and the short ends behind wagged to and fro like tails. I could see every rib, the joints of their limbs were like knots in a rope; each had an iron collar on his neck, and all were connected together with a chain whose bights swung between them, rhythmically clinking. Another report from the cliff made me think suddenly of that ship of war I had seen firing into a continent. It was the same kind of ominous voice; but these men could by no stretch of imagination be called enemies. They were called criminals, and the outraged law, like the bursting shells, had come to them, an insoluble mystery from over the sea. All their meager breasts panted together, the violently dilated nostrils quivered, the eyes stared stonily uphill. They passed me within six inches, without a glance, with that complete, deathlike indifference of unhappy savages. Behind this raw matter one of the reclaimed, the product of the new forces at work, strolled despondently.

(64)

160 Consume and commodify

And:

> Black shapes crouched, lay, sat between the trees, leaning against the trunks, clinging to the earth, half coming out, half effaced within the dim light, in all the attitudes of pain, abandonment, and despair.
>
> (66)

And:

> One, with his chin propped on his knees, stared at nothing, in an intolerable and appalling manner: his brother phantom rested its forehead.
>
> (67)

And:

> Looking past that mad helmsman, who was shaking the empty rifle and yelling at the shore, I saw vague forms of men running bent double, leaping, gliding, distinct, incomplete, evanescent.
>
> (111)

This well-known description of the zombie-like black men, chained to each other, indifferent to suffering having long gone past their limits, is a process of ghostification. With disease and exhaustion the black bodies have been reduced to mere skeletal frames, and Marlow notes their 'moribund shapes', 'black bones' and 'bundles of acute angles'.[14] The blacks have been reduced to ghosts in their own country, climate and setting. (I will have reason to return to this description later, in Chapter 5.)

Avery Gordon has persuasively argued that ghosts represent the haunting reminders of modernity's violence (1997). Other critics like Bishnupriya Ghosh argue that ghosts force us to ask 'questions of political justice and hope' (2004: 205). Labouring bodies in Conrad are, metaphorically, ghosts, lacking any person-hood. This is also the Other-object, shadowy and insubstantial. Although not exactly invisible, Conrad's metaphors of shadows, vague forms, evanescence and hollowed-out bodies, I suggest, render them almost immaterial matter. They are, in Conrad's words, 'raw matter' but it is matter that is amorphous, intangible and therefore immaterial.

Ethical matter

William Cowper in 'Sweet Meat has Sour Sauce, or, the Slave Trader in the Dumps' (1837) spoke of the trader to the Caribbean who discovers the system of slavery that kept his trade afloat. After a detailed account of the sufferings of the slaves in the ships' hold – which includes a 'notable engine to open his jaws' when the slave refuses to eat – he decides to sell his stock. But before this the trader refers to the 'sweetening' of tempers in a direct reference to British consumption of blood-stained sugar. The Empire's 'sweetmeats' (the title of the poem) was produced through blood and suffering and British consumption was always an unethical one, suggests Cowper (1994: 295–7). The language of sentiment that we see in Cowper reflects a larger discourse of the victimhood and suffering of the racial, cultural Other which simultaneously projected the Englishman and woman in particular ways.

The arguments in this section take their cue from two significant works on sentimentality and Empire. Lynn Festa's work on sentiment and the British Empire has demonstrated how the indigenous individuals and populations were objectified as victims, although there was considerable anxiety that unregulated sympathy might be a source of threat to the very identity of Englishness (2006). Andrew Rudd (2011), similarly, has shown us the key role 'sympathy' played in the construction of colonial subjects in the 1770–1830s period. English sentiments towards the racial, cultural Other might be deemed to be a globalizing move in and of itself, an imperialism of affect, to which, as we shall see in the concluding chapter, a discourse of improvement would come to be added from the early eighteenth century.

By the mid-eighteenth century the slave body gets appropriated into a different discourse of objectification.[15] In anti-abolition tracts and literature the slave body comes to signify, in addition to the corruption and decadent morality of the Empire, the possibility of ethical behaviour and emancipatory idealism of the English. The subject–object relationship here is significantly different from the discourse of slavery because now the slave body is re-evaluated as a vulnerable object demanding ethical treatment. Retaining the hierarchy of master–slave the subject–object relationship makes this shift. This discourse relies heavily on the slave body being constructed as a vulnerable and suffering object, insecure creature, towards whom a particular set of attitudes (compassion, mainly) need to be shown by the English. Thus, in this form of engagement with the slave body as Other-object, the Englishman or woman fashions him-/herself as the benevolent master. Without the construction of the suffering, pitiable body of the black Other-object there would be no such identity for the English. 'Ethical matter' is the black body as the Other-object deserving of, pleading for, charity as the irrational-but-feeling object of white sentiments. The English now construct themselves as compassionate and 'feeling' people, possessing both imaginative sympathy (defined as the 'faculty of mind whereby a person can enter into the thoughts and feelings of another through the exercise of imagination') and sensibility (which might be defined as the capacity to 'feel' (Rudd 2011: 2)).

Robinson Crusoe's Xury is one of the original characters who would come to typify the docile and vulnerable abject-object black individual in English literature. Xury swears to be faithful to Crusoe, promising to go around the world with him. Crusoe sells Xury to the Portuguese captain, although it is never clear (as Daniel Carey notes, 2009: 114), how exactly Crusoe, himself a slave with Xury in Salé, comes into *ownership* of Xury. The captain agrees to free him after a ten-year indenture

162 Consume and commodify

but only if he converts to Christianity. Then, says Defoe in Crusoe's words: 'upon this, and Xury saying he was willing to go to him, I let the captain have him'. This is a complicated transaction where the 'slave' expresses willingness for participating in the transfer. He *voluntarily* accepts his sale, as Defoe's novel suggests. Defoe's objectification of the Xury-body, I propose, is contingent upon a peculiar sense of the word 'willing'. On the promise of eventual freedom, depending on his conversion, the slave agrees to his commodification. Although Crusoe does not quite 'own' Xury, Xury allows Crusoe to make a profit by making him, Xury, property through the transaction. A nominal 'voice' and agency granted to Xury in Defoe's text attributed choice to the 'slave', and the slave *willingly* takes the role of a piece of property. Defoe then records Crusoe's *sentiments* at this commercial and racially-inflected transaction: 'I was very loath to sell the boy's liberty who had assisted me so faithfully in procuring my own' (1975: 29).

The sentimentalization of racial dynamics of the eighteenth and early nineteenth century offers us interesting insights into the subject–object relationship between whites and black bodies. In the anti-slavery poetry of the 1760–1840 period the slave is not the despised, exotic Other-object. William Blake in 'The Little Black Boy' writes:

> My mother bore me in the southern wild,
> And I am black, but O! my soul is white;
> White as an angel is the English child;
> But I am black as if bereav'd of light.

> (1973: 125)

Here, Blake contrasts the black boy (and its collateral, the 'dark continent', that would serve as a metaphor for Africa for over two centuries) with the white one but also suggests that the soul of the black boy is as white as could be. In the new morality of the humanitarian regime, the black boy/man/woman becomes the site of this new morality, and the white anti-slavery individual the signifier of Britain's new subject. This new British subject who engages with the racial other within the context of the anti-slavery campaign and colonialism, is the sentimental subject, and the black body becomes the object towards which all white sentiment and charity can be directed.

What is also to be noted is that these representations of black bodies portray them as loyal, affectionate and vulnerable. An illuminating incident occurs in Edgeworth's 'The Grateful Negro' which demonstrates the true affections of the black slave:

> Caesar [the slave] had no knife. 'Here is mine for you,' said Mr. Edwards, 'It is very sharp,' added he, smiling; 'but I am not one of those masters who are afraid to trust their negroes with sharp knives.'
>
> These words were spoken with perfect simplicity: Mr. Edwards had no suspicion, at this time, of what was passing in the negro's mind. Caesar

received the knife without uttering a syllable; but no sooner was Mr. Edwards out of sight than he knelt down, and, in a transport of gratitude, swore that, with this knife, he would stab himself to the heart sooner than betray his master!

> (http://ebooks.adelaide.edu.au/e/edgeworth/maria/grateful-negro/)

Later Caesar is described thus:

> The principle of gratitude conquered every other sensation. The mind of Caesar was not insensible to the charms of freedom: he knew the negro conspirators had so taken their measures that there was the greatest probability of their success. His heart beat high at the idea of recovering his liberty.
>
> (http://ebooks.adelaide.edu.au/e/edgeworth/maria/grateful-negro/)

It is the loyal slave who ensures that the slave violence does not spiral out of control.

It is sensation, feeling and imaginative sympathy, that is constantly being described here. We also see in several of the poems a social cause and project of the white person (we shall return to the welfarist discourses of the Other in a separate chapter) founded on Christian goodness and compassion even though colonial profits – which necessitated slavery in the Caribbean plantations – remained the higher agenda. Moira Ferguson has tellingly argued that slavery provided a context for the British middle-class woman to 'intensify their involvement in philanthropy' (1992: 108). Such an involvement, as illustrated in the anti-slavery poems of the period, revolves around constructing the subject–object relationship within sentiment.

James Grainger's *The Sugar-Cane* proposes:

> to every slave assign
> Some mountain-ground: or, if waste broken land
> To thee belong, that broken land divide.
> This let them cultivate, one day, each week.

Such an act, coupled with some generosity, suggests Grainger, would win the white man the slave's loyalty, and the slave would then thwart the attempt of other disaffected blacks:

> But let some antient, faithful slave erect
> His sheltered mansion near; and with his dog,
> His loaded gun, and cutlass, guard the whole:
> Else negro-fugitives, who skulk 'mid rocks
> And shrubby wilds, in bands will soon destroy.
> Thy labourer's honest wealth; their loss and yours.
>
> (unpaginated, http://mith.umd.edu/eada/html/display.php?docs
> =grainger_sugarcane.xml)

164 Consume and commodify

Maria Edgeworth's 'The Grateful Negro' epitomizes the sentimentalization of the subject–object in the period through which the Englishman fashions himself as the compassionate subject. Mr Edwards in the novel articulates the politics of sentiment. Slaves, he says, should be treated 'with all possible kindness' (unpaginated). The slaves crave families, domesticity and protection. They possess 'simplistic mentalities' and exemplify 'rank powerlessness' (Ferguson 1992: 238). They are irrational, unthinking, and by extension apolitical, *matter*, not mind. G.A. Henty in *By Sheer Pluck* offers us an account of the innocent, vulnerable and gullible – essentially, unthinking – Africans:

> Just like children … They are always laughing or quarreling. They are good-natured and passionate, indolent, but will work hard for a time; clever upto a certain point densely stupid beyond. The intelligence of an average negro is about equal to that of a European child of ten years old. A few, a very few, go beyond this, but these are exceptions, just as Shakespeare was an exception to the ordinary intellect of an Englishman. They are fluent talkers but their ideas are borrowed. They are absolutely without originality, absolutely without inventive power. Living among white men their imitative faculties enable them to attain a considerable amount of civilisation. Left alone to their own devices they retrograde into a state little above their native savagery.
>
> (cited in Huttenback 1965: 73)

But what is more important is the forging of a sentimental bond between the benevolent white subject and the powerless and craving-for-affection black object. While it might be argued that the portrayal of the black body as possessing of sentiment does suggest a measure of agency, it could also be read as the *reduction* of the black to a mass of harmless sentiment, but minus anger or rebelliousness: none of these poems depict angry, ready-to-fight slaves, what we see are only snivelling and weeping-for-comfort blacks. (We shall return to the amelioration theme of abolitionism in Chapter 6.)

In Hannah More's 'The Sorrows of Yamba, or The Negro Woman's Lamentation' (1797), the slave woman describes her journey on the Middle Passage, and then 'driven like cattle to a fair' (Nayar 2013b: 56) to be sold, as children are separated from their mothers, 'all for love of filthy Gold' (56). More resignifies the black body here in terms of a contradiction: the black woman's voice, which embodies her subjectivity, speaks of her animalization and the objectification in terms of money. But More also takes care to represent Yamba as an individual who is primarily bemoaning her victim status, and thus remains an abject presence throughout the tale. Yamba's tale also foregrounds African family and domestic life in More's attempt to humanize them and thereby offers a nominal attempt at equality. Then the English missionary comes along and convinces Yamba to convert. Yamba then becomes the forgiving – and therefore unthreatening – black woman who only wishes 'o if Massa would repent' (58). Yamba now becomes ready to even 'forgive [her] cruel capture', and would rather:

count thy mercies o'er,
Flowing thro' the guilt of man.

(58)

because 'all [her] former thoughts [she] abhorred' now (59). More alleviates any possible anxiety around the angry and vengeful black by presenting the black woman as forgiving and Christian, and with no other thought than peace for all. The rhetoric of objectification here not only constructs the English missionary as the compassionate subject but also offers a minimal subject-position to the converted black by demonstrating her capacity for forgiveness once she has acquired the white man's religion. Towards the end of the poem Yamba prays:

True of heart, and meek and lowly,
Pure and blameless let me grow!
Holy may I be, for Holy,
Is the place to which I go.

(Nayar 2013b: 59)

More deploys the rhetoric of objectification in order to present the black body as sentimental and vulnerable but also cringing and quiescent matter in these lines. In another poem, 'Slavery: A Poem', More begins by proposing that the blacks have the power of rationality, and then smoothly elides this feature for their characteristic 'passions':

they have heads to think, and hearts to feel,
And souls to act, with firm, tho' erring, zeal;
For they have keen affections, kind desires,
Love strong as death, and active patriot fires;
All the rude energy, the fervid flame,
Of high-soul'd passion, and ingenuous shame:
Strong, but luxuriant virtues boldly shoot
From the wild vigour of a savage root.

(Wu 1997: 45)

Foregrounding African domesticity as a mode of proving their humanity, More claims: 'In all the love of home and freedom reign' (Wu 1997: 46). 'Tho' dark and savage, ignorant and blind', she says about the blacks, they 'still are men' (460), although More's description suggests they are unthinking men, or therefore implicitly, *matter*. More sees the problem of slavery and oppression not as a matter that requires deep thought about politics, economy and racial relations. Rather, these require feeling and a sentimental response:

There needs no logic sure to make us feel.
The nerve, howe'er untutor'd, can sustain
A sharp, unutterable sense of pain.

(47)

166 Consume and commodify

Calling for a return to Christian virtues, More promises mercy's grace upon the repentant and reformed English:

> On *feeling hearts* she sheds celestial dew,
> And breathes her spirit o'er th' enlighten'd few;
> From soul to soul the spreading influence steals,
> Till every breast the soft contagion *feels*.

> (49, emphasis added)

This reformation is an emotional one, so that a new subjectivity (an affective one) is forged for the Englishman in the crucible of a sentimental relationship with the slave-object. More's poem too calls for a mix of both imaginative sympathy and sensibility.

In Amelia Opie's 'The Negro Boy's Tale' (1795), the black boy wishes to go on the ship to England, for then he would be free. The white girl, Anna, wishes she could help, but her father refuses and the boy, desperately trying to get on the ship, drowns and dies. The poem is structured around the boy's tale, about being snatched from his mother, his subsequent slavery, his dreams of returning to his mother, but it is equally structured around the politics of the white girl's sentiment. Just as Yamba yearns to return to her 'spouse' in More's poem, Opie's Zambo wishes to return to his mother. The heart of the poem is the boy's plea to the white girl and the white girl's request to her father, that she should be allowed *one* black friend who could, ostensibly, be the object of her charity:

> 'I know', she cried, 'I cannot free
> The numerous slaves that round me pine;
> But one poor negro's friend to be,
> Might (blessed chance!), might now be mine'.

> (Wu 1997: 357)

What Anna seeks is not only redemption of Zambo but of herself, the chance to be his friend. It is as much about Zambo as it is about her role as a Christian English girl, bravely battling a cruel system (that she is alone in voicing support for Zambo, in the teeth of patriarchy – she is arguing with her father – and a system is significant).

Wordsworth's poem on the 'mad mother' (titled 'Her Eyes Are Wild', included under 'Poems Founded on the Affections' in the Hutchinson-Selincourt edition of the *Poetical Works*) is narrated from the point of view of the mother. The poem is in the form of the mother's consoling words to her child about the two of them being abandoned by the father. The mother, described as possessing 'coal-black hair' in the second line of the poem, is someone who has come 'far from over the main'. She later asks a rhetorical question: 'but thou will love with me in love,/and what if my poor cheek be brown?' Wordsworth also emphasizes that she speaks in the 'English tongue'. Together these accounts seem to suggest that the mother is an African. With Wordsworth focusing almost entirely on the mother's sentiments towards the child a throwaway line offers a puzzle: 'to thee I know too much I owe;/I cannot work thee any woe'. But the mother is also alarmed that the child has certain 'wicked looks' that she says 'never, never came from me' (Wordsworth 1969: 115). Is this a suggestion that it is the progeny of a white man who is a slave owner? Critics like Debbie Lee (2002) have proposed that the mother is speaking after she has killed or is on the verge of killing her child so that there will be no enslavement for the baby (200). Sentimentalizing the mother's story Wordsworth also foregrounds the horrific modes slaves were willing to use to escape enslavement. Lee proposes a connection between Wordsworth's 'mad mother' of the poem 'Her Eyes Are Wild' and Elizabeth Barrett Browning's 'The Runaway Slave at Pilgrim's Point'. Browning's mother complains that her child's face was 'far too white … too white for me'. Then she explains why the complexion troubles her:

> In that single glance I had
> Of my child's face … I tell you all,
> I saw a look that made me mad …
> The master's look, that used to fall
> On my soul like his lash … or worse!
>
> (2014: 68)

Like Wordsworth's mother, Browning's mother also kills her child ('I twisted it round in my shawl'). Lee argues that this 'destructive and despairing mother-infant dyad [is] a stereotype that functioned as the most powerful sentimental campaigning tool in abolitionist literature' (2002: 200). Similar images of despairing mothers and the death of the children of slaves are found in Helen Maria Williams' 'On the Bill which was Passed in England for Regulating the Slave Trade' (1788). Williams writes:

> And woman, she, too weak to bear
> The galling chain, the tainted air,—
> Of mind too feeble to sustain
> The vast, accumulated pain,—
> No more, in desperation wild,
> Shall madly strain her gasping child;
> With all the mother at her soul,
> With eyes where tears have ceas'd to roll,
> Shall catch the livid infant's breath,
> Then sink in agonizing death!
>
> (Wu 1997: 238)

The despairing black slave is at the heart of the rhetoric of objectification here where all we have is the feeling individual, no more and no less.

William Cowper, having referred to the 'cargoes of despair' – thus constructing the Middle Passage almost entirely in affective terms – offers his first description of the slave (in 'Charity'):

168 Consume and commodify

> The sable warrior, frantic with regret
> Of her he loves, and never can forget,
> Loses in tears the far-receding shore.

Cowper's advice to the slaves is interesting in itself:

> Bid suffer it a while, and kiss the rod,
> Wait for the dawning of a brighter day,
> And snap the chain the moment when you may.
> Nature imprints upon whate'er we see,
> That has a heart and life in it, Be free!
> The beasts are charter'd—neither age nor force
> Can quell the love of freedom in a horse:
> He breaks the cord that held him at the rack;
> And, conscious of an unencumber'd back,
> Snuffs up the morning air, forgets the rein;
> Loose fly his forelock and his ample mane;
> Responsive to the distant neigh, he neighs;
> Nor stops, till, overleaping all delays,
> He finds the pasture where his fellows graze.
> (http://quod.lib.umich.edu/e/ecco/004792651.0001.000/1:8?rgn
> =div1;view=fulltext)

David Brion Davis detects in these lines 'an artful blend of British primitivism and natural rights philosophy' (1999: 370). The account is an excellent example of the rhetoric of objectification for its portrait of the slave as an animal. The horse straining at the reins might represent for Cowper the urge for freedom, but the animalizing of the slave in the analogy establishes an easy equivalence between the slave and the animal. Demonstrating raw physical power both the animal and the black slave can only fight in purely physical terms the restrictions placed on them. It also recalls the older stereotyping of the black man as animal. The savagery implicit in the Cowper account, while ostensibly for purposes of abolitionist rhetoric, partakes of the analogy and metaphor of an entire discourse of colonialism and slavery in its account of the non-Europeans.

Robert Burns' 'The Slave's Lament' (1792) uses as its refrain, the phrase, 'And alas! I am weary, weary O!' (1971: 515). Thomas Day and John Bicknell's 'The Dying Negro' (which went into its third edition by 1775) portrays the black man's grief as he prepares to shoot himself in order to avert a voyage to slavery in America. Ann Yearsley's 'A Poem on the Inhumanity of the Slave Trade' (1788) also constructs a family for the slave-object so as to suggest a recognizably human character even among native Americans (called simply 'Indians' in the poem). Yearsley in her prefatory letter addressed to Rev Frederick, Earl of Bristol, calls for 'Ideas of Justice and Humanity [that] are not confined to *one* Race of Men' (emphasis in original). Starting her story of the 'Indian Luco' Yearsley writes, 'Of his too humble home, where he had left/His mourning father', and his Incilanda, Luco curses the English slave traders:

Curse
On him who from a bending parent steals
His dear support of age, his darling child;
Perhaps a son, or a *more tender* daughter,
Who might have clos'd his eyelids, as the spark
Of life gently retired.

(Wu 1997: 159)

Yearsley, like the other abolitionist poets of her age, deplores the ready equation between gold and human lives when she describes the glee on the Englishman's face after concluding a successful transaction:

see what horrid joy
Lights up his moody features, while he grasps
The wish'd-for gold, purchase of human blood!

(160)

Numerous references to 'tears' and 'woe', sorrow, 'pangs' reinforce the sentimental politics of abolition in which the Indian/black become objects of pity. Dramatizing Luco's disappearance Yearsley focuses on the emotional trauma of the family left behind. She also paints a portrait of the Indian family as close-knit. She does this by speaking of Luco's courtship of and marriage with Incilanda:

For Incilanda, Luco rang'd the wild,
Holding her image to his panting heart;
For her he strain'd the bow, for her he stript
The bird of beauteous plumage; happy hour,
When with these guiltless trophies he adorn'd
The brow of her he lov'd. Her gentle breast
With gratitude was fill'd, nor knew she aught
Of language strong enough to paint her soul,
Or ease the great emotion; whilst her eye
Pursued the gen'rous Luco to the field,
And glow'd with rapture at his wish'd return.

(161)

Then Yearsley, like others, calls for a new subjectivity among the English: a feeling subjectivity.

Why Luco was belov'd: then *wilt thou feel,*
Thou selfish Christian, for thy private woe,
Yet cause such pangs to him that is a father?

(160, emphasis added)

170 Consume and commodify

Throughout the poem Yearsley addresses the absence of feeling among the English, their cold commerce that results in such suffering among people who are essentially, in her depiction, emotional beings. And, like other similar portraits of the willing slave/labourer, Yearsley gives us the following image:

> He strives to please,
> Nor once complains, but greatly smothers grief.
> His hands are blister'd, and his feet are worn,
> Till ev'ry stroke dealt by his mattock gives
> Keen agony to life; while from his breast
> The sigh arises, burthen'd with the name
> Of Incilanda. Time inures the youth,
> His limbs grow nervous, strain'd by willing toil;
> And resignation, or a calm despair,
> (Most useful either) lulls him to repose.
>
> (163)

The Indian, like the black slave, is docile, emotional *matter*, no more:

> In piteous imag'ry, his aged father,
> His poor fond mother, and his faithful maid:
> The mental group in wildest motion set
> Fruitless imagination; fury, grief,
> Alternate shame, the sense of insult, all
> Conspire to aid the inward storm; yet words
> Were no relief, he stood in silent woe.
>
> (163)

Yearsley offers an inventory of emotions here, and thus calls attention to the sentimental native. Towards the end of the poem Yearsley calls for a different sentimental response to the conditions of West Indian trade:

> Thy softest emanations, pity, grief,
> Lively emotion, sudden joy, and pangs,
> Too deep for language, are thy own: then rise,
> Thou gentle angel! Spread thy silken wings
> O'er drowsy *man*, breathe in his *soul*, and give
> Her God-like pow'rs thy animating force,
> To banish Inhumanity.
>
> (166–7)

Then, says Yearsley, the Englishman

> shall melt,
> Yea, by thy sympathy unseen, shall feel

Another's pang: for the lamenting maid
His heart shall heave a sigh; with the old slave
(Whose head is bent with sorrow).

(167)

The 1805 poem 'The Poor Negro Sadi' by Charlotte Dacre (Charlotte Byrne née King) exemplifies the argument I have been proposing about the self-fashioning of the English as the compassionate subject in relation to the vulnerable victim slave object. The poem deals with the sufferings of a black man who has been 'torn like a wretch from his innocent dwelling' and was forced to leave his wife and cosy domesticity. Right from the title with its 'poor negro', Byrne presents us with not just the black individual but an abject one. Sadi escapes and, saved by a ship, arrives in Britain. The heart of the poem's sentimental politics is the English existence of the black man. Sadi is at the mercy of the nation that would be the land of the free (by law, a slave landing on the shores of Britain would be free from the moment of landing):

Oh, Britons! So fam'd in the annals of glory,
The poor negro Sadi is cast on your plains—
Oh, Britons! If just be your fame or your glory,
The poor negro Sadi shall bless your domains.

(Wu 1997: 366)

It is here, however, that Sadi discovers his complete and total abjection.

As yet see he wanders forlorn and in sadness,
By many scarce seen, and unpitied by all;
No glance yet his sunk heart has flutter'd with gladness,
Nor voice sympathetic on him seem'd to call.
In vain, wretched negro! Thou lookest around thee—
In vain, wretched negro! So lowly dost bend;
Tho' a thousand cold faces for ever surround thee,
Among them not one is, poor Sadi, thy friend.
Three nights and three days had he wander'd despairing.
No food nor no shelter the victim had found;
The pangs of keen hunger his bosom were tearing,
When, o'erpower'd with torture, he sunk on the ground.
He clasp'd his thin hands, now no longer imploring
The succour which all had so basely denied,
In hopeless submission had finish'd deploring
The suff'rings he felt must so shortly subside.

(366)

He wanders the streets of the English city, cold and starving. In a scene that would bring to mind postcolonial theory's attention to the 'invisibility' of blackness, Sadi

172 Consume and commodify

is ignored by the English: 'by many scarce seen' (366). Surrounded by 'cold faces' (366), he finds no friend and no pity (recalling Yearsley's description of the slave owner as a 'remorseless Christian' in 'A Poem on the Inhumanity of the Slave Trade'). Eventually lying down to die in a doorway he is thrown out from the minimal shelter he finds. Sadi dies, 'unaided, alone' (367). Despite his tone of prayer and agony being 'unchristian' (367), says Dacre, they are 'pure' (367). Byrne's poem criticizes the English for not offering compassion to Sadi. The abject black man in the land of the free dies alone and friendless. The sentimentalization of the politics of emancipation that is visible in the poem renders the black body abject but 'pure', not angry or rebellious but quiet and vulnerable. It is in the construction of the vulnerable and *docile* black body that Byrne presents the object for compassion. We do not see blacks, slaves or Indians making political pleas or arguments in these abolitionist poems. In almost every case they appeal, emotionally, to the sentiment of the English for better treatment or the chance to reunite with their families. The docile, 'simplistic mentalities' that Moira Ferguson identifies in some poems and which I have traced in numerous poems above is a *reduction* of the black body, I suggest, to just matter – a portrait that (1) alleviates the anxiety of possible political subjectivity among them and (2) sentimentalizes the relationship between the rational, enlightened, Christian and politically informed English and the emotional, unthinking primitive Other.

When critiquing the slave trade what these poets do is to elide the question of political economy or morality and focus almost entirely on the sentiments that the British slave owners and plantation owners need to have. Occluding the economic foundations of slavery the poets call not for equality but charity, not for freedom of the slaves but benevolent paternalism, as we shall see in the last chapter. The subject–object relation of white man–black man needs to be recast, suggest the poems, as an appropriately sentimental relationship of protective benevolence. This enables a construction of the sentimental-but-political British subject when s/he encounters and engages with the purely sentimental indigenous object. The rhetoric of commodification then is the narrativization of this new subject–object relationship that enables the self-fashioning of the English as benevolent in connection with the vulnerable and docile slave-object/racial Other.

**

What emerges from these studies, although selective, is that England's engagement with the world and the globality of its literature relied heavily upon the import, circulation, assimilation and signification of material objects. Saree Makdisi reading Byron's *Childe Harold's Pilgrimage* has argued that:

> Byron narrates a voyage to two different and mutually-exclusive spatial-temporal constructs ... first, the Levant as the cultural and historical ancestor of Europe; and second, the Levant as the space and territory of the Oriental other ... the first implies the re-possession and the appropriation of the space

of the Levant for a Eurocentric vision of history, in which Europeans claim to assimilate other peoples, cultures, and histories into the history of modernity – a history to be narrated and understood from the standpoint of Europe; while the second implies the coexistence of distinct though related cultures and histories, spaces, and times.

(1998: 127–8)

Makdisi's argument could be tweaked here to suggest that this 'assimilation' that leads to what he calls the theme of a 'universal empire' in the Romantics, and the modernization of England and the world, was to be found at home in the form of assimilated products and people. It did not necessitate a journey: England's modernization and the rise of both capitalist modernity and consumer culture was made possible through the domestic circulation and assimilation of products from the Other. Objects from foreign shores, bodies cast as objects and objects resignified in particular ways – profit-generating, sympathy-eliciting, anxiety-inducing – meant that the English constantly developed their subjectivity in *relationships* with these objects. Globality was therefore, at least partly, a *globality of objects* that enabled particular forms of self-fashioning of the English.

Notes

1 In Krista Lysack's reading of how 'capital sought to incite women's participation in Empire, as it attempted to inscribe women within its imperial project through the construction of women as consumers of oriental goods' (2005: 143) we can see how Laura's shopping expedition could also include the purchase of commodities whose provenance lie outside the British Isles but which have become commonplace goods for purchase by all.
2 In fact the demand for tea was so high by the 1780s that vast quantities were smuggled into Britain, with some accounts computing the quantity at 7,500,000 pounds a year, and the other, between 4,000,000 and 6,000,000 pounds (Mui and Mui 1968: 44).
3 'Habit' here is clearly aligned with Pierre Bourdieu's formulation of the *habitus*, where embodied predispositions of individuals incorporate social conditions. *Habitus*, which informs individual behaviour, is thus essential to the maintenance or furthering of one's social position through repetition.
4 Maxine Berg notes that tea-drinking was initially also a domestic event by the mid-eighteenth century, but later even the labouring and working classes began consuming it as a form of polite behaviour. More interesting, Berg notes that tea-drinking became a public ritual in tea- and coffee-houses (2007: 230).
5 It was not only England that had a sustained interest in China and Chinese products. East Asia and China were central to *Europe's* transpacific imaginings. See Markley (2006) and Christine Lee (2012).
6 An antecedent for such a process of making an alien out of a European would be the character of Tamora in Shakespeare's *Titus Andronicus*. Tamora is a European who has been rendered alien and rechristened Semiramis. I am grateful to Anna Kurian for this reference.
7 John Whale's reading of the Hazlitt essay argues that:

> Hazlitt's sense of cultural difference serves to differentiate the Brahmans from the jugglers in order to support the self-centred nature of the mechanical … the jugglers are in danger of losing their Indian identity. In so far as they are endorsed by

174 Consume and commodify

> Hazlitt's sense of the mechanical, which is rooted in the material world, they forfeit their cultural particularity. Defined as mechanical, the jugglers also lose the imprint of identity and the possibility of historical self-consciousness.
>
> (2005: 215)

By focusing on the purely mechanical, in other words, Hazlitt is able to erase the specificity of their identity: as Hindu.

8 Artisans, described as 'rude mechanicals' in Shakespeare's *A Midsummer Night's Dream*, were treated as akin to 'matter', innately formless (Parker 1996: 43–4).

9 See D.B. Davis, *The Problem of Slavery in Western Culture* (1966).

10 One of the key texts in which labour is first foregrounded is Milton's *Paradise Lost* (1667), as Maureen Quilligan has argued and which I rely on here. Satan seeks to make an entire population his slaves (Book IV, 381–92). Adam and Eve are alert to the fact that in order to utilize the fertility of the garden they need more 'hands' (a synecdoche for labour, Book IV, 623–9). Through the rest of the poem Adam constantly emphasizes the quality and nature of their labour, notes Quilligan.

11 There was also a certain anxiety about possible white slavery in novels like Penelope Aubin's *The Noble Slaves* (1722).

12 Grainger's advice to planters on keeping slaves happy proceeded from white insecurity around slave behaviour. There were, as studies show, increasing attempts to restrict slave activity. In a study of the legal system in Jamaica in the mid-eighteenth century Diana Paton shows how 'from drumming, to hunting, to gathering after dark' were criminalized (2001: 224). Slave violence was seen as a threat to the social order of the plantation and the colony itself and hence more severe punishment was meted out for every presumed misdemeanour.

13 Elizabeth Kim reading this passage argues that the benevolent paternalism Edgeworth offers as 'an antidote to [the] strained master-slave relationship' also 'celebrates the colonialist values of hard work and individualist responsibility for the land' (2003: 113). The labouring body of the black is only raw matter with some emotions and considerable loyalty. The 'party scene' shows minstrel bodies, dancing bodies, serving bodies and labouring bodies in harmony, but no *persons*.

14 Conrad, however, also represents the colonial bodies as degenerating. Kurtz, when Marlow first sees him, looks thus:

> I saw the thin arm extended commandingly, the lower jaw moving, the eyes of that apparition shining darkly far in its bony head that nodded with grotesque jerks. … I could see the cage of his ribs all astir, the bones of his arm waving. It was as though an animated image of death carved out of old ivory had been shaking its hand with menaces at a motionless crowd of men made of dark and glittering bronze.
>
> (1974: 133–4)

M.H. Dutheil de la Rochère notes Conrad's 'description of human beings as lacking human presence and corporeal substance on both sides of the colonial divide'. Rochère adds: 'the characterization of Africans and Europeans alike as disembodied beings inevitably complicates the politics of Conrad's novel, and invites us to reconsider accusations of racism in recent Conrad criticism' (2004: 195).

15 The slave body in such poetry is distinctive from the vulnerable Indian (Native American) body we see in poems of the age – such as Wordsworth's 'Complaint of the Forsaken Indian Woman' or Southey's 'Dirge of the American Widow' – discussed in Chapter 3.

5

DISEASE AND DEGENERATION

The pathologized Other

Within the discourse of globality of the English Romantic writers it is possible to discern a major concern over the arrival of migrants in England. In 'The Emigrant Mother' (1802) Wordsworth sketches the sorrows of a French Lady separated from her child:

> a Lady driven from France did dwell;
> The big and lesser griefs with which she mourned,
> In friendship she to me would often tell.
> This Lady, dwelling upon British ground,
> Where she was childless.
>
> (Wordsworth 1969: 95)

Similarly, in 'Emigrant French Clergy' (1827) Wordsworth paints England as a refuge for 'good' emigrants. He writes:

> More welcome to no land
> The fugitives than to the British strand,
>
> —
>
> while the moral tempest roars
> Throughout the Country they have left, our shores
> Give to their Faith a fearless resting-place.
>
> (1969: 353)

In another poem, 'September 1, 1802', Wordsworth's headnote would denounce the 'capricious acts of tyranny' by which France 'chas[ed]' the blacks out of the country:

> We had a female Passenger who came
> From Calais with us, spotless in array,

176 Disease and degeneration

> A white-robed Negro, like a lady gay,
> Yet downcast as a woman fearing blame;
> Meek, destitute, as seemed, of hope or aim
> She sate, from notice turning not away,
> But on all proffered intercourse did lay
> A weight of languid speech, or to the same
> No sign of answer made by word or face:
> Yet still her eyes retained their tropic fire,
> That, burning independent of the mind,
> Joined with the lustre of her rich attire
> To mock the Outcast – O ye Heavens, be kind!
> And feel, thou Earth, for this afflicted Race.

(1969: 243)

Wordsworth sees England as a space of refuge to which victims of oppression turn. Charlotte Smith in *The Emigrants* (1791) also depicts England as a space of refuge when she speaks of the traumatized migrants from France:

> Men
> Banish'd for ever and for conscience sake
> From their distracted Country, whence the name
> Of Freedom misapplied, and much abus'd
> By lawless Anarchy, has driven them far
> To wander.

(1793: 7–8, http://digital.lib.ucdavis.edu/projects/bwrp/
Works/SmitCEmigr.htm)

Smith refers to them as 'Poor wand'ring wretches' and as 'ill-starr'd wanderers', most 'dwelling on [what they have] lost'. The speaker hears from across the English Channel 'the deep groans/of martyr'd Saints and suffering Royalty'.[1] It is the 'emigrant' theme, it is possible to argue, that enables Wordsworth and Smith to reflect on *England's* own contexts in what could be an additional layer to the transnational theme. Constructing the English nation as a bastion of freedom and embracing many faiths, welcoming of emigrants, Wordsworth and Smith project an English *moral identity* when taken in conjunction with its role in accommodating difference in the form of emigrants and victims of oppression. The French migration in the wake of the Revolution, in other words, serves as a key moment in the English self-fashioning of a moral, cultural and socio-political identity as a nation of freedoms.

However, this thematic of self-fashioning of English identity as accommodating and assimilatory was not the dominant form of depicting the migrants. The arrival of the migrant, in the form of commodities, people or, as we shall see, pathogens, from the Other space frequently induced panic and anxiety – and this was a dominant theme in England's pathologized discourse of globality. Difference was

Disease and degeneration **177**

the subject of a pathogenic discourse, especially when this difference *entered* the British home, family, street and public space, very often in the form of the inhuman, the monstrous, the addictive or, in a very special thematic, in the form of the corrupted, dehumanized Englishman himself. The Other space was now, one could say, 'at home' in England.

The anxiety over the Other's space where the English either become dehumanized or become the cause of their subjects' dehumanization that climaxes with Joseph Conrad's Kurtz in *Heart of Darkness* has a long genealogy. It begins to make its appearance as early as the sixteenth century with fears over the deculturation – the loss of their 'native' culture when they took to the cultures of their Asian or African location – of the Englishmen. English soldiers and traders into the Mediterranean were, when captured, converted to Islam. In other cases they went willingly and 'turned Turk'. Daniel Vitkus writes:

> English Protestants, who had no coreligionists in the region except for merchants and factors, engaged in a kind of cultural and commercial adaptivity that was not a religious conversion, but it was a milder form of 'turning Turk.' Something akin to what was later called 'going native,' this kind of hybridity was necessary to maintain the flow of profits back to investors in England, and so a whole new class of people emerged who adopted Turkish or Moorish ways in order to do business.
>
> (2007: 80)

The renegado and the Christian-turned-Turk – incidentally, titles of two popular plays of the period – were criticized for their abandonment of their culture in a foreign land (Vitkus 2007). Earlier, in Chapter 3, we saw instances where European women masqueraded as Turks for their own benefit, again producing a discrepant geography where English/European identity was subverted.

The theme of the Englishman's corruption in the colonies was not, it must be noted, only about Africa or Asia. Ben Jonson's plays (for example *Eastward Ho!* and the rewriting of *Bartholomew Fair* as *The New Inn*) often depicted the degeneration of the white man in Virginia. On the one hand, in Rebecca Bach's words, the 'Virginia Company attempted to promote [a certain English identity] between a virtuous London that would support the colonial endeavor and a pure Virginia colony that would civilize the Indians around it', but on the other 'the population of the city posited an equivalence between London's underworld inhabitants and the dangerous presences in the colonies – both Indians and "corrupted" Englishmen' (1997: 289). In *Bartholomew Fair*, therefore, Wasp tells Bartholomew Cokes that his tenants are 'civil savages that will part with their children for rattles, pipes and knives' (Jonson 1968: 79). While this dimension of self-fashioning in a transnational frame is certainly visible in the literary writings of the 1780s–1830s period the dominant register is of anxiety at migration. Migrations from all over the world are represented in many literary texts as sources of anxiety and even 'revulsion' (Mary Shelley's term in *The Last Man*), and result in a *thematic of invasion*, the subject of

178 Disease and degeneration

the present chapter. This thematic is of transnational terror, the terror's aetiology being England's multiple and varied international linkages, with the literature seeking to fashion an English identity around the idea of a 'threatened' nation/ culture.

The arrival of 'savages' in England – first recorded visits date to 1501 when three men from Newfoundland were brought by Bristol fishermen into the country – was not, it must be noted, seen as a source of threat. As Kate Fullagar (2008) points out, at least until the early seventeenth century, 'this savagery refracted contemporary British civilization – specifically, how it shed light on Britain's transition to a commercial economy, reliant on expansion into overseas markets, and its attendant creation of a sophisticated public sphere' (213). So commentators like Addison and Steele pointed to the manners and behaviour of the English in the age of commercial expansion by contrasting these with the 'savages'.

In Shakespeare's *The Comedy of Errors* Egeon speaks of his profession and his home:

> In Syracusa was I born, and wed
> Unto a woman, happy but for me,
> And by me, had not our hap been bad.
> With her I lived in joy; our wealth increased
> By prosperous voyages I often made
> To Epidamium, till my factor's death
> And the great care of goods at random left
> Drew me from kind embracements of my spouse.
>
> (I.1, ll. 36–43)

While Egeon's trafficking in goods across the world brings him material prosperity it seems to have produced havoc in his domestic domain, where he is 'drawn' (away) from his spouse. Shakespeare here seems to direct our attention to the risks involved in transnational mercantile engagements – which alter the peace and quiet domesticity of the home. Transnational commerce leads to domestic chaos, what we gain as a network of connections costs us in terms of disconnects in the family.

Thomas de Quincey in *Confessions of an English Opium Eater* (1821) writes:

> Under the connecting feeling of tropical heat and vertical sun-lights, I brought together all creatures, birds, beasts, reptiles, all trees and plants, usages and appearances, that are found in all tropical regions, and assembled them together in China or Indostan. From kindred feelings, I soon brought Egypt and all her gods under the same law. I was stared at, hooted at, grinned at, chattered at, by monkeys, by paroquets, by cockatoos. I ran into pagodas: and was fixed, for centuries, at the summit, or in secret rooms; I was the idol; I was the priest; I was worshipped; I was sacrificed. I fled from the wrath of Brama through all the forests of Asia: Vishnu hated me, Seeva laid wait for me. I came suddenly upon Isis and Osiris: I had done a deed, they said,

which the ibis and the crocodile trembled at. I was buried, for a thousand years, in stone coffins, with mummies and sphynxes, in narrow chambers at the heart of eternal pyramids. I was kissed with cancerous kisses, by crocodiles; and laid, confounded with unutterable slimy things, amongst reeds and Nilotic mud.

(1985: 73)

De Quincey here describes the heterogeneous collection of objects he gathers in his vision under the influence of the narcotic opium. The vision shows the European's notional control of knowledge being taken away, eroded by 'objects' (animals and birds) he thought he controlled by putting them in a museum. As Sanjay Krishnan notes, the animals mock him, and soon cause him to discover the limits of his ability to control them. The European's epistemological and even ontological certainty breaks down when faced with the non-European, non-human Other. In his trafficking with global creatures, the Englishman loses a sense of self (Krishnan 2006).[2] In both cases the Englishman attributes the *loss* of self, of identity and attachments, domesticity and family, to his links with foreign products, places and actions, whether it is an involvement in foreign trade in the case of Egeon or the consumption of opium in the case of de Quincey. Then, later, English womanhood would be threatened by invasion of (the East European) Dracula. Kipling, Conrad and others express in their writings anxieties over the Englishman 'going native' in the colony. England collapses due to pathogenic, ideational, demographic and cultural *invasions*. In other words, pathologizing and projecting the fears of dissolution onto a racial–cultural Other, whether out there or at home, was a key form of England's engagement with the globe in every age.[3]

An entire cultural imaginary of the porosity of one's bodily and geopolitical borders, and a concomitant vulnerability of its internal integrity – biological, psychological, cultural – was made possible through the recognition and discursive constructions in literary and other texts of the unavoidable negative, or pathogenic, consequences of international travel and trade. *Stigmatizing the foreign body – whether commodity or human – in literature as a biological, moral or cultural pathogen has been an expression, this chapter proposes, of the anxieties over England's transnational identity-making processes* right from the Early Modern period. That is, England's mercantile, soldierly, political, social linkages and their *deleterious* effects were a key element in the process of defining Englishness. The chapter further demonstrates how the theme of corruption was also embodied in the depiction of the Englishman/woman him/herself *becoming 'foreign'* to England and Englishness. The chapter therefore examines the pathologizing discourses that construct an English identity as being under threat. The eroded or eroding English identity, whether due to invasion or corrupted Englishness, is linked discursively to the threatening presence of and interaction with a racial–cultural Other. The racial–cultural Other is the origin, or a conduit, of a *moral contagion*, whether in the form of cultural practices like tea-drinking or religious conversion, both of which 'corrupt' national character. The moral contagion is the foundational trope of all cultural anxieties resulting from transnational encounters.

180 Disease and degeneration

Foreign matter/s

In an earlier chapter we noted how a vocabulary of foreign/imported things and certain kinds of objectification rhetoric intertwines commodities and objects into the lives and homes of Englishmen/women, and inserts other lives – such as that of slaves – as objects deserving of pity and compassionate treatment and erases the possibility of political subjectivity among other races. Thus foreign objects and people-as-objects were woven as narrative elaborations into the lives of English characters, and their (i.e. English) identities were often hinged on this set of engagements with foreign objects. Yet, such engagements with foreign objects did not only take the form of consumption or compassionate activism (exemplified by the anti-abolitionist writings of the late eighteenth century) – very often they also took the form of an anxious discourse of the Other as a threat.

Borders were crossed by commodities, people, ideas and, as the nineteenth century finally acknowledged, pathogenic creatures. Their entry into the host 'body' as foreign objects altered the equilibrium of the host, whether in terms of revolutionary ideas or degenerative disease. Continuing to explore in a different key the English concerns with foreign objects, I examine in this section the *material* threats as documented in English literature, where the 'material' could range from sugar and tobacco to bacteria. The transition of Oriental, New World and other goods from luxury to mass consumption during the seventeenth century meant, as I have suggested above, the incorporation of these products into English everyday life across classes. What used to be the purview of elite consumption slowly became items in working-class life as well, and this, I suggest, is the source of the anxiety about Other-objects that we can discern as a parallel tradition in the vocabulary of things in English writings. Material threats as seen in these writings were not only about the undermining of English economy, production and consumption, they were also about the decadence, corruption and degradation of English *qualities* or character. An entire variety of foreign objects has, at some point or other, induced anxieties in England regarding their corrupting influence. In what follows I examine a few of these Other-objects as represented in literary texts.[4]

Philip Massinger in 'London's Lamentable Estate' was one of the earliest to speak of England's deplorable transition to immoral luxury through conspicuous consumption:

> From all parts of the world, thou hadst supplie
> Of what was wanting to thy luxurie:
> Barbary, Sugars: Zant, Oile: tapestrie
> T'adorne thy prowd walls, Brabant made for Thee:
> Now were the Indies slowe to feed thy sence
> With cassia, mirrhe (farr'fetch'd with deere expence):
> The sea, her pearle: and many a boystrous knock
> Compelled the sparckling diamond, from the Rock,

> To deck thy daughters: in a word th'adst all
> That could in compasse of thy wishes fall.
> But theis great guifts (abus'd) first bredd in thee
> A stupid sloth, and dull securitie
> The parent of destruction.
>
> (2012: 399–400)

Massinger makes it clear that the global trade that might have benefited the economy of England had also induced corruption. In what is surely an indictment of the first stage of British mercantile expansion and trade Massinger faults not the trade per se but the weakness of English character that had allowed the love of luxury to 'dull' their security and engineer destruction through excessive consumption. Massinger's inventory of foreign objects ranges from food to décor and jewellery, thus suggesting that a variety of products was responsible. Massinger transforms the wonder of the world's variety seen in the travelogues of the age (Greenblatt 1992, Sell 2006, Nayar 2008) into an *anxiety* over this same material variety. Instead of the *hortus conclusus* of a perfect garden in which many varieties of plants are arranged in harmonious order, Massinger shows the prodigious variety as multiplying England's problems.

If Massinger was offering an entire catalogue of Other-objects that threatened to corrupt England, one particular product came in for sustained attention for its ability to instil addiction: tobacco. John Goodman's survey (1993) documents the cultures of tobacco, and the literature of Early Modern England seems to suggest a culture of anxiety around this particular foreign object.[5] In this connection, James I's *A Counter-blaste to Tobacco* (1604) offers us a prototype of what I have called material anxieties. James I in his address to the Reader justifies his stance by declaring that the body-politic, like the body, was prone to diseases and as the physician of the nation it was his duty to cure the sickness. And, he writes, 'surely in my opinion, there cannot be a more base, and yet hurtfull, corruption in a Countrey, then is the vile use (or other abuse) of taking Tobacco in this Kingdome'. James argues that things with godly, necessary or honourable grounds can be imported into England, but tobacco originates in a land of 'base corruption and barbarity' (the American land) and was invented by 'barbarous Indians' as an antidote to filthy diseases they in particular suffered from such as the 'pox' (Jeffrey Knapp points out that this was a standard trope in the Early Modern narratives about savages: that they 'always hold the wrong thing in "precious estimation" – not gold, for instance, but trifles', 1988: 35).[6] James then uses the Other-object tobacco to speak of different cultures:

> what honour or policy can move us to imitate the barbarous and beastly manners of the wild, godless, and slavish *Indians*, especially in so vile and stinking a custom? Shall wee that disdain to imitate the manners of our neighbour *France* ... and that cannot endure the spirit of the Spaniards (their King being now comparable in largeness of Dominions, to the great

182 Disease and degeneration

> Emperor of *Turkie*) ... shall we, I say, without blushing, abase our selves so far, as to imitate these beastly *Indians*, slaves to the *Spaniards*, refuse to the world, and as yet aliens from the holy Covenant of God? Why doe we not as well imitate them in walking naked as they do? in preferring glasses, feathers, and such toys, to gold and precious stones, as they do? yea why do we not deny God and adore the Devil, as they do?
>
> (unpaginated, http://www.laits.utexas.edu/poltheory
> /james/blaste/blaste.html)

He thus rejects the arguments about tobacco's medicinal benefits and proposes that the English who took to it did so merely because of the novelty (the word occurs four times in this short piece) of this product. To adapt a practice because it is foreign and novel, argues James, is absurd. James warns that tobacco has become a *habit* and an addiction for several English:

> many in this kingdom have had such a continual use of taking this unsavoury smoke, as now they are not able to forbear the same, no more than an old drunkard can abide to be long sober, without falling into an incurable weakness and evil constitution: for their continual custom hath made to them.
>
> (http://www.laits.utexas.edu/poltheory/james/blaste/blaste.html)

It 'disables' the body of the Englishman for himself and the country, and thus causes him to renege on his responsibilities. It is uncivil – and therefore contrary to English manners – to smoke at dining tables, puffing out smoke at each other. Eventually, says James, this would lead to England becoming the subject of contempt among other cultures, 'wondered at by all foreign civil Nations, and by all strangers that come among you, to be scorned and condemned'.

James' treatise dismisses tobacco for being of base origins (i.e. among barbaric foreign nations), addictive, contrary to accepted medical theories, novel and for being a practice that strikes at the root of English civility and manners. An object that disturbs English manners and bodies, his thesis states, cannot be of any value no matter how wondrous its novelty might be. James' rejection of tobacco, born of an anxiety of invasion by foreign products, is cast as a defence therefore of English identity itself. The values or beliefs of the English, he seems to say, are at stake in the consumption of tobacco. Clearly, then, the Other-object is invested with far more than edible or nutritional values. In fact tobacco consumption is linked to the spread of a moral contagion of addiction and is therefore to be condemned, as seen in his rhetoric, not only in biomedical and religious terms but also moral ones.

If James I warned the English public against the loss of Englishness due to the consumption of tobacco, John Donne's elegy (Elegy 11), 'The Bracelet, Upon the Loss of His Mistresses Chain, for which He Made Satisfaction' (1633), argues a case against foreign coins and currency that, according to Donne, damage English economy and habits. Donne makes a comparison between English currency and foreign ones:

Were they but crowns of France, I carèd not,
For most of these their country's natural rot,
I think, possesseth; they come here to us
So pale, so lame, so lean, so ruinous.
And howsoe'er French kings most Christian be,
Their crowns are circumcised most Jewishly.
Or were they Spanish stamps, still travelling,
That are become as Catholic as their king.

(Donne 1975: 108)

Yet these coins circulate, and this induces Donne's anxiety about foreign matter.
Donne claims that people might be persuaded by foreign currency to betray their
own country: 'with foreign gold bribed to betray/Thy country', thus indicating
corruption that arrives in the form of foreign monies – material – that then
undermine English sovereignty. As instances of the ruinous effect of these foreign
bodies Donne writes:

As streams, like veins, run through th' earth's every part,
Visit all countries, and have slily made
Gorgeous France, ruin'd, ragged and decay'd,
Scotland, which knew no state, proud in one day,
And mangled seventeen-headed Belgia.

(1975: 108)

True, as Stephen Deng observes (2009: 268–9), there is in Donne's diatribe an
anxiety about the pernicious economic and political impact of foreign gold and
currency, but what is more significant for our purposes is Donne's focus on the
symbolic value of foreign matter, of the additional significance and cultural realities
he associates with the coins: in particular, of English morality and religion, and thus
how he foregrounds the threat of a moral contagion.

Within the discourse of consumption, exemplified in Donne's poem about foreign currency and gold being absorbed into English usage, several Other-objects
were treated as disruptive of English domesticity. Here we see the resignification of
the Other-object and the rituals of English consumption into something troubling
of English identity. If, as de Grazia *et al.* argue, objects 'can be made to absorb
other evanescent cultural realities' (1996: 9), then these resignifications gesture at
the complicated shifts in gender and class identity in England's society. Foreign
objects, whether in James I's diatribe against tobacco or Donne's against foreign
currency, are not simply material intrusions: they represent a *moral* contagion as
well because they corrupt, through temptation, the vulnerable English citizenry.
Here of course English identity is projected as vulnerable and open to influences,
and malign ones at that. But the point is that English identity's stability (or lack of
it) hinges on the consumption of foreign products and by implication the linkages
with foreign trade. Here the presumed 'realities' of Eastern or non-European

184 Disease and degeneration

cultures are deemed to be embedded in the object which then transmits these (contaminating) realities to England. The moral contagion is coded as the greed, the temptation, the love of luxury and the reinvention of lifestyle made possible by the circulation of foreign commodities, although in several cases authors located the pathogen in England's own character with external aetiologies.[7]

Take for instance Congreve's *The Double Dealer*. In the play Congreve satirizes women who drink tea as the ladies retire to 'tea and scandal, according to their ancient custom'. This suggests that the entire ritual of *women's* tea-drinking and gossip – at least in Congreve's imagination – marked a disruption of quiet, quiescent English domesticity (Kowaleski-Wallace 1994: 132). In Eliza Haywood's *The Female Spectator* she echoes this sentiment that tea might alter the Englishwoman's taste irrevocably and thus ruin the peace of the home. A letter from 'John Careful' in *The Female Spectator* mourns the fact that 'the tea table ... costs more to support than would maintain two children' (quoted in Kowaleski-Wallace 1994: 137). Edward Young, more famous for his *Night Thoughts*, would damn the tea-drinking woman thus: 'For her own breakfast she'll project a scheme, Nor take her tea without a strategem' (*Love of Fame*, Satire vi, 1752: 114). A sustained expression of the anxiety around the female consumer is seen in John Gay's 'To a Lady on Her Passion for Old China' (1725):

> What ecstasies her bosom fire!
> How her eyes languish with desire!
> How blest, how happy should I be,
> Were that fond glance bestow'd on me!
> New doubts and fears within me war:
> What rival's near? a *China* jar.
> *China*'s the passion of her soul;
> A cup, a plate, a dish, a bowl,
> Can kindle wishes in her breast,
> Inflame with joy, or break her rest.
> Some gems collect; some medals prize,
> And view the rust with lover's eyes;
> Some court the stars at midnight hours;
> Some dote on Nature's charms in flowers!
> But ev'ry beauty I can trace
> In *Laura*'s mind, in *Laura*'s face;
> My stars are in this brighter sphere,
> My lily and my rose is here.
> Philosophers more grave than wise
> Hunt science down in Butterflies;
> Or fondly poring on a Spider
> Stretch human contemplation wider;
> *Fossiles* give joy to *Galen*'s soul,
> He digs for knowledge, like a mole;

In shells so learn'd that all agree
No fish that swims knows more than he!
In such pursuits if wisdom lies,
Who, *Laura*, shall thy taste despise?
When I some antique Jar behold,
Or white, or blue, or speck'd with gold,
Vessels so pure and so refin'd,
Appear the types of woman-kind:
Are they not valu'd for their beauty,
Too fair, too fine for houshold duty?
With flowers and gold and azure dy'd,
Of ev'ry house the grace and pride?
How white, how polish'd is their skin,
And valu'd most when only seen!
She who before was highest priz'd,
Is for a crack or flaw despis'd;
I grant they're frail, yet they're so rare,
The treasure cannot cost too dear!
But Man is made of coarser stuff,
And serves convenience well enough;
He's a strong earthen vessel made,
For drudging, labour, toil, and trade;
And when wives lose their other self,
With ease they bear the loss of *Delf*.
Husbands more covetous than sage
Condemn this *China*-buying rage;
They count that woman's prudence little,
Who sets her heart on things so brittle.
But are those wise-men's inclinations
Fixt on more strong, more sure foundations?
If all that's frail we must despise,
No human view or scheme is wise.
Are not Ambition's hopes as weak?
They swell like bubbles, shine and break.
A Courtier's promise is so slight,
'Tis made at noon, and broke at night.
What pleasure's sure? The Miss you keep
Breaks both your fortune and your sleep.
The man who loves a country life,
Breaks all the comforts of his wife;
And if he quit his farm and plough,
His wife in town may break her vow.
Love, *Laura*, love, while youth is warm,
For each new winter breaks a charm;

186 Disease and degeneration

> And woman's not like *China* sold,
> But cheaper grows in growing old;
> Then quickly chuse the prudent part,
> Or else you break a faithful heart.
>
> (1822: 108–10)

The woman, Laura, wastes her attentions, desires and ambitions on mere china, and thereby neglects the man. To invest in 'brittle' substances like chinaware, the poet argues, is to demonstrate a 'little' mind. As the woman continues in her pursuit of china, the poet warns that all this might cause her to defer more important matters, such as love, marriage and domesticity. When the poem concludes Gay argues that like china, age causes increased fragility in women, and so to wait until tomorrow might not be wise. Laura should abandon this foolish quest and settle into domesticity – 'the prudent part' is the part of 'wife' he expects her to play – quickly. Just as James I warned that English civility was at stake with increasing tobacco consumption at dinner tables, Gay forges a link between the woman's love of china and the consequent threat to domesticity.

Even though, as noted above, luxury had lost some of its potency as evil and wicked, anxieties continued to swirl around luxury goods. When John Gay prayed, 'o Britain, chosen Port of trade/May luxury ne'er thy sons invade! ('The Man, the Cat, the Dog and the Fly', Gay 1889), he was worrying about the loss of an austere Englishness to the vice of luxury.

In other cases the increasing circulation of luxury goods from the outposts of the Empire were treated by some commentators as signs of British corruption. In a minor poem, *Tea and Sugar of the Nabob and the Creole* (1792), Timothy Touchstone writes:

> Thus, Britons are procured those eastern wares,
> Your ivory cabinets and your ivory chairs,
> Your silks, your costly gems and baneful tea …
> Which for gain, thousands of Indians bleed,
> And base corruption's ready-growing seed
> Is largely sewn over Britain's famous land
> By an unprincipled, a savage band.
>
> (qtd. in Eaton 2006: 239)

Alexander Pope's *Windsor Forest* also seems to capture this anxiety of invasion by different cultures, peoples and their material objects. Converting the spectacle of cultural encounters into a source of anxiety at multiple fashions, physiognomies and lifestyles, Pope writes:

> The time shall come, when free as seas or wind
> Unbounded *Thames* shall flow for all mankind,
> Whole nations enter with each swelling tyde,

And seas but join the regions they divide;
Earth's distant ends our glory shall behold,
And the new world launch forth to seek the old.
Then ships of uncouth form shall stem the tyde,
And feather'd people croud my wealthy side,
And naked youths and painted chiefs admire
Our speech, our colour, and our strange attire!

(Pope 1963: 209–10)

Reversing the so-called colonial gaze (that postcolonial critics discern in English writings about non-European nations), Pope here speculates upon the English becoming the subject of non-European gazes. The Englishman's attire, their speech and skin colour become the spectacles for the amusement of the rest of the world.

Another dimension to this thematic of English corruption due to exposure to foreign objects might be read into the concerns expressed in numerous texts about English greed for gold and profits. William Cowper in 'Charity' castigates the English for focusing entirely on their profits to the detriment of their human impulses. Hannah More in 'Slavery: A Poem' (1788) writes of how the 'sordid lust of gold their fate controls-/The basest appetite of basest souls' of the English (Wu 1997: 46). In his poem 'Sweet Meat has Sour Sauce, or, the Slave Trader in the Dumps', William Cowper imaged the sugar from the Caribbean, produced through slave labour, as 'blood sugar' (1994: 295–7). The threat trade poses is to (mythic) English virtue and Christian humanity in abolitionist poetry such as this.

Thomas de Quincey of course documents the addictive effects of an Eastern product – opium. Ironically his 'corruption' into an addict occurs not in the East but in Wales. The hybridization of his diet, as Alan Bewell notes, is 'born in the very heart of an English national ideal' (1999: 157) where 'Englishness produces its very opposite; the hybridity implicit in the very idea of an "English opium eater"' (157).

Wilkie Collins' *The Moonstone* revolves around the corruption and disaster that arrives in an English house as a result of the precious stone, whose origins are in India. This is one account of the influence of the stone (I have cited this in Chapter 2): 'here was our quiet English house suddenly invaded by a devilish Indian diamond – bringing after it a conspiracy of living rogues, set loose on us by the vengeance of a dead man'. Originating from the 'forehead of an Indian idol' it has now invaded English domesticity. What makes the stone even more of a problem for English domesticity is that it is not comprehensible, not amenable to English rational processes: it falls outside English epistemic prowess. Here is the first full-fledged account of the diamond:

Lord bless us! It WAS a Diamond! As large, or nearly, as a plover's egg! The light that streamed from it was like the light of the harvest moon. When you looked down into the stone, you looked into a yellow deep that drew your eyes into it so that they saw nothing else. It seemed unfathomable; this jewel,

188 Disease and degeneration

that you could hold between your finger and thumb, seemed unfathomable as the heavens themselves. We set it in the sun, and then shut the light out of the room, and it shone awfully out of the depths of its own brightness, with a moony gleam, in the dark. No wonder Miss Rachel was fascinated: no wonder her cousins screamed. The Diamond laid such a hold on ME that I burst out with as large an 'O' as the Bouncers themselves. The only one of us who kept his senses was Mr. Godfrey. He put an arm round each of his sister's waists, and, looking compassionately backwards and forwards between the Diamond and me, said, 'Carbon Betteredge! Mere carbon, my good friend, after all!'

(1982: 68–9)

The account speaks of the mesmerizing effect of the stone upon the English imagination, emotion and rationality. Godfrey's attempt at bringing it into the ambit of English scientific rationality – 'mere carbon' – is an attempt to assert English control over the 'devilish' Other-object. In an astute reading Ashish Roy notes how the entire English household needs to place the stone under constant surveillance. The stone, having been brought there by English travellers, is now the object of careful scrutiny and constant investigation. It marks, in Roy's words, an 'apprehension of the primitive' within a 'more modern system of control' (1993: 661). Thus Rachel Verrinder wonders if she should 'put the Indian diamond in the Indian cabinet, for the purpose of permitting two beautiful native productions to admire each other' (1982: 85). This suggests not just the *witnessing* of the two Indian curios – the cabinet and the diamond – but also organizes a common narrative that apprehends them within English domesticity and 'cabinet culture' preliminary to an inquiry into their stories. The stone is of course a spectacle, a curio for exhibition, but at the same time represents an 'unfathomable' (Collins' term, in the above passage) thing that might just *escape* comprehension. Yet the attempt of the English household seems to be to domesticate it, display it as a family heirloom or exhibition but, in all cases, domesticate it. If the domestic is, as noted at the beginning, exclusive of the foreign as Collins' text seems to suggest, I believe that the foreign has come to reside, worryingly, at the heart of the domestic.

As should be clear from the above discussion, material objects, while desired, profitable and status-determining, were also treated in some quarters as endangering English domesticity, feminine virtues, health and moral character by inducing addiction and even greed. The imported material object corrupts, corrupts absolutely.

Foreign bodies

Other forms of invasion also figure in English literature's sustained engagement with racial-cultural Others. In many cases this Other is an unnameable, amorphous 'thing'. Its ontological category might be uncertain, but its palpable effect is frightening.

Material culture, as noted above, originating elsewhere is seen in English literature as constituting a threat to the moral, social and psychological identity of the English. The foreign is the one that, through absorption, disrupts. While in the above cases there is a clear material object to be pathologized, in other cases a rhetoric of objectification transforms pathogens, humans and organic identity into unknowable but palpably threatening, if unnameable, *things*.

Unnameable things

How does one name a disquiet, an uncertain anxiety or an inexplicable fear, around a *figure, even the figure of an object*? If the construction of the slave-object/racial Other as an irrational vulnerable thing within a rhetoric of objectification enabled the simultaneous self-fashioning of the English as benevolent, a second mode within this rhetoric demonstrates a different form of engagement with the Other. While it continues the thematics of racial and cultural anxiety around Other-objects that I have already examined, the rhetoric also on occasion might objectify that which cannot be named or even identified as the foreign or the outside.

In Chapter 2 I examined tropes of the social and cultural monstrous wherein fantastic geographies in English literature demarcated and characterized new lands and fantastic ethnographies of cannibals and monsters. However, there is in English literature a tradition of identifying the unclassifiable Other as not just a cannibal or a monster but as something unnameable, whose abilities and properties seem to escape (Western) explanations and therefore comprehension. More importantly this Other is not out there like a monster patrolling the borders and peripheries of the known world: the Other is one that is at least partly with(in) us. As Bill Brown tells us, we need to confront the 'indeterminate ontology where things seem slightly human and humans seem slightly thing-like' (2003: 13). There is indeed an indeterminate ontology of *different* things in English literature.

Take the famous case of *The Tempest* in which Caliban is addressed as: 'this thing of darkness'. Immediately following this objectifying rhetoric is the odd possessive and proprietary phrase: 'I acknowledge mine'. What exactly is the thing being possessed here? What does possessing and therefore a relationship with such a thing involve? The possession of some-thing Caliban shifts it from the outside and the periphery into the life of the European, and yet maintains a peculiar outsider identity within the relationship.

Victor Frankenstein christens the being he creates as just the 'creature' before eventually terming it a monster. From elsewhere is an account of the arrival of a child in an English household:

> We crowded round, and over Miss Cathy's head I had a peep at a dirty, ragged, black-haired child; big enough both to walk and talk: indeed, its face looked older than Catherine's; yet when it was set on its feet, it only stared round, and repeated over and over again some gibberish that nobody could

190 Disease and degeneration

> understand. I was frightened, and Mrs. Earnshaw was ready to fling it out of doors: she did fly up, asking how he could fashion to bring that gipsy brat into the house, when they had their own bairns to feed and fend for? What he meant to do with it, and whether he were mad? ... Not a soul knew to whom it belonged, he said; and his money and time being both limited, he thought it better to take it home with him at once, than run into vain expenses there: because he was determined he would not leave it as he found it. Well, the conclusion was, that my mistress grumbled herself calm; and Mr. Earnshaw told me to wash it, and give it clean things, and let it sleep with the children.
>
> (36–7)

The repeated use of 'it' in the description dehumanizes the child, who will eventually become Heathcliff (*Wuthering Heights*, 1847).

In each of these cases we can discern a concern with something terrifyingly unnameable. This unnameable being that is at once with us and outside and inside ('mine', a child among other children in the family and a being created by a scientist) is a Thing. Studying the role of the Thing in Gothic fiction Gary Farnell proposes a definition:

> that amorphous, chaotic, meaningless physical level beyond all reference that both resists and provokes symbolisation ... it may be at once inside and outside one's home, one's family, or one's self ... Its extimacy is what gives rise to our ambivalent sense of pleasure and horror, or beauty and disgust, at the prospect of an encounter with the unnameable Thing ... It is what must *not* happen and must never even be mentioned, though it must often be implied in a ghostly way, in order for what *does* happen to take place.
>
> (2009: 113–14)

It is a taboo that is never mentioned (hence outside) but at the same haunts the imagination, action and events (hence inside) as a 'foundation' (Farnell's term). Related to this Thing in Gothic fiction is the uncanny. Nicholas Royle proposes that the 'foreign' is integral to the uncanny, and elicits horror for being at once inside and familiar and external and unfamiliar (2003: 12).

I propose that the rhetoric of objectification foregrounds (1) this unnameable absence in the centre of lives, places and events and (2) the oscillation between inside and outside of the unnameable as a part of the family and as the unknown and unknowable belonging. Tracking this form of objectification I further propose that the racial and cultural Other is the Thing haunting numerous texts. The Thing might not necessarily be a concrete, embodied object. It can be simply a prohibition or an anxiety about, say, a colour (in *The Tempest*). I am here yoking together Tilley's suggestion of objectification as the embodiment of an idea that then shows how subjects and objects *relate* to each other with theories of the Thing to argue that the racial Other is the embodiment of ideas of invasion, corruption and

Disease and degeneration **191**

pollution through which a relationship is being forged with the world at large. The Thing is the absence at the heart of the engagement with the world, and the Thing is perhaps the *colour* black (or yellow or brown).[8]

Kim Hall (1995) tracing the history of 'blackness' tells us that by the mid-sixteenth century 'black' was culturally ambiguous, conflating negroes and Moors. On the one hand there was the Elizabethan order to expel the blacks from England, and on the other blackness was a marketable feature that was therefore imitated by men and women on the stage, blackening themselves in, for instance, Jonson's *The Masque of Blackness* (1605). There was a suggestion also, Richmond Barbour notes, of a licentious and lustful blackness (2003: 82). Barbour goes on to argue that 'in appropriating blackness, the masque [by Jonson] expresses not strategic attention to geography and ethnicity but rather a British desire to embrace, and thereby to refine, the greater world' (83). That is, blackness had entered England in various ways, but was not sufficiently or accurately traceable to Africans, Moors or specific races. Such interpretations as Hall's, Barbour's and Nussbaum's (about the eighteenth century in which she speaks of the 'portability' of races and racial types, 2009) tend to see the conflation and confusion of categories as exoticization: 'exotic splendor, not ethnographic precision, was its concern' (Barbour 2003: 87).

However, I propose that blackness represented both desire and fear, exotic and threat, just as in Gary Farnell's argument, the Thing is at once evocative of beauty and disgust, desire and horror. Blackness comes into the cultural imagination of England, gets coded in multiple ways with little attention to detail or accuracy, and is sufficiently powerful as a signifier to evoke strong emotions. The conflation of varieties of blackness is not merely about splendour but about the *generic* threat 'black' represents, not a specific source of the threat. The variants of blackness do not matter: what matters is that *all* forms and shades of black are unknowable, desirable and frightening. The conflation can be read as a resistance to identifying specific causes, teleologies (national, regional, racial) so that Shakespeare's account of England as 'this precious stone set in the silver sea' as being the 'envy of less happier lands' might be read as envy folding into a threat of the invasive darkness. The conflation, I propose, suggests not a singular threat, but a plurality. If, as Farnell and others propose, the Thing is an unknowable 'absence', then black as a signifier of the absence of light (and Enlightenment) contrasts dangerously with Britain which is:

> Ruled by a sun that to this height doth grace it,
> Whose beams shine night and day, and are of force
> To blanch an Ethiop, and revive a corse,
> His light sciential is, and, past mere nature,
> Can salve the rude defects of every creature.

(Jonson 1975a: 56)

It is in the ambiguity of blackness, its uncertainty and radical difference from the 'lighted up' England that blackness functions as a Thing, intimate and unknowable,

192 Disease and degeneration

foreign and insider. Such figurations *of the unfigurable blackness in English writing, I argue, must be treated as a form of objectification.* The Thing is my name for the anxiety of something foreign, something Other, undefined but no less real for all that, in English writings about ghosts, spectres and shadowy figures.

Take Thomas de Quincey's Malay sequence as an instance of the unnameable anxiety represented by the East. The Malay turns up at de Quincey's door – of Wordsworth's Dove Cottage, incidentally – and the description goes thus: 'the sallow and bilious skin of the Malay, enamelled or veneered with mahogany by marine air, his small, fierce, restless eyes, thin lips, slavish gestures and adorations' (1985: 56). The Malay is received by an English girl, and he 'placed himself nearer to the girl than she seemed to relish' (56), and thus de Quincey gestures at a sexual anxiety about the girl's safety as well. Later he feeds the Malay opium too and the Malay leaves. Critics have noted that de Quincey neutralizes the threat of the East by consuming, in the form of opium, a bit of the East itself (Barrell 1991: 16), while others suggest that the Malay and the Englishman are both linked by the 'same disease of diet – the love of opium' (Bewell 1999: 159). But this reading mostly ignores the passage immediately following the Malay incident. De Quincey writes:

> because this Malay (partly from the picturesque exhibition he assisted to frame, partly from the anxiety I connected with his image for some days) fastened afterwards upon my dreams, and brought other Malays with him, worse than himself, that ran 'a-muck' at me, and led me into a world of troubles.
>
> (1985: 58)

Although, as de Quincey claims, he has 'taken happiness both in a solid and liquid shape, both boiled and unboiled, both East India and Turkey' and 'inoculated myself, as it were, with the poison of 8000 drops of laudanum per day' (58), one visit from the Malay, whether real or imagined, leaves him with an anxiety for several days afterwards. The Malay, like opium, also serves as a pathogen that infects de Quincey. Unnameable, unidentified, uncategorizable as a person or thing, the 'Malay' is a foreign 'body' infecting/infesting Dove Cottage *and* de Quincey's mind (the nightmares I cited from de Quincey at the opening of this chapter). The uncanny nature of the visit and the aftermath – a ghostly remains, a revenant – is the foreign at the heart of England itself in de Quincey's near-Gothic account.[9]

In an astute reading of Ann Radcliffe's *The Italian* (1797) Eugenia deLamotte notes that despite the fact that the African races are not the theme or setting for the novel, the colour 'black' (and its correlates) is the single most common colour in the tale. It becomes associated with evil and wicked acts (2004: 21). Heathcliff is said to possess a 'black countenance' and 'sharp cannibal teeth' when he appears at Isabella's window in *Wuthering Heights*. Jane Eyre's nemesis seems to be the dark-skinned Bertha Mason. The moment of the being's coming-to-life is described thus in *Frankenstein*:

It was already one in the morning; the rain pattered dismally against the panes, and my candle was nearly burnt out, when, by the glimmer of the half-extinguished light, I saw the dull yellow eye of the creature open; it breathed hard, and a convulsive motion agitated its limbs.

How can I describe my emotions at this catastrophe, or how delineate the wretch whom with such infinite pains and care I had endeavoured to form? His limbs were in proportion, and I had selected his features as beautiful. Beautiful! Great God! His yellow skin scarcely covered the work of muscles and arteries beneath; his hair was of a lustrous black, and flowing; his teeth of a pearly whiteness; but these luxuriances only formed a more horrid contrast with his watery eyes, that seemed almost of the same colour as the dun-white sockets in which they were set, his shrivelled complexion and straight black lips.

Yellow, black and shadows ('half-light'), except for the being's teeth, characterize the being. When the creature visits Frankenstein the scientist is shocked by the appearance:

by the dim and yellow light of the moon ... I beheld the wretch—the miserable monster whom I had created. He held up the curtain of the bed; and his eyes, if eyes they may be called, were fixed on me. His jaws opened, and he muttered some inarticulate sounds, while a grin wrinkled his cheeks.

(Shelley 1996: 35)

Mary Shelley describes a beast, and has the scientist finally give 'it' a classificatory term: 'monster'. Shelley's novel abounds in images of darkness: from the dark icy wastes of the Pole to the 'deepest gloom' (14) on Frankenstein's face. Variants of 'black' also occur frequently, to describe everything from the weather ('black and comfortless sky', 35) to the black ballots that condemn Justine to the gallows and the 'black mark of fingers' of the creature on a human he kills. Blackness, one would think, is the Thing that haunts Frankenstein as symbolic of the species-Other (it must be noted that Frankenstein had hoped to create a 'new species'): the 'monster', that is at once inside and outside Frankenstein. It belongs and yet does not. It is the taboo that underlies all his anxieties and about which he cannot speak but cannot exorcise either. The Thing is a thing of blackness, a species-Other, that haunts humanity in the tale.

In John Keats' famous *Lamia* (1820) the Thing is the uncertain quality of a creature that metamorphoses and there possesses an undefinable quality. The serpent is clearly an attractive, exotic creature:

Vermilion-spotted, golden, green, and blue;
Striped like a zebra, freckled like a pard,
Eyed like a peacock, and all crimson barred;
And full of silver moons, that as she breathed,

194 Disease and degeneration

> Dissolved, or brighter shone, or interwreathed
> Their lustres with the gloomier tapestries.
>
> (Keats 1973: 162)

Such a description, according to a critic, points to Lamia's 'destabilizing transformation' (Lee 2002: 127). But, I propose, the transformation is what is unsettling for it leaves it uncertain as to the true 'nature' of the serpent. With its origins in Africa (as already noted), Keats complicates the identity of this mesmerizing creature by refusing to give it an essence. The Thing, as we have seen, is the absence at the heart and this is precisely what Keats is gesturing at: the unknowable, unnameable absence that is Lamia.

Similar to *Frankenstein* is Stoker's classic *Dracula* (1897), which once again relies on the Thing of blackness as the inside-outside of all people, lives and events, which belongs and yet does not. Dracula is at once a foreigner with clear plans of invading England. His 'corruption' of the English woman – stereotypically the boundary-marker of security and invasion – suggests the role of contaminant by an unnameable thing. His features make him appear akin to both Jewish ·and Irish, according to some critics. It also suggests, they argue, that the entire threat of vampirism implies not only feeding off, but also sexual liaisons with Britons (Wasson 1966, Hatlen 1980, Zanger 1991: 36, Valente 2002, cited in Bollen and Ingelbein 2009: 408). The dark knowledge and forces that Dracula of Transylvania (literally, 'the land beyond the forest') represents might defeat the forces of English rationality and morality. Burton Hatlen's early critique proposed that Dracula is the very epitome of Otherness, representing all the 'dark, foreign (i.e., non-English) races; all "dark", foreign (i.e. non-bourgeois) classes' (1980: 92). Never racially named or coded, Dracula represents the unnameable and the unidentifiable Thing. The 'Thing' nature of the vampire is highlighted through another mode: his beastly connections and conjunctions. Harker's first inkling of this animal-connection is described in the following passage:

> I saw around us a ring of wolves, with white teeth and lolling red tongues, with long, sinewy limbs and shaggy hair. ... How he came there, I know not, but I heard his voice raised in a tone of imperious command, and looking towards the sound, saw him stand in the roadway. As he swept his long arms, as though brushing aside some impalpable obstacle, the wolves fell back and back further still.
>
> (Stoker 1997: 20)

Although this could be dismissed as a preternatural ability some humans might possess in dealing with animals there is more evidence to suggest that Dracula's own beastly nature is what the animals respond to. His ability to mimic lizards and crawl up and down walls and his ability to transform himself into a pack of rats or even a large dog (when he arrives in England) suggest that shape-shifting is central to his 'nature'. Further, as critics have noted, *Dracula* offers numerous suggestions of

Disease and degeneration **195**

disease (Sparks 2002, Willis 2007), and therefore the unnameable Thing is a contagion in the novel. Finally, and strangely, the Count is described as a throwback, in Van Helsing's terms: "'Well for us, it is, as yet, a child-brain ... However, he means to succeed, and a man who has centuries before him can afford to wait and to go slow'" (1997: 264). Akin to accounts of blacks as possessing subhuman intelligence – and therefore being just 'things' – and biological theories about the evolutionary scale of life, Stoker presents a Thing that cannot be named, described or comprehended. Its magic and its 'dark powers' render it beyond rational explanation. The Englishmen and women's relationship with 'it' suggests the presence of the Thing inside English culture. It is therefore certain that Dracula represents a threat at the heart of England. The rhetoric of objectification treats Dracula as anything but human, everything but human: and he is now *inside* London.[10]

David Punter has proposed that stories like Stevenson's 'Dr Jekyll and Mr Hyde' also articulate an anxiety about the foreign (1980: 241). Patrick Brantlinger argues that the ape-like Hyde is the 'stereotype of the shillelagh-wielding Irish hooligan' (2009: 48). While these critics trace specificities of threat discourse to racial and even geographical sites, there are often generic accounts of such threats. This leads William Hughes to argue that Transylvania in Bram Stoker is *not* the Orient and therefore, the

> invasion script of *Dracula* is most effective when read not as an incident- or racial-group-specific incursion, but as an abstracted conflict of Orient against the Occident – a conflict which may unite the representatives of the West against any challenge to the latter's cultural integrity or hegemony.
>
> (2003: 92)

While Gothic and horror tales like *Dracula* and *Frankenstein* are explicitly set in European spaces, Conrad's *Heart of Darkness*, which, as I shall argue, also demonstrates anxieties about the Thing, is set in interior Africa. As I shall argue in the final chapter, the novel shows a darkness at the heart of civilized London and, interestingly, Africa is the place where the European *performs* barbaric acts and himself turns barbarian. Kurtz's primitivization is symbolic of Europe's loss of values and self. But besides this theme of the primitivization of the European there is also a thingification of Kurtz that needs to be examined. In Conrad's rhetoric of objectification, Kurtz becomes increasingly immaterial and unsubstantial. Marlow employs various descriptors for Kurtz: 'disinterred body', a 'ghost', a 'shade', an 'initiated wraith from the back of Nowhere', 'an animated image of death', a 'shadow', an 'atrocious phantom', an 'apparition', 'a vapour exhaled by the earth' and an 'eloquent phantom'. J.S. Romero, addressing this spectrality of Kurtz, writes of:

> [Marlow's] concomitant loyalty to Kurtz's ghost not as an ethical obligation to avoid totalising temptations and keep the field of otherness open, but as Marlow's last-ditch attempt to preserve the coherence of the British and

196 Disease and degeneration

imperialist culture in which he is embedded and from which he derives his identity.

(2011: 45)

Marlow's contradictory attitudes towards imperialism, Romero believes, are the reason why he cannot let the ghost go. Marlow has already anticipated the insubstantiality of Kurtz:

He was just a word for me. I did not see the man in the name any more than you do. Do you see him? Do you see the story? Do you see any thing? It seems to me I am trying to tell you a dream—making a vain attempt, because no relation of a dream can convey the dream-sensation, that commingling of absurdity, surprise, and bewilderment in a tremor of struggling revolt, that notion of being captured by the incredible which is of the very essence of dreams.

(74)

If Romero gestures at the spectral in representations of Kurtz, Stephen Skinner, reading the above passage, refers to the story's thematic: 'a suggested truth is dimly perceived in the distance, pushed back and shrouded by language which hints at that truth but primarily emphasizes its own inadequacy in pursuing it' (Skinner 2010: 93–4). The real experience itself, in Skinner's argument, cannot be captured in words, and thus begins to resemble 'dream-sensations'.

I extend Romero's and Skinner's readings to suggest that Kurtz's ghost represents not Kurtz but *the legacy of imperialism which will not be laid to rest*. Further, I want to argue that the experience of the Other enters the unconscious but cannot be apprehended or appropriated within language. Conrad's novel, in other words, is about the Thing – blackness, as African, as imperial ideology, as the condition of Kurtz, all this and much more – that enters England in the form of Kurtz's ghost, but also Marlow's experience. The novel is as much about England and the Englishman's inability to comprehend the blackness of the entire imperial experience. It is, in Skinner's term, 'unsayable', but that does not in any way mean it is unreal.

Take for example the scene of Marlow's encounter with Kurtz's 'Intended'. Marlow experiences the presence of Kurtz's spectre even here:

For her he had died only yesterday. And, by Jove! the impression was so powerful that for me, too, he seemed to have died only yesterday—nay, this very minute. ... I saw him clearly enough then. I shall see this eloquent phantom as long as I live.

(Conrad 1974: 157)

Kurtz as ghost is the blackness at the heart of England, a point Conrad makes a few pages prior to the above incident:

It was written I should be loyal to the nightmare of my choice. I was anxious to deal with this shadow by myself alone,—and to this day I don't know why I was so jealous of sharing with any one the peculiar blackness of that experience.

(141)

The 'peculiar blackness of ... experience' is the Thing that haunts London, the Intended and Marlow. Kurtz as the Englishman-gone-primitive arrives as a ghost, even as the discrepant geography of Africa where the primitivization of civilized Englishmen occurs is now inside London. Unknowable, unfathomable, intimate and yet foreign, insubstantial and yet material, the heart of darkness in London is the Thing, the name of the unnameable Other. When Marlow says he will stay loyal to the nightmare he is proposing that he does not have an option. Kurtz and imperialism constitute the non-material Thing of nightmares. It is the return not only of the repressed but of the *different* that was always at the heart of England. One could perhaps think of the Thing as something that has been *domesticated*, made a part of the home, even as an unexplained absence.

The pathogenic Other

In *The Comedy of Errors*, while everybody acknowledges Spain's prosperity, this wealth is also imaged as disease:

> O, sir, upon her nose, all o'er embellished with rubies, carbuncles, sapphires, declining their aspect to the hot breath of Spain, who sent whole armadoes of carracks to be ballast at her nose.
>
> (III.2, ll. 129–36)

If a nation were to embark on trade with Spain, with her 'hot breath' suggestive of inflammation and fever, it runs the risk of contamination. That is, mercantile profits are always at risk from the disease of participating nations.[11] In the Dutch Church Libel of 1593 (attributed to Christopher Marlowe) we see a direct link being forged between Jews, foreign trade and disease. The Libel opens with the image of consumption/incorporation: 'And like the Jewes, you eate us up as bread'. And then continues thus:

> You transport goods, & bring us gawds good store
> Our leade, our vitaille, our ordenance & what nott
> That Egipts plagues, vext not the Egyptians more
> Than you doe us.
>
> (Cited in Harris 2004: 62–4)

The Libel then accuses the Jews in England of being diseased (the poem is addressed to the foreigners resident in London, and corrupting its mercantile and social body):

> With Spanish gold, you all are infected.
>
> (Cited in Harris 2004: 62–4)

198 Disease and degeneration

Jonathan Gil Harris, reading the above Libel, argues that the diatribe against foreigners and immigrants contains a discourse of national economy, even as it 'fantasizes an English nation under siege by foreign artisans and merchants' (2004: 64). This threat, as Harris notes, is due to England's participation in a transnational economy of trade and exchange. National economy and national borders are both, in this reading, vulnerable to corruption and contagion. Ben Jonson's Sir Politic-Would-Be in *Volpone* plans to develop a scheme to detect plague arriving in ships coming from the Orient:

> How t'enquire, and be resolved,
> By present demonstration, whether a ship,
> Newly arrived from Soria, or from
> Any suspected part of all the Levant,
> Be guilty of the plague.
>
> (IV.1, ll. 100–4. Jonson 1977: 99)

Jonson links mercantile profit with the threat of disease in the above speech, symbolically treating the desire for profits itself as a kind of infection. Earlier in the play Lady Politic-Would-Be had already warned of the risks of assimilating foreign bodies – that would then induce disease and instability:

> in politic bodies,
> There's nothing more doth overwhelm the judgment,
> And cloud the understanding, than too much
> Settling and fixing, and, as 'twere, subsiding
> Upon one object. For the incorporating
> Of these same outward things, into that part,
> Which we call mental, leaves some certain faeces
> That stop the organs, and as Plato says,
>   Assassinate our Knowledge.
>
> (III.3, ll. 104–12. Jonson 1977: 177–8)

As Harris notes, it is not simply a pathological condition accruing in the body due to the *consumption* of foreign 'bodies' but a veritable infection of the body politic, i.e. country, as well (2004: 133). But what is crucial here is to note that it is not simply the biological pathogen or humoral disturbances (since this rhetoric of the Libel and Shakespeare is well *before* the germ theory of disease) that pose a threat to the national body but the *moral contagion* of usury, greed and fascination for profits and foreign gold that enters the moral fibre of the English body and social order.

In the early 1820s Robert Southey in the first of several sonnets on the slave trade would speak of the disease of greed infecting English houses and families:

> the pale fiend, cold-hearted Commerce there
> Breathes his gold-gendered pestilence afar,

Disease and degeneration **199**

And calls to share the prey his kindred Daemon War.

> (www.pitt.edu/~ebb8/southey/poemsSlaveTrade.html)

Here Southey explicitly references international trade and its concomitant slavery as serving the greed of consumption – sugar and other products – within England. The moral contagion of 'blood sugar' (as it was called, see Morton 2005) had seeped into the English constitution in eighteenth- and early nineteenth-century abolitionist poetry. In another sonnet (Sonnet III) Southey would write:

> The scorching Sun,
> As pityless as proud prosperity,
> Darts on him his full beams; gasping he lies
> Arraigning with his looks the patient skies,
> While that inhuman trader lifts on high
> The mangling scourge. Oh ye who at your ease
> Sip the blood-sweeten'd beverage! thoughts like these
> Haply ye scorn: I thank thee Gracious God!
> That I do feel upon my cheek the glow
> Of indignation, when beneath the rod
> A sable brother writhes in silent woe.

> (www.pitt.edu/~ebb8/southey/poemsSlaveTrade.html)

Here Southey first documents the tropics (the scorching sun), terms prosperity 'pityless' and moves on to the whipping (scourge, which also has echoes of disease and pestilence). He explicitly targets people who use sugar thoughtlessly as they sip the 'blood sweeten'd beverage', and then consoles himself for possessing a conscience. The moral contagion here is directly connected to England's distant interests, out there under the scorching sun.[12] Thus Southey (and other abolitionist poets) shows how peripheral colonies are *not* distant because they actually infect England's soul.

Richard Clarke's poem, 'The Nabob', subtitled 'The Asiatick Plunderers', described the character of the English ruling class in the colonies as follows:

> Clime, colour, feature, in my bosom find
> The friend to all
> Why rob the Indians and not call it theft?
> ——
> Christians 'gainst pagan heretics claim right
> By war to plunder, or famine kill.

> (1773: 30)

And concludes with: 'low thoughted commerce! Heart corrupting trade' (41).

Keats in *Isabella, or The Pot of Basil* would, like Southey, remind England that its profits and products came from labourers toiling themselves to death on distant shores:

200 Disease and degeneration

For them the Ceylon diver held his breath,
And went all naked to the hungry shark;
For them his ears gushed blood; for them in death
The seal on the cold ice with piteous bark
Lay full of darts; for them alone did seethe
A thousand men in troubles wide and dark
Half-ignorant, they turned an easy wheel
That set sharp racks at work to pinch and peel.

(Keats 1973: 182)

The racial geography of globalizing trade and threatening disease inaugurated in Shakespearean England gathers strength in later centuries, as the literature indicates. For example the English Romantic poets had a considerable interest in pathologies of colonialism, often transposing tropical climates, diseases and even plants into the English countryside. In 'The Ruined Cottage', Alan Bewell notes, Wordsworth's account of 'bursting gorse' and 'insect host' seems to reference a tropical rather than an English setting (Bewell 1999: 52–3). The excess of wilderness and uncontrolled growth represents, for Bewell, the Romantic anxiety over the tropicalization of England's otherwise temperate landscape. In poems like 'To Autumn', for instance, Keats speaks of overripe gardens, fruits practically rotting on trees and a 'conspiring' (1973: 218–19. 'Conspiring', as Bewell notes, has connotations of 'breathing together' but also, in this case, a breathing of heavily miasmic air of the excessive vegetation, 1999: 177).

But when abolitionists gave voice to slaves, as Cowper does in 'The Negro's Complaint', the images recall those of disease from the Early Modern – specifically the use of terms like 'taint' which, as Harris has noted, also referred to pathology (2004: 52). Cowper's slave tells the English:

Deem our nation brutes no longer
Till some reason ye shall find
Worthier of regard and stronger
Than the colour of our kind.
Slaves of gold, whose sordid dealings
Tarnish all your boasted pow'rs,
Prove that you have human feelings,
Ere you proudly question ours!

(http://www.yale.edu/glc/aces/cowper2.htm)

Contemptuously dismissing them as 'slaves of gold' the black man addresses the 'tarnishing', or tainting, of their (English) powers. Similarly combining images of disease and moral contagion is Anna Laetitia Barbauld in 'To William Wilberforce, Esq':

Nor less from the gay East, on essenc'd wings,
Breathing unnam'd perfumes, Contagion springs;
The soft luxurious plague alike pervades

The marble palaces and rural shades;
Hence, throng'd Augusta builds her rosy bowers,
And decks in summer wreaths her smoky towers;
And hence, in summer bow'rs, Arts costly hand
Pours courtly splendours o'er the dazzled land:
The manners melt – One undistinguished blaze
O'erwhelms the sober pomp of elder days;
Corruption follows with gigantic stride,
And scarce vouchsafes his shameless front to hide:
The spreading leprosy taints ev'ry part,
Infects each limb, and sickens at the heart.
Simplicity! most dear of rural maids,
Weeping resigns her violated shades:
Stern Independence from his glebe retires,
And anxious Freedom eyes her drooping fires;
By foreign wealth are British morals chang'd,
And Afric's sons, and India's, smile aveng'd.

(Nayar 2013b: 52)

William Hutchenson in 'The Princess of Zanfara' (1792), speaking of the Caribbean slave ships, depicts crowds of sick and pathogenic (i.e. carrier) bodies entering the English ships – evidently headed for English shores and thus spreading contagion:

New cargoes crowd our shores, and on the beach
The squalid multitudes are pouring forth,
From over-loaded ships, which, like the curse
Of vile Pandora's box, bring forth disease,
With misery, and pallid want,
Crippled and maimed, whose ulcerating sores
Cling to the canker'd chains, that rankle deep.

(cited in Lee 2002: 61)

Similarly in Helen Maria Williams' 'Poem on the Bill Lately Passed' she sees contagion spreading *outward* from the guilt of the man in charge of the slave ship: 'beams direct, that on each head / The fury of contagion shed' (http://digital.lib.ucdavis.edu/projects/bwrp/Works/WillHPoems.htm#p166). In James Montgomery's 'The West Indies' (1807) a similar source of disease is located:

The Eternal makes his dread displeasure known,
At his command the pestilence abhorr'd
Spared poor slaves, and smites the haughty lord.

(1823: 47)

Montgomery, while organizing immunity in racially differentiated ways here – the black bodies spared of affliction, the white one struck down – also sees the disease

202 Disease and degeneration

as punishment for slavery. Eventually, warns Montgomery, the Englishman's body (and, by extension its *body politic*) will be destroyed by these diseases:

> Foreboding melancholy sinks his min,
> Soon at his heart he feels the monster's fangs,
> They tear his vitals with convulsive pangs ...
> Now frenzy-horrors rack his whirling brain,
> Tremendous pulses throb through every vein;
> The firm earth shrinks beneath his torture-bed,
> The sky in ruins ruses o'er his head;
> He rolls, he rages in consuming fires,
> Till nature, spent with agony, expires.
>
> (48)

Robert Southey in his *A Tale of Paraguay*, Canto 1, imaged smallpox as the curse the African races sent against the English as punishment for slavery:

> the lamentable pest
> Which Africa sent forth to scourge the West,
> As if in vengeance for her sable brood
> So many an age remorselessly oppresst.
>
> (1827: 22)

Elsewhere, in 'To the Genius of Africa' (1795) Southey called upon the African climate to avenge the enslavement of its peoples by infecting European slavers with disease:

> And o'er the unholy host with baneful breath
> There Genius thou hast breath'd the gales of Death.
>
> (1823: 41)

This is in order to avenge 'the demon avarice' of England's commerce and colonization (40).

In Thomas Pringle (the Scotsman who lived in South Africa for some years and is sometimes acknowledged as a pioneer South African poet) we see the slave dealer overcome with remorse at his actions:

> From ocean's wave a Wanderer came,
> With visage tanned and dun:
> His Mother, when he told his name,
> Scarce knew her long-lost son;
> So altered was his face and frame
> By the ill course he had run.
> There was hot fever in his blood,

And dark thoughts in his brain;
And oh! to turn his heart to good
That Mother strove in vain,
For fierce and fearful was his mood,
Racked by remorse and pain.

(1839: 58)

The 'fever in the blood' links disease with a consciousness of his immoral and inhuman acts.

Slavery thus is the *source* of contagion in such abolitionist rhetoric, and England by being involved in slavery is responsible, in a sense, for its own pathology.

If abolitionists saw the contagion as the result of England's guilt, greed and inhumanity that took its individuals beyond its borders (and thus bringing contagion in from the outside), others continued to identify distant places as the source of contagion. In Mary Shelley's apocalyptic *The Last Man* (1826), the plague is clearly racially marked in its origins: it 'raised its serpent-head on the shores of the Nile' (2004: 139). It is the 'contagion from the east' (178). When Perdita hears that Raymond is setting out for the wars, she immediately thinks of the East as the source of infection: 'One word … alarmed her more than battles or sieges … PLAGUE' (139). When the Greeks enter Constantinople the Turks curse them:

> Take it, Christian dogs! Take the palaces, the gardens, the mosques, the abode of our fathers – take plague with them; pestilence is the enemy we fly; if she be your friend, hug her to your bosoms.
>
> (152)

Conquest and military triumph become, that is, modes of acquiring *pathogenic territory*, even as the very source of Europe's survival – colonies – 'dries up', for 'in New Holland, Van Diemen's Land, and the Cape of Good Hope, plague raged' (187). Yet the novel is more than about disease. In the figure of Evadne, a Greek princess, we can see the moral contagion that infects 'true' Englishness, for there is another threat to the Englishman who stirs beyond his country's borders: women of other cultures. In this case it is Evadne. Lord Raymond, described early as 'an adventurer in the Greek wars' (30), is susceptible to Evadne's influence. Shelley writes:

> His spirit was as a pure fire, which fades and shrinks from every contagion of foul atmosphere: but now the contagion had become incorporated with its essence, and the change was the more painful.
>
> (100)

In Bewell's reading, Evadne, whom Raymond meets when she is in a penurious state, in the working-class district of London, poses a sexual threat to his Englishness

204 Disease and degeneration

(1999: 299). The imagery of his interest and subsequent moral crisis are cast in pathological language. This is Shelley's account of Raymond after a showdown with his wife Perdita regarding his liaison with Evadne:

> He slowly recovered himself; yet, at last, as one might from the effects of poison, he lifted his head from above the vapors of fever and passion into the still atmosphere of calm reflection.
>
> (2004: 101)

Eventually of course everything is wiped out by the plague. Shelley's novel therefore combines several pathogenic elements: foreign women, wars and imperial ambitions (the war is against the Turks) and of course the plague itself. It is in England's constant interactions with other cultures, even if European (embodied in Evadne), that the source of various kinds of contagion might be found, suggests Shelley. Shelley's account of London's streets captures the desolation:

> On the twentieth of November, Adrian and I rode for the last time through the streets of London. They were grass-grown and desert. The open doors of the empty mansions creaked upon their hinges; rank herbage, and deforming dirt, had swiftly accumulated on the steps of the houses; the voiceless steeples of the churches pierced the smokeless air; the churches were open, but no prayer was offered at the altars; mildew and damp had already defaced their ornaments; birds, and tame animals, now homeless, had built nests, and made their lairs in consecrated spots. We passed St. Paul's. London, which had extended so far in suburbs in all direction, had been somewhat deserted in the midst, and much of what had in former days obscured this vast building was removed. Its ponderous mass, blackened stone, and high dome, made it look, not like a temple, but a tomb. Me thought above the portico was engraved the *Hic jacet* of England. We passed on eastwards, engaged in such solemn talk as the times inspired. No human step was heard, nor human form discerned. Troops of dogs, deserted of their masters, passed us; and now and then a horse, unbridled and unsaddled, trotted towards us, and tried to attract the attention of those which we rode, as if to allure them to seek like liberty. An unwieldy ox, who had fed in an abandoned granary, suddenly lowed, and shewed his shapeless form in a narrow door-way; every thing was desert; but nothing was in ruin. And this medley of undamaged buildings, and luxurious accommodation, in trim and fresh youth, was contrasted with the lonely silence of the unpeopled streets.
>
> (265)

When Verney becomes truly the last man it is in Europe, away from England, wandering from Switzerland across Rome and other places.

In H.G. Wells' classic *The War of the Worlds* (1898) the arrival of the Martian vehicles is described in the following terms:

In the centre, sticking into the skin of our old planet Earth like a poisoned dart, was this cylinder. But the poison was scarcely working yet. Around it was a patch of silent common, smouldering in places, and with a few dark, dimly seen objects lying in contorted attitudes here and there. Here and there was a burning bush or tree. Beyond was a fringe of excitement, and further than that fringe the inflammation had not crept as yet. In the rest of the world the stream of life still flowed as it had flowed for immemorial years. The fever of war that would presently clog vein and artery, deaden nerve and destroy brain, had still to develop.

(2005: 36–7)

Wells images the alien invasion of planet earth as a poisoning, and goes on to describe the inter-species war in pathological terms. The alien brings disease and the invasion must be seen as the crossing of intergalactic or interstellar space as infection, the transmission of poisonous chemicals and agents of decay and death.[13]

Cultural invasion

The closest interpretation to a reading of the imperialism-produced blackness – or Kurtz, if you will (which produces a half-rhyme with 'curse') – that haunts the centre of Victorian England is Melissa Free's (2006) reading of *The Moonstone*. In my reading of the novel above I noted that the Indian stone has come to reside at the heart of English domesticity, organizing lives around it, even when it produces a 'legacy of trouble and danger'. Free draws attention to the fact that the stone is *not* cursed. Free then writes: 'empire, not the moonstone, is the family curse and the real "family scandal" … centered around – and illuminated by – the spoils of empire' (343). Free also thereby gestures at the curse around which English domesticity and its history itself seems to be centred. Nobody would speak of the stone as stolen (by one of their ancestors), where nobody admits to this scandal of the family or the illegitimacy of their legacy. If *The Moonstone* embodies the Thing – the blackness of the curse of Empire – Conrad leaves it spectral, a palpable but phantasmatic presence alongside Marlow and within London. The 'blackness' that Conrad describes is the shame of Kurtz, a product of imperialism's worst moments. Kurtz, with the 'barren darkness of his heart' (147) and his 'impenetrable darkness' (149), as Marlow describes it, is now in England itself. It is this Kurtz/curse that has come to reside in England now, and as a family spectre, so to speak, is a permanent fixture of English domesticity. The Thing is not frightening because it is out there as an external threat. On the contrary the Thing frightens because it is a part of us, intimate with us, domesticated and yet alien, like a Kurtz whom Marlow remembers as this primitivized creature he saw in the deepest blackness of Africa but who is now a part of England. We ought to recall that Marlow begins by a similar reference to London: 'And this also … has been one of the dark places of the earth.' The last lines of the novel read:

206 Disease and degeneration

> The offing was barred by a black bank of clouds, and the tranquil waterway leading to the uttermost ends of the earth flowed somber under an overcast sky—seemed to lead into the heart of an immense darkness.
>
> (162)

London, it would seem, with its legacy of Empire, would always have at its heart a darkness, an unnamed Thing. We will have reason to return to this 'new' London in a while.

In other cases, the foreign 'thing' that corrupts is racially and culturally marked indelibly – as Jew, as African, as Gypsy, as Indian, etc. – and this history of representation goes back to the seventeenth century.

Ben Jonson's masque *The Gypsies Metamorphosed* (1621) introduces the gypsies thus: 'Enter a gypsy leading a horse laden with five little children bound in a trace of scarfs upon him; a second leading another horse laden with stolen poultry, etc' (1975b: 318). In the course of the masque, of course, the spectators lose their wallets and other belongings (351).

In Marlowe's *The Jew of Malta* Barabas compiles a list of evils he has supposedly committed:

> Sometimes I go about and poison wells;
> Being young I studied physic, and began
> To practice first upon the Italian;
> There I enriched the priests with burials,
> And always kept the sexton's arms in ure
> With digging graves and ringing dead men's knells:
> And after that I was an engineer,
> And in the wars 'twixt France and Germany,
> Under pretence of helping Charles the Fifth,
> Slew friend and enemy with strategems.
> Then after that I was an usurer,
> And with extorting, cozening, forfeiting,
> And tricks belonging unto brokery,
> I filled the jails with bankrouts in a year
>
> (II.3, ll. 179–95. 1975: 378–9)

Of course the entire passage reads like a boast, and Barabas is painting himself as a thoroughly wicked Jew (usury for a long time was associated with Jews). But the larger point here is that Barabas is speaking of a cultural invasion that overturns and even destroys the receiving society, just as Aaron does in *Titus Andronicus*. With his mercantile interests spread throughout the Mediterranean region, Barabas represents the truly globalized Jew whose cultural impact, as a result of his economic power, is also global – from Italy through France and Germany. Cultural invasion as described by Barabas must be seen as an *extension* of the commodity invasion

Disease and degeneration **207**

and material threats already discussed above. From wells and drinking water to usury, the Jew contaminates everything, if Barabas is to be believed.

The capture of Christians by the Turks during Marlowe's time is the context in which, in the play, Del Bosco inventories his slaves: 'Grecians, Turks, and Afric Moors' (II.2, l. 9. 1975: 370). The conversion of many Christians to Islam ('turning Turk', as it came to be called) was seen as a cultural invasion of Christianity by Islam.[14] This cultural invasion manifests as the threat of 'going native' by those Englishmen and Europeans who had lived for a long time in other cultures, as we shall see in the next section.

The description of the child as a 'gypsy brat' of unknown origins in *Wuthering Heights* also names an anxiety: of a foreigner insinuating himself into the family. The gypsy is the quintessential foreigner, and Europe's internal Other, in much English literature from the mid-eighteenth century. As Jodie Matthews (2010) has noted, following the work of Laura Peters (2000) on orphans in Victorian literature, 'the orphan is used to reassert the idea of family via the expulsion of a threatening, foreign outsider, an attitude usually directed at the Gypsy' (141).[15] The child's language – described as 'gibberish' in the above passage – suggests a foreignness of uncertain provenance, even as the 'gypsy' reference partook of an existing discourse where it 'metaphorically … mean[t] any kind of dark stranger' (Matthews 2010: 141). The gypsy woman's sexuality threatens, as Abby Bardi argues, the 'purity of virginal female characters' (2006: 34). As in the case of the later novel, the gypsies first appearing in the encounter in *Emma* are children, but no less threatening for all that, Austen suggests, given the delicate sensibility of English womanhood.

> Miss Smith, and Miss Bickerton, another parlour boarder at Mrs. Goddard's, who had been also at the ball, had walked out together, and taken a road, the Richmond road, which, though apparently public enough for safety, had led them into alarm.—About half a mile beyond Highbury, making a sudden turn, and deeply shaded by elms on each side, it became for a considerable stretch very retired; and when the young ladies had advanced some way into it, they had suddenly perceived at a small distance before them, on a broader patch of greensward by the side, a party of gipsies. A child on the watch, came towards them to beg; and Miss Bickerton, excessively frightened, gave a great scream, and calling on Harriet to follow her, ran up a steep bank, cleared a slight hedge at the top, and made the best of her way by a short cut back to Highbury. But poor Harriet could not follow. She had suffered very much from cramp after dancing, and her first attempt to mount the bank brought on such a return of it as made her absolutely powerless—and in this state, and exceedingly terrified, she had been obliged to remain.
>
> (Austen 1971: 300)

Austen continues:

> How the trampers might have behaved, had the young ladies been more courageous, must be doubtful; but such an invitation for attack could not be

resisted; and Harriet was soon assailed by half a dozen children, headed by a stout woman and a great boy, all clamorous, and impertinent in look, though not absolutely in word.—More and more frightened, she immediately promised them money, and taking out her purse, gave them a shilling, and begged them not to want more, or to use her ill.—She was then able to walk, though but slowly, and was moving away—but her terror and her purse were too tempting, and she was followed, or rather surrounded, by the whole gang, demanding more.

In this state Frank Churchill had found her, she trembling and conditioning, they loud and insolent. By a most fortunate chance his leaving Highbury had been delayed so as to bring him to her assistance at this critical moment. The pleasantness of the morning had induced him to walk forward, and leave his horses to meet him by another road, a mile or two beyond Highbury—and happening to have borrowed a pair of scissors the night before of Miss Bates, and to have forgotten to restore them, he had been obliged to stop at her door, and go in for a few minutes: he was therefore later than he had intended; and being on foot, was unseen by the whole party till almost close to them. The terror which the woman and boy had been creating in Harriet was then their own portion. He had left them completely frightened; and Harriet eagerly clinging to him, and hardly able to speak, had just strength enough to reach Hartfield, before her spirits were quite overcome.

(300–1)

Critics have perspicaciously suggested that Harriet being threatened thus by the gypsy woman and the child serves as a metaphor not only for English femininity but for English nationhood as well (Kramp 2004, Bardi 2006), for Harriet Smith represents the 'future promise of her local and national community' (Kramp 2004: 148). It throws Harriet at Frank Churchill's mercy, and he extends his protection. The gendered nature of the encounter – Englishwoman held near-captive by gypsies – is what draws the attention of the critics here. Englishness is threatened when English women are threatened, especially by 'foreigners'. (Churchill brings Harriet to Hartfield, the ancestral place, once again reinforcing the stability of the English home in the face of racial threat as embodied in the nomadic gypsies.) As Bardi notes the gypsies are situated outside the village, associated with nature and thus 'pose a threat to social mores', even a subtle sexual threat in *Emma* (2006: 35) since, in Deborah Nord's words, gypsies mark 'not only cultural difference but a deep sense of unconventional, indeed aberrant femininity' (1998: 190). Similarly when she wishes to highlight Maggie's 'wildness' in *The Mill on the Floss*, George Eliot shows the girl running away to join the gypsies. In Walter Scott's *Guy Mannering* (1815) the gypsies are involved in a kidnap (kidnapping, as Bardi and Matthews point out, is seen as an inherent trait of the gypsies as a race). Gypsies represent, therefore, a cultural invasion that threatens femininity and class boundaries but also, by extension, the credibility of the nation. In Doyle's 'The Speckled Band', on hearing of the death of Roylott's stepdaughter, Julia, Holmes asks: 'were there gypsies in the plantation at the time?' (1986a: 102). Helen, telling the story to Holmes, thinks her sister's reference, before dying, to a speckled band 'referred to some band of people, perhaps to these very gypsies in the plantation' (102).

Other than Jews and the Romany, certain Africans also posed a threat to England if Victorian literature is to be believed, due to England's own connections with these other races. A preeminent account of this threat is available in Rider Haggard's *She* where Ayesha plans to ransack England and depose Queen Victoria. Then, in another passage, Ayesha discusses the possibility of conquering England:

> 'And now tell me of thy country—'tis a great people, is it not? with an empire like that of Rome! Surely thou wouldst return thither, and it is well, for I mean not that thou shouldst dwell in these caves of Kôr. Nay, when once thou art even as I am, we will go hence—fear not but that I shall find a path—and then shall we journey to this England of thine, and live as it becometh us to live. Two thousand years have I waited for the day when I should see the last of these hateful caves and this gloomy-visaged folk, and now it is at hand, and my heart bounds up to meet it like a child's towards its holiday. For thou shalt rule this England —'
>
> 'But we have a queen already,' broke in Leo, hastily.
>
> 'It is naught, it is naught,' said Ayesha; 'she can be overthrown.'
>
> At this we both broke out into an exclamation of dismay, and explained that we should as soon think of overthrowing ourselves.
>
> 'But here is a strange thing,' said Ayesha, in astonishment; 'a queen whom her people love! Surely the world must have changed since I dwelt in Kôr.'
>
> Again we explained that it was the character of monarchs that had changed, and that the one under whom we lived was venerated and beloved by all right-thinking people in her vast realms. Also, we told her that real power in our country rested in the hands of the people, and that we were in fact ruled by the votes of the lower and least educated classes of the community.
>
> 'Ah,' she said, 'a democracy—then surely there is a tyrant, for I have long since seen that democracies, having no clear will of their own, in the end set up a tyrant, and worship him.'
>
> 'Yes,' I said, 'we have our tyrants.'
>
> 'Well,' she answered resignedly, 'we can at any rate destroy these tyrants, and Kallikrates shall rule the land.'
>
> (2008: 224–5)

While Joseph Bristow is right in his assessment that the entire passage suggests an 'intolerance towards democracy' (1991: 143) – which is characterized as a tyrant – he misses the gendered threat that Holly and Leo are attempting to ward off here. England, like their own masculinity, is under threat from an imperious non-European *woman* with mystical-magical powers.[16] What they mount is not only, therefore, a defence of the realm, but also a defence of a certain racial masculinity itself.

210 Disease and degeneration

Stephen Arata has proposed that invasion narratives are responses to a cultural guilt, where British culture sees 'its own imperial practices mirrored back in monstrous forms' (1990: 623). The primitivism of the Other that many such invasion narratives, especially vampire tales like Stoker's and Marryat's but also works like Haggard's *She*, highlight reflects an anxiety over the regressive movement of civilization itself (Brantlinger 1988: 228–9). The famous British rationality has failed to stem the tide of the cultural Other's primitivism and savagery. What is significant is that the vampire figure itself is treated in Stoker as an instantiation of Europe's own invasion-lust. As Van Helsing points out, in *Dracula*, the Count merely 'follow[s] the wake of the berserker Icelander, the devil-begotten Hun, the Slav, the Saxon, the Magyar' (1997: 211). In just this one sentence Stoker locates Dracula's threat to England as the inevitable consequence of *Europe's* history of invasion and colonization. Dracula himself declares, with not inconsiderable pride in the military history of the area: 'there is hardly a foot of soil in all this region that has not been enriched by the blood of men, patriots, or invaders … Is it a wonder that we were a conquering race?' (27). That is, Europe's *history of transnational, global military movements has now climaxed in a situation wherein England is under threat.* It is a racial history originating in the Carpathians that climaxes in England.

It is important to note, as Arata does, that Eastern Europe's polyracial history – what Dracula calls 'the whirlpool of European races' (Stoker 1997: 33) – is bloody (Arata 1990: 629). Dracula's vampirism is only one instance of the savagery, decay and destruction of *previous* conquerors. And, since England is now on the verge of decay, vampirism would 'naturally' surface in the country, Stoker seems to suggest.[17]

'Going native'

In Smollett's *Humphrey Clinker*, Lishmahago returns from colonial America and trades on his experiences there (war, torture by Indians) to gain a social foothold in England. He dresses up his bride Tabitha as an Indian bride, in a 'fur cloak of American sables' (unpaginated, http://ebooks.adelaide.edu.au/s/smollett/tobias/clinker/complete.html). Commentators have noted that these, and other incidents, suggest a 'going native' theme in Smollett (Sussman 2000: 85–6, Fulford 2006: 109–10). In Charles Reade's *A Simpleton* (1873) the Boers have 'degenerated into white savages' and even the Kaffir 'savages' are 'socially superior' to the whites. When Conrad's Kurtz starts off, he is full of (European, colonial) ideas of progress but ends with the imperative 'exterminate the brutes' but – and this is important – he becomes one himself. Africa transforms him into the very brute he hated. In Rudyard Kipling's 'The Mark of the Beast' an Englishman is transformed into a werewolf due to the curse of a local seer/priest. In Doyle's *The Sign of Four* Jonathan Small becomes part of a crime syndicate along with Indians. Jekyll's transformation into the savage Hyde has been seen by some critics (Brantlinger 1988) as a representation of an anxiety about the degeneration of England and Englishness into something primitive.

A key element in each of the above instances is the anxiety over the *loss of English character and identity through a process of 'going native'*, a description of deculturation and deracination. This anxiety begins in the Early Modern age itself when traders and travellers into Istanbul, Basra and other places, it was believed, might turn 'renegade' English when they turned Turk. In Philip Massinger's *The Renegado* the pirate is one who has made a pact with the Islamic/Turkish devil. When Gazet tells Vitelli that he has lived in England, Spain, France, Rome, Geneva, Vitelli asks him if in Tunis then, he (Gazet) would turn Turk. Clem in Thomas Heywood's *Fair Maid of the West* is castrated (when he tries to stand in for Spencer) and dons a Turkish dress, thus prompting critics like Jean Howard to claim that he is castrated for 'going native' (cited in Harris 2004: 156). English traders often adapted local customs, clothing and habits for their business interests in the Asian markets. Robert Daborne's *A Christian Turn'd Turk* examined the life of John Ward, one time pirate, in the form of such a 'gone native' Englishman. Eventually of course, in a moral lesson to those Englishmen who would replace patriotism and national identity with financial profits and mercantile identity, Ward is betrayed by his Muslim wife. In an attempt to regain a measure of dignity, he commits suicide. Daniel Vitkus' comment on this conclusion to the play is particularly incisive:

> Ward does not want to become a Muslim, but he is pressured and seduced until he gives in. In the fantasy world of the London playhouses (unlike the real world), those who turn Turk are punished. And yet, even these theatrical fictions of conversion and punishment indicate that Islamic sponsorship leads to genuine freedom for men like Ward whose ambition and high spirits were confined and frustrated while they remained obedient to the English social order. To 'turn Turk' was to break free from the claustrophobic environment created by the English social hierarchy.
>
> (2007: 87)

Vitkus' reading is anticipated in an early passage in the play when the Frenchmen whom Ward is trying to recruit to his pirate gang plead with him to be allowed to return to their country. To which Ward's man Gismund responds thus:

> Who would not smite
> To heare this piece of wretchedness boast his wounds?
> How farre he went to purchase them with what honour
> He put them on, and now for sustenance,
> Want of a little bread, being giving up
> His empty soule, should joy yet that his Country
> Shall fee him breath his last: when that aire he termes his
> Ungratefully doth stifle him.
>
> (Daborne 1612: unpaginated)

'Going native' as Daborne's play seems to suggest was not always a mere slippage into another role-play tempted by the possibilities of a new identity: it was necessitated, for people like Ward, by social and economic hardships in England.

212 Disease and degeneration

The discrepant geography of failure or cruelty was not always of the Other place – it could be at the heart of England itself, as Charlotte Smith seems to suggest in her depiction of Orlando's return in *The Old Manor House*. The European as the monstrous or the space of England as alien, barbaric and monstrous also constitutes a discrepant geography. A good example of such a discrepant geography with the Other within is visible in Conrad's *Heart of Darkness*.[18]

When Marlow, having seen the 'dark continent', returns to England, he discovers its discrepant geography. Kurtz's 'Intended', the white woman, resembles Kurtz's African woman. The topography of the city with its tall houses lining the city streets resemble, strangely, the posts with human heads on them at Kurtz's Inner Station. Even the beating of his heart, Marlow believes, echoes the beat of primitive drums heard in the depths of the jungle. Homi Bhabha refers to this as a 'discourse of daemonic doubling' (2009a: 305) where for Marlow London is also a place of darkness. But to simply treat Marlow's version of London as a fantasm repeated from its African setting is to miss the discrepancy initiated in his vision *because* of his African experience. If nearly two centuries before Marlow, Swift's Gulliver and Defoe's Crusoe found themselves unable to adapt to London after their sojourn in Other places, Conrad's Marlow recasts London geography as the Other place. It is not mere fantasmatic doubling as much as the introduction of a discrepant geoaesthetics: London is always the Other, inverted, only it took an Africanized Marlow to discover this. 'The tranquil waterway leading to the uttermost ends of the earth flowed sombre under an overcast sky–seemed to lead into the heart of an immense darkness', says Marlow of the Thames (1974: 162. Years later D.H. Lawrence in his 'On Coming Home', 1923, would echo Marlow's feelings: 'so still! So remote-seeming! Across what mysterious belt of isolation does England lie! … And that is how it seems, as you slowly steam up the Sound in the night, and watch the little lights that must be land, on the unspeaking darkness,' cited in Childs 2007: 39).

If 'going native' and cultural hybridization as effects of England's transnational connections produced an anxiety as far back as the Early Modern, another cause for anxiety was the contamination of English identity through miscegenation and marriage. Interracial sexual liaisons, a commonplace in the Empire since the 1780s, became the subject of much political and public debate in the nineteenth century. It is within the contexts of these debates that we need to situate the iconic *Dracula* and Florence Marryat's *The Blood of the Vampire* (1897).

Bloodline contamination and racial identity

The first major portrait of a Creole hybrid in English settings is that of Bertha Mason in Charlotte Brontë's *Jane Eyre* (1847). What the white, and the epitome of English femininity, Jane Eyre, sees is a 'clothed hyena' on all fours, sometimes rising onto its 'hind feet'. She is unsure 'whether [it were] beast or human being' (2010: 250). 'It snatched and growled like some strange wild animal … it was covered with clothing; and a quantity of dark, grizzled hair, wild as a mane, hid its head and face' (250). Elsewhere Rochester describes his 'embruted partner' (249) and Bertha Mason is compared to a dog, a wolf, a tigress, and 'a carrion-seeking bird of prey' (179). Bertha Mason prefigures Florence Marryat's and Bram Stoker's vampires when Jane Eyre explicitly images her as a vampire, because she is reminded of 'the foul German spectre – the Vampyre' (242. Later of course Bertha Mason attacks and bites her brother). Bertha Mason represents an invasion of England, its domesticity and its femininity, in the form of a racial hybrid of uncertain parentage, family and community. She poses a threat to Rochester, his home and his future generations. That is, Bertha Mason invades not just Rochester's home as his wife but also the future generations of English children, who might also be of mixed race.[19]

H.L. Malchow, writing about vampire fiction and race in the nineteenth century, argued that 'the most emotive threat of the novel [Marryat's] is, in fact, that of racial pollution' (1996: 169). It is not Mason's racial hybridity but the possibility of it being transmitted, and therefore contaminating English blood- and family lines, that produces the horror of the novel. Bertha Mason is a racial-sexual threat, in other words, that arrives in England as a result of the Rochester family's *transnational* connections, specifically with Jamaica. Colonization, trade and travel produce a Bertha Mason, in short, that then begins to disrupt the English pastoral idyll.

As the Victorian age moved on the Bertha Mason model was to be replicated. In Florence Marryat's *The Blood of the Vampire* (1897) the account of Harriet's mother – her father is a Swiss vivisectionist – establishes the primitive origins of the vampire who would come to trouble Europe:

> She was a fiend, a fitting match for Henry Brandt ... a fat, flabby half-caste, who hardly ever moved out of her chair but sat eating all day long ... I can see her now, with her sensual mouth, her greedy eyes, her low forehead and half-formed brain, and her lust for food ... she thirsted for blood, she loved the sight of it, the smell of it, she would taste it on the tip of her finger when it came in her way ... a sensual, self-loving, crafty and bloodthirsty half-caste.
>
> (2010: 68)

Harriet, the half-caste daughter of this union, is described as being 'lissom' with lips of 'a deep blood colour' and 'small white teeth' (4). The animal imagery used to describe Bertha Mason is deployed for Harriet as well: Harriet eats like 'a cormorant' (6) and 'a pig' (9). She is variously a 'coiling snake', a 'puma cub', a 'panther', a 'lynx', a 'sly cat'. As Brenda Hammack, citing these descriptions, puts it, Harriet is an 'analogically uncertain being' (2008: 893–4).

When Harriet sits next to anybody, Marryat writes, that person 'become[s] fainter and fainter ... as if something or someone were drawing all ... life away' (2010: 18). When Harriet approaches people, exclaims Olga Brimont, 'some times I tell her I think she would like to eat them' (58). She even poses a threat to European women, but more worryingly, Harriet attracts men, and men engaged to be married to others promptly abandon their fiancées and gravitate towards her.

214 Disease and degeneration

Harriet thus poses a threat to the establishment or potential for establishing a 'proper' English family, as the Pullens discover. Malchow is right in his assessment that Harriet is a monster, like Shelley's creature in *Frankenstein*, who tries to pass (as normal) but cannot (1996: 171). Writes Malchow:

> Both vampire and half-breed [pose] hidden threats – disguised presences bringing pollution of the blood. Both may be able to 'pass' among the unsuspecting, although both bear hidden signs of their difference, which the wary may read.
>
> (168)

Harriet is a 'gothic unnatural' (Malchow 1996: 172) because she defies categories – racial, national and even species. But more worryingly, she can *pass* as white, and thus insinuate herself into families and bloodlines.

This hybrid import from Jamaica is thus one more effect of Europe's transnational linkage, and is, unlike the spices and silks, a threat that will not be appropriated. The vampire represents the uncategorizable, inter-species creature (between human and animal). She threatens Englishmen and women alike, and eventually saps their lives. Associating a malignity with Harriet and her hybrid origins Marryat thus proposes a racial threat to white supremacy at the level of sexuality, sexual union and the family. Further, as Sarah Willburn notes (2008), by associating her protagonist's racial identity with the occult and the supernatural Marryat positions Harriet within the traditional stereotype of the irrational, incomprehensible racial-cultural Other.

Other versions of 'going native' also figure in English writing, especially of the late nineteenth and early twentieth century. Take Kipling's classic 'The Mark of the Beast'. Fleete is turned into a werewolf as a result of a curse laid upon him for defiling a Hindu temple/idol. Yet this is really not the point of the tale, as far as I can see. The tale opens with the following paragraph:

> East of Suez, some hold, the direct control of Providence ceases; Man being there handed over to the power of Gods and Devils of Asia, and the Church of England Providence is only exercising an occasional and modified supervision in the case of Englishmen.
>
> (1964: 240)

Kipling has already warned the English that their gods do not operate well in the East/colonies. Fleete is an Englishman who unlike others does not 'go native', whose 'knowledge of natives was … limited' (241). As a result of the curse he becomes a wolf-like creature and has to be treated by Strickland and other English as such: 'We bound this beast with leather thongs of the punkah-rope, and tied its thumbs and big toes together, and gagged it with a shoe-horn' (251). Eventually the leper, under threat of his life from Strickland, takes back the curse

Disease and degeneration **215**

and Fleete is cured. Strickland realizes that he has given up the civilized Englishman role for that of a brutal colonizer: '[we] had disgraced ourselves as Englishmen forever' (258). As Paul Battles rightly points out, while the story opens with binaries of civilized English versus primitive East, these polarities collapse, and the English have not only lost all claims to 'Englishness' but also discovered that 'the Beast lies within themselves, not in the Indians' (1996: 340).

In Kipling's tale the 'going native' is the result of the collapse of *English* values in the colony – not unlike Kurtz's collapse (he also appears as an animal, it must be remembered) – and not the 'curse' of the Other. That is, Fleete, like Kurtz, has become the Other to England and its ideals when given the opportunity to do so in the colonies. The evil lies within *English character as their greed, arrogance and incompetence become the sources of the degenerative disease of Empire.*

Returning servicemen

'I fear thee, ancient Mariner', says the Wedding Guest in Coleridge's famous poem (1973: 196). Alan Bewell locates the Guest's fear in *disease*: he worries that the Mariner might be carrying some pathogen, having returned from pathogenic spaces (1999: 103–8). The poem, according to Debbie Lee, links fever, very specifically yellow fever, with slavery (1998). It was believed that yellow fever spread from returning mariners and voyagers. The crossing of geographical borders meant a crossing into the region of pathogens.[20] (This incident of the Ancient Mariner's ship and its damaged survivor is echoed in Mary Shelley's *The Last Man* where a ship from the Americas arrives at Portsmouth with its sole survivor, a 'nearly black' man with 'matted hair and bristly beard' who falls down dead as soon as he steps on to land, 2004: 173.)

Bewell goes on to locate in the 'serviceman's return' poems of Wordsworth ('The Discharged Soldier', 'The Brothers' and the *Salisbury Plain* poems) and others a national anxiety over 'the vagrancy, sickness, broken bodies, and alienation' accompanying such homecomings (1999: 111). In the *Salisbury Plain* poems Wordsworth mourns the wastes of England, the result of its wars (Bewell 1999: 109). When the soldiers, having served the Empire and Britain, come back home, they are viewed as 'less than human' (113). In R.T.'s 'The Worn Soldier' (1808) the soldier comes back 'from many long toilsome years'. What he carries in his mind on the return journey are memories of his home as he had left it:

> How sweet are his green native hills,
> As they smile to the beams of the west

He expects cheers on his return:

> For already in fancy, he enters his home,
> 'Midst the greetings of tender friends

216 Disease and degeneration

But all of this hope is destroyed:

> For he found the dear cottage a tenantless waste,
> And his kindred all sunk to the grave.
> Lend a sigh to the soldier's griefs,
> For now he is helpless and poor,
> And, forc'd to solicit a slender relief,
> He wanders from door to door.
> To him let your answers be mild,
> And, O! to the suff'rer be kind,
> For the look of indiff'rence, the frown of disdain,
> Bear hard on a generous mind.
> (http://www.rc.umd.edu/editions/warpoetry/1808/1808_3.html)

In his absence his home is a 'waste'. He is reduced to the status of a beggar seeking 'slender relief'. The poet then pleads that he be treated with some compassion. The poem suggests that what is cruel is not the war or the injuries of war but the wastes greeting a soldier's return. All signs of his existence once in that spot are erased, he is a stranger to the town he grew up in. In Robert Burns' 'The Soldier's Return' (1793) he refers to the 'stranger':

> The brave poor sodger ne'er despise,
> Nor count him as a stranger;
> Remember he's his country's stay,
> In day and hour of danger.
> (http://www.robertburns.org/works/401.shtml)

In Charlotte Smith's *The Old Manor House*, when Orlando, who had been in battle during the American Revolution, returns home, he is unrecognizable. Taken to be a stranger by the people he meets, Orlando is shell-shocked and his beloved home itself seems 'loaded with the groans of all he had ever loved, or revered' (1969: 399). Smith suggests that England itself is irrevocably changed by its returning soldiers and travellers – seen also in Wordsworth's Discharged Soldier and Coleridge's Ancient Mariner – due to the effect of the distant places on its people, a theme that would find resonance in Conrad's Marlow. As Simon Parkes puts it, 'the war has destroyed his link with the place by displacing him: he has not existed in this particular locale' (2011: 770). This 'displacement' is not only Orlando's physical relocation to America but also a re-relocation back to an *unrecognizable England*. The returning Englishman returns a foreigner because he has been 'touched' and altered irrevocably by his experiences of the Other space. In Robert Merry's 'The Wounded Soldier' the wounded soldier returns to his home expecting to find it all wasted, his parents dead and his beloved Lucy married elsewhere. But he is pleasantly surprised:

> He reach'd the threshold of his parents' shed,
> Who knew not of his fate, but mourn'd him lost,

> Amidst the number of the *unnam'd dead*.
> Soon as they heard his well-remember'd voice,
>   A ray of rapture chas'd habitual care:
> 'Our HENRY lives – we may again rejoice!'
>   And LUCY sweetly blush'd, for she was there.
> But when he enter'd in such horrid guise,
>   His mother shriek'd, and dropp'd upon the floor:
> His father look'd to heav'n with streaming eyes,
>   And LUCY sunk, alas! to rise no more.
> O, may this tale, which agony must close,
>   Give due contrition to the self-call'd great,
> And show the poor how hard the lot of those
>   Who shed their blood for *ministers of state*!
>   (http://www.rc.umd.edu/editions/warpoetry/1799/1799_12.html)

In Bewell's reading the soldier's return 'destroys the rural cottage life that he sought to recover' (1999: 111). But the point is that nowhere in the poem's conclusion is there a clue that the cottagers *recognize* him, although they recognize his voice. Like the Ancient Mariner who has become 'long, and lank, and brown', and Orlando in *The Old Manor House* who is ghostly, Merry's soldier arrives in a 'horrid guise'. Wordsworth's discharged soldier in 1850 *Prelude* (Book 4), or 'veteran', as the poem's narrator calls him, is described almost like a ghost:

> Long were his arms, pallid his hands; his mouth
> Looked ghastly in the moonlight.
>
> (1969: 520)

We are told he had served in the 'Tropic Islands'. A few lines later, he is described as 'ghostly': 'His ghostly figure moving at my side' (520). The narrator guides him to a refuge when the poem ends. In 'The Female Vagrant' (published in the *Lyrical Ballads* and then incorporated into *Guilt and Sorrow, or Incidents Upon Salisbury Plain*, 1842) the woman tells the narrator how her husband had been forced to join the army, mainly as an effort to clear the streets of vagrants: 'to sweep the streets of want and pain' (1969: 23). Wordsworth thus erases any national ideal that prompted conscription, instead suggesting that the journey overseas for the vagrant's husband was a cruel strategy to remove signs/sights of poverty. Even before they leave England's shores the ships with the miserable soldiers on them are devastated by sickness:

> There were we long neglected, and we bore,
> Much sorrow ere the fleet its anchor weighd;
> Green fields before us and our native shore,
> We breathed a pestilential air, that made
> Ravage for which no knell was heard.
>
> (23)

218 Disease and degeneration

The woman loses her entire family in a year:

> The pains and plagues that on our heads came down;
> Disease and famine, agony and fear,
> In wood or wilderness, in camp or town,
> It would unman the firmest heart to hear.
> All perished – all, in one remorseless year,
> Husband and children! one by one, by sword
> And ravenous plague, all perished: every tear
> Dried up, despairing, desolate, on board
> A British ship I waked, as from a trance restored.

(23)

In poems such as these the 'plague' is as much an import as any commodity. But more significantly Wordsworth shows how, even without disease, the very migration or travel of young men outward, away from England, brought enough plague-like destruction on the family and communities they left behind.

In other cases, such as Charlotte Smith in *The Old Manor House* and the returning servicemen poems, it is not a disruption due to the return as much as a disruption produced by the arrival of a stranger/foreigner. Although to the soldier the home is exactly as he left, to the inhabitants he is a stranger. The foreigner is *not the racial, cultural Other but one of 'our own' who has been Othered to ourselves in the course of a transnational and global journey.*

In each of these cases what we perceive is the effect an overseas stay has on England's young men and their inability to return to the England of their memories. Further, while they were away in the service of the country, on military or trade voyages, England moves on, changes and is unrecognizable. The returning serviceman poem serves an important function in that it suggests that England's transnational activities changes its men and ensures that they can never return *as they were*, as a consequence of which they become strangers to their home. Thus the physician Roylott in Doyle's 'The Speckled Band', when he returns from Calcutta, India, has been transformed into a man with a 'large face, scarred with a thousand wrinkles, burned yellow with the sun, and marked with every evil passion' (1986a: 104). That is, the transnational linkage deracinates the Englishman in such a way that he comes back as a ghost, or as an embodiment of evil itself. The Ancient Mariner is practically a stranger, or foreigner, to the English when he returns, looking diseased, deranged and possessed. There is, in an apposite phrase of Debbie Lee's about Coleridge's Ancient Mariner, 'alterity carried in the blood under dark skin' (1998: 682), when they return from their overseas trips. What comes back to England in the 'guise' of the discharged soldier, the merchant or the sailor is Otherness itself.

Transnational networks of vice

> A crowd of shivering slaves of every nation,
> And age, and sex, were in the market ranged;

Each bevy with the merchant in his station:
Poor creatures! their good looks were sadly changed.
All save the blacks seem'd jaded with vexation,
From friends, and home, and freedom far estranged;
The negroes more philosophy display'd,—
Used to it, no doubt, as eels are to be flay'd.

(Byron 1975: 712–13)

This is Byron's description, in *Don Juan*'s Canto 5, of the Black Sea ('Euxine' is the ancient Greek name for the Black Sea) area, separating eastern Europe from western Asia. The place is cosmopolitan, and yet this cosmopolitanism is one built on an *immoral transnational linkage*: the slave trade. Europe has been 'cosmopolitanized' but through the aggregation of suffering Others.

In Charlotte Smith's *The Old Manor House*, in a passage I quoted earlier (Chapter 3), Mr Jamieson tells Orlando that of all the unfair advantages the English sought in the war against the Americans 'there was none that seemed so unjustifiable as that of sending forth the Indians against them' (1969: 360–1). Troy Bickham quotes a poem on the American Revolution which expresses this same sentiment and attacks Britain for hiring the savage Native Americans:

Her [Britannia's] name struck terror ev'n in barren soils,
And Indians Trembled when Britannia frown'd;
But now, even savages partake our spoils,
And England's annals with disgraces crown'd.

(2005: 256)

Here in Byron, Smith's novel and the poem cited above, England's (and Europe's) overseas connections, however self-serving and temporary these were, are presented as networks of vice, cruelty and 'unBritish' behaviour. Britain has been shamed due to its overseas connections. 'Even savages partake our spoils' says the author of the above verse, thus gesturing at an unholy connection of Britain with the savage races.

In 'Eighteen Hundred and Eleven' (1812) Anna Laetitia Barbauld writes:

Wide spreads thy race from Ganges to the pole,
O'er half the Western world thy accents roll:
… Thy stores of knowledge the new states shall know,
And think thy thoughts, and with thy fancy glow;
Thy Lockes, thy Paleys shall instruct their youth,
Thy leading star direct their search for truth;
Beneath the spreading Plantain's tent-like shade,
Or by Missouri's rushing waters laid,
'Old father Thames' shall be the Poet's theme,
Of Hagley's woods the enamoured virgin dream,

220 Disease and degeneration

And Milton's tones the raptured ear enthrall,
Mixt with the roar of Niagara's fall.

(Wu 1997: 12)

Barbauld is speaking of England's magnificent reach – from the New World to the East Indies. Yet it was precisely this extent, this connection across spaces, that was also interpreted as the source of several of England's scourges, from disease to moral degradation. We have also noted how in Wordsworth the very fact of England's young men conscripted into the navy or even international voyages causes the degeneration and decay of the family and community left behind, irrespective of whether disease from the tropics does arrive in England. It is enough to have young men involved in transnational linkages and have them go away, Wordsworth suggests in 'The Brothers', 'The Female Vagrant' and other poems.

Variations of this theme of ruinous transnational networks occur throughout English writings from the 1780s.

Mary Shelley's *The Last Man* opens thus:

> I am the native of a sea-surrounded nook, a cloud-enshadowed land, which, when the surface of the globe, with its shoreless ocean and trackless continents, presents itself to my mind, appears only as an inconsiderable speck in the immense whole; and yet, when balanced in the scale of mental power, far outweighed countries of larger extent and more numerous populations. So true it is, that man's mind alone was the creator of all that was good or great to man, and that Nature herself was only his first minister.
>
> (2004: 5)

Jonathan Elmer correctly points out that this is the fantasy of 'sovereign extension' (2009: 358), where the speaker's 'projective power' reaches far beyond the limits of his country's limits to spread across 'countries of larger extent'. While Elmer focuses on the sovereignty and individuation that Shelley ostensibly foregrounds, Shelley's own rhetoric of imaginative and material expansion is tethered to a context of transnational linkages that are real and material, and not just imaginative, as Elmer seems to think.

This projective expansion of England is traceable back to the Early Modern period, as already noted in Chapter 2. What is crucial is that this rhetoric is tied in to actually existing networks of exchange – of trade, slaving, wars and travel.

In Shakespeare sexual and financial economies merge in many plays as prostitution, marriage and sex become inseparable in discourses of profit, mercantilism and investment. Reading his *Comedy of Errors*, Jonathan Gil Harris detects a 'syphilitic economy', where there is the attempt at a compromise formation that 'mediates between residual moral discourse of appetitive economy and an emergent systemic discourse of global trade' (2004: 49). Thus profits generate anxiety as well in the Early Modern period as England gets drawn into these networks.

Thomas de Quincey's narrator and Arthur Conan Doyle's Sherlock Holmes are both addicts to products that enter England through transnational routes: opium and cocaine.[21] In both cases the imperial network undermines English identity and character, although Doyle refuses to portray Holmes as *only* an addict. The subjugation of English character to a drug might very well be seen as the invasion or infection of England by an Oriental/Other drug. De Quincey thus confesses that he indulged in the 'sensual pleasure' of opium to 'an excess' (1985: 2).[22]

If drugs such as opium and cocaine reconfigure English character they are also instrumental in altering the public spaces of London with its addicts and suppliers. As Christopher Keep and Don Randall put it, 'cocaine is ... the archetypal colonial product: it traces an arc from raw substance originating on the ill-defined periphery of empire to the imperial center where it is refined and sold for profit in the domestic marketplace' (1999: 210). Jewellery, money, drugs are all products – made from the sufferings of slaves, as abolitionist poetry pointed out endlessly – from the edge of the Empire to the centre, facilitated by England's own licit as well as illicit transnational networks of trade, travel and trafficking of soldiers that then contribute to an alteration of the cultural landscape of England, and the quiet degeneration of English character.

By the Victorian era the peripheries of the Empire had arrived in the metropolis, as numerous historians have demonstrated (Burton 1998, Hall 2002). No longer was India or Burma 'out there', rather it was very much present in various forms at the heart of English London. The anxiety over this shift in the nature of English London from a bastion of white privilege and racial 'purity' to a multicultural space is expressed in the literature of the age. The metropolis, writes Joseph McLaughlin in his study of this literature of invasion and multiculturalization of London, became 'a dangerous jungle of ethnic confusion' (2000: 29).

Let me turn to particular key – and popular – texts of the age: Wilkie Collins' *The Moonstone*, Bram Stoker's *Dracula*, Rider Haggard's *She* and Arthur Conan Doyle's novella, specifically *The Sign of Four*, to examine how the degeneration of London/England into a multicultural and ethnically confused space is imaged in invasion tropes, or tropes of transnational wickedness and corruption.

In Collins' *Moonstone*, in a passage I have had reason to cite (twice) earlier, he writes:

> here was our quiet English house suddenly invaded by a devilish Indian diamond – bringing after it a conspiracy of living rogues, set loose on us by the vengeance of a dead man. ... Who ever heard of the like of it – in the nineteenth century, mind; in an age of progress, and in a country which rejoices in the blessings of the British constitution? Nobody ever heard the like of it, and, consequently, nobody can be expected to believe it.
>
> (1982: 36–7)

The English home is possessed by a demonic stone which pollutes the quiet domesticity of the space. However, what is clear from the novel is that it is the

222 Disease and degeneration

Englishman's greed that brings the stone with its so-called devilish attributes into the English home. Collins gives us the context of the stealing of the stone:

> The camp-followers committed deplorable excesses; and, worse still, the soldiers found their way, by a guarded door, into the treasury of the Palace, and loaded themselves with gold and jewels. It was in the court outside the treasury that my cousin and I met, to enforce the laws of discipline on our own soldiers. Herncastle's fiery temper had been, as I could plainly see, exasperated to a kind of frenzy ... I got to an open door, and saw the bodies of two Indians (by their dress, as I guessed, officers of the palace) lying across the entrance, dead.
>
> A cry inside hurried me into a room, which appeared to serve as an armoury. A third Indian, mortally wounded, was sinking at the feet of a man whose back was towards me. The man turned at the instant when I came in, and I saw John Herncastle, with a torch in one hand, and a dagger dripping with blood in the other. A stone, set like a pommel, in the end of the dagger's handle, flashed in the torchlight, as he turned on me, like a gleam of fire. The dying Indian sank to his knees, pointed to the dagger in Herncastle's hand, and said, in his native language—'The Moonstone will have its vengeance yet on you and yours!' He spoke those words, and fell dead on the floor.
>
> (1982: 4–5)

The next day even upon questioning by his superior officer, Herncastle does not admit to any wrongdoing. The narrator hints that Herncastle might actually have killed the Indian guards but has no evidence to back this theory. What is clear is that the stone comes into England through the horrific war-time conduct of English soldiery itself. Thus the 'invasion' that Collins terms the arrival of the stone into England is a gross misnomer: the stone's *imperial English antecedents of murder and dishonourable behaviour* are what come to haunt England and Englishness.

In Doyle's *The Sign of Four* Jonathan Small the Englishman and his four Indian friends come across a vast treasure in the anti-Mutiny battles of 1857–8. The task of finding and securing the treasure until such time as Small and his companions arrived in England falls to Sholto. Sholto, says Small in his account to Holmes: 'had stolen it all without carrying out one of the conditions on which we had sold him the secret' (1988a: 143). The evil that follows, murder and death, at the heart of London are the effects of this betrayal by an *Englishman*. Joseph McLaughlin's reading proposes that the ill-gotten wealth of Sholto and his family becomes 'symbolic of England's corruption' (2000: 59). While Tonga the cannibal Andamanese might seem to be the threat to English identity and lives in Doyle's narrative, I propose that Tonga is incidental to the real tale, which is that of an Englishman's degeneration and abandonment of codes of ethical conduct. Sholto is the Herncastle of Doyle's tale. I am more in resonance with Benjamin O'Dell's interpretation of the text that Victorian domesticity in the novel is 'disrupted' through its 'intimate relationship to contemporary networks of vice' (2012: 994). Small himself, O'Dell points out, is not an innately wicked man: he is forced to turn to a life of crime when, invalided out of the army due to an injury, he finds himself with little support. O'Dell thus sees Small as symbolic of the 'failure of the ideological mission of England' (992–3). Tonga as the murdering savage only fits into the existing (Oriental) stereotype of the savage native. But the key point is that it is *England's* and the *Englishman's* transnational dealings – whether soldiery, politics or trade – that perpetuate the horrific events of the tale because these dealings are now evacuated of the high idealism on which the Empire was founded. In 'The Speckled Band' Roylott, with his temper and fascination for Turkish slippers, 'Indian animals' (1986a: 100) and 'strong Indian cigars' (101) is yet another instance of the Englishman not only 'gone native' but one who has degenerated into an animal. He is the villain of the tale, and his murder weapon, famously, is the Indian swamp adder. After Roylott, says Doyle, returned to England – having beaten his native butler to death in India (100) – a 'morose and disappointed man' (100), he became, due to his temper, 'the terror of the village' (100). Doyle clearly points to Roylott's *Indian* connections and obsessions as the source of the evil.[23] It should be noted that Doyle's first mention of the Roylott family is prefixed with the descriptive 'well-known' (97), while a member of the family admits that 'four successive heirs were of a dissolute and wasteful disposition, and the family ruin was eventually completed by a gambler' (99). Thus, old English families are *already* degenerating, and their implication in transnational network merely speeds up rather than initiates the ruin.

In Collins and Doyle the degeneration of England is actually, in the tales' subtexts, engineered and initiated from *within* albeit with 'support' from a transnational network. When the Empire's soldiers, epitomized in Herncastle and Sholto, insert themselves into the networks of vice they automatically expel themselves from whatever philanthropic or benevolent capitalist networks the Empire had originally relied on. In other words, I am reading Collins and Doyle as implicitly signalling the arrival of the 'urban jungle' of London with the *shift in the nature of Englishness itself*, and not in any external threat.

We see a similar case of the 'networks of vice' that harm the nation from inside in Daphne du Maurier's Gothic tale, *Jamaica Inn* (1936). Smuggling links specific classes of England (it is set in Cornwall), its people, illicitly, to other unscrupulous black-marketers across the world. The creation of a separate, underground economy subverts national policy and is often treated as a social ill. As Dianne Armstrong notes in her study of the novel (2009), smuggling serves as a 'reverse Gothic invasion motif' in the novel because the instability to England comes from within its borders. Like *Moonstone* and *Sign of Four, Jamaica Inn* might also be read as the articulation of an anxiety about the descent of England into un-English behaviour.

While not strictly speaking either a 'reverse invasion' or the 'networks of vice' motif, Stoker's *Dracula* also offers a version of the degeneration of England story. Count Dracula's invasion of England of course, as noted earlier, is in keeping with

224 Disease and degeneration

the pathologizing of the Other theme. When Harker enters the library the sight that meets his eyes is one of extensive English materials:

> A table in the centre was littered with English magazines and newspapers, though none of them were of very recent date. The books were of the most varied kind—history, geography, politics, political economy, botany, geology, law—all relating to England and English life and customs and manners. There were even such books of reference as the London Directory, the 'Red' and 'Blue' books, Whitaker's Almanac, the Army and Navy Lists, and—it somehow gladdened my heart to see it—the Law List.
>
> (1997: 25)

Dracula, it would seem, was preparing for an immigration test preliminary to acquiring an English citizenship. But what might escape our attention is the fact that it is the *English* mercantile-financial and real estate corporate bodies that are seeking to facilitate Dracula's acquisition of estates in England. Peter Hawkins, who is Harker's boss, is described by Dracula as 'my friend' (26). Dracula requests Harker: 'by our talking I may learn the English intonation; and you tell me when I make error, even of the smallest, in my speaking' (26). Dracula has specifications about the estate he wishes to acquire in England. And this is precisely what Harker informs him they have procured:

> At Purfleet, on a by-road, I came across just such a place as seemed to be required, and where was displayed a dilapidated notice that the place was for sale. It is surrounded by a high wall, of ancient structure, built of heavy stones, and has not been repaired for a large number of years. The closed gates are of heavy old oak and iron, all eaten with rust. The estate is called Carfax, no doubt a corruption of the old *Quatre Face*, as the house is four-sided, agreeing with the cardinal points of the compass. It contains in all some twenty acres, quite surrounded by the solid stone wall above mentioned. There are many trees on it, which make it in places gloomy, and there is a deep, dark-looking pond or small lake, evidently fed by some springs, as the water is clear and flows away in a fair-sized stream. The house is very large and of all periods back, I should say, to mediæval times, for one part is of stone immensely thick, with only a few windows high up and heavily barred with iron. It looks like part of a keep, and is close to an old chapel or church. I could not enter it, as I had not the key of the door leading to it from the house, but I have taken with my kodak views of it from various points. The house has been added to, but in a very straggling way, and I can only guess at the amount of ground it covers, which must be very great. There are but few houses close at hand, one being a very large house only recently added to and formed into a private lunatic asylum. It is not, however, visible from the grounds.
>
> (28–9)

What we see here is the replication in England of Dracula's isolated castle/manor in Transylvania, with the cooperation of England's real estate agent. In my interpretation this too marks a veiled degeneration-of-England theme wherein Stoker points to the active collusion, for profit, of the English market with foreigners of dubious ethnicity – not to mention gastronomic tastes. It is this transnational network that brings England to the verge of disaster when Dracula makes the crossing into the island nation. Harker recognizes this complicity when he records his horror at Dracula's presence on English soil:

> This was the being I was helping to transfer to London where, perhaps for centuries to come, he might, among its teeming millions, satiate his lust for blood, and create a new and ever widening circle of semi-demons to batten on the helpless.
>
> (53–4)

Thus, the degeneration of England in these novels is not simply a 'narrative of reverse colonization' as Stephen Arata terms it in his essay on Stoker (1990). Rather it is a narrative of England's transnational engagement that produces specific linkages and opens up the borders for invasion. The primitive and the atavistic – the Indians of *Moonstone*, Tonga of *The Sign of Four*, the murdering smugglers of *Jamaica Inn*, the vampire of *Dracula* – are not setting out to colonize imperial England (Senf 1979) on their own. Their *'invasion' is facilitated and even invited by the actions of Englishmen who have for various reasons been a part of (licit and/or illicit) networks of a transnational nature.* Further, it is not simply an invasion by foreigners, it is an invasion by degenerate Englishmen like Small, Roylott and others.[24]

The 'Parliament of Monsters' and the degeneration of London/England

> The English, whether travellers or residents, came pouring in one great revulsive stream, back on their own country; and with them crowds of Italians and Spaniards. Our little island was filled to bursting.
>
> (Shelley 2004: 188)

This is Mary Shelley's description in *The Last Man* of the migrants and refugees fleeing into London, and away from plague-ridden European cities. Where England had attracted wealth once it was now receiving migrants in a form of invasion that arouses a particular anxiety. Shelley's anxiety over the 'stream' of immigrants that seem to cross the English Channel with frightening ease echoes Wordsworth's anxiety over the proximity of France in the wake of large-scale emigration of aristocrats and others in the years after the Revolution. Wordsworth wrote in 'September 1802' (not to be confused with 'September 1, 1802'):

Inland, within a hollow Vale, I stood,
And saw, while sea was calm and air was clear,

> The Coast of France, the Coast of France how near!
> Drawn almost into frightful neighbourhood.
> I shrunk, for verily the barrier flood
> Was like a Lake, or River bright and fair,
> A span of waters; yet what power is there!
> What mightiness for evil and for good!
>
> (1969: 243)

What is clear from the above texts is that disease, as imported or as punishment for slavery, was only one form of invasion that England would have to be worried about. Immigration was a key concern from the 1780s, and while many saw England presenting its best face as the space of refuge and last bastion of freedom as we shall see, the writings do exhibit considerable anxiety over the multiculturalization of their nation.

The degeneration of England as visualized by, say, the abolitionists or poets like Coleridge and Wordsworth, is attributable not only to disease but also to returning servicemen/mariners and migrants. That is, there occur different images of the pathogenic Other that threatens bodies and the body politic in England's literature.

George Eliot's *Daniel Deronda* (1876), Walter Besant's *All Sorts and Conditions of Men* (1882), the fiction of Margaret Harkness are articulations of the immigrant theme in Victorian England. David Glover (2012), tracing the cultural history of the 1905 Aliens Act that sought to regulate immigrant entry into the British Isles, has demonstrated how the figure of the Jew comes to dominate the popular imagination as the 'quintessential foreigner' (10) even as the word 'alien' became a 'national-racist epithet' (10). Glover's study shows how feelings about the 'invasion' (demographic, cultural) of England ran high and it was its literary and periodical culture that drove the emotional responses to the figure of the alien. In Margaret Harkness' *In Darkest London* (echoing the title of William Booth's evangelist tract, *In Darkest England and the Way Out*), she portrays the *threat* to London's poor consisting, Glover notes, of Hottentots, Algerians, Indians and Polish Jews. Even the London vagrant and slummer, in Harkness' portrait, would be happy to 'kick the foreigner back to "his own dear native land" ' if only Government would believe in "English for English" and give all foreigners notice' (qtd. in Glover 2012: 68–9). In another Harkness socialist text demonstrating sympathies for the London working class and poor, the target of attack remains the foreigner: 'the country's going to the dogs along of these foreigners. I'd like to weed 'em out' (qtd. in Glover 2012: 69).

These expressions of Victorian rage over the alien and the foreigner and the influx of the cultural-racial Other into its spaces might be traced back to an anxiety over the degeneration of England/London of an earlier era. This is the Wordsworthian age when London's transformation through immigration from the country is gathering pace. He writes of London in Book 8 of 1850 *Prelude*:

That vast metropolis,
The fount of my country's destiny and the world's;
That great emporium, chronicle at once
And burial-place of passions, and their home
Imperial, and chief living residence.

(1969: 554)

And in 'Composed Upon Westminster Bridge, September 3, 1802' he would exclaim: 'The very houses seem asleep;/And all that mighty heart is lying still!' with a play on 'lying': even when London is asleep it seems to lie because it is so degenerate in its heart (1969: 214). His London in Book 7 of 1850 *Prelude* is characterized by numerous people flowing through its streets, crowded and clogging: the 'endless stream of men, and moving things' (1969: 539). He uses the word 'swarm' to describe the imperial metropolis' inhabitants and writes of their 'undistinguishable world ... / amid the same perpetual flow / Of trivial objects' (1969: 546). As Saree Makdisi points out, for Wordsworth it is '*precisely* because this flow has "no law, no meaning, and no end" that it constantly threatens to transform itself into the (supposedly) equally "disorderly" and "meaningless" working-class mob' (1998: 29, emphasis in original), and the 'space of London turns into the space of Empire' (31). But this crowd is not only of working-class immigrants, as we have noted above: it often includes crowds of emigrant clergy and aristocrats, especially in the wake of the French Revolution.

In most cases, however, the metropolis' imperial role manifests in the form of the Empire's peripheries 'coming home', so to speak. What Joseph McLaughlin (2000) identifies as the preeminent Victorian thematic of London's 'urban jungle' due to the excessive arrivals from the outposts of Empire is prefigured in Wordsworth's palpable anxiety over the degeneration of the city in Book 7 of 1850 *Prelude*. Wordsworth writes:

See, among less distinguishable shapes,
The begging scavenger, with hat in hand;
The Italian, as he thrids his way with care,
Steadying, far-seen, a frame of images
Upon his head; with basket at his breast,
The Jew; the stately and slow-moving Turk,
With freight of slippers piled beneath his arm!
Enough;—the mighty concourse I surveyed
With no unthinking mind, well pleased to note
Among the crowd all specimens of man,
Through all the colors which the sun bestows,
And every character of form and face:
The Swede, the Russian; from the genial South,
The Frenchman and the Spaniard; from remote
America the hunter-Indian; Moors,

228 Disease and degeneration

Malays, Lascars, the Tartar, the Chinese,
And negro ladies in white muslin gowns.

(1969: 540)

Wordsworth is describing an unending flow of cultural and racial Others through
the streets of London. The passage expresses a particular kind of anxiety: that
London is no more a purely English space. To cite Makdisi's comment on the
above passage: this 'is also a destabilizing and ultimately a terrifying vision. Once
the colonial flood-gates have been opened, once Britain has gone out into
the world, there is nothing at all to prevent the world flooding and crashing back
into Britain' (1998: 31). Elsewhere Wordsworth would speak of London's 'Parliament
of [multicultural] Monsters', in Book 7 of the 1850 *Prelude*:

> What a shock
> For eyes and ears! what anarchy and din,
> Barbarian and infernal, – a phantasma,
> Monstrous in colour, motion, shape, sight, sound!
> Below, the open space, through every nook
> Of the wide area, twinkles, is alive
> With heads; the midway region, and above,
> Is thronged with staring pictures and huge scrolls,
> Dumb proclamations of the Prodigies;
> With chattering monkeys dangling from their poles,
> And children whirling in their roundabouts;
> With those that stretch the neck and strain the eyes,
> And crack the voice in rivalship, the crowd
> Inviting; with buffoons against buffoons
> Grimacing, writhing, screaming, – him who grinds
> The hurdy-gurdy, at the fiddle weaves,
> Rattles the salt-box, thumps the kettle-drum,
> And him who at the trumpet puffs his cheeks,
> The silver-collared Negro with his timbrel,
> Equestrians, tumblers, women, girls, and boys,
> Blue-breeched, pink-vested, with high-towering plumes. –
> All moveables of wonder, from all parts,
> Are here – Albinos, painted Indians, Dwarfs,
> The Horse of knowledge, and the learned Pig,
> The Stone-eater, the man that swallows fire,
> Giants, Ventriloquists, the Invisible Girl,
> The Bust that speaks and moves its goggling eyes,
> The Wax-work, Clock-work, all the marvellous craft
> Of modern Merlins, Wild Beasts, Puppet-shows,
> All out-o'-the-way, far-fetched, perverted things,
> All freaks of nature, all Promethean thoughts

Of man, his dulness, madness, and their feats
All jumbled up together, to compose
A Parliament of Monsters.

(1969: 546)

From Wordsworth's diatribe against the multiculturalization of London coded as degeneration ('Parliament of Monsters') to Doyle's notorious account of London in 'A Study in Scarlet' (1887) as 'that great cesspool into which all the loungers and idlers of the Empire are irresistibly drained' (Doyle 1988c: 3) is but a step. London degenerates into chaos and terrifying plurality precisely as a result of its transnational engagements.[25]

In Shelley's *The Last Man*, England is invaded by migrants hoping that its climate will ensure their safety from the pandemic plague. The ports of Ireland are clogged with vessels 'rotting on the lazy deep' (2004: 236). Shelley writes:

A number of people from North America, the relics of that populous continent, had set sail for the East with mad desire of change, leaving their native plains for lands not less afflicted than their own. Several hundreds landed in Ireland, about the first of November, and took possession of such vacant habitations as they could find; seizing upon the superabundant food, and the stray cattle. As they exhausted the produce of one spot, they went on to another. At length they began to interfere with the inhabitants, and strong in their concentrated numbers, ejected the natives from their dwellings, and robbed them of their winter store. A few events of this kind roused the fiery nature of the Irish; and they attacked the invaders. Some were destroyed; the major part escaped by quick and well ordered movements; and danger made them careful. Their numbers ably arranged; the very deaths among them concealed; moving on in good order, and apparently given up to enjoyment, they excited the envy of the Irish. The Americans permitted a few to join their band, and presently the recruits outnumbered the strangers—nor did they join with them, nor imitate the admirable order which, preserved by the Trans-Atlantic chiefs, rendered them at once secure and formidable. The Irish followed their track in disorganized multitudes; each day encreasing; each day becoming more lawless. The Americans were eager to escape from the spirit they had roused, and, reaching the eastern shores of the island, embarked for England. Their incursion would hardly have been felt had they come alone; but the Irish, collected in unnatural numbers, began to feel the inroads of famine, and they followed in the wake of the Americans for England also. The crossing of the sea could not arrest their progress. The harbours of the desolate sea-ports of the west of Ireland were filled with vessels of all sizes, from the man of war to the small fishers' boat, which lay sailorless, and rotting on the lazy deep. The emigrants embarked by hundreds, and unfurling their sails with rude hands, made strange havoc of buoy and cordage. Those who modestly betook themselves to the smaller craft, for

230 Disease and degeneration

the most part achieved their watery journey in safety. Some, in the true spirit of reckless enterprise, went on board a ship of an hundred and twenty guns; the vast hull drifted with the tide out of the bay, and after many hours its crew of landsmen contrived to spread a great part of her enormous canvass— the wind took it, and while a thousand mistakes of the helmsman made her present her head now to one point, and now to another, the vast fields of canvass that formed her sails flapped with a sound like that of a huge cataract; or such as a sea-like forest may give forth when buffeted by an equinoctial north-wind. The port-holes were open, and with every sea, which as she lurched, washed her decks, they received whole tons of water. The difficulties were increased by a fresh breeze which began to blow, whistling among the shrowds, dashing the sails this way and that, and rending them with horrid split, and such whir as may have visited the dreams of Milton, when he imagined the winnowing of the arch-fiend's van-like wings, which increased the uproar of wild chaos. These sounds were mingled with the roaring of the sea, the splash of the chafed billows round the vessel's sides, and the gurgling up of the water in the hold. The crew, many of whom had never seen the sea before, felt indeed as if heaven and earth came ruining together, as the vessel dipped her bows in the waves, or rose high upon them. Their yells were drowned in the clamour of elements, and the thunder rivings of their unwieldy habitation—they discovered at last that the water gained on them, and they betook themselves to their pumps; they might as well have laboured to empty the ocean by bucketfuls. As the sun went down, the gale increased; the ship seemed to feel her danger, she was now completely water-logged, and presented other indications of settling before she went down. The bay was crowded with vessels, whose crews, for the most part, were observing the uncouth sportings of this huge unwieldy machine—they saw her gradually sink; the waters now rising above her lower decks—they could hardly wink before she had utterly disappeared, nor could the place where the sea had closed over her be at all discerned. Some few of her crew were saved, but the greater part clinging to her cordage and masts went down with her, to rise only when death loosened their hold.

(235)

Shelley continues:

Such incursions struck the English with affright, in all those towns where there was still sufficient population to feel the change. There was room enough indeed in our hapless country for twice the number of invaders; but their lawless spirit instigated them to violence; they took a delight in thrusting the possessors from their houses; in seizing on some mansion of luxury, where the noble dwellers secluded themselves in fear of the plague; in forcing these of either sex to become their servants and purveyors; till, the ruin complete in one place, they removed their locust visitation to another.

Disease and degeneration **231**

When unopposed they spread their ravages wide; in cases of danger they clustered, and by dint of numbers overthrew their weak and despairing foes. They came from the east and the north, and directed their course without apparent motive, but unanimously towards our unhappy metropolis ...

The van of our invaders had proceeded as far as Manchester and Derby, before we received notice of their arrival. They swept the country like a conquering army, burning—laying waste—murdering. The lower and vaga-bond English joined with them. Some few of the Lords Lieutenant who remained, endeavoured to collect the militia—but the ranks were vacant, panic seized on all, and the opposition that was made only served to increase the audacity and cruelty of the enemy. They talked of taking London, con-quering England—calling to mind the long detail of injuries which had for many years been forgotten. Such vaunts displayed their weakness, rather than their strength—yet still they might do extreme mischief, which, ending in their destruction, would render them at last objects of compassion and remorse ...

Gorgon and Centaur, dragon and iron-hoofed lion, vast sea-monster and gigantic hydra, were but types of the strange and appalling accounts brought to London concerning our invaders. Their landing was long unknown, but having now advanced within an hundred miles of London, the country people flying before them arrived in successive troops, each exaggerating the numbers, fury, and cruelty of the assailants. Tumult filled the before quiet streets—women and children deserted their homes, escaping they knew not whither—fathers, husbands, and sons, stood trembling, not for themselves, but for their loved and defenceless relations. As the country people poured into London, the citizens fled southwards—they climbed the higher edifices of the town, fancying that they could discern the smoke and flames the enemy spread around them.

(237–8)

My reading proposes that the plague is *not* the only pathologizing trope that Mary Shelley deploys to speak of the end of England. The flow of refugees is invasion too, of a different kind. London, imagined as a city of refuge, suffers a 'locust vis-itation', as she puts it, from the people fleeing the plague in other parts of the world. What is important to see here is that Shelley is articulating a *reverse* coloniza-tion, as Bewell notes (1999: 306), but also, in my view, foregrounds the intransigent and irreducible nature of transnational linkages. Shelley, therefore, *demonstrates how England's own transnational linkages, its interests in colonization or trade, have opened its doors to refugees now.* That is, where England once controlled the flow of popula-tions across the world, whether in terms of slave trading, mercantile voyages or soldiering, it was now at the receiving end of such a flow. It is not simply a reversal of colonial demographics as much as an outcome of England's own travels. This is the plague-ridden, and plague-driven, urban jungle where the heart of the Empire is now an 'unhappy metropolis' (Shelley 2004: 237).

232 Disease and degeneration

Further, Shelley, I believe, underscores the connectedness of England with other nations in an ironic comment:

> The plague is in London; the air of England is tainted, and her sons and daughters strew the unwholesome earth. And now, the sea, late our defence, seems our prison bound; hemmed in by its gulphs, we shall die like the famished inhabitants of a besieged town. Other nations have a fellowship in death; but we, shut out from all neighbourhood, must bury our own dead, and little England become a wide, wide tomb.
>
> (198)

While ostensibly she refers to how even a tiny island has become a 'wide, wide tomb' it is significant that she proffers this image after describing a 'fellowship in death' of other nations. The earth itself is therefore the wide tomb. If, as Jonathan Elmer proposes, the novel speaks of the impossibility of sovereignty (2009: 359), then the above account seems to propose that in the age of transnational trade, and transnational disease, there is a fellowship of suffering.

In Stoker's *Dracula* Harker is worried that once on English soil, Dracula would 'create a new and ever widening circle of semi-demons to batten on the helpless' (1997: 53–4). The anxiety is not only of the *arrival* of the vampire but of the arrival as marking the opening moments of an *empire of vampires feeding off a decaying England*, it is the anxiety – as would be typical, in fact, of science fiction – over the reproduction/replication of the monster invader. Renfield and Lucy (and Mina, almost), victims of Dracula's pursuits and evil ambitions, epitomize the degeneration of England.[26] Harriet, like Stoker's Renfield who eats flies and other creatures, behaves like a 'restless animal' (Marryat 2010: 176). She seems to have a preternatural fascination for eating (4), and is also another instance of a human degenerating into animal-like behaviour.[27] That is, *Dracula* (or Harriet Brandt in Marryat's tale) instantiates an anxiety over the possibility of the 'Parliament of Monsters', an entire race of monsters taking over England, having arrived from across the continent. The anxiety is about *the multiculturalization of England and the species cosmopolitanism – from humans to vampires and animals* – that is likely to follow in the wake of Dracula. The 'reverse colonization' and deracination – the loss of racial characteristics of the English race as a result of the vampire bites (Arata 1990) – is the effect of the widespread dissemination of new *races* across England.[28] In the words of Florence Marryat, it is the deadly combination of 'black blood and of the vampire's blood' (2010: 156) that spells ruin for England, thus combining in one description the racial *and* vampiric threat posed to the nation by the foreigner, or a creature from the ancient past. Thus Dracula is an ancient evil and the Baskerville hound is an ancient curse. It is important to note that 'reverse colonization' and England's subsequent-consequent degeneration is attributed to both a racial-cultural Other as well as a temporally distanced Other (in Chapter 2, I had pointed to the temporal distancing as an important rhetorical strategy). The 'primitive past' serves as a code for both Dracula the foreigner *and* the hound in Victorian writing. As

Nils Clausson (2005) notes in his study of Doyle, these Gothic elements indicate a cultural anxiety that evolution and progress do not always move smoothly *forward* – for there are always 'irrational', primitive – atavistic – elements that enter the frames of any culture.

By the time we enter the mid-twentieth century these anxieties have solidified and might be seen in Enoch Powell's famous 'rivers of blood' talk and the anti-immigrant sentiments in England. The anxiety over a 'decolonizing' England – and its attendant amusement for other races – is captured so wonderfully in Jamaican-English poet Louise Bennett's 'Colonization in Reverse'. The poem begins with the speaker expressing joy that Jamaicans are now colonizing England, coming to the former colonial power in hundreds and 'tousan'. They seek jobs in what they see as their 'mother lan'. These immigrants, writes Bennett, 'turn history upside dung!' as they 'immigrate an populate/De seat a de Empire'. The poem concludes with:

> Wat a devilment a Englan!
> Dem face war an brave de worse,
> But me wondering how dem gwine stan
> Colonizin in reverse.
>
> (http://louisebennett.com/colonization-in-reverse/)

Commentators have argued that T.S. Eliot's attempts to reiterate a common European tradition and its strengths was a response to the imminent collapse of Empire but also of so-called established English/European values (MacPhee 2011: 37–8), even though there was in many works a nostalgic craving for non-European primitivism.

**

Haunted by degenerate Europeans, such as Dracula (Stoker), Jonathan Small and Roylott (Doyle), Harriet Brandt (Marryat), England begins to lose its cultural cohesiveness and identity, and the anxiety over this loss is captured in the literature of the Victorian age. However, this kind of anxiety over 'reverse colonization', cultural degeneration and invasion has always been a component of England's identity-making process, as we have seen in the representations of Jews (Marlowe) or renegade English John Ward (Daborne) in the Early Modern period. Whether as usurer or as vampire the Other as pathogenic threat is intrinsic to the making of English identity. More worryingly, as we shall see (Chapter 6) in the characters of Heathcliff (*Wuthering Heights*) and Rochester (*Jane Eyre*), the corruption of England's masculinity is already underway in the form of the 'oriental despot'.

This chapter has argued that transnational linkages and global networks in which England was embedded since the Early Modern period, while producing profits in terms of commodities, markets and people, also produced particular anxieties about the racial, cultural Other. The pathologized Other is a multi-layered discourse of borders, border-crossings, pathogens and invasions that climaxes with an anxiety of the corruption, hybridization, multiculturalization and degeneration of Englishness

234 Disease and degeneration

through its interactions with the racial, cultural Other. Invasion rhetoric that is central to the expression of these anxieties takes various forms. Commodity cultures contaminate England as effectively as pathogens from across the seas. Moral contagions in the form of greed for profit and gold available from the transnational linkage and activities alter English character for the worse. Returning servicemen become strangers to their own country and home. The thematic of invasion by vampires and half-breeds climaxes in an anxiety over the loss of Englishness as the city of London, under the assault of new races and different cultures, becomes a 'Parliament of Monsters'. England, in this reading of the pathologized Other, *fashions itself as an identity in threat of dissolution.*

Notes

1 Michael Wiley points out that writers like Charlotte Smith, while projecting England as a space of freedom, are also conscious of the possible loss of such freedoms for the English themselves unless major political and social reforms are instituted (2008: 22–3).
2 For a masterly reading of the linkage between opium and Empire in de Quincey see John Barrell's *The Infection of Thomas de Quincey: The Psychopathology of Imperialism* (1991).
3 This 'invasion' rhetoric acquires a different valence in the abolitionist writing of the 1780–1840 period when it is Europe that is believed to have invaded the otherwise peaceable African peoples. Thus, James Grahame and others were of the firm belief that:

    in that fair land of hill, and dale, and stream,
    the simple tribes from age to age had heard
    no hostile voice

    as Grahame put it in 'Africa Delivered; or, The Slave Trade abolished' (1809, cited in Brantlinger 1988: 176). While this kind of portrait does deploy the stereotype of the simple, primitive African it also paints the European arrival in Africa as an unwanted, unwarranted *invasion*. There were other critiques as well. Samuel Johnson, for example, in an essay in *The Idler* created a fictional Indian (Native American) in order to critique colonialism, and especially England's treatment of the Native Americans. The Indian in Johnson's text speaks of an imminent moment 'when the pride of usurpation shall be crushed, and the cruelties of invasion shall be revenged' (cited in Fulford 2006: 20).
4 Daniel Vitkus argues that the expansion of the Ottoman Empire, which had won territory from Venice and Spain in the sixteenth century and conquered Egypt, was colonizing the European territories during the era when European nations were looking at the New World and the Indies for trade and/or conquest. Vitkus' is an important intervention in Early Modern studies for his focus on Turkish-European tensions but also for his revisioning of the proto-colonial movements by speaking of these kinds of reversals (Vitkus 1997). For English literature's, more specifically Spenser's, engagements with Turkey in the Early Modern period see Hollings (2010).
5 Tobacco's connection with Britain's imperial project has also been studied. See Knapp (1988). *The Worke of Chimney Sweepers* (anonymous, identified only as 'Philaretes') compared the effects of tobacco to the soot that caused illness in chimney sweepers. As response Roger Marbrecke wrote *A Defence of Tabacco* (1602).
6 This view of the indigenous people, whether of Africa, Asia or America, as valuing baubles and fetishizing what the European took to be mere trifles, gathered discursive strength post-1700s. The Europeans described any object valued by the Africans as 'fetishes' and this grew out of a context where a shared value of commodities for trade had to be established. For a study of Western representations of African, specifically Asante fetishes in the colonial era, see Engmann (2012).

Disease and degeneration 235

7 Thus, Charles Dickens, notes Mary Burgan, while he 'feared infection from abroad and chaos from the colonies ... his most specific descriptions of contagion centered on England and the threat of disease from domestic poverty and deprivation' (2002: 839). In a reading of Daniel Defoe's key pathogenic text, *A Journal of the Plague Year* (1722), 'The circulation of capital becomes the instrument of plague, as it spreads in the marketplace and trade routes ... Defoe's protagonist H.F., a businessman dependent on the circulation of capital, becomes a figure of the plague' (Boluk and Lenz 2010: 131).

8 On the invasion theme in nineteenth-century literature, especially of the Gothic variety, see Brantlinger (1988, 2009: 47–9).

9 Barrell writes: '[De Quincey] was terrorised by the fear of an unending and interlinked chain of infections from the East, which threatened to enter his system and to overthrow it, leaving him visibly and permanently "compromised" and "orientalised"' (1991: 15). The nightmares de Quincey describes and which I have already cited earlier in this chapter are examples of the infections. It is in this context of a fear of pathogens that de Quincey's reference to 'inoculation' and Barrell's own reading of the 'infections of de Quincey' that we need to locate the nightmarish consumption of the Eastern product.

10 In the era of decolonization immigrant writers such as Louise Bennett would treat this invasion theme in interesting ways. Bennett in 'Colonization in Reverse' (1966) will speak of the Jamaican colonization of England. But Bennett suggests that when the Jamaicans begin to see England as their new mother land ('Everybody future plan/Is fe get a big-time job/An settle in de mother lan') they perform not only amnesia but disloyalty towards their culture.

11 The play itself, Jonathan Gil Harris notes, has numerous references to syphilis, and these references are often cast in economic and financial terms (2004: chapter 2).

12 Patrick Brantlinger notes that the 'constant association of Africa with the inhuman violence of the slave trade did much to darken its landscape even before the Romantic period' (1988: 175). Thus the 'dark continent', one could say, was the darkening of the land-scape through European practices. The Gothic 'potential' of African lives and landscape shifted the darkness *away* from European practices to African ones.

13 Ironically of course the Martians are defeated by earth's bacteria. Their red weed, writes Wells, dies due to a 'cankering disease ... [induced by] certain bacteria' (2005: 145). The Martians themselves were 'dead! – slain by the putrefactive and disease bacteria against which their systems were unprepared ... slain, after all man's devices had failed, by the humblest things that God, in his wisdom, has put upon this earth' (168).

14 Daniel Vitkus points to numerous captivity narratives by men enslaved in Muslim areas that provide the context for Daborne's and Massinger's plays (Vitkus 2006: 65).

15 On the Victorian obsession with the 'roving' gypsies see Behlmer (1985).

16 English/European masculinity in crisis, or at least in flux, with cross-dressing and homoeroticism would reach its climactic moment with figures like T.E. Lawrence.

17 However, it is also possible to see, as Attila Viragh does (2013), *Dracula* as a novel about cultural extinction of the East European races. In an insightful essay that flies in the face of several readings that only focus on the English end of things – where Dracula is the threat – Viragh treats Dracula as a *victim*. Viragh writes:

> *Dracula* can be seen as a prescient depiction of a globalizing world in which minority cultures and languages are increasingly threatened with assimilation and extinc-tion ... The Szèkely, with whom Dracula initially claims kinship, are one such Hungarian-speaking people whose culture has been threatened in Transylvania, where they face pressure to adopt the language and culture of Romania ... Trans-ylvania is in Dracula's words a 'whirlpool of European races,' in the sense of a place of cultural blending, drowning and annihilation ... Dracula can be viewed as a subaltern struggling against cultural loss. As the sole heir of a disappearing civilization,

236 Disease and degeneration

he is losing his own historical record even as he attempts to learn the dominant, imperial language and culture of the British Empire.

(232)

At one point in the tale Van Helsing does compare Dracula to a slave: 'He can do all these things, yet he is not free. Nay, he is even more prisoner than the slave of the galley, than the madman in his cell' (211). Also see Ken Gelder on Stoker's theme of vampires, national identity and reverse colonization (1994: 11–13).

18 The imperialist ideology underpinning Conrad's novel has been the subject of considerable debate, with many arguing for its racism and colonial politics (Achebe 1977) and others detecting a certain ambiguity in them (Said 1994). Others note that Marlow distinguishes between the more liberal English who achieve some practical good in Africa, and the other Europeans who simply plunder (Lewis 1998).

19 I am not pursuing the gender angle to Bertha Mason's portrait.

20 It must be remembered that mariners and naval officers were also projected and treated as heroes in this same period of Coleridge and Shelley and in the popular novels of Frederick Marryat. Figures like Nelson and Alexander Bell, notes Tim Fulford, represented 'moral exemplars for the domestic and imperial spheres' (1999: 162). It is therefore possible to see the Ancient Mariner and the returning servicemen figures of Wordsworth, Coleridge, Merry and Burns as subtly reversing the heroic motif, within the context of Britain's imperial schema.

21 In a recent work Emrys Chew notes how the imperial arms trade in the Indian ocean area was a central feature of the nineteenth-century global expansion of Europe (Chew 2012). So in addition to opium we now have arms movement and trade as part of the mercantile-imperial expansion of Empire.

22 Yet, even addictions to these products are sometimes converted into symbols of English resilience. Thus, despite his addiction to cocaine, Doyle's Holmes triumphs over all. A better case would be de Quincey's addict. In the very opening pages of his *Confessions* de Quincey's addict speaks of how he escaped his addiction:

> I have struggled against this fascinating entrapment with a religious zeal … and have, at length, accomplished what I never yet heard attributed to any man – have untwisted, almost to its final links, the accursed chain which fettered me. Such a self-conquest may reasonably be set off in counterbalance to any kind or degree of self-indulgence.
>
> (1985: 2)

Thus the addict demonstrates strength of character in escaping the self-indulgence and addiction, and thus reinforces the power of English character in defying, rejecting and overcoming an Oriental product's power. In both Holmes and de Quincey, the addiction does no permanent damage to the Englishman's character: the former continues to be the brilliant criminalist and the latter asserts his character again. Daniel O'Quinn's reading of de Quincey suggests that the opening pages of *Confessions* that show his 'struggl[e] from subordination' also portray the addict as exemplary (2003: 264). O'Quinn establishes a connection between de Quincey's rhetoric of bondage and escape and abolitionist discourses of the age, to argue that, like abolitionist rhetoric, de Quincey 'stage[s] exemplary freed men and women to testify first to the stripping away of their humanity, and second to their eventual reconstitution as free Christian subjects' (264).

23 Lesli Favor has argued that Doyle 'others' both the foreign and the female in several of his stories in order to 'assert the eminence of the English over the Other-than-English and the Male over the Other-than-male' (2000: 398).

24 The theme of the degeneration of England and English character was the stuff of massive polemical writing. See Harpham (1976) and Brantlinger (1988: 230).

25 The curate in Wells' *The War of the Worlds*, having seen what the Martians could do, loses his mind and begins to rant:

> It is just, O God! ... It is just. On me and mine be the punishment laid. We have sinned, we have fallen short. There was poverty, sorrow; the poor were trodden in the dust, and I held my peace. I preached acceptable folly – my God, what folly! – when I should have stood up, though I died for it, and called upon them to repent.
>
> (2005: 137)

The curate suggests that the desolation wrought upon London is justified, as punishment for being a wicked city, one whose heart, wrote Wordsworth in a perhaps unintentional pun, 'lies still' even when asleep. This portrait of a desolate London/England as the end-product of its own sins is a common theme in Victorian literature, but this sinning is linked to England's transnational actions (I have already noted the abolitionist poetry's focus on English guilt regarding slavery and the pathogenic retribution that is England's lot). While Wells' curate offers theological explanations for the apocalypse other authors provide more prosaic – and political – reasoning for England's collapse.

26 On trauma and Otherness in Dracula see Khader (2012).

27 It is therefore interesting that at the same time that Doyle, Dracula and others were mapping the degeneration of European humans into animal-like states, H.G. Wells would write *The Island of Dr. Moreau* – the novel appears a year before *Dracula*, in 1896 – with the vivisectionist's attempts to de-animalize the animals of the island so that they would become more like humans. Wells' novel has been examined as a novel about race and origins (see Christensen 2004).

28 I am not addressing here the intersection of vampiric racial discourse and sexuality. Since Dracula's primary victims are all women, and women represent the possibility of racial continuity, the process of invasion involves, evidently, sexual dynamics as well (see Craft 1984 and Stevenson 1988). One critic has proposed that 'the novel does lead us to consider Lucy's sexuality as responsible for her own infection, nowhere more so than when she attempts to seduce Lord Godalming while under Dracula's influence, an episode that reinforces the connection between her diseased state and her sexual assertiveness' (Willis 2007: 315).

6

CIVILIZE AND COLLAPSE

Improveable Others, disintegrating English

In Edmund Spenser's *The Faerie Queene* (Book 2, Canto 7) Mammon shows Guyon the 'Great heapes of gold, that neuer could be spent' (1984: 224) being extracted through slave labour:

> One with great bellowes gathered filling aire,
> And with forst wind the fewell did inflame;
> Another did the dying bronds repaire
> With yron toungs, and sprinckled oft the same
> With liquid waues, fiers Vulcans rage to tame,
> Who maistring them, renewd his former heat;
> Some scumd the drosse, that from the metall came;
> Some stird the molten owre with ladles great;
> And euery one did swincke, and euery one did sweat.
> But when as earthly wight they present saw,
> Glistring in armes and battailous aray,
> From their whot worke they did themselues withdraw
> To wonder at the sight: for till that day,
> They neuer creature saw, that came that way.
> Their staring eyes sparckling with feruent fire,
> And vgly shapes did nigh the man dismay,
> That were it not for shame, he would retire,
> Till that him thus bespake their soueraigne Lord & sire.

(Spenser 1984: 230)

In Maria Edgeworth's 'The Grateful Negro' she describes the progressive plantation owner Mr Edwards thus:

This gentleman treated his slaves with all possible humanity and kindness. He wished that there was no such thing as slavery in the world, but he was convinced, by the arguments of those who have the best means of obtaining information, that the sudden emancipation of the negroes would rather increase than diminish their miseries. His benevolence, therefore, confined itself within the bounds of reason. He adopted those plans for the amelioration of the state of the slaves which appeared to him the most likely to succeed without producing any violent agitation or revolution. For instance, his negroes had reasonable and fixed daily tasks; and when these were finished, they were permitted to employ their time for their own advantage or amusement. If they chose to employ themselves longer for their master, they were paid regular wages for their extra work. This reward, for as such it was considered, operated most powerfully upon the slaves. Those who are animated by hope can perform what would seem impossibilities to those who are under the depressing influence of fear. The wages which Mr. Edwards promised, he took care to see punctually paid.

(http://ebooks.adelaide.edu.au/e/edgeworth/maria/grateful-negro/)

In H.G. Wells' *The Island of Dr. Moreau* (1896) the doctor mourns that he cannot burn out the 'emotions' in the animals (2002: 106–7. I shall return to this passage later in the chapter).

Spenser focuses on the labour that produces the 'fountaine of the worldes good', as Mammon calls it. Edgeworth develops the double stereotype of the kind plantation owner and his slave, the latter grateful for the ameliorative measures that the white master initiates on his plantation. In Wells the aim of the white man is to 'evolve' out of the native beasts a 'rational creature' of his own, through an interventionary process of 'burn[ing] all the animal'.

The three examples here, chosen randomly over nearly 300 years, construct particular images of the racial, cultural Other in English literature, and a concomitant self-fashioning. Spenser, in Maureen Quilligan's perceptive reading of the above passage, is in fact presenting 'New World wealth as it really was', with a base in 'forced labor' (2001: 23) by creatures that might be slaves or demons. Edgeworth shifts the terms of the debate around slavery away from outright emancipation ('the sudden emancipation of the negroes would rather increase than diminish their miseries') to amelioration. And Wells' Moreau seeks to accelerate the process of evolution wherein the beast folk of the island, from their natural 'animal' state (or 'negroid' – the term is used to describe one of the beast people) must be made into rational creatures that *he* can comprehend, and perhaps control. What is common to the three examples cited here are the interlinked discourses of enslavement, amelioration and improvement. These discourses mark a whole new aspect of globality in English literature, and constitute one of the two poles of this chapter.

After travelling to the ends of the earth and bringing much of it under its control as colonies, dominions and subjects, Europe from the 1780s developed yet another dimension of globality. The world, as England saw it from the 1780s (Lester 2000,

2012), was a field for the English to work at improving, whether in the plantations of Jamaica or in the colonies of South Asia. The space of the *interracial, intercultural encounter now included a specific form of engagement with the Other: welfare, the civilizational mission and 'improvement'*. The racial-cultural Other was now, besides being discovered, exoticized, commodified and pathologized, an *improveable Other*, just as the imperialist was the heroic, battling-all-odds, stoic Englishman seeking to improve the suffering Other. This improveable, racially-culturally different Other was to be found mainly in England's and Europe's *colonies* where they possessed the authority to improve the *subjects*. Thus this chapter narrows the focus of the book's study of English globality to its colonial possessions where there were any number of natives and any number of cultural defects that could be erased, ameliorated or replaced by better (i.e. English) cultural practices.

The imperialist-hero stereotype emerged, especially in the late nineteenth century, in the discourse of rescue, improvement and civilizing-the-savages in England's colonies in Africa and South Asia. The hero was not just the military conqueror of the General Gordon variety. The selfless missionary, doctor, teacher, nurse, reformer and social worker was also the 'imperial hero'. Thus, it might be argued that *central to England's transnational engagements, was a discursive binary constructed around the figures of the to-be-improved native and the improving-Englishman or woman*. The world was the space of such philanthropic, stoic, selfless and 'moral' engagements on the part of the English: so the improving Englishman was a whole new category of English identity. The Englishman would labour, literally and figuratively, under what Rudyard Kipling would famously characterize as 'the white man's burden' in an 1899 poem of the same title.

The improveable Other in English writings included a diverse variety of non-Europeans: slaves, Native Americans, Hindus and Muslims of the 'East Indies', to mention a few. This 'improvement' discourse cut across numerous domains: economy, agriculture, the law, public health, education, and included various efforts directed at 'social evils' or the regulation of rampant sexuality and towards the 'character-building' of natives. Even domains such as animal breeding and botanic gardens were seen as 'tokens of the righteousness of property and empire' (Drayton 2005: 87).

However, it is within this ideology of improvement and the taxonomy of the 'improveable native'/'improving Englishman' that the fissures and contradictions within England's transnational engagements make their appearance most powerfully. What this chapter, the final one of the book, therefore does is to trace a contradiction, or a counter-discourse, alongside the dominant one of improvement. It argues that from the 1890s, but prefigured in texts much earlier, England's transnational engagements with the racial, cultural Other, besides the discourse of improvement and the civilizational mission, also had to account for a certain discrepant geography where the English were the cause of native ruin *and* themselves experienced disintegration, dehumanization and death. That is, even as the discourse of moral imperialism manifests in English literature in the form of the theme of the civilizing mission, we can detect a deeper anxiety that England's distant engagements with cultural Others were also producing savages out of the 'pukka sahib' and destroying their moral-cultural values. *Globality therefore has two clear axes: of the 'improvement discourse' and the 'disintegrating English' discourse.*[1]

The disintegrating Englishman could be of various types: the bloodthirsty and savage English persuading Native Americans to bloodier acts of cruelty (in Charlotte Smith's *The Old Manor House*), the animalized Kurtz (Joseph Conrad's *Heart of Darkness*), the emotionally unstable John Flory (George Orwell's *Burmese Days*), the failed missionary Edwina Crane (Paul Scott's *The Raj Quartet*) and boys 'gone primitive' (William Golding's *Lord of the Flies*).

This chapter has two parts, one dealing with the avowedly imperial discourse of improvement and the second dealing with a discrepant geography where England finds its transnational engagements untenable in terms of English ideals of moral superiority. The discourse of improvement relies heavily on a rhetoric of deficiency, cultural defects and suffering as a *prehistory* of colonial humanitarianism and imperial intervention. The discourse of discrepant geographies thematizes English decadence, corruption and disintegration in the colonies as well as at home (this last – of the collapse of English at home – we have already noted in Chapter 5).

Before we move to examine the discourse of improvement and its components, it is essential to study the project of moral imperialism, which makes its presence felt in English literature from around the late eighteenth century.

The global project of moral imperialism

William Blake saw the first moments of the global capitalist Empire emerging. In *Vala, or the Four Zoas*, Blake would offer a horrific vision of these moments:

> First Trades & Commerce ships & armed vessels he builded laborious
> To swim the deep & on the Land children are sold to trades
> Of dire necessity still laboring day & night till all
> Their life extinct they took the spectre form in dark despair
> And slaves in myriads in ship loads burden the hoarse sounding deep
> Rattling with clanking chains the Universal Empire groans.
>
> (1973: 333)

The 'universal empire' is of exploitation, profit, suffering and labour, and echoes for different reasons Edmund Spenser's account of the labouring slaves producing gold in Mammon's caves. Blake saw the proto-empire as evil, as David Erdman's brilliant reading (*Blake: Prophet against Empire*, 1977) has shown. If Blake produced one of the first *moral* interpretations of globalizing capitalism (as Makdisi proposes, 1998), it marked a moment in England's literary history where similar moral readings of the alternate possibilities of Empire began to appear.

> 'Tis a design humanely just and kind,
> Worthy to share each free-born Briton's mind:

242 Civilize and collapse

> Each free-born Briton the design maintains,
> To break inglorious Slav'ry's galling chains;
> To cheer the woe-fraught soul, to sooth distress,
> With Freedom's ray far-distant climes to bless.
>
> (unpaginated, http://www.oac.cdlib.org/view?docId=kt638nc0hv;
> NAAN=13030&doc.view=frames&chunk.id=d0e4696&
> toc.depth=1&toc.id=d0e3939&brand=oac4)

This is Elizabeth Bentley in 'On the Abolition of the African Slave Trade, July 1789'. Note how Bentley proposes a unification of Britain under the aegis of abolition: 'each free-born Briton's mind'. Further Bentley sees the unification of Britons as the anterior moment to the unification of the world as Britain's project: 'far-distant climes'. What we discern here is a totalizing vision, a moral imperialism in British abolitionist writing that brings the distant parts of the world into Britain's civilizational domain. The poem's conclusion reiterates this project:

> High as the fairest sons of Europe's lands.
> O! may sweet Mercy's angel form divine,
> Deign o'er the world with softest beams to shine;
> May heav'n-inspir'd Philanthropy increase,
> And through each realm spread Liberty and Peace.

Abolitionist discourse imbued with heavy sentiment was a part of England's national project of improving the world (Ferguson 1992, Colley 1992, Richardson 1998), just as a universal conception of history and modernization was underway in England, and one that felt compelled to incorporate – as Saree Makdisi has demonstrated of the English Romantics (1998) – India and other regions into its narrative. In Lynn Festa's words: 'sentimental texts helped create the terms for thinking about agency and intent across the geographic expanse of the globe by giving shape and local habitation to the perpetrators, victims, and causal forces of empire' (2006: 2). Sentimentality and its consequence, improvement, was a mode of global conquest as well, bringing together empire builders, victims, oppressors, 'primitives', emancipators and colonial subjects. Sentimentality had a global reach, and was accompanied by the global ameliorative-emancipatory project, and conversely, 'colonization was a project of amelioration' (Drayton 2005: 92).

Abolitionist discourses very clearly embody the transnational theme that this book has been pursuing when they foreground England's *global* role in the emancipation of slaves. Poetry dealing with the suffering of the slaves and the impieties of the slave trade position England as the moral leader of the campaign against the system. With this effort, it was believed, there would be a 'global renewal from a moralized British imperialism' (Tomko 2007: 27), but what can also be thought of as a necessary supplement to England's imperial project because it both completed England's conquest of the world, even as it constituted a necessary excess to the mercantile capitalism that drove the Empire.

Hannah More's *Slavery: A Poem* (1788) opens with a series of questions:

> If heaven has into being deign'd to call
> Thy light, O LIBERTY! to shine on all;
> Bright intellectual Sun! why does thy ray
> To earth distribute only partial day?
> [...]
> Why are thy genial beams to parts confin'd?
>
> While the chill North with thy bright ray is blest,
> Why should fell darkness half the South invest?
> Was it decreed, fair Freedom! at thy birth,
> That thou shou'd'st ne'er irradiate *all* the earth?
> While Britain basks in thy full blaze of light,
> Why lies sad Afric quench'd in total night?

(Wu 1997: 43)

More is mapping here the *geography of both morality and depravation*: the intellectual sun – a reference to the polemics of liberty and equality – does not appear in Africa. Not only is freedom denied the African continent, the very *debates about freedom within Britain seem to ignore that thousands of Africans are slaves under the yoke of Britain itself.*

A sense of this globalizing project of Britain's moral imperialism might be seen in William Roscoe's (1787) abolitionist poem *The Wrongs of Africa*. Roscoe's speaker addresses Humanity (and not just Africa/Africans):

> Offspring of love divine, Humanity!

(1853: 25)

He then pleads:

> may the kind contagion widely spread,
> Till in its flame the unrelenting heart
> Of Avarice, melt in softest sympathy;—
> And one bright blaze of universal love,
> In grateful incense, rises up to heaven.

(26)

Roscoe suggests that the entire Humanity is to be held responsible for spreading this 'universal love'. Michael Tomko proposes that such 'totalizing visions of worldwide British benevolence enabled abolitionists to overlook individual or regional difference' (2007: 28). But one could also see Roscoe, like Hannah More, employing the language of moral imperialism, and one that would be spearheaded by Britain.

244 Civilize and collapse

This moral imperialism was the project of those Englishmen and women endowed with specific qualities. In other words, and as seen in the preceding chapter, the project of the colonial enabled the *self-fashioning* of the Englishman in particular ways: principled, brave, compassionate, sentimental, sympathetic, etc. Poets therefore argued that Britons must establish themselves as different from the other nations and cultures, especially in the way they dealt with their colonies. For example Thomas Campbell's *The Pleasures of Hope* (1799) said:

> When Europe fought your subject realms to gain,
> And stretch'd her giant sceptre o'er the main,
> Taught her proud barks their winding way to shape,
> And brav'd the stormy spirit of the Cape;
> Children of Brama! then was mercy nigh
> To wash the stain of blood's eternal dye?
> Did Peace descend, to triumph and to save,
> When free-born Britons cross'd the Indian wave?
> Ah, no! to more than Rome's ambition true,
> The Nurse of Freedom gave it not to you!
> She the bold route of Europe's guilt began,
> And, in the march of nations, led the van!
>
> (unpaginated, http://spenserians.cath.vt.edu/Text
> Record.php?textsid=37917)

Campbell here deplores the fact that unlike the 'nurse of freedom' that Britain *ought* to have been, she has been like a Roman conqueror. The Indians, described in Orientalist terms as 'children' (who of course need a 'nurse'), have been betrayed by 'the manifest inconsistency of Britons who boast of liberty but do not grant it to their Indian subjects' (Rudd 2011: 5). The reference to Rome is not simply about betrayed promises, as Rudd suggests, but gestures at a wholly different order of imperialism that Britain ought to put together: a *moral* imperialism. This would require not just power over subjects but also compassion, sympathy and sensibility – without which British imperialism would be like any other. It requires a certain kind of Englishman to execute the moral imperialism.

Thus in *Jane Eyre* the eponymous heroine mourns the fact that St John Rivers, burning with missionary zeal, which would make him just one more cog in the imperial project, lacks sympathy and compassion. A missionary seeking to improve the lot of the heathens – Rivers is to go out to India – must be, above all else, a man of sentiment and feeling. As Jane puts it: 'Feeling without judgment is a washy draught indeed; but judgment untempered by feeling is too bitter and husky a morsel for human deglutition' (Brontë 2010: 202). She herself cannot marry him because, even with his high principles, he is essentially a man without 'spirit':

> Can I receive from him the bridal ring, endure all the forms of love (which I doubt not he would scrupulously observe) and know that the spirit was quite

absent? Can I bear the consciousness that every endearment he bestows is a sacrifice made on principle? No: such a martyrdom would be monstrous.

(345)

The project of moral imperialism can be performed, according to Jane, only by certain kinds of Englishmen and women. Thus the encounter with and the improvement of racial–cultural others first demands a self-fashioning by the English. It is in transnational projects, in other words, that English character is to be built, even as the development of a type of character is central to the transnational interests that England now possesses. English identity itself emerges from carrying the white man's burden – the amelioration and civilization of the primitive races of the earth. If, as noted in Chapter 4, sentimentality towards the hapless victims – the natives, the racial, cultural Other – itself signalled a certain imperialism of affect by the English, improvement proves to be the logical extension of this form of imperialism.

Much abolitionist discourse, of course, forgives colonialism in the same breath as it proposes an amelioration of the condition of slaves, or if possible, an end to England's slave trade. (In the previous chapter I noted the construction of the slave body as pure matter or sentimental creature and the self-fashioning of the Englishman/woman as the 'feeling' person.) England, the discourse proposes, needs to ameliorate the slave's condition, but not necessarily end colonialism *in toto*. Thus Roscoe, as noted above, calls for 'sympathy'. Mary Birkett Card in her 1792 work 'A Poem on the African Slave Trade' (unpaginated, http://www.brycchancarey.com/slavery/mbc1.htm) called for 'benevolence' and for greater compassion ('A sorrowing sympathy surrounds my heart,/And mild compassion bleeds in every part').[2] Such a rhetoric evades the thorny issue of the linkage of colonialism with slavery. Instead it proposes an ameliorative and philanthropic system where the plantation owner is morally responsible for the way he treats his slaves. By switching the register to what might be thought of as an *affective morality*, the abolitionist discourse smoothly elides the prospect, and potential, of a *political morality*. The world will be united under Britain's benevolent colonialism. To return once more to Birkett's poem:

Plant there our colonies, and to their soul,
Declare the God who form'd this boundless whole;
Improve their manners – teach them how to live,
To them the useful lore of science give;
So shall with us their praise and glory rest,
And we in blessing be supremely blest;
For 'tis a duty which we surely owe,
We to the Romans were what to us Afric now.

If God created the 'boundless whole' it now becomes Britain's duty to make sure that the manners of the people occupying this 'boundless whole' are 'improved', according to Birkett. The emphasis here is of course on the moral duty to be extended across the known world, and might be seen as an instantiation of a

246 Civilize and collapse

moral imperialism which builds on an imperialism of affect. Hence, for people like St John Rivers in *Jane Eyre*, a preeminent text of the moral imperialist variety, England is too limited: his domain is the world itself. Jane, who has been warned by St John Rivers not to take too much effort at domesticity, thinks this of him:

> 'This parlour is not his sphere,' I reflected: 'the Himalayan ridge or Caffre bush, even the plague-cursed Guinea Coast swamp would suit him better. Well may he eschew the calm of domestic life; it is not his element: there his faculties stagnate – they cannot develop or appear to advantage. It is in scenes of strife and danger – where courage is proved, and energy exercised, and fortitude tasked – that he will speak and move, the leader and superior. A merry child would have the advantage of him on this hearth. He is right to choose a missionary's career – I see it now.'
>
> (Brontë 2010: 335)

This English self-fashioning of sentimental, compassionate and benevolent paternalism entailed and facilitated the deployment of the actionable discourses of emancipation, amelioration and rescue. Having first established the necessity of a moral imperialism, they fashioned themselves as the sentimental colonizers who could arguably 'execute' such an imperialism.

Amelioration and improvement

> And who in time knows whither we may vent
> The treasure of our tongue, to what strange shores
> This gaine of our best glorie be sent,
> T'nrich unknowing Nations with out stores?
> What worlds in th' yet unformed Occident
> May come refin'd with th' accents that are ours?

Samuel Daniel's lines from *Musophilus* (1599, cited in Greenblatt 2013: 22) might well be the slogan of the colonial enterprise itself. Greenblatt is accurate when he argues that Daniel's lines suggest that 'in place of the evangelical spirit … Daniel would substitute a linguistic mission, the propagation of English speech' (23). It is English language and speech that would in the long run become England's greatest gift to the world, if Daniel's fantasy is to be believed. Barbarians – traditionally, those who did not speak the Greek language were deemed by the Greeks to be 'barbarians' – would reach a level of civilization, thanks to this linguistic evangelism of the English. Spenser (*Faerie Queene* Book 6, Canto 4) would show us how such a barbarian would be on par with an animal:

> For language had he none, nor speech,
> But a soft murmer, and confused sound
> Of senselesse words, which Nature did him teach.
>
> (1984: 649)

The 'salvage man' who is being described here crouches low on the ground, and is more animal than even wild man. But without this 'salvage man' or a Caliban without human (English/European) language, there would be no colonial project of civilizing the native. Hence Miranda would chastise Caliban after his abortive rape attempt on her:

> I pitied thee,
> Took pains to make thee speak, taught thee each hour
> One thing or other; when thou didst not, savage,
> Know thine own meaning.
>
> (Shakespeare, *The Tempest* I.2)

The savage did not know 'its own meaning' because its own meaning can come only through a self-recognition in the European's language – which the savage has to first acquire.

In each of these three Early Modern texts we witness the opening moments of colonialism's civilizational mission. If the Early Modern texts foreground linguistic gifts and learning imparted to the savages, later projects would include Christianizing them as well (although the Virginia Charters in the New World included Christianizing as integral to the project). The discourses of colonial conquest, domination and hegemony from the 1780s would always be coterminous with the discourse of improvement that the Early Modern texts anticipate.

But the discourse of improvement, benevolent paternalism, compassion and amelioration that we see emerging in the 1780s has another anterior moment. In order to establish the necessity for colonial/English improvement it was essential to provide a prehistory, which took the form of a discursive construction of the primitive, antiquated, repressed nature of the native.

Improvement and development: a prehistory

A key constituent of the prehistory of English and colonial improvement was the inventory of cultural defects that we see articulated across English literary texts. Superstition, irrationality, barbaric treatment of women, the absence of private property, despotic kings, indolence, waste and decline were frequently recorded as 'observations' as early as the seventeenth century, especially in English travel writings on South Asia, eventually tying in with the project of Empire most visibly from the 1780s.

Cultural defects

> The empire of the Turks may be truly affirmed to be more barbarous than any of these. A cruel tyranny, bathed in the blood of their emperors upon every succession; a heap of vassals and slaves; no nobles, no gentlemen, no freemen, no inheritance of land ... a people that is without natural affection,

248 Civilize and collapse

and, as the Scripture saith, that regardeth not the desires of women: and without piety or care towards their children: a nation without morality, without letters, arts, or sciences; that can scarce measure an acre of land, or an hour of the day: base and sluttish in buildings, diets, and the like; and in a word, a very reproach of human society.

(Bacon 1860: 198)

This is Francis Bacon's inventory of the cultural defects of the Turks in 'An Advertisement Touching a Holy War' (1629). The Turks in Bacon's assessment are not to be included within humanity at all. Nearly two centuries later we have Maria Edgeworth in 'The Grateful Negro' speaking of the superstitious black races, establishing their primitivism by referring to their credulity towards mysticism.

The enlightened inhabitants of Europe may, perhaps, smile at the super-stitious credulity of the negroes, who regard those ignorant beings called *Obeah* people with the most profound respect and dread; who believe that they hold in their hands the power of good and evil fortune, of health and sickness, of life and death. The instances which are related of their power over the minds of their countrymen are so wonderful, that none but the most unquestionable authority could make us think them credible.

(unpaginated, http://ebooks.adelaide.edu.au/e/edgeworth/
maria/grateful-negro/)

Edgeworth sees this as a cultural defect where an entire race seems to function from within this premodern belief system. In this section I shall examine a few instances of such cultural defects as they figure in English writings about the racial, cultural Other of the 'East Indies'. Cultural defects, in English rhetoric, held a vice-like grip on the minds of the natives, what John Stuart Mill in 'On Liberty' (1859) would describe as a 'despotism of custom' (unpaginated, https://ebooks.adelaide. edu.au/m/mill/john_stuart/m645o/). No improvement of the Arab, the Asian or the African was possible without first freeing them from these 'mind-forg'd manacles' that William Blake wrote about in another context ('London'). In Walter Scott's *The Surgeon's Daughter* he speaks of Islam:

The Mahometans have a fanciful idea, that the true believer, in his passage to Paradise, is under the necessity of passing barefooted over a bridge composed of red-hot iron. But on this occasion, all the pieces of paper which the Moslem has preserved during his life, lest some holy thing being written upon them might be profaned, arrange themselves between his feet and the burning metal, and so save him from injury. In the same manner, the effects of kind and benevolent actions are sometimes found, even in this world, to assuage the pangs of subsequent afflictions.

(http://ebooks.adelaide.edu.au/s/cott/walter/surgeon)

Scott's tone suggests that this is a cultural defect, of the irrational Muslims.

Civilize and collapse **249**

A prominent cultural defect that finds its early expressions in Aphra Behn is the non-European's view of women. In Aphra Behn's *Oronooko* Imoinda serves as a symbol of African cultural defects, and is slave to the customs dictated by these defective cultural beliefs. The rhetoric suggests that the role of the woman is that of the (traditional) repository of tribal and cultural values. Oroonoko, pondering his strategies, if he should fail in his attack on the English, also worries over the consequences that might be visited on Imoinda:

> He considered, if he should do this deed, and die either in the attempt or after it, he left his lovely Imoinda a prey, or at best a slave to the enraged multitude; his great heart could not endure that thought. 'Perhaps,' said he, 'she may be first ravaged by every brute; exposed first to their nasty lusts, and then a shameful death.'
>
> (1994: 67)

Then he reveals his plans to his wife:

> He told her his design, first of killing her, and then his enemies, and next himself, and the impossibility of escaping, and therefore he told her the necessity of dying. He found the heroic wife faster pleading for death that he was to propose it, when she found his fixed resolution; and, on her knees, besought him not to leave her a prey to his enemies.
>
> (67)

In Anne Fogarty's words, 'his sexual ownership of her [Imoinda] justifies the sacrificial mutilation of her body' (1994: 12). This is of course indisputable – the woman is the place-holder for the male ego, and this is manifest as the sexual ownership of the woman's body. However, missing from Fogarty's analysis is an attention to Behn's comments on the *enslavement to a cultural belief*:

> while tears trickled down his cheeks, hers were smiling with joy she should die by so noble a hand, and be sent into her own country (for that's their notion of the next world) by him she so tenderly loved, and so truly adored in this: for wives have a respect for their husbands equal to what any other people pay a deity; and when a man finds any occasion to quit his wife, if he love her, she dies by his hand; if not, he sells her, or suffers some other to kill her. It being thus, you may believe the deed was soon resolved on; and 'tis not to be doubted but the parting, the eternal leave-taking of two such lovers, so greatly born, so sensible, so beautiful, so young, and so fond, must be very moving, as the relation of it was to be afterwards.
>
> (1994: 67–8)

The subsequent brutal ritual killing and mutilation of Imoinda, by Oroonoko, suggests the gendered *culture* of subjugation. That is, it is not simply Oroonoko's

250 Civilize and collapse

brutal behaviour that is described by Behn: it is the social monstrous where both Oroonoko and Imoinda are enslaved by their cultural beliefs in the woman's sacrifice. The racial, cultural Other is marked by a strange *cultural* notion of love, suggests Behn's text, which entails the ritual death of the woman at the hands of the one who purportedly loves her. But, as we shall see, this does not adequately explain the novel because Oroonoko was, right at the beginning, depicted as culturally nearer to Europeans than to Africans.

The emotional African or Indian serves as the stereotype for the English to suggest the backwardness of the cultures. Even when they possess the language to express their feelings, the men and women of these races are so overwhelmed by their sentiments that even language fails them. For example in Edgeworth's 'The Grateful Negro' the slave Caesar, for so long traumatized by his cruel master, discovers that he has been bought by the much kinder Mr Edwards. Edgeworth writes:

> Caesar perfectly understood all that Mr. Edwards said; but his feelings were at this instant so strong that he could not find expression for his gratitude: he stood like one stupefied! Kindness was new to him; it overpowered his manly heart; and at hearing the words 'my good friend,' the tears gushed from his eyes: tears which no torture could have extorted! Gratitude swelled in his bosom; and he longed to be alone, that he might freely yield to his emotions.
>
> (unpaginated, http://ebooks.adelaide.edu.au/e/edgeworth/ maria/grateful-negro/)

It is the culture of sentiment that deprives Caesar of even basic speech. (Later of course Caesar demonstrates his gratitude when the slaves on the plantation rise up in revolt against the white owners, and he stands by his master.)

Being conditioned to cultural practices such as these, English writings imply, the African or the East Indian is enslaved by irrationality, superstition and primitivism, or just plain greed and indulgence. When these become characteristics of monarchs then we see the Oriental despot emerging from within the culture of cruelty and greed.[3] The cruel monarch is a cultural defect of Asian and African cultures as represented in English literature.

Here is William Beckford's opening account of such an Oriental despot in *Vathek*:

> Vathek, ninth Caliph of the race of the Abassides, was the son of Motassem, and the grandson of Haroun Al Raschid. From an early accession to the throne, and the talents he possessed to adorn it, his subjects were induced to expect that his reign would be long and happy. His figure was pleasing and majestic; but when he was angry, one of his eyes became so terrible that no person could bear to behold it; and the wretch upon whom it was fixed instantly fell backward, and sometimes expired. For fear, however, of

depopulating his dominions, and making his palace desolate, he but rarely gave way to his anger.

Being much addicted to women, and the pleasures of the table, he sought by his affability to procure agreeable companions; and he succeeded the better, as his generosity was unbounded and his indulgences unrestrained.

(1970: 1)

Beckford paints a portrait of a wealthy ruler whose every characteristic has to do with excess: his wealth, his indulgences and his anger. Other Oriental despots in English writings on Asia, Arabia and Africa include Amurath, the Ottoman sultan in James Ridley's *The Tales of the Genii* (1766). In keeping with the stereotype of the despot, Ridley portrays the sultan as capable only of excess, where Oriental monarchs can only describe themselves in hyperbolic terms like Ridley's Amurath who declares: 'the sun knows no shadow, and Asia's monarch knows no restriction' (67). Or elsewhere, in South India, Tipu Sultan became the synonym for monstrous cruelties in British India. Henty's novel, *The Tiger of Mysore* (1895), opened its description of him as follows:

Tippoo ... revelled in acts of the most abominable cruelty. It would seem that he massacred for the very pleasure of massacring, and hundreds of British captives were killed by famine, poison, or torture, simply to gratify his lust for murder.

And later:

Tippoo ... is a human tiger. He delights in torturing his victims, and slays his prisoners from pure love of bloodshed.

(unpaginated, http://www.gutenberg.org/files/18813/ 18813-h/18813-h.htm)

Henty takes care to ensure that the rage and murderous sensibility of the Oriental king is not within the context of war, but is driven by psychopathological reasons. That is, the despotism is the result of a flawed personality – 'lust for murder', 'the pleasure of massacring' and the 'pure love of bloodshed'. The focus stays on the irrational behaviour of the tyrannical monarch. (Considerable space was expended in Henty's novel on Tipu's tyrannical behaviour towards English captives.)

It was not always the monarch's bloodlust that is represented as the cultural defect of the non-European. The African's savagery in their tribal battles came in for some attention in the nineteenth century. Patrick Brantlinger (2003) has noted how there was an entire discourse of African extermination. The 'myth of extreme [African] savagery' was coterminous, he argues, with what we can think of as the discourse of improvement where 'the only cure for savagery is conquest and government by the white, civilized, ruling race' (92).

The tyranny of the monarch was, in these discourses that find their origins in the mid- to late eighteenth century, only one of the causes of the decline of economic

252 Civilize and collapse

prosperity of the region. The natives themselves with their indolence and their inability to appreciate the wealth in their grasp were responsible, according to colonial writings, for the enormous wastage visible in most parts of the Asian subcontinent.

Natives were deemed to be ignorant of the value of their landscape and other precious possessions. A discourse of deficiency – whether in terms of labour (the trope of the lazy Oriental), in their ability to value correctly – runs through the moralizing rhetoric of English writing about the Asian and African Other. In his novel about the South Indian monarch who rebelled against the English, Tipu Sultan, Philip Meadows Taylor declares: 'The natives of India are perhaps heedless of natural beauties' (21). The discourse of deficiency as cultural defect is also brought to bear on the question of agriculture, where the natives are depicted as lazy and therefore unable to produce better harvests by sheer effort (see Arnold 2005a).

Deficiency and decline go together in numerous English texts on Asia and especially on India. John Dryden's *Aureng-zebe* (1675), like Marlowe's *Tamburlaine* (1587), mapped the glory and eventual decline and collapse of the Mughals. This decline is characterized by a very important theme in the play, as Ros Ballaster has noted (2005: 277). Instead of conquest and military glory, the Mughals have now begun to focus on domestic matters and passions. Aurangzeb, says Dryden in his opening note, 'enjoyed the plenitude of authority originally vested in the Emperor of India' (1808a: 169). From this position of authority Aurangzeb, instead of consolidating his authority, becomes a dreamer, but not a visionary meditating on the possible glories of his rule/realm. Instead, the dreams are of excesses, of pleasure in the present (Ballaster 2005: 284. On dreaming and fantasy in the play see Jennifer Brady 2004). The following dialogue between Aurangzeb and Indamora (I. 1) is worthy of some analysis for the English presentation of native cultural defects:

> Indamora:
> Love is an airy good, opinion makes;
> Which he, who only thinks he has, partakes:
> Seen by a strong imagination's beam,
> That tricks and dresses up the gaudy dream:
> Presented so, with rapture tis enjoyed;
> Raised by high fancy, and by low destroyed.

Aurangzeb responds with:

> If love be vision, mine has all the tire,
> Which, in first dreams, young prophets does inspire:
> I dream, in you, our promised paradise:
> An age's tumult of continued bliss.
> But you have still your happiness in doubt;
> Or else 'tis past, and you have dreamt it out.

(Dryden 1808a: 202–3)

Ballaster's reading of it proposes that 'trapped in an eternal present of romantic love … may limit his ability to unify a political state' (2005: 285), an argument that gestures at once to the risks of being a dreamer-monarch as well as the English preference for such a dreamer rather than a political ruler. Aurangzeb in the play recognizes the erosion of his authority, and he:

> mourns his former vigour lost so far,
> To make him now spectator of a war.
>
> (I.1. Dryden 1808a: 193)

From a military leader, the Mughal emperor is a mere 'spectator' during times of war. Dryden, mapping the decline of the great Mughals, focuses on the wasting away of military prowess in what might be read as a proto-colonial fantasy about Asian empires. Elsewhere they would seek the reasons for this wasting away.

Decadence and imminent collapse of the great Empire in such texts is also attributed to the evil-doings of the native women. We have already noted (in Chapter 2) Beckford's representation of the queen Carathis in *Vathek*. Nearly a hundred years before Beckford's uncharitable representation, Dryden's play opens with a reference to the 'cursed cabal of women' that 'strove/to draw the king to partial love'.[4]

While Dryden does see Aurangzeb as a hero, the play also implicitly suggests the erosion of the might of the Mughals, at a time when the British were looking to consolidate their presence and power in the subcontinent. Presenting the racial, cultural Other – and one who, in this particular case, is an emperor – as poised on the cusp of collapse enables the discourse of improvement and the necessity of British intervention to follow. The native's cultural practices, religion and beliefs become cultural *defects* – which need to be removed by offering a whole new culture for the native. 'Improvement' then consists of cultural interventions by the Englishman in the lifeworlds of the native.

Important to the prehistory of improvement and reform, in the case of a 'cultural defect' such as *sati*, was the portrayal of the dutiful – that is, a wife indoctrinated into her sense of wifely duty by the culture – Hindu wife, whose unquestioning attitude to her own ritual death was deemed irrational and therefore needing 'remedy'. An early instance of the *sati* discourse in literary representations occurs in Dryden's *Aureng-zebe*.[5] Aurangzeb himself sees *sati* as a sign of the wives' loyalty (V.1):

> 'Tis the procession of a funeral vow,
> Which cruel laws to Indian wives allow
> When fatally their virtue approve;
> Cheerful in flames, and martyrs of their love.
>
> (1808a: 279)

Then Melesinda, the Muslim wife of Morat, commits *sati*. Ignoring much historical evidence that the Muslims were against the practice of *sati* Dryden goes ahead and

254 Civilize and collapse

gives an account of the dutiful wife ending her life alongside her husband. Melesinda is warned that the sacrifice is wasted because her husband was 'not kind', as Indamora puts it (279). Melesinda replies:

> Had he been kind, I could no love have shown:
> Each vulgar virtue would as much have done.
> My love was such, it needed no return;
> But could, though he supplied no fuel, burn.
> Rich in itself, like elemental fire,
> Whose pureness does no aliment require.
> In vain you would bereave me of my lord;
> For I will die: Die is too base a word,
> I'll seek his breast, and, kindling by his side,
> Adorned with flames, I'll mount a glorious bride.
>
> (279–80)

Strangely, the death of another Muslim woman, Nourmahal, is also cast in the form of a *sati* by Dryden:

> burn, I more than burn; I am all fire.
> See how my mouth and nostrils flame expire!
> I'll not come near myself
> Now I'm a burning lake, it rolls and flows;
> I'll rush, and pour it all upon my foes.
> Pull, pull that reverend piece of timber near:
> Throw't on, 'tis dry, 'twill burn
> Ha, ha! how my old husband crackles there!
> Keep him down, keep him down; turn him about:
> I know him, he'll but whiz, and strait go out.
> Fan me, you winds: What, not one breath of air?
> I'll burn them all, and yet have flames to spare.
> Quench me: Pour on whole rivers. Tis in vain:
> Morat stands there to drive them back again:
> With those huge billows in his hands, he blows
> New fire into my head: My brain-pan glows.
> See! see! there's Aureng-Zebe too takes his part;
> But he blows all his fire into my heart.
>
> (280)

The two deaths occur side by side, literally, for Nourmahal's death immediately follows Melesinda's declaration of her decision to commit *sati*. Both deaths, of Muslim women in the form of the Hindu practice of *sati*, present a decadent India. Some critics propose that the deaths of the two women protagonists who represent 'the more incendiary and destructive aspects' of the Mughal emperor's dreaming might constitute a 'proto-colonial' fantasy of the British (Ballaster 2005: 291). However, it is also possible to read, if we align Dryden's text with Beckford's, the British fantasy of the collapse of Oriental monarchies/empires slightly differently. I propose that the *British fantasy attributes the collapse of great Oriental empires and monarchs to the dominance of women in their royal households*. Further, it is sexual politics – in both the texts here – that drives monarchs to their ruin. Carathis and Nourmahal are both figures of active female power and, in British eyes, subversive of masculinity itself.[6]

The cultural defect here, then, is the *excessive* role played by emotionally charged *domestic, marital and sexual politics* of Oriental monarchs that interferes with the larger, supposedly rational project of military conquest, political stability and ordered societies. It is this personalized and emotional rule, embodied in *Vathek* and *Aureng-zebe*, that the impersonal, systematized and masculine British system would replace as an 'improvement'.

If cultural practices such as ritual killing (say *sati*, widow-burning in India) were indices of the primitivism of the African and Asian, then the system of despotic governance was treated as the mark of decadent political modernity.

Sati and the self-sacrificing native woman was an exemplification in English writing of a cultural defect that pointed to the irrational, superstitious and hyper-emotional character of the natives/colonized subjects. The native was, according to other texts, unable to acquire political maturity because of this same sentiment. That is, even when the native seeks to assert a nationalist sentiment, he is reduced to disorderly rants, as we see in the case of E.M. Forster's *A Passage to India*.

Despite his humanism, Forster portrays Oriental sentimentality as a cultural defect when the educated Dr Aziz performs in the role of a caricature of a nationalist:

> Down with the British anyway. That's certain. Clear out, you fellows, double quick, I say. We may hate one another, but we hate you most. If I don't make you go, Ahmed will, Karim will, if it's fifty-five hundred years we shall get rid of you, yes, we shall drive every blasted Englishman into the sea.
>
> (1970: 317)

Lidan Lin interprets this Aziz speech/performance as follows:

> Aziz is shown to have no better way of responding than to 'dance this way and that, not knowing what to do' but to 'cr[y]' out a series of anti-British slogans. Second, the actual wording of this statement lays bare Aziz's deferential habit of playing down Indianness in order to sound English by mimicking bonafide English idioms such as 'you fellows, double quick, I say,' even in his most anti–British moment.
>
> (1997: 144)

256 Civilize and collapse

Forster reinstates the stereotype of the highly sentimental Indian here, and thus reinforces the absence of a political rationality/modernity even among India's educated classes. Enslaved by their emotions and their blind aping of their colonial masters, the Indians' nationalism, Forster implicitly suggests, is less a political consciousness than a matter of gushing sentimentality. While Aziz had earlier described himself and all Indians as 'monkeys' (1970: 130) – and Forster depicts him 'beside himself', screaming for his friend, Fielding, who has missed the train and mewling 'piteously, like a child' (131) – the comic strain is extended into the nationalist speech Aziz gives. Aziz is child-like, animal-like, but essentially a comic figure in this account, a portrait through which Forster suggests that nothing much distinguishes the 'monkeying' around, so to speak, of Aziz, whether he is playing the fool on the train or expressing a nationalist dislike of the British. I shall have reasons to return to Aziz's tomfoolery later.

There is an additional feature of the discourse of cultural defects that needs to be addressed, and this is the importation and incorporation of tropes of these Asian or African defects to describe *English* culture and character.

Tropes such as the Oriental despot and the language of tyranny begin to be used to describe *European* men in nineteenth-century fiction. Elsie Michie's (1992) study of *Wuthering Heights* and *Jane Eyre* notes how Heathcliff is described as being of uncertain, undecidable racial origins, called variously a heathen, a lascar, a gypsy and an Indian or Chinese prince. Rochester in *Jane Eyre*, on the other hand, is described as possessing a 'dark face' (Brontë 2010: 96), 'broad and jetty eyebrows' (102) and 'full nostrils' (102). Later Jane sees him this way:

> his dark eyes and swarthy skin and Paynim features suited the costume [of Eliezer during the charades] exactly; he looked the very model of an Eastern emir, an agent or a victim of the bow-string.
>
> (156)

Both accounts, argues Michie, seem to echo prevalent descriptions of Irishmen (129–30). Outsiders in terms of looks and origins (Heathcliff is an orphan and Rochester is the second son, and unlikely to inherit), both have to acquire property in the manner of Oriental despots, writes Michie in an innovative argument, through 'conquest or appropriation' (1992: 135). But both the Brontës use the language associated with Oriental despotism.

> The tyrant grinds down his slaves and they don't turn against him, they crush those beneath them. You are welcome to torture me to death for your amusement, only allow me to amuse myself a little in the same style.
>
> (Heathcliff to Cathy in *Wuthering Heights*: 112)

And Rochester tells Jane in *Jane Eyre*: 'when once I have fairly seized you, to have and to hold, I'll just—figuratively speaking—attach you to a chain like this (touching his watch-guard)' (231).[7] Other characters in this novel are also associated with a certain despotic and imperial bearing. Thus Mrs Reed has an 'imperious, despotic eyebrow' (196) and Blanche Ingram's mother has a 'truly imperial dignity' (146). Jane herself sees the 'despotism' in Rivers after he has proposed to her (234), a despotism that expected her to exhibit a 'lamb-like submission and turtle-dove sensibility' (234). Michie concludes:

> The Brontë novels suggest that that stereotype functions as a screen onto which the Victorians could project a variety of fantasies, in the case of *Wuthering Heights* and *Jane Eyre*, fantasies of overcoming class and gender difference both through access to power and rebellion.
>
> (1992: 140)

While Michie's is an interesting mode of reading the tyrannical male figures in these novels, it might also be apposite to consider how England's transnational engagement could be read into the above novels. On the one hand the discourse of improvement positioned the geographically distant racial-cultural Other as being in *need* of *English* intervention (embodied in St John Rivers in *Jane Eyre*), but on the other hand novels like the above seem to suggest that models of despotism, enslavement and tyranny exist *within* England itself. Individuals like Heathcliff and Rochester who occupy marginal positions within English society fall prey to the despotic strain as well, even as the epitome of English superiority – St John Rivers – goes out to India, to improve *that* space. But what is also significant, as Michie has suggested in the case of Rochester and Heathcliff, is that despotism exists in the case of Englishmen as well. It is Jane Eyre who speaks of the impossibility of marrying somebody like St John Rivers, who is as tyrannical – despotic – as anybody else. Rivers does speak like a man who seeks to dominate: 'I want a wife: the sole helpmeet I can influence efficiently in life and retain absolutely till death' (Brontë 2010: 346).[8]

The cultural defects of a distant space are now part of England too, perhaps because of its transnational engagements. For instance, like masculine despotism, the Indian ritual of widow-burning, critiqued and eventually banned by the British government in 1830, finds its horrific double in England as well. In *Jane Eyre*, Jane compares herself to a *sati*:

> 'I considered it a very natural and necessary one: he had talked of his future wife dying with him. What did he mean by such a pagan idea? *I* had no intention of dying with him—he might depend on that.'
>
> 'Oh, all he longed, all he prayed for, was that I might live with him! Death was not for such as I.'
>
> 'Indeed it was: I had as good a right to die when my time came as he had: but I should bide that time, and not be hurried away in a suttee.'
>
> (233)

Mary Ellis Gibson comments: 'in Bronte's novel the line between Christian and heathen becomes oddly porous. Jane stands accused by Brocklehurst of being worse

258 Civilize and collapse

than a heathen before Juggernaut, and she imagines herself a suttee' (1999: 425). Thus we can think of an *imported* cultural defect here where, as a result of England's cultural encounters with Hinduism, its women begin to see themselves as aligned, however temporarily, with the Hindu women.

Over a century later, Edwina Crane in Paul Scott's *The Raj Quartet*, having seen her own failure in the civilizational mission, commits suicide. Scott writes of her death:

> She dressed for the first time in her life in a white saree, the saree for her adopted country, the whiteness of widow-hood and mourning ... She locked herself in and soaked the walls with paraffin and set them alight and died.
>
> (1978: 123)

Scott terms it 'suttee' (123), thus establishing a symbolic equivalence between England and India, which leads at least one commentator to argue: 'her death is ... the assertion of a heartfelt connection with India that she had hitherto not experienced' (Mezey 2006: 342).

When Ronny Heaslop in *A Passage to India* (1924) sets the British up as 'gods' he also appropriates the despotic roles of the native male, and thus erodes the image of the upright English gentleman. This 'infection' of the English gentleman by the Oriental model of masculinity as portrayed by the Brontës suggests a *transnationalization and transplantation of the colonial stereotype, ostensibly generated to describe the Asian or African, into England.*[9]

Novels embodying the social imaginary of the age, such as *Wuthering Heights* and *Jane Eyre*, could well be read as both expressions of an anxiety over this cultural 'infection' and as a (quasi?) feminist criticism of English patriarchy that enslaves and tyrannically controls English women in the same fashion as the men of distant cultures that the British claim are primitive.

Having established the racial, cultural Other as primitive and defective, the discourse of improvement now emerges as a kind of discursive response and responsibility towards this Other.

Amelioration and benevolent paternalism

> I love to hear my uncle talk of the West Indies. I could listen to him for an hour together ... Did you not hear me ask him about the slave trade last night? ... But there was such a dead silence.

This is Fanny Price reporting a conversation about the subject of the slave trade in Austen's 1814 novel *Mansfield Park* (1970: 177–8). Edward Said's reading proposes that Austen 'assum[es] the importance of an empire to the situation at home' (1994: 106), and the English domestic space 'requires overseas sustenance' (107).

The 'dead silence' that follows Fanny Price's question, in Said's reading, 'suggest[s] that one world could not be connected with the other since there was simply no common language for both' (115).[10] But, as George Boulukos points out, the entire section seems to suggest that Sir Thomas, to whom Fanny Price had posed the question, had responded positively to her (although her cousins had not), and might be read as a nuanced 'distinction between slavery itself': of ameliorative and improveable slavery and the 'irredeemable ... slave trade' (2006: 366–7). It is not the system of slavery *in toto* that is the subject of discussion, but rather the improvements possible within the system that attracts attention, according to Boulukos.

Thus the kind slaveowner Edwards in Edgeworth's story 'The Grateful Negro' asks the cruel Jeffries:

> Granting it to be physically impossible that the world should exist without rum, sugar, and indigo, why could they not be produced by freemen as well as by slaves? If we hired negroes for labourers, instead of purchasing them for slaves, do you think they would not work as well as they do now?

Edwards suggests: 'we can endeavour to make our negroes as happy as possible' (unpaginated, http://ebooks.adelaide.edu.au/e/edgeworth/maria/grateful-negro/). Edwards represents the epitome of colonial paternalism, where, despite acknowledging the necessity of slavery as an economic system, he pleads for ameliorating the lot of the slaves.

England's transnational engagements and perceptions of the globe involved the system of slavery. From the 1780s the theme of globality is marked by the arrival of a new discourse: amelioration and improvement, revolving, mostly, around the slave question but also around issues of African and Asian cultural defects. Freeing the native from their cultures was therefore central to the project of improvement itself.

Deculturation, reconstruction and improvement

G.A. Henty in his *A Roving Commission* has this to say about African cultures:

> Fetish worship and human sacrifices are carried on in secret, and the fairest island in the western seas lies sunk in the lowest degradation – a proof of the utter incapacity of the Negro race to evolve, or even maintain, civilization, without the example and the curb of the white population among them.
>
> (cited in McMahon 2010: 159–60)

Here Henty makes the African a slave to 'primitive' cultural practices. These practices prevent the 'evolution' of the African into a full human, according to Henty. Any escape from this debilitating 'incapacity' for the African requires the firm hand of the white man. What Henty's prose proposes is this: the English

260 Civilize and collapse

engagement with the African involves a deliberate deculturation of the latter. Rescue is coded here as the evacuation of cultural values from the African's life and mind.

But well before Henty's portrait of the 'improved' native – which seems to bring to a climax the discourse of improvement – other antecedent texts seem to suggest a deculturation of the natives. We have already cited Aphra Behn's famous account of Oroonoko, but the passages are worth revisiting for the ideology of the improveable native they encode:

> He had an extreme good and graceful mien, and all the civility of a well-bred great man. He had nothing of barbarity in his nature, but in all points addressed himself as if his education had been in some European court ... He was pretty tall, but of a shape the most exact that can be fancied: the most famous statuary could not form the figure of a man more admirably turned from head to foot. His face was not of that brown rusty black which most of that nation are, but of perfect ebony, or polished jet. His eyes were the most awful that could be seen, and very piercing; the white of 'em being like snow, as were his teeth. His nose was rising and Roman, instead of African and flat. His mouth the finest shaped that could be seen; far from those great turned lips which are so natural to the rest of the negroes. The whole pro-portion and air of his face was so nobly and exactly formed that, bating his color, there could be nothing in nature more beautiful, agreeable, and handsome. There was no one grace wanting that bears the standard of true beauty. His hair came down to his shoulders, by the aids of art, which was by pulling it out with a quill, and keeping it combed; of which he took parti-cular care. Nor did the perfections of his mind come short of those of his person; for his discourse was admirable upon almost any subject: and whoever had heard him speak would have been convinced of their errors, that all fine wit is confined to the white men, especially to those of Christendom.
>
> (Behn 1994: 11–12)

From physiognomy to behaviour and attitude, Oroonoko demonstrates a greater affinity with the Europeans (and Romans) than with his own countrymen and race. If the savages, as argued in Chapter 3, represent the European exoticizing of difference, the exoticization was also woven with its apparently contradictory dis-course – of the *erasure of difference*.

Behn appears to contradict herself here. As noted above, Oroonoko's ritual killing of Imoinda suggests a cultural defect – primitivism and sexual enslavement of women – in the man. But Behn also portrays Oroonoko as culturally proximate with Europeans and Romans. Then the cultural defect within the man seems a residual one that does not ever disappear. This means Behn presumes both an innate primitivism that needs excision-as-improvement and a more 'noble' substrate.

Another instance, a century after Behn's portrait of the nearly-decultured Oroonoko, of a native narrative that offers an ethnographic account of his tribe but in terms that would appeal to the European stereotypes of the 'innocent' and the African, is Ouladah Equiano's *The Interesting Narrative of the Life of Olaudah Equiano* (1789). Equiano casts his African people in the mould of innocence, in a sharp departure from the savage stereotype. He claims that their 'manner of living is entirely plain', they are 'modest' and 'unacquainted with those refinements in cookery which debauch the taste' (http://www.gutenberg.org/files/15399/15399-h/15399-h.htm). In another extraordinary passage Equiano, when reading the Bible, exclaims: 'I was wonderfully surprised to see the laws and rules of my country written almost exactly here' (http://www.gutenberg.org/files/15399/15399-h/15399-h.htm). Emily Donaldson Field argues that Equiano's descriptions are less about Africans than of Africans akin to the English, more accurately, of contemporary Britons (2009). With this strategy, argues Field, he distances himself from the primitivism of African and moves closer to the English. I suggest that Equiano's text is an exercise in discursive deculturation so as to suggest the potential for improvement among (even) the Africans. The disavowal of African ways of life, the attempts to show their cultural kinship with the Europeans and, above all, the self-portrait of the African-as-innocent-savage, cohere into a discourse, I suggest, of *improveability* that necessitates the shedding of cultural values, practices and beliefs by the native. Even before the Europeans' active intervention, according to Equiano's text, the ground has been prepared by the natives themselves.

In the case of *sati* or widow-burning, the British (as Lata Mani, 1998, and others have noted) sought to find the justification for their rule in the rescue act they *had* to perform in order to save the poor Hindu woman. But in literary representations of *sati*, it was proposed that the remedying of cultural defects in Hinduism could be achieved by reforming the Hindus into Christianity. Adopting the rhetoric of sentimentality – that I have already noted in the preceding chapter as being integral to the abolitionist poetry of the period – such texts presented the 'reform' as part of the sentimental Briton's response to the cultural defects.

Such cultural defects as religion, superstition and irrationality needed to be treated firmly. Deculturation therefore involves active intervention in the natives' belief systems so as to save their souls. The moral imperialism of the nineteenth century was underwritten by the firm conviction that England had to evangelize extensively, so that a global missionary effort was the keystone of its transnational identity.

In General Mainwaring's 1830 novel, *The Suttee*, the reform of cultural defects is clearly stated early in the text's Preface itself: the task of the English is to 'emancipate the Hindoos from the bondage of superstition' (cited in Herman 2005: 248). Hinduism is the cultural defect here, and the British solution is of course Christianity. The reform is, in fact, initiated as a Hindu's sentimental response to Christianity where Nuradda's heart feels 'a void, which Christianity alone was capable of filling up' (Herman 2005: 27). Nuradda's English friend advises him to persuade Temora, Nuradda's wife, not to commit *sati* and instead turn to Christianity. As Jeanette Herman puts it:

262 Civilize and collapse

> In Mainwaring's representation of Nuradda's conversion through his rejection of sati, she presents a vision of colonial India that involves the religious, cultural, and political assimilation of the Hindu population into the national identity and way of life of the British conquerors.
>
> (2005: 249)

Simply put, the project of reform involves deculturation of the natives through the conversion to Christianity.[11]

Deculturation involves not simply an unmooring of the native from her/his cultural roots, but an entire reconstruction, from the psyche and behaviour upwards. Reconstruction is the imparting of specific qualities (qualities believed to be valuable according to the English), to the slave or the brown man.

One of the earliest examples of this reconstructive effort on the part of the English/European may be found in Shakespeare. Prospero's anger against Caliban is not, Shakespeare's *The Tempest* suggests, only because of the latter's attempt to rape Miranda. Prospero states:

> I have used thee,
> Filth as thou art, with human care, and lodged thee
> In mine own cell, till thou didst seek to violate
> The honour of my child.
>
> (I.2, ll. 345–7)

The anger here is not about Caliban's unbridled sexuality (which is itself monstrous) but about his *ingratitude* towards Prospero. Mark Burnett has persuasively argued that Caliban is '"monster" because he fails to respect the gift of an accommodating paternal protection' (2002: 133). As arguably one of the first examples of the reconstruction of a 'primitive' (colonized) subject in English literature, Caliban's monstrosity is less about his undecidable ontological identity (he is on occasion deemed to be a tortoise, and a fish with 'long nails', as Burnett notes, 134) than about the continuity of his primitive nature despite Prospero's kindness. That is, despite the education imparted by Prospero (Shin 2008), Caliban has reverted to his *original* primal-primitive self. It/he has not been successfully reconstructed.

Caliban responds, it must be noted, first, like an animal, to physical kindnesses ('Thou strok'st me, and made much of me'). Later Prospero teaches him language, Miranda reminds him ('I endow'd thy purposes/with words that made them known' (I.2, ll. 359–60)). It is through this reconstruction and the concomitant erasure of Caliban's primitive consciousness that Shakespeare presents the 'evolved' native. Caliban is now educated enough to say to Prospero:

> This island's mine, by Sycorax my mother,
> which thous tak'st from me. When thou cam'st first,
> thou strok'st me, and made much of me; wouldst give me
> water with berries in't; and teach me how

to name the bigger light, and how the less,
that burn by day and night: and then I lov'd thee,
and show'd thee all the qualities o' th' isle,

———

For I am all the subjects that you have,
Which first was mine own King: and here you sty me
In this hard rock, whiles you do keep from me
The rest o' the' island.

(I.2, ll. 333–46)

Learning about heredity and property rights from Prospero (who speaks of his title, his rights and their violation), Caliban begins to recognize the exact nature of his relationship with the European.

Caliban's rebellion, like the attempted rape of Miranda, signifies two dimensions of the civilizational process: (1) the intellectual reconstruction or evolution – it is never clear whether Caliban is a beast, a humanoid, or a 'slave' (Prospero calls him that and later he will be called 'servant-monster') – and (2) the (re)turn to savage impulses and anger as part of his rebellion against the master–slave relationship. Shakespeare would put this (re)turn as follows: 'as with age his body uglier grows,/so his mind cankers' (IV.1, ll. 191–2). He is also, of course, a 'born devil' (IV.1, l. 188).

Whether Shakespeare sees it as a *relapse* on the part of the now-civilized 'monster' or the irreducible and innate beastliness of the native is unclear. (Alan Lester, 2012, has argued that the civilizational mission which gathers strength in the late eighteenth century was equally divided between universalist theories, which argued that every race had a capacity to progress, and innatist views, which argued that aptitudes and abilities of different races were immutable.)

In staging the failure of Prospero Shakespeare suggests the failure of the civilizing mission itself: that the native will not be tamed. Thus, despite being taught the language, Caliban acquires not the identity of a sophisticated subject but that of a 'servant-monster' (III.2, l. 4).[12] He 'learns', of course, to 'curse', in the phrase postcolonial critics have made much of. However, even as a servant, dependent on Prospero, Caliban fails when he is described as: 'a very shallow monster' (II.2, l. 138), a 'very weak monster' (II.2, l. 139), a 'credulous monster' (II.2, l. 140), a 'most perfidious and drunken monster' (II.2, l. 144–5), an 'abominable monster' (II.2, l. 153) and a 'howling monster' (II.2, l. 174). In short, the transformation into a manageable domestic, albeit a quasi-monster, seems to fail. The primitive will not be domesticated and will *remain* a species of monster.[13] Hence when Prospero presents the monster to the king, he refers to him as 'demi-devil'. Prospero offers Caliban pardon for his rebellion and violence, but on the condition that he remain a slave – Prospero does not offer Caliban freedom, perhaps founded on the assumption that Caliban cannot be reconstructed enough to be a free 'man'.

The reconstruction of the savage and the primitive involved remedying the moral and cultural defects of the racial, cultural Other. This might involve, as in

264 Civilize and collapse

the case of Shakespeare's play, bestowing the gift of language, an adoptive family (to Caliban, by Prospero) so that the wildness might be tamed and *reconstructed* in the model and function demanded by the European – with the native in the status of a domestic, in the case of Caliban. It involved, in the late nineteenth century, the physical transformation of the country (Africa, India) through the heroic efforts of the Englishman and later the Englishwoman so that a triumphalist geography of the world might be produced (see Chapter 1 for the triumphalist geography argument).

Even when the 'savage' was presented as possessing a fairly decent worldview and religion, this deculturation and reconstruction by the European was deemed to be essential. An excellent example of such a theme may be found in Robert Southey's narrative poem, *A Tale of Paraguay* (1825). The poem actually offers an idealized state of innocence and robust lifeworlds of the Guarani tribe of Amerindians. At the beginning of the poem a couple survive an epidemic and have to bring up their son in isolation after their entire tribe has been decimated. They are, writes Southey, of 'healthy heart and righteous mind'. However, despite this idyllic life and culture – close to nature, as Southey constantly emphasizes – the Jesuit priest manages to convert them. Southey says:

> They on the Jesuit, who was nothing loth,
> Reposed alike their conscience and their cares;
> And he, with equal faith, the trust of both
> Accepted and discharged. The bliss is theirs
> Of that entire dependence that prepares
> Entire submission, let what may befall;
> And his whole careful course of life declares
> That for their good he holds them thus in thrall,
> Their Father and their Friend, Priest, Ruler, all in all.
>
> (1827: 112)

The emergence of the native into the world is portrayed thus:

> Day comes, and now a first and last farewell
> To that fair bower within their native wood,
> Their quiet nest till now. The bird may dwell
> Henceforth in safety there, and rear her brood,
> And beasts and reptiles undisturb'd intrude;
> Reckless of this, the simple tenants go,
> Emerging from their peaceful solitude,
> To mingle with the world.
>
> (106)

Tim Fulford (2001) correctly points to the contradiction in Southey's poem: 'the Indians' state of nature is so joyful, innocent, virtuous and instinctively religious that it is difficult to see why they need to be "rescued" from the forest by the Jesuits' (unpaginated).[14] However, one needs to see Southey's narrative as revealing a deeper subtext of anxiety about the 'innocent' Native American.

The poem, I argue, is a narrative about modernization. The natives themselves will be like 'children under wise parental sway', says Southey. Even with, or maybe because of, their naive relationship with nature (that nurtures but also gave them disease), they need to be civilized. The poem suggests a march towards the modernization of the native, choreographed and regulated by the European. The colony's agricultural, political, economic progress is contingent upon the Englishman overseeing their homes, villages and communities. Retaining portions of the Paraguayan/Amerindian world in the original, supposedly 'pure', state would render the English project of moral imperialism incomplete.

In the eighteenth century English travellers noted the devastation and wastage produced by native incompetence and senseless war-mongering (Nayar 2008: 75), thus preparing the ground for the colonial master's rescue act. By offering systematic legislation and extensive protection the colonial rule in Africa and India ensured prosperity (Arnold 2005a) – because the farmers returned to their fields with no fear of predators, attacks by other tribes and/or unfair landlords.

> Some of the young men grumble, but the old ones rejoice at the change. Formerly they had to go to the plough with their spears and swords beside them because they never knew what marauders from the hills might sweep down, besides, when there was war they might be called away for weeks, while the crops were wasting upon the ground ... Now the Rajah has no longer to squeeze the cultivators; therefore they pay but a light rent for the lands, and the Rajah is much better off than his father was; so that on all sides there is content and prosperity.
>
> (unpaginated, http://www.gutenberg.org/files/18813/18813-h/
> 18813-h.htm)

Henty's account here, from *The Tiger of Mysore*, encapsulates the discourse of improvement in all its dimensions. The farmer is saved from his enemies, the community from other communities. But they are also saved from the exploitative landlord – Henty's portrait of the Rajah here is that of the typical 'Oriental despot'.

In another Henty novel, *Through the Sikh War* (1893), it is the native who endorses the necessary role of English's improving mission:

> What a blessing it [English rule] would be to the country! In the first place, there would be neither over-taxation nor oppression. All would live and till their lands and work their loom, secure of enjoying their earnings in peace. Money would flow into the country, for the sahibs would come in great numbers from the plains for health and for sport, and would spend money freely, and would buy our manufactures from the weavers and silversmiths at

266 Civilize and collapse

first hand, while now they have to be sent down to the market at great expense, and in troublous times at great risk.

(1902: 215)

The land is improveable, just as there is still hope in the wretched native. The local Rajah says of his son in *The Tiger of Mysore* that he (the prince) acquired courage during his last adventure with the Englishman, Dick. Says the Rajah: 'he attained rank and position, and has returned with these valuable gifts' (unpaginated, http://www.gutenberg.org/files/18813/18813-h/18813-h.htm). It only requires the firm, guiding hand of the white man. Thus character-building, which might be read as the 'reconstruction' of the native, is part of the process of improvement initiated by the Englishman.[15]

Reconstruction of this kind might result in new behaviour on the part of the blacks/slaves. Once again I return to Maria Edgeworth's 'The Grateful Negro'. Here Caesar is moved by his master, Edwards', kindness and trust – Edwards gives him a knife with the words 'I am not one of those masters who are afraid to trust their negroes with sharp knives'. At this Caesar, says Edgeworth, 'swore that, with this knife, he would stab himself to the heart sooner than betray his master!' (unpaginated, http://ebooks.adelaide.edu.au/e/edgeworth/maria/grateful-negro/). Edgeworth here shows how the savage African is completely transformed by the act of kindness and trust. This Caesar is the improved Caesar, with only feelings of gratitude and loyalty towards the white master. Edgeworth offers us the psyche of the improved slave:

> The mind of Caesar was not insensible to the charms of freedom: he knew the negro conspirators had so taken their measures that there was the greatest probability of their success. His heart beat high at the idea of recovering his liberty: but he was not to be seduced from his duty, not even by this delightful hope; nor was he to be intimidated by the dreadful certainty that his former friends and countrymen, considering him as a deserter from their cause, would become his bitterest enemies.
>
> (unpaginated, http://ebooks.adelaide.edu.au/e/edgeworth/
> maria/grateful-negro/)

Edgeworth also shows the improved slave as being able to overcome the temptation of freedom, and instead preferring to be loyal to the white master. She also portrays Caesar as abandoning his racial affiliations: an act that would, in Edgeworth's subtext, be symptomatic of his reconstruction. This reading is invited by what Edgeworth proceeds to do. The sorceress Esther tells him his wife Clara would die if he didn't cooperate in the slave rebellion. Edgeworth writes:

> Caesar appeared to be more and more agitated. His eyes were fixed upon Clara. The conflict in his mind was violent: but his sense of gratitude and duty could not be shaken by hope, fear, or ambition; nor could it be vanquished by love. He determined, however, to appear to yield.

Caesar has been 'improved' enough here to perform two things: playing the role of defeated and cooperative rebel and preserving his 'essence' of the grateful slave. What is significant is that he overcomes his 'natural' impulses in order to do so. Edgeworth thus suggests that the reconstructed black man is able to fight down his impulses and allow his more 'rational' responses – the pretence of being subdued and his gratitude towards the white man – to dominate him and his actions.

If self-sacrificing gratitude such as Caesar's was a symbol of the improved savage under the ameliorative and paternalist colonial then another sign of the improved native was civility and civil behaviour. Anindyo Roy (2005) has argued that civility in the native was treated at once as a sign of improvement under the British influence and as a 'mask concealing an aggressive and deceptively ambitious mind' (5). The native 'vacillated between being aggressive and being excessively civil and obsequious' (5. Also see Homi Bhabha 2009b). It is an intentional distortion, under the guise of imitation, of the colonizer's practices and norms. Roy, following Bhabha, is no doubt accurate in his reading of the ambivalence of the colonial towards the civil native. However, the narratives of Kipling, Forster and Orwell seem to *satirize* rather than admire the English-educated, civil native. Thus it is possible to see the *native's civility in colonial fiction as representing the final product of the colonial project of improvement*. While Roy seems to see the civility as a mask concealing a deeper evil, I suggest that the civility and formal conversational modes that sound clearly out-of-place and 'textbookish' mark not evil but the limits of the improvement project. Even though these texts by Forster, Kipling, Orwell are anti-imperialist in many ways, they are unable to imagine a native who can be so completely decultured and thus made to resemble English civil behaviour. But this might also be read as a call to *continue* the project – the native's improvement is still an unfinished project.

Writing about Hurree Chunder Mookerjee, Rudyard Kipling demonstrates this unfinished project of modernizing and civilizing the savage. Mookerjee has to undertake some ethnographic studies, but is uncertain of the magic and mystic elements of the local cultures.

> 'How am I to fear the absolutely non-existent?' said Hurree Babu, talking English to reassure himself. It is an awful thing still to dread the magic that you contemptuously investigate—to collect folk-lore for the Royal Society with a lively belief in all Powers of Darkness.
>
> (1965: 197)

Here, despite talking English to 'reassure' himself, and armed with the Royal Society's backing to 'contemptuously investigate' the local cultures, Hurree Babu finds himself awed and frightened. Later, Hurree Babu is described as smiling 'ingratiatingly' (197), using idiomatic expressions native to the English ('jolly beastly', 'by Jove'). At one point he admits: '"That is all raight. I am only Babu showing off my English to you. All we Babus talk English to show off," said Hurree, flinging his shoulder-cloth jauntily' (200). Kipling makes Hurree Babu a

268 Civilize and collapse

self-aware native subject, who recognizes his feigned obsequiousness. If the colonial project was to civilize the native, the native in this case recognizes the limitations of the project and simply goes along with it when/because it suits him. That Hurree Babu recognizes the English need to civilize him is made evident when Kipling portrays a radical transformation in the man:

> The Hurree Babu of his knowledge—oily, effusive, and nervous—was gone; gone, too, was the brazen drug-vendor of overnight. There remained—polished, polite, attentive—a sober, learned son of experience and adversity.
>
> (246)

This is hardly colonial mimicry or 'sly civility'. The civility is the native's *role-playing* and self-conscious acquiescence to the colonial project of improvement so that he is able insinuate himself into the power structures of the Empire (Hurree Babu in *Kim*) or acquire for his purposes the friendship of the English Flory so that he can gain access to the Europeans-only Club (Veraswami in *Burmese Days*). The 'showing off' to the English that Hurree Babu admits to draws *English* attention to the colonized subject's intense awareness of what is going on. Thus, while on the one hand Kipling satirizes the 'improved' colonial subject he also underscores the native's alertness to this project of improvement. Like Caliban who has learnt how to curse, Hurree Babu has learnt the art of both self-deprecation and showing off, in the master's tongue.

In *Burmese Days* the Indian doctor Veraswami is described as possessing a voice 'eager and bubbling' (Orwell 1981: 35). When Flory asks him if he may come into the house, Veraswami responds:

> If you may come up! Of course, of course, come up this instant! Ah, Mr Flory how very delightful to see you! Come up, come up. What drink will you have? I have whisky, beer, vermouth, and other European liquours. Ah, my dear friend, how I have been pining for some cultured conversation.
>
> (35)

In an earlier section I had pointed, via Lidan Lin's arguments, to Dr Aziz in *A Passage to India* where there is considerable comic miming of English civil exchanges and conversation. Lin proposes that Aziz's demeanour suggests a native sentimentality (therefore Lin accuses Forster of employing the regular colonial stereotype here). I suggest that Aziz is *aware* that he is playing the role of a sentimental native so that he is able to make the politically unacceptable observations about the British being driven away. Aziz has been reconstructed as a civil native, and so he uses the civility that is exaggerated and overly obsequious to reveal that he knew he was a colonial project, that he was aware of his reconstruction, and went along with it because it served his purposes of deploying a political language. To me it seems as though Hurree Babu, Flory and Aziz represent not simply the limits of the civilizational project of reconstructing the native but also indicate the *native's political maturity in recognizing the benefits of the civilizational mission.* To phrase it differently, the native does not passively go along with the civilizational process: rather he finds in it the weapons and instruments of political modernity. We can therefore see native civility, apparently instilled by Western education and training under the Empire, as a form of England's engagements with the racial, cultural Other, but one in which the native seems to have an equal and decisive role to play.

(It must be noted that contextually these 'civil' figures in colonial fiction emerge in post-1857, i.e. post-'Mutiny', India. From the aggressive, sly and deceitful native, armed and ready to wreak revenge on the white man, we see a shift in portrayals here. The civil native is the less-dangerous native, but this on no account can be read as passive acquiescence or as a sign of native naivety.)

But perhaps the most violent reconstruction of the native and the primitive is exemplified in H.G. Wells' *The Island of Dr. Moreau.* A tale evidently influenced by Darwinian theories of evolution, Wells' novel deals with the attempt to expel the 'animality' – by immersing the animals in the 'bath of pain' – in the creatures so that they can become more human-like. Moreau tells Prendick:

> For it is just this question of pain that parts us. So long as visible or audible pain turns you sick, so long as your own pains drive you, so long as pain underlines your propositions about sin, so long, I tell you, you are an animal, thinking a little less obscurely what an animal feels.
>
> (2002: 100)

When the story opens the island is peopled by 'beast-people', neither fully human yet, but not really animal any more. They have formed communities and have developed a ritual of reciting the 'Law'. The Law, Prendick reports, is a chant:

> Not to go on all-Fours; *that* is the Law. Are we not men?
> Not to suck up Drink; *that* is the Law. Are we not men?
> Not to eat Flesh or Fish; *that* is the Law. Are we not men?
> Not to claw the Bark of Trees; *that* is the Law. Are we not men?
> Not to chase other Men; *that* is the Law. Are we not men?
>
> (79–80)

The rhetorical force of the iterated question 'Are we not men?' suggests that it is in the observance of the Law, which we may read as a metonym for social norms and codes, that humanity is forged, for the oral performance of the Law stages their subjectivity as distinct from animals. But the 'not', iterated, expresses uncertainty over the efficacy of rhetorical strategies to 'make' men out of animals (Christensen 2004: 581).

It should, however, be noted that the beast-people, as Wells' characters Moreau and Prendick describe them, seem to be racially aligned with blacks. One is described as a 'fair specimen of the negroid type' (2002: 103), while another possesses 'a black negroid face' (34). (Prendick asks Montgomery when he first sees them,

270 Civilize and collapse

'what race are they?', 48.) Thus, the beast-people occupy an ontological category between animals and 'negroid' races before they become, Moreau hopes, fully human. Furthering this evolutionary process that would 'produce' humans from animals is the white man's job.

Not only do Moreau's experiments result in the reconstruction of animals into near-humans, they also produce social structures among animals. Moreau says: 'They build themselves their dens, gather fruit and pull herbs – marry even' (108). The human social order is replicated by the beast-people as well. But Wells' doctor-hero also recognizes that the bestial foundations of the beast-people are not ever fully erased or transformed:

> But I can see through it all, see into their very souls, and see there nothing but the souls of beasts, beasts that perish—anger, and the lusts to live and gratify themselves. ... Yet they're odd. Complex, like everything else alive. There is a kind of upward striving in them, part vanity, part waste sexual emotion, part waste curiosity. It only mocks me.
>
> (108)

The 'upward striving' seems to suggest a human-like aspirational condition of the beast-people, but Moreau seems unsure of what it is: residual (bestial?) sexual emotion perhaps, or even (human) curiosity. Later, elaborating on this impossible nature of their identity, Moreau says:

> [T]here is still something in everything I do that defeats me, makes me dissatisfied. ... And least satisfactory of all is something that I cannot touch, somewhere—I cannot determine where—in the seat of the emotions. Cravings, instincts, desires that harm humanity, a strange reservoir to burst suddenly and inundate the whole being of the creature with anger, hate, or fear. ... Each time I dip a living creature into the bath of burning pain, I say: this time I will burn out all the animal, this time I will make a rational creature of my own.
>
> (106–7)

Timothy Christensen points out that Moreau admits to being unable to change the 'cravings, instincts, desires' of the beasts into social or religious duty (2004: 579). Like Victor Frankenstein, Moreau seeks a 'rational creature of my own', without specifying *why* he should have a creature of his own (Frankenstein hopes the life he creates would be beholden to him as creator).

When Prendick returns to London he says of his encounter with the beast-people: 'I could not persuade myself that the men and women I met were not ... Beast People, animals halfwrought into the outward image of human souls' (2002: 182).

Such a reconstruction involves the bridging of gaps and distances across species and races, as Wells' novel suggests, but a reconstruction whose overall direction and control is retained by the improving Englishman. A key scene in the reconstruction of interracial space in the colony may be found in *A Passage to India*. The setting is the Club, where the Indian women and some men have also gathered. Forster's description goes thus:

> A little group of Indian ladies had been gathering in a third quarter of the grounds, near a rustic summer-house, in which the more timid of them had already taken refuge. The rest stood with their backs to the company and their faces pressed into a bank of shrubs. At a little distance stood their male relatives, watching the venture. The sight was significant: an island bared by the turning tide, and bound to grow.
>
> (1970: 41)

The Indian women, and their male relatives, form an island alongside the English. Several things are striking about the above description. One, the Indians are islands made visible by the 'turning tide': isolated thus far but increasingly *visible*. That Forster shows Indian women 'coming out', so to speak, suggests a reconstruction of Indian cultural space where (1) the circumscribed yet public space of the British Club is now 'open' in limited ways to Indians and (2) Indian women, for long sequestered in their home, come out into this space. Two, Forster's throwaway line, that these islands are 'bound to grow', suggests a reconstruction in the form of increasing visibility and therefore modernization of the Indian woman. Encouraged and facilitated by the British Club, however restricted and oppressive this imperial structure itself might be, a slow remedying of a cultural defect – the Indian woman's invisibility in public spaces – is underway, implies Forster.

Prendick, Kurtz, Fielding, Flory, Merrick represent the exact obverse – and the subverted ideal – of English heroism, the civilizational mission and the project of improvement. Globality in English literary texts from the end of the nineteenth century expressed anxieties about the failure of the moral imperialist ideal, and more often than not saw the world in terms of its discrepant geographies where Englishness disintegrated in the face of the Other, and partly as a result of the very ideals they set out to execute. Thus, I am arguing here that the *discourse of improvement is concomitant with the discourse of failed Englishness and the ruins of English identity in various parts of the world.* Mrs Lackersteen's comment to Mr MacGregor in *Burmese Days* summarizes this dualism: 'we seem to have no authority over the natives nowadays with all these dreadful Reforms' (Orwell 1981: 28).

This collapse of English authority that Mrs Lackersteen mourns is, however, one element in a larger collapse of Englishness in which the moral depravity that undermines the myth-illusion-ideal of the civilizational mission is perhaps a larger component. This collapse or depravity constitutes a whole new transnational engagement for England where the world is mapped in terms of the discrepant spaces where Englishness disintegrates.

272 Civilize and collapse

Discrepant geographies

> Pox Britannica ... Pox Britannica is its proper name.
>
> (Orwell 1981: 39)

William Blake's *Visions of the Daughters of Albion* begins with the lament of enslaved (white) women:

> Enslav'd, the Daughters of Albion weep a trembling lamentation
> Upon their mountains; in their valleys, sighs toward America.
> For the soft soul of America.
>
> (1973: 189)

What is interesting is that Oothon-as-America and the daughters of Albion are both united in their slavery. Steven Vine is accurate when he notes that the cries of Oothon are heard by her 'patriarchal and colonial oppressor, Bromion' who is a mixture of 'British imperialism and masculinist aggression' (1994: 40). As the poem proceeds Blake merges colonialism with slavery, in the form of Oothon's rape by Bromion as she struggles towards Theotormon, her beloved:

> Bromion rent her with his thunders. On his stormy bed
> Lay the faint maid, and soon her woes appalld his thunders hoarse
> Bromion spoke. Behold this harlot here on Bromions bed,
> And let the jealous dolphins sport around the lovely maid;
> Thy soft American plains are mine, and mine thy north & south:
> Stampt with my signet are the swarthy children of the sun:
> They are obedient, they resist not, they obey the scourge:
> Their daughters worship terrors and obey the violent.
>
> (1973: 190)

In Blake's language of enslavement Bromion is at once slaveowner, rapist and imperialist ('Thy soft American plains are mine, and mine thy north & south'). Sexual enslavement is conflated with the enslavement of lands in Blake's work. Women are united in their slavery, whether they are American or British. Slavery therefore is a horrific transcendental signifier of the woman's condition.

In Charlotte Brontë's *Jane Eyre*, early in their childhood, Jane objects to John Reed's tyrannical behaviour. Her protests – and name-calling – go thus:

> 'Wicked and cruel boy!' I said. 'You are like a murderer—you are like a slave-driver—you are like the Roman emperors!'
>
> I had read Goldsmith's History of Rome, and had formed my opinion of Nero, Caligula, etc.
>
> (2010: 8–9)

Jane conflates categories here – slavery, imperialism, extreme violence (murder) – in her denunciation of Reed. She is of course punished – incarcerated in the

Red-room – for her behaviour. Bronte's point is subtly conveyed – the woman's oppression at the hands of the males of the household ought to recall *global* issues of enslavement and tyranny, of racial, masculine and imperial varieties, even as the metaphor of slavery is transferred across racial categories (from blacks to the white Jane). That is, the language of enslavement here places the white woman alongside the black slave and the colonial subject.

An entire grammar of enslavement and oppression that seemingly cuts across classes and races is captured in the above passages from Blake and Brontë. The state of Englishwoman's oppression produced within English social-cultural conditions in these two texts demands a language, a language readily furnished by the larger contexts of the slave trade and slavery. To phrase it differently, Blake and Brontë's language of enslavement is a clear sign of England's transnationalized culture wherein the slavery of the blacks was a well-known fact: for Blake and Brontë to take recourse to the language of enslavement it would have been essential for a current discourse of slavery to circulate. Much of this discourse was built on an implicit argument about cultural defects which in turn produced the improvement and amelioration discourse of the 1780s and after. What the above examples point to is the language of cultural defect itself, borrowed from England's transnational connections.

In Chapter 2 we noted how poets used the deaths of Englishmen in foreign spaces to transform those spaces into sites of celebration: of English triumphs, sacrifice, heroism and valour. The Other space becomes a triumphalist geography of Englishness in such literary representations where the end of English itinerancy is the embracing of heroic death. However, this triumphalist geography was often countered by a very different view of the space of the Other.

Byron's *Don Juan*, a sterling example of Romantic cosmopolitanism that I have cited before, foregrounds the necessity of expansive thinking, and of acknowledging the 'narrowness' of England's sense of itself:

> To our Theme.—The man who has stood on the Acropolis,
> And look'd down over Attica; or he
> Who has sail'd where picturesque Constantinople is,
> Or seen Timbuctoo, or hath taken tea
> In small-eyed China's crockery-ware metropolis,
> Or sat amidst the bricks of Nineveh,
> May not think much of London's first appearance—
> But ask him what he thinks of it a year hence?
>
> (1975: 789)

Byron here, writes Kirsten Daly (1998), opposes the narrow, even parochial, pretentiousness of London culture to the expansive nature of the world outside – a world the truly cosmopolitan has seen and experienced (198). London becomes, in this binary, the *lesser* of the cultures as a result of the Englishman's travels.

274 Civilize and collapse

Another paradigmatic poem that offers us a different kind of space is Rudyard Kipling's 'Chant-pagan'. In the opening stanza the speaker asks:

'Ow can I ever take on
With awful old England again
An' 'ouses both sides of the street,
And 'edges two sides of the lane,
And the parson an' gentry between
An' touchin' my 'at when we meet–
Me that 'ave been what I've been?

(1977: 212)

The speaker then goes on to describe the places he has been (South Africa) and the deaths he has witnessed and the events he has experienced:

Me that saw Barberton took
When we dropped through the clouds on their 'ead,
An' they 'ove the guns over and fled—
Me that was through Di'mond 'Ill,
An' Pieters an' Springs an' Belfast—
From Dundee to Vereeniging all—
Me that stuck out to the last
(An' five bloomin' bars on my chest)—
I am doin' my Sunday-school best,
By the 'elp of the Squire an' 'is wife
(Not to mention the 'ousemaid an' cook),
To come in an' 'ands up an' be still,
An' honestly work for my bread,
My livin' in that state of life
To which it shall please God to call
Me!

(213)

The poem ends with a denunciation and rejection of England:

That the sunshine of England is pale,
And the breezes of England are stale,
An' there's somethin' gone small with the lot;
For *I* know of a sun an' a wind,
An' some plains and a mountain be'ind,
An' some graves by a barb-wire fence;
An' a Dutchman I've fought 'oo might give
Me a job were I ever inclined,
To look in an' offsaddle an' live

Where there's neither a road nor a tree—
But only my Maker an' me,
And I think it will kill me or cure,
So I think I will go there an' see.
Me!

(214)

The poem celebrates an English heroism, but it does so in order to demonstrate how the spaces of the colony are spaces of opportunity where a man can be a Man. It is, of course, the space of death and the entire area is marked by graves but, says the speaker, there seems to be a greater authenticity to life (and death) in the Other space. The man back from foreign spaces also finds it impossible, like Crusoe and Gulliver before him, to be at home in England. England itself is being re-evaluated as a result of the man's off-shore experiences. The Other space, so to speak, has come to haunt England, just as Coleridge's Ancient Mariner comes back to tell his horrible tale and transform complacent Englishmen into 'sadder and wiser' men. (I have examined this theme of the 'returning' Englishman in Chapter 5.)

'Discrepant geography' is my term for a particular cluster of discourses around Other spaces. First, as we can see in the Kipling poem the discourse of discrepant geography suggests that very often the English find greater honesty and opportunity not back 'home' but in the Other space. Second, in a discrepant geography the mapping project, the descriptive account and the ethnography (already discussed in Chapter 2) do not appear to fully apprehend or comprehend the Other's space. Third, it maps the space of the Other wherein the European in the 'new world' becomes the Other to the 'native', a space not where the black or the brown is studied but where the *European* is subject to scrutiny and control, and experiences injury, derangement and even death. Fourth, it is a spatial discourse where the interruptions and disruptions, the barbarism and the wildness of the land are the effects of *European* interventions. Finally, in such a discourse the wild and the darkness are located within England itself, as evidenced in particular texts by Kipling, Hardy and Conrad.

Occasionally the discourse of knowledge by the European of the Other world is cast as a two-way transaction. The space of the Other, and travel itself, serves, in Mary Louise Pratt's famous term, as a 'contact zone', where the cultural encounter with difference occurs. 'Discrepant geographies', as I think of the contact zone, are the spaces where the European, expecting the Other, *discovers himself to be the Other*. But in the discourse of discrepant spaces it is the European who is wholly the tourist, the visitor, the anomaly, the spectacle – the Other.

Here the geoaesthetics of wonder is inverted where the European becomes the wonderful or the monstrous. Francis Bacon in *The New Atlantis*, for instance, invests European voyages with a wholly different project: the chance for the natives of these places to study the European, rather than the other way round. The Spaniards therefore are kept in isolation, their movements closely observed and their interactions, including conversations with the Bensalemites, regulated and

276 Civilize and collapse

kept to a minimum. On the day of their transport to Strangers House, the Spaniards have the first taste of being the *observed*:

> there were gathered some people on both sides, standing in a row; but in so civil a fashion, as if it had been, not to wonder at us, but to welcome us; and divers of them.
>
> (Bacon 1862: 364)

Later the narrator puts it this way:

> For they have by commandment (though in form of courtesy) cloistered us within these walls for three days: who knoweth whether it be not to take some taste of our manners and conditions? and if they find them bad, to banish us straightways; if good, to give us further time. For these men that they have given us for attendance may withal have an eye upon us.
>
> (367)

Clearly, this reverses the colonial trope of discovery.[16] However, one needs to ponder over the structure of discovery that Bacon seems to present fairly explicitly. It is possible to see Bacon's text as encoding a double fantasy: the 'discovery' of a utopian space and an Other, but also the fantasy of being discovered. The narrator's emphasis on being observed and monitored gestures at the island being a laboratory where strange new arrivals are subject to the same kind of laboratory testing and internment as animal or plant species. Thus, Bacon's trope of expansion of territory and of knowledge (in this particular text the two go together) seamlessly welds together the European politics of gazing with the natives' curious gaze. In this visual narrative of *The New Atlantis* we can think of the expansion of territory as a code for the two-directional gaze of Europe and its Other.

In Behn's *Oroonoko* the white female narrator records:

> They had no sooner spied us but they set up a loud cry, that frighted us at first; we thought it had been for those that should kill us, but it seems it was of wonder and amazement. They were all naked; and we were dressed, so as is most commode for the hot countries, very glittering and rich; so that we appeared extremely fine.
>
> (1994: 53)

Similar to the experience of the Spaniards in Bacon and of Behn's narrator is that of Lemuel Gulliver in Lilliput, Brobdingnag and other places. The news of his arrival in Lilliput, says Gulliver, had spread all over the country:

> As the news of my arrival spread through the kingdom, it brought prodigious numbers of rich, idle, and curious people to see me; so that the villages were almost emptied; and great neglect of tillage and household affairs must have

ensued, if his imperial majesty had not provided, by several proclamations and orders of state, against this inconveniency.

(Swift 1960a: 25–6)

In Brobdingnag, instigated by a miserly neighbour, his local guardian decides to exhibit Gulliver as a marketable spectacle. Having already been subject to the scrutiny of the courtiers and the monarch, Gulliver finds himself now transformed into a commercial spectacle. The farmer's daughter, Glumdalclitch, sympathizes with Gulliver, understanding how, with his 'modest nature', 'what an indignity [he] should conceive it to be exposed for money as a public spectacle to the meanest of the people' (78). He is exhibited and forced to entertain visitors. Europeans, it would seem, are equally subject to non-European exoticization in Swift's tale.

The condition of becoming/being a spectacle in these narratives performs an interesting inversion of the geography of monstrosity: the European is made aware of his own strangeness. Gulliver is the monstrous in the landscapes of Lilliput and Brobdingnag. Over a century later R.M. Ballantyne in *The Coral Island* would similarly present the boys on the island as akin to both pirates and savages: 'Little did we imagine [says Ralph] that the first savages who would drive us into it would be white savages, perhaps our own countrymen' (unpaginated, http://ebooks.adelaide. edu.au/b/ballantyne/rm/coral-island/). Here whites have not only degenerated into pirate-like figures, they have even begun to resemble 'savages' (for this theme see the 'going native' section of Chapter 5).

We need to keep in mind that discrepant geographies where the English 'lost' their civilization was as old a theme as the triumphalist geography of the New World. Richard Middlemas in Walter Scott's *The Surgeon's Daughter* is so corrupted by the Orient – and Scott seems to tone down European corruption here by making him a Jew of dubious origins – that he stoops to collaborating with Montreville to sell Menie Gray, the English girl, to Tipu Sultan. Middlemas dresses in native costume 'so remote from all European costume'. He is described as a 'double traitor', who would 'betray thy betrothed to the Prince, in order to obtain the means of betraying the Prince to the English, and thus gain thy pardon from thy countrymen'. Later Adam Hartley and Esdale see Middlemas' 'abandoning a British subject to the fraud of renegades, and the force of a tyrant' as the height of treason by a Briton. Hartley sees him as an 'apostate' when he beholds Middlemas serving as Montreville's servitor in the presence of Tipu, thus conveying the complete and utter degradation of the white man in India (http://ebooks.adelaide.edu. au/s/cott/walter/surgeon).[17]

In Mary Shelley's *The Last Man* (1826) Adrian tells Perdita and Lionel Verney of the horrors of war where he saw Englishmen, fighting side by side with Greeks (against the Turks), 'contend for a girl, whose rich dress and extreme beauty excited the brutal appetites of these wretches' (2004: 128), thus suggesting that they had been debased by the context and setting (Constantinople) into animals. This theme reaches its climax, arguably, in Conrad's *Heart of Darkness*.

278 Civilize and collapse

My reading of Conrad's classic is more sympathetic to Tony Brown's persuasive reading where he argues that 'Marlow performs a perversion of the West's ideal-image of itself as the true seat of civilization and light – a perversion which offers a certain critical leverage for interrupting the perpetuation of this self-image' (2000: 15). My argument is, first, Marlow does not simply interrupt the perpetuation of London's self-image, he inverts its genealogy, topography and history. He makes London not just the mirror-image of Africa, but suggests that Africa enables the traveller to discover the darkness at the heart of civilization. Here Africa functions as the provider of both a prospective and a retrospective vision. 'Prospective' because like his predecessors (Hythlodaeus, Crusoe, Gulliver, Leo) Marlow's pro-spects lie in Africa. Viewing Africa, like Kurtz, he sees potential. But it is also ret-rospective because Africa enables him to reflect upon London when in London, and makes its darkness visible. Second, and in line with Brown's reading, the darkness and the horror in the space of the Other is traced by Conrad to two causes (or 'oscillates', to use Brown's term, between these two causes): colonial intervention in Africa and the environment itself (Brown 2000: 16–18). The second cause, of course, fits right in with colonial discourse's construction of the geography of monstrosity. But the first produces what I am calling a discrepant geography.

> Black shapes crouched, lay, sat between the trees, leaning against the trunks, clinging to the earth, half coming out, half effaced within the dim light, in all the attitudes of pain, abandonment, and despair … These moribund shapes were free as air- and nearly as thin. I began to distinguish the gleam of the eyes under the trees. Then, glancing down, I saw a face near my hand. The black bones reclined at full length with one shoulder against the tree, and slowly the eyelids rose and the sunken eyes looked up at me, enormous and vacant, a kind of blind, white flicker in the depths of the orbs, which died out slowly … Near the same tree two more bundles of acute angles sat with their legs drawn up. One, with his chin propped on his knees, stared at nothing, in an intolerable and appalling manner: his brother phantom rested its forehead, as if overcome with a great weariness; and all about others were scattered in every pose of contorted collapse, as in some picture of a massacre or a pestilence.
>
> (Conrad 1974: 66)

This description suggests, Brown argues, that the frontier is where *European civili-zation cannot assert itself anymore*: 'the colonial frontier manifests as a stumbling block for civilization in *Heart of Darkness* in the form of, or rather in the formless presence of, a void which forecloses upon European culture' (2000: 19). Kurtz's return to the darkness, according to Brown, marks the 'deferral necessary in asserting the authority of civilization's codes when displaced to the fundamentally different location beyond civilization's margins' (22). Yet there is more to the account of the zombie-like black figures in the African environment, or Kurtz being claimed by

Africa. Marlow's encounter teaches him that it is the colonial who is responsible for the leaching processes that drain the Africans of their life. The discrepant geography in this case is also the devitalization of the African environment with the arrival of the European. Contrast, in order to detect the discrepant geography of the colonial's travels, the above passage with Henry Stanley's dreams for Africa in 1885:

> On the 14th of August, 1879, I arrived before the mouth of this river [the Congo] to ascend it, with the novel mission of sowing along its banks civilised settlements, to peacefully conquer and subdue it, to remould it in harmony with modern ideas into National States, within whose limits the European merchant shall go hand in hand with the dark African trader, and justice and law and order shall prevail, and murder and lawlessness and cruel barter of slaves shall for ever cease.
>
> (cited in Lewis 1998: 224)

Stanley saw the white man's mobility into and through Africa as heralding the arrival of civilization. Kurtz seems to have shared this vision, as his 'Report to the International Society for the Suppression of Savage Customs' indicates: 'we whites ... must necessarily appear to them [savages] in the nature of supernatural beings ... By the simple exercise of our will we can exert a power for good practically unbounded' (Conrad 1974: 118). The Report, however, concludes with a simple injunction: 'exterminate all the brutes' (118). Conrad's account of Kurtz and the so-called 'humanitarian mission' (which, as Alan Lester (2000) has noted, produced its own geography of compassion and intervention), however, demonstrates the limits and, more significantly, the dangers of colonial intervention. In Conrad it is the geography not of Africa but of the *European in Africa* who, by his mobility and redrawing of the border, introduces monstrous disruptions. The geography of monstrosity, in other words, was originally constructed (in the age of exploration and discovery and until the eighteenth century) in representations by the European of the *distant* Other lands, but Conrad shows how the monstrous geography is really an effect of the mobility and settlement by/of the *European* in these lands. If the Spaniards and Gulliver were the monstrous spectacles – implying a passive object of viewing – in Bacon and Swift, in Conrad they are *active* monstrosities, intervening in the land. Hence the 'colony' also marks the geography, or the spatial extent, of white man's cruel, mad or civilizational acts.

> I always ask leave, in the interests of science, to measure the crania of those going out there ... Ever any madness in your family? ... It would be ... interesting for science to watch the mental changes of individuals on the spot, but ... I have a little theory which you Messieurs who go out there must help me to prove.
>
> (Conrad 1974: 58)

280 Civilize and collapse

The Company Doctor, who says these words to Marlow before examining his cranial shape, seems to be proposing a type of colonial personality or even a racial determinism: certain kinds of Europeans are headed for the spaces of Africa and the colony.[18]

Further, Kurtz's return to the wilds is not merely indicative of the necessity of colonial imposition on the barbaric space. It also indicates, in geographical terms, the limits of the colonial project. Kurtz recognizes these limits and retreats into the wilds, and *away* from colonial spaces. The frontier is not where the colonial needs to push forward but where Africa (1) pushes the colonial back or (2) draws the colonial into the 'barbaric' space. This last, in *Heart of Darkness*, is the triumph of Otherness that draws the so-called modern European into itself.

The world's geography must hereafter list those spaces where the European meets and engages with the Other but also loses a sense of singularity (racial or national identity) and is creolized. The nativization of the European in the wilds of Africa, seen in the fiction of Edgar Rice Burroughs and Conrad, is also a form of discrepant geography in English representations. I have already discussed in Chapter 2 the possibility of reading the white man's masquerade (as native) not as a sign of a stable colonial identity and its dominance but as symbolic of a desire to escape the confines of this (English, colonial) identity. It is the space of Asia and Africa that offers the colonial the opportunity to move away from 'pure' Englishness and towards creolization, initially in dress but also in language. This reading also contributes to the sense of the colonized space as a discrepant geography where Englishmen lose, modify or tone down their Englishness.

Haggard's Allan Quatermain declares that he can 'tolerate England no more' and would prefer to live and die 'among the wild game and the savages'. He is tired, he claims, of the 'prim English country, with its trim hedgerows and cultivated fields, its stiff formal manners, and its well-dressed crowds' (unpaginated, https://ebooks. adelaide.edu.au/h/haggard/h_rider/allan/). The desire to abandon a 'civilized' space for the so-called 'savage' spaces of Africa, therefore, continues the theme of the desirable space of the Other. Jim, Conrad's eponymous hero in *Lord Jim*, finds salvation in the Malayan region of Patusan. While admittedly, Conrad shows how nativization enables Jim to become the local Tuan or Lord, he also proposes that the Englishman is able to achieve a semblance of happiness in this Other space.

But this Other-space-as-salvation is missing in Conrad's *Heart of Darkness*. In Conrad's description of Kurtz's transformation we see the European's mobility as producing an entire new geography of the African continent as the space of the non-singular, of the hybrid and of the deracinated:

> The wilderness had patted him on the head, and, behold, it was like a ball – an ivory ball; it had caressed him, and – lo! – he had withered; it had taken him, loved him, embraced him, got into his veins, consumed his flesh, and sealed his soul to its own by the inconceivable ceremonies of some devilish initiation. He was its spoiled and pampered favourite ... How many powers of darkness claimed him for their own ... The wilderness ... had whispered to

him things about himself which he did not know ... the whisper had proved irresistibly fascinating. It echoed loudly within him because he was hollow at the core ... The heavy, mute spell of the wilderness ... seemed to draw him to its pitiless breast by the awakening of forgotten and brutal instincts, by the memory of gratified and monstrous passions.

(1974: 115)

That eventually Kurtz is represented more as an animal than a civilized European (like a quadruped, 'crawling on all-fours', writes Conrad, 142) suggests a primitivization of the European that recalls the European-as-monstrous of Gulliver or the Spaniards in Bacon that I have already alluded to.[19] Discrepant geography is the geography of this creolization where European identity and its pride in its purity, chivalry, valour and enterprise are muted and modified in such representations where the European is a spectacle, a hybrid and a source of mockery, laughter, savagery or alteration.

Yet another discourse of English itinerancy and the discrepant geography of the Other is visible in English writings from the eighteenth century. Edmund Burke warned the English Parliament:

In carrying on the war in the West Indies, the hostile sword is merciful: the country in which we engage is the dreadful enemy. There the European conqueror finds a cruel defeat in the very fruits of his success. Every advantage is but a new demand on England for recruits to the West Indian grave. In a West India war, the Regicides have for their troops a race of fierce barbarians, to whom the poisoned air, in which our youth inhale certain death, is salubrity and life. To them the climate is the surest and most faithful of allies.

(Burke 1796)

S.T. Coleridge's famous *The Rime of the Ancient Mariner* documented the suffering of colonialism, specifically of the suffering of English soldiers, sailors and travellers who go out towards the tropics. Alan Bewell notes that the Mariner has been traumatized by the voyage – into the 'silent sea' (the Pacific) and the tropics, and its attendant colonial experience (1999: 100). The guilt of the Mariner, argues Bewell, enacts a colonial 'economy of complicity and guilt' (101). Bewell also reads the Mariner's disease experience (that leaves him 'long, lank, and brown') as a critique of the English nation's colonial mobility that caused these sailors to move into and across 'pathogenic spaces' (103). Thus, as we have noted in the case of Crusoe and Gulliver, the corporeal encounter with the New World is repeated in the Ancient Mariner's life story, and represents the space of English mobility and its attendant suffering – a discrepant geography where instead of conquest, profit or dominance, they encounter pain, trauma and suffering. The landscape of opportunity is now a landscape of pain – although, as Elaine Freedgood has demonstrated, in the nineteenth century the English embraced adventure tourism, mountaineering

282 Civilize and collapse

and such as a 'collective means of preemptively expressing and relieving anxiety …
a voluntary and knowing experience of danger' (2000: 105).

The collapse of Englishness when in adverse situations is the key theme of
Orwell's *Burmese Days*. The English are referred to in pejorative and abusive terms
by Flory throughout the novel: 'nasty, poodle-faking, horseless riffraff' (1981: 191),
'boozing, womanizing, yellow-faced loafers' (193), being some of them. Flory's
own ragged birthmark on the cheek is a source of some shame and embarrassment
for him, even when he is with the supposedly inferior natives.

William Golding's *Lord of the Flies* (1954) is an excellent example of a modern-
day discrepant geography that critiques the colonial civilizational illusion. Extending the themes of adventure tales from Ballantyne, Kipling and Conrad, Golding
demonstrates how the veneer of sophistication and civilization worn by the English
collapses absurdly fast when they are 'outside' their geopolitical domains. In the
novel the boys initially decide that they have to be properly behaved. Says Jack:

> We've got to have rules and obey them. After all, we're not savages. We're
> English; and the English are best at everything. So we've got to do the right
> things.
>
> (1999: 43–4)

Slowly, of course, they slide towards the very savagery and barbarism they wished
to avoid:

> They heard him [Piggy] stamp. 'What are we? Humans? Or animals? Or
> savages? What's grown-ups going to think? Going off – hunting pigs – let-
> ting fires out – and now!'
>
> (99)

The boys even begin to have 'tribal' gatherings, complete with body-paint and a
Chief:

> The chief was sitting there, naked to the waist, his face blocked out in white
> and red. The tribe lay in a semicircle before him. … 'To-morrow,' went on
> the Chief, 'we shall hunt again.' He pointed at this savage and that with his
> spear. … A savage raised his hand and the chief turned a bleak, painted face
> towards him.
>
> (181)

While on the one hand Golding seems to be mocking the smugness over their so-
called civilization, critics note that *Lord of the Flies* is an imperialist text because he
posits a slide towards *African*, and therefore non-European, savagery. That is, the
collapse of a European civilization is equated with and measured in terms of *African*
savagery. No other 'version' of savagery exists for Golding. Thus Stefan Hawlin
writes: 'The boys should have created white civilisation and constitutionalism, and

instead they have fallen back down the hierarchies, regressed to Africanness' (1995: 133). In addition to mapping the discrepant geographies where English collapse occurs, the text remains grounded in imperialist binaries of civilized English/savage African.

In texts like Graham Greene's *The Heart of the Matter* (1948) Africa becomes the space not of the great English humanitarian project but of the existential struggles of the Englishman, Henry Scobie. Thus, Greene's sympathies appear to lie with the Englishman in the colony and in the novel itself the theme of decolonization is actually marginalized in favour of the theme of national decline (MacPhee 2011: 27). That this national decline should occur in those spaces where once the humanitarian impulse had found its most legible expression suggests, in my reading, a discrepant geography of the Empire and the post-imperial condition.

The collapse of Englishness in terms of what the English do to the natives has historical antecedents in literature.

The theme of violent mutilation and dismemberment of the African body, by the English, inaugurated in Behn's *Oroonoko*, repeated in a different fashion in Defoe's *Robinson Crusoe* and climaxing in Henty, Haggard and Conrad, deserves mention. I propose that while these accounts do contribute to a triumphalist geography where the Englishman triumphs over the land and the body of the Other, it is also possible to see the violence as symbolic of the voluntary or involuntary degeneration of the white man in the colonial context. Thus the discrepant geography I examine here is the geography of European violence, both essential and gratuitous, and barbarism.

In Behn's *Oroonoko* the execution of the African prince-slave is described in vivid detail:

> And the executioner came, and first cut off his members, and threw them into the fire; after that, with an ill-favored knife, they cut off his ears and his nose and burned them; he still smoked on, as if nothing had touched him; then they hacked off one of his arms, and still he bore up, and held his pipe; but at the cutting off the other arm, his head sunk, and his pipe dropped, and he gave up the ghost, without a groan or a reproach.
>
> (1994: 72)

Later, they 'cut Caesar in quarters, and sent them to several of the chief plantations' (64).

Crusoe catalogues scrupulously the animals he kills for food. When he spies the savages on the island he considers how he might kill them. He records: in 'the night I dreamed often of killing the savages and of the reasons why I might justify doing it'. However, he realizes that such a gratuitous murder would make him 'no less a murderer than they were in being man-eaters—and perhaps much more so'. When he eventually does kill one of the savages this is how Defoe describes it: 'I perceived presently he had a bow and arrow, and was fitting it to shoot at me: so I

284 Civilize and collapse

was then obliged to shoot at him first, which I did, and killed him at the first shot' (158). Defoe then converts this killing into an act not only of self-defence but one through which Crusoe saves a native life, and ensures the native's loyalty and perpetual servitude. This is done through a symbolic marking of the body: 'he kneeled down again, kissed the ground, and laid his head upon the ground, and taking me by the foot, set my foot upon his head; this, it seems, was in token of swearing to be my slave for ever'. If, as Laura Franey (2003) proposes, European sovereignty is achieved at least partly through tattooing and other such markings upon the native body, Defoe's protagonist achieves precisely this. By saving the man's life − when he kills the other 'savages' − and the symbolic gesture of servitude on the part of the native, Crusoe inscribes the man with his authority. The landscape's triumphal geography here hinges on the dualism of a space of brutal violence and of symbolic subjection leading to real subjection.

In Charlotte Smith's *The Old Manor House* she explicitly links the destruction of the American landscape with the English war against the Revolutionaries:

> The country, lately so flourishing, and rising so rapidly into opulence, presented nothing but the ruins of houses, from whence their miserable inhabitants had either been driven entirely, or murdered! ... Even from [their] wretched temporary abodes they were often driven, to make way for the English soldiers; and their women and children exposed to the tempest of the night, or, what was infinitely more dreadful, to the brutality of the military ... [T]he country appeared almost depopulated, [and] the few stragglers, who yet lingered round the places most eagerly contended for, had been habituated to suffer till they had almost lost the semblance of humanity.
>
> (1969: 356)

The savagery here is, it needs to be noted, of the *English*, and is no different from that of any non-European savages.

We have already noted Ballantyne's description of the white savages. In Haggard's *King Solomon's Mines* the battle between Twala and Sir Henry ends thus:

> Once more Twala came on, and as he came our great Englishman gathered himself together, and swinging the heavy axe round his head, hit at him with his force. There was a shriek of excitement from a thousand throats and, behold! Twala's head seemed to spring from his shoulders and then fell and came rolling and bounding along the ground towards [Umbopa], stopping just at his feet. For a second the corpse stood upright, the blood spouting in fountains from the severed arteries; then with a dull crash it fell to the earth, and the gold torque from the neck went rolling away across the pavement.
>
> (unpaginated, http://ebooks.adelaide.edu.au/h/haggard/h_rider/
> king/index.html)

In *She* Haggard's Holly recounts his killing of a native:

> I … hacked at the head of one man with my hunting-knife, which was almost as big and heavy as a short sword, with such vigour, that the sharp steel … split his skull down to the eyes, and was held so fast by it that as he suddenly fell sideways the knife was twisted right out of my hand.
>
> (2008: 97)

And in the case of others:

> My arms were round the two swarthy demons, and I hugged them till I heard their ribs crack and crunch up beneath my gripe. They twisted and writhed like snakes, and clawed and battered at me with their fists, but I held on. Lying on my back there, so that their bodies might protect me from spear thrusts from above, I slowly crushed the life out of them.
>
> (97)

I have already cited Ballantyne's account from *The Gorilla Hunters*.[20]

In this geography of English brutality from *Oroonoko* to *Heart of Darkness* the Africans/Others are of course savages, aggressive, powerfully built and even devilish (Haggard calls them 'swarthy demons' in *She*). Thus the violence is cast in the rhetoric of triumph where it is the white man's superior prowess, in some cases enabled by technology, that enables him to defeat the Other. The dismemberment and killing of the Other marks the triumph of the Englishman over the body-space of the Other and therefore by extension over the territory of the Other. Yet, I would suggest, we can also see the spaces of violence enacted here in such detail as indicating the flawed foundations of European sovereignty: it is only in violence that Europeans can find their sovereign identities. It is in these acts of dehumanization where the Other is reduced to dead bodies or zombies (in *Heart of Darkness*) or the inhuman-animal that Englishness seems to assert itself.

'Discrepant geography' is the geography of European savagery and the concomitant geography of the Other's dehumanization and abjection.[21] It is discrepant in another sense as well. While there are instances of African violence upon the Europeans these mostly remain ineffective (Franey 2003: 100). Thus the geographies of heroism, triumph, profit and benevolent imperialism and expansion have now merged with the geographies of European cruelty and violence and thus perform the geography of European transformation. It is, once again, Conrad who points out this new geography in Marlow's description of an El Dorado expedition:

> It was reckless without hardihood, greedy without audacity, and cruel without courage. There was not an atom of foresight or of serious intention in the whole batch of them, and they did not seem aware these things are wanted for the work of the world. To treasure out of the bowels of the land

286 Civilize and collapse

was their desire, with no more moral purpose at the back of it than there is in burglars breaking into a safe.

(1974: 87)

By the time of the twentieth century with its anti-colonial struggles and decolonization processes, representations of the geography of the Other in English writing change even more drastically. These spaces now become either spaces of nostalgia (say in Graham Greene) or clearly discrepant. In E.M. Forster's *A Passage to India* the landscape physically separates the Englishman (Fielding) and the Indian (Dr Aziz). In the colony, where the British are still in power – but the Empire is beginning to shake by the time of the Forster novel – the landscape seems to possess a life of its own, with ideas about the mixing of races. This makes it a discrepant one because, somehow, Forster suggests that the Indian landscape (which is characterized as female in the novel, according to at least one critic, Sainsbury 2009: 63) escapes control, or even the ambition of racial mixing. In Orwell's *Burmese Days* (1934), the British in Kyauktada are completely debauched and as far from the 'pukka sahib' of the former halcyon days of the Empire (Flory's suicide at the end of the novel seems to be symbolic of the collapse of the imperial Englishman ideal itself).[22] It becomes discrepant because it gets coded in Forster and Orwell as a landscape of failure – of the British colonial project – just as Conrad's landscape of failure maps the dehumanization of the colonial and the colonized thereby recalling the history of British ideals such as the civilizational mission in the colony. As Robin White puts it in Paul Scott's *The Jewel in the Crown* (1966): 'We were in India for what we could get out of it … The onus of moral leadership falls naturally on the people who rank as superior' (1978: 340). In another space the English assumed moral superiority and then reneged on the promise this same assumption entailed, as the *Quartet* demonstrates. The cost of this reneging is often paid by the whites themselves: Daphne Manners and Edwina Crane in *The Raj Quartet*, where their ruin marks India out as a discrepant geography where English liberal humanist ideals of a paternal colonialism had failed.

We have already noted how the deaths of Englishmen outside their national boundaries enabled the Victorian poets to transform the distant space into triumphalist spaces of English heroism. These same events of suffering and death, however, in poets like Thomas Hardy are treated as transformative where the distant shores are spaces of just plain suffering. If in the previous instance the sailor and soldier travelling out took England with him and mapped England, in terms of its so-called virtues, on the Other space, then Hardy and anti-war poetry refused to valorize such forms of engagement with the Other. Take a poem like 'The Souls of the Slain' (1899). Hardy presents the spirits of dead soldiers (killed in South Africa) who return to England expecting to be fêted for their glorious deaths on the distant shores. But, says Hardy, this was not quite the case. They are informed that:

your kin linger less
On your glory arid war-mightiness
Than on dearer things.

The 'dearer things' turn out to be mothers' memories of the soldiers' childhood and the way they were at home. A father wishes:

> Would I had set him
> To some humble trade,

instead of allowing him to enlist. As for their sweethearts:

> Some fickle and fleet hearts
> Have found them new loves.

Then the soldiers conclude:

> Alas! Then it seems that our glory
> Weighs less in their thought
> Than our old homely acts,
> And the long-ago commonplace facts
> Of our lives – held by us as scarce part of our story,
> And rated as nought!

(Hardy 1994: 84–7)

If Rupert Brooke in the early twentieth century would have us believe that a distant corner of the world would remain England because its soldiers died there, Hardy believes that ordinary acts at home triumph over the so-called glorious deaths abroad. The suffering of soldiers in an elsewhere does not redeem the distant shore into the scene of triumph or victorious British identity, it simply makes the Other space a space of suffering and loss.

The space of the Other is also, especially in English novels on India, a space of exile and protracted suffering, for both men and women, but especially for the women. Very far from the triumphalist-conquistador view of the land, these texts – James Grant's *First Love, Last Love* (1860), H.S. Cunningham's *The Chronicles of Dustypore* (1877), B.M. Croker's *Mr Jervis* (1894), Flora Annie Steel's *On the Face of the Waters* (1896), to mention a few – document the conditions of exile, the traumatic domesticity (see the reading of Alice Perrin's empire fiction in Chapter 3 of this book), the separation from their children (the children were sent home to England around the age of seven or eight, see Buettner 2004) and the interactions with the natives.[23]

Later Auden would also refuse to treat the formerly colonized spaces as triumphal. When Auden has to account for such a formerly colonized space in 'Fleet Visit' (1951) he identifies it first as an 'unamerican place/where natives pass with laws/and futures of their own' (1976: 420). As Graham MacPhee points out, the poem replaces British presence in the unnamed third world nation with the American one. The visitors are neither humanitarian workers (as was the case with the English missionaries) nor conquerors but tourists being pestered by the

288 Civilize and collapse

'whore and the ne'er-do-well' (Auden 1976: 421). They have no orders as to who to kill: 'without a human will/to tell them to whom to kill' (421), which MacPhee reads, correctly, as the irrelevance of the interests of the inhabitants to the visitors (2011: 21). (We see Philip Larkin in his 1969 poem, 'Homage to a Government', note how 'it's been decided nobody minds' what happens to the former colonies, and anyway when the West sent soldiers to the colonies they 'only made trouble happen', clearly evacuating any heroism from the West's contention of benevolent imperialism. Larkin 2003: 141.) However, it is also possible to read this landscape of the twentieth-century former colony as a discrepant one that continues to attract the Westerner but one that constantly *recalls* former regimes of violence in that space. It is a landscape of memory, of killing fields, savagery and so-called civilization. The reference to killing and violence suggests that the present form of Western mobility into the former colony is always already inscribed into the history of other kinds of mobility. Although now it is the American fleet and sailors that visit, the memories of such arrivals are, Auden suggests, written into the landscape itself where the 'ships on the dazzling blue/of the harbor' are a present 'just-in-case'. The ominousness of Auden's poem – borne out in the latter decades of the twentieth century with American interventions, 'just wars' and such – converts the landscape of the un-American place into the space of *incipient* savagery and violence.

Occasionally, as we can see in Paul Scott's *The Raj Quartet*, or in Orwell's *Burmese Days*, this discrepant geography of the Empire is the space where the English *fail* to fulfil the promises they have made to their subjects. In Orwell's novel Flory says of the Empire:

> Look at our schools – factories for cheap clerks. We've never taught a single useful manual trade to the Indians ... we're not civilizing them, we're only rubbing our dirt on to them. Where's it going to lead, this uprush of modern progress?
> (1981: 39–40)

Flory debunks the myth of the civilizing mission, instead pointing to the damage wrought by the Empire in the name of improvement and civilization. He is painting Burma as the scene of British selfishness and failure.

In Scott's *The Jewel in the Crown*, Edwina Crane, the missionary woman, fails to protect her loyal assistant, Mr Chaudhuri:

> 'I can't help it,' she said, as if to him, when he lay bloody and limp and inhuman in the place she had dragged him to. 'There's nothing I can do, nothing, nothing,' and turned away and began to walk with long unsteady strides through the rain, past the blazing car, toward Mayapore. As she walked she kept saying, 'Nothing I can do. Nothing. Nothing.'
> (1978: 69)

In Scott's vision this 'nothing I can do' is not an individual betrayal, but a metonym for the failure of the entire paternalist project in whose name the Raj conducted its operations among the colonized subjects. Elsewhere Daphne Manners, around whose rape the first volume of the *Quartet* revolves, writes similar sentiments in her diary in *The Jewel in the Crown*:

> I said, 'There's nothing I can do, nothing, nothing,' and wondered where I'd heard those words before, and began to run again, through those awful ill-lit deserted roads that should have been leading me home but were leading me nowhere I recognised; into safety that wasn't safety because beyond it there were the plains and the openness that made it seem that if I ran long enough I would run clear off the rim of the world.
>
> (436)

Janis Haswell rightly argues that Daphne Manners here runs not only to save herself but to save the Indian man she has been with just before her rape, Hari Kumar (2001: 205). Both Crane and Manners, of course, fail, suggesting that the very structure of the Empire, and its irreducible racism and greed, ensures that any attempt to protect the native from the scourge that is the Raj, was bound to fail: and those English who seek to protect because they believe in their mission towards the natives, will die. It is, to word it differently, the failure of the discourse of improvement.

**

This chapter has argued that the discourse of the civilizational mission that implicitly positioned the English as morally superior was often accompanied by a discourse of collapsing Englishness. The space of the culturally defective and therefore improveable Other becomes transformed, especially from the late nineteenth century, into the space of the disintegrating Englishman. While the pathologized Other was part of the invasion discourse (Chapter 5) the collapse of English ideals seen in Conrad, Forster, Orwell, Scott and Auden suggests that the improveable Other is what proves to be England's undoing.

Globality in English literature, therefore, is the global civilizational mission of England's moral imperialism, the intrusion of the Other's cultural defects into England's vocabulary and discourses, and, finally, the disintegration of the English character and identity in various parts of the globe. Even as English literature depicts a global geography of English compassion it also gives us a global geography of the collapse of Englishness.

Notes

1 Daniel Pick's *Faces of Degeneration* (1989) is one of the leading studies of this discourse of disintegration and ruin.
2 Birkett's poem also calls attention to the biological-anatomical similarities of all human forms:
Look at the Negro's sun-burnt, grief-worn frame!
Examine well each limb, each nerve, each bone,

290 Civilize and collapse

Each artery – and then observe *thy own*;
The beating pulse, the heart that throbs within,
All, (save the sable tincture of his skin,)
Say, Christians, do they not resemble you?
If so, their feelings and sensations too.

3 For a genealogy of the 'Oriental despot' in European thought see Venturi (1963), Rubiés (2005) and Curtis (2009). Rubiés argues that the interest in 'Oriental despots' might be contextually traced to Europe's own concerns over monarchical power so that 'the fundamental concern with setting limits to royal power often appears under the guise of criticism of "tyrannical" or "absolute" monarchical power' (112). Much of the European writing on this theme was influenced by François Bernier's *Travels in the Mughal Empire, 1656–1668*.

4 The play devotes substantial space to accounts of the sensual excesses of Aurangzeb, Indamora and Nourmahal (see particularly Act IV).

5 Alexander Dow, the East India Company official who also wrote a history of Mughal India, produced a volume of tales, *Tales, Translated from the Persian of Inatulla of Delhi* (1768), where he retold the story of the Rajput princess, Rani Padmini, and her famous *sati*. Dow also clearly critiques Muslim/Mughal despotism. In later texts we have cheerful *satis*. The widow, in some cases, goes smilingly to her death in 'The Tomb of Suttee':

E'en now one shudder as she mounts the pile:
The struggle passes; with a calm delight
She takes his head upon her breast – her smile
Is hid by flames that, odorous and bright,
Rise canopied with smoke.

(Keene 1868: 133)

In G.H. Trevor's 'The Suttee of Gorah's Wife' (1894) the young widow, on seeing her husband's body on the pyre, and 'the spirit of the Rajput glowing/within her breast that swelled with love and pride' says 'my Lord will chide me for delay' and 'sprang on the pyre' (33). (But in Rudyard Kipling's 'The Last Suttee' we see a queen unwilling to face the thought of death by burning, and she has to be cut down by a sword instead.)

6 Shawn Maurer writes about Dryden's play and its sexual politics:

the competition over women serves as a surrogate for, and correlative of, the struggle for political power. The fabricated sexual subplot, in which father and sons vie for the same woman, brings to center stage the familiar trope of sexual contention among men.

(2005: 151)

7 Carl Plasa reading this little speech argues that in the novel 'to be a woman under patriarchy – whether governess, lover, mistress or wife – is to have the place of a slave' (1994: 74)

8 But Rivers, whom Jane recognizes as 'martyr-like', demands a martyrdom from Jane as well. She says:

if forced to be his wife, I can imagine the possibility of conceiving an inevitable, strange, torturing kind of love for him: because he is so talented; and there is often a certain heroic grandeur in his look, manner, and conversation. In that case, my lot would become unspeakably wretched.

(354)

9 Ironically the men who actually come from the East and of hybrid identities – such as Mason in *Jane Eyre* – are the very opposite of the Oriental despot, being more like emasculated (British) males. I am grateful to Anna Kurian for pointing this out to me.

Civilize and collapse **291**

10 For differing views from Said's see Trumpener (1997). Boulukos (2006) summarizes the critical positions arguing for and against Said's (n. 13, n. 14, n. 15).

11 There was also, interestingly, the equation of certain rituals and customs of the British that were deemed to be akin to the practices of the barbaric cultures. In this category we can see *sati* used as a metaphor for the Englishwoman's condition, in Charlotte Brontë, Antony Trollope and others. See Gilmartin (1997).

12 Burnett notes that a wall-painting from the 1580s represented a domestic as a *hirocervus*, a union of a man, hog, deer and ass (2002: 139).

13 At the turn of the twentieth century, under the influence of Darwinism, Caliban was regarded and represented in the staging of *The Tempest* as a monster with 'human yearnings' and the evolutionary missing link (Christine Dymkowski, cited in Erika Rundle 2007: 52).

14 But Fulford also points out that a substantial theme in the poem is of the scientific progress of the European that would aid the natives. But this science, Fulford notes, is also imaged as contamination and disease in Southey, thereby implying an ambivalence towards the entire project of evangelical emancipation/reconstruction.

15 Oddly, the discourse of rescue often constructed moral hierarchies amongst Europeans. G.A. Henty in *A Roving Commission; or, Through the Black Insurrection of Hayti* (1900), for example, suggested the French were better colonizers:

> Nowhere were the slaves so well treated as by the French colonists, and they soon discovered that, so far from profiting by the massacre of their masters and families, they were infinitely worse off than before. They were still obliged to work to some extent to save themselves from starvation; they had none to look to for aid in the time of sickness and old age; hardships and fevers had swept them away wholesale; the trade of the island had dwindled almost to nothing; and at last the condition of the Negroes in Hayti has fallen to the level of that of the savage African tribes. Unless some strong white power should occupy the island and enforce law and order, sternly repress crime, and demand a certain amount of labour from all able-bodied men, there seems no hope that any amelioration can take place in the present situation.
>
> (cited in McMahon 2010: 157)

Henty suggests that within the larger European engagement with the project of amelioration and emancipation of the wretched African, the French were better than other Europeans. Establishing a hierarchy of humanitarianism, Henty's text suggests that under French rule the Africans had managed to survive. But with the massacre of their European masters – i.e. presumed independence from colonialism – instead of progressing to an advanced stage of humanity, they had slid back to the level of African savages. Henty reaffirms the need for the civilizational mission here.

16 Denise Albanese (1990) points to this reversal of the colonial trope in Bacon.

17 In the novel it is significant that Hyder Ali, Tipu's father, stops the enslavement of Menie Gray. He appears at the opportune moment and, in the role of the greater authority, strips Tipu of his power, executes Middlemas and ensures the safety of Menie. Scott seems to suggest a native who is nobler than the English Middlemas, particularly when it comes to the safety of women.

18 In the 1960s psychologist Octave Mannoni would write of the colonial type, Europeans with a particular personality who thrived in the colonial environment because it gave them dependent and vulnerable natives to exploit and brutalize. See his *Prospero and Caliban: The Psychology of Colonization* (English translation, 1964).

19 On the primitive in Conrad and Victorian fiction see Elbarbary (1993).

20 The novel also makes no distinction between the Englishman's destruction of various kinds of life. Ralph Rover informs his friends that, since their last adventures (in *The Coral Island*), he has been 'fighting with the Caffirs, and the Chinamen, and been

292   Civilize and collapse

punishing the rascally sepoys in India, and been hunting elephants in Ceylon and tiger shooting in the jungles, and harpooning whales in the polar seas, and shooting lions at the Cape' (unpaginated, http://www.gutenberg.org/files/21736/21736-h/21736-h. htm). What Ballantyne does in such fiction is to map the Englishman's geography of violent and triumphalist adventure.

21 In a reversal of this theme Ronald Merrick, the class-conscious, repressed homosexual policeman of Paul Scott's *The Raj Quartet*, claims that the corruption of the English ruling class in the colonies lay in their wilful *dilution* of imperial-racial ideology. In the course of his torture of Hari Kumar/Harry Coomer, the Westernized upper-class Indian, he says (as reported later by Kumar in the last volume, *The Day of the Scorpion*):

> The true corruption of the English is their pretence that they have no contempt for us, and our real degradation is our pretence of equality ... The permutations of English corruption in India were endless: affection for servants, for peasants, for soldiers, pretence at understanding the intellectual or sympathizing with nationalist aspirations, but all this affection and understanding was a corruption of what he called the calm purity of their contempt.
>
> (1979: 307–11)

22 The Club at Kyauktada itself is symbolic of the collapse of imperial splendour and authority in the colony, see Gopinath (2009). For the centrality of the Club in the colony see Sinha (2001).

23 After the Indian 'Mutiny' of 1857, of course, the image of the threatened Englishwoman gained considerable literary presence, thus adding to the sense of a discrepant geography. See Sharpe (1991), Paxton (1992).

BIBLIOGRAPHY

Abu-Lughod, J. *Before European Hegemony: The World System, AD 1250–1350*. New York: Oxford University Press, 1989.

Achebe, C. 'An Image of Africa: Racism in Conrad's *Heart of Darkness*'. 1977. In R. Kimbrough (ed.) *Heart of Darkness*. New York: WW Norton, 1988. 3rd ed. 251–61.

Addison, C. '"Elysian and Effeminate": Byron's *The Island* as a Revisionary Text', *SEL* 35 (1995): 687–706.

Albanese, D. '*The New Atlantis* and the Uses of Utopia', *ELH* 57.3 (1990): 503–28.

Alloula, M. *The Colonial Harem*. Trans. M. Godzich and W. Godzich. Minneapolis: University of Minnesota Press, 1986.

Altinck, H. *Representations of Slave Women in Discourses on Slavery and Abolition, 1780–1838*. London and New York: Routledge, 2007.

Anderson, B. *Imagined Communities: Reflections on the Origins and Spread of Nationalism*. London and New York: Verso, 1991.

Arata, S.D. 'The Occidental Tourist: *Dracula* and the Anxiety of Reverse Colonization', *Victorian Studies* 33.4 (1990): 621–45.

Aravamudan, S. 'Fiction/Translation/Transnation: The Secret History of the Eighteenth-Century Novel', in P.R. Backscheider and C. Ingrassia (eds) *A Companion to the Eighteenth-Century English Novel and Culture*. Malden: Blackwell, 2005. 48–74.

——'Response: Exoticism Beyond Cosmopolitanism?', *Eighteenth-Century Fiction* 25.1 (2012): 227–42.

Armstrong, D. 'The Myth of Cronos: Cannibal and Sign in *Robinson Crusoe*', *Eighteenth-Century Fiction* 4 (1992): 207–20.

——'The Inverse Gothic Invasion Motif in Daphne du Maurier's *Jamaica Inn*: The National Body and Smuggling Disease', *Women's Studies* 38 (2009): 23–42.

Arnold, D. 'Agriculture and "Improvement" in Early Colonial India: A Pre-History of Development', *Journal of Agrarian Change* 5.4 (2005a): 505–25.

——*The Tropics and the Travelling Gaze: India, Landscape, and Science, 1800–1856*. New Delhi: Permanent Black, 2005b.

Auden, W.H. *Collected Poems*. Ed. Edward Mendelson. London: Faber & Faber, 1976.

Austen, J. *Sense and Sensibility*. 1811. The University of Adelaide Library. http://ebooks.adelaide.edu.au/a/austen/jane/a93s/. 20 July 2014.

——*Mansfield Park*. Ed. John Lucas. London: Oxford University Press, 1970 [1814].

——*Emma*. Ed. David Lodge. London: Oxford University Press, 1971 [1815].

294 Bibliography

Avramescu, C. *An Intellectual History of Cannibalism*. Trans. A.I. Blyth. Princeton: Princeton University Press, 2011.

Azim, F. *The Colonial Rise of the Novel*. New York: Routledge, 1993.

Bach, R.A. 'Jonson's "Civil Savages"', *Studies in English Literature, 1500–1900* 37.2 (1997): 277–93.

Bacon, F. *The Great Instauration*. 1620. https://ebooks.adelaide.edu.au/b/bacon/francis/instauration/. 1 December 2014.

——'Of Travel', in *The Works of Francis Bacon*. Ed. J. Spedding, R.L. Ellis and D.D. Heath. Vol. XII. Boston: Brown and Taggard, 1860. 137–9.

——*The New Atlantis*, in *The Works of Francis Bacon*. Ed. J. Spedding, R.L. Ellis and D.D. Heath. Vol. V. Boston: Brown and Taggard, 1862. 347–414.

——*The Advancement of Learning*, in *The Works of Francis Bacon*. Ed. J. Spedding, R.L. Ellis and D.D. Heath. Vol. VI. Boston: Brown and Taggard, 1863. 77–412.

——'An Advertisement Touching a Holy War', in *The Works of Francis Bacon*. Ed. J. Spedding, R.L. Ellis and D.D. Heath. Vol. XIII. Boston: Houghton Mifflin, 1860. 173–219.

——*Brief Discourse Touching the Happy Union of the Kingdoms of England and Scotland*. 1603. In *The Letters and the Life of Francis Bacon, Including all his Occasional Works*. Ed. J. Spedding. Vol. III. London: Longmans, Green, Reader, and Dyer, 1868. 90–99.

Baillie, J. 'Lines to a Teapot', *Fugitive Verses*. 1840. British Women Romantic Writers Project. University of California, Davis. http://digital.lib.ucdavis.edu/projects/bwrp/Works/BailJ Fugit.htm#p161. 20 July 2014.

Ballantyne, R.M. *The Coral Island: A Tale of the Pacific Ocean*. 1858. The University of Adelaide Library. http://ebooks.adelaide.edu.au/b/ballantyne/rm/coral-island/. 19 July 2014.

——*The Young Fur Traders*. 1856. Project Gutenberg. http://www.gutenberg.org/files/21712/21712-h/21712-h.htm. 19 July 2014.

——*The Gorilla Hunters*. 1861. Project Gutenberg. http://www.gutenberg.org/files/21736/21736-h/21736-h.htm. 19 July 2014.

Ballaster, R. *Fabulous Orients: Fictions of the East in England, 1662–1785*. Oxford: Oxford University Press, 2005.

Barbour, R. *Before Orientalism: London's Theatre of the East 1576–1626*. Cambridge: Cambridge University Press, 2003.

Bardi, A. 'The Gypsy as Trope in Victorian and Modern British Literature', *Romani Studies 5* 16.1 (2006): 31–42.

Barnes, G. 'Curiosity, Wonder, and William Dampier's Painted Prince', *Journal for Early Modern Cultural Studies* 6.1 (2006): 31–50.

Barrell, J. *The Infection of Thomas de Quincey: The Psychopathology of Imperialism*. New Haven and London: Yale University Press, 1991.

Bartolomeo, J.F. '"New People in a New World"?: Defoe's Ambivalent Narratives of Emigration', *Eighteenth-Century Fiction* 23.3 (2011): 455–70.

Battles, P. '"The Mark of the Beast": Rudyard Kipling's Apocalyptic Vision of the Empire', *Studies in Short Fiction* 33.3 (1996): 333–44.

Beaumont, J. *The Metamorphosis of Tabacco*. 1602. English Poetry 1579–1830: Spenser and the Tradition. http://spenserians.cath.vt.edu/TextRecord.php?action=GET&textsid=33000. 20 July 2014.

Beckford, W. *Vathek*. Ed. Roger Lonsdale. London: Oxford University Press, 1970.

Bedad, A. *Belated Travelers: Orientalism in the Age of Colonial Dissolution*. Durham, NC: Duke University Press, 1994.

Behlmer, G.K. 'The Gypsy Problem in Victorian England', *Victorian Studies* (1985): 231–53.

Behn, A. *Oroonoko and Other Writings*. Ed. Paul Salzman. Oxford: Oxford University Press, 1994 [1688].

——*The Widow Ranter, or, the History of Bacon in Virginia*. 1690. *Electronic Texts in American Studies*. Paper 45. http://digitalcommons.unl.edu/etas/45. 19 July 2014.

Bell, D.S.A. 'Dissolving Distance: Technology, Space, and Empire in British Political Thought, 1770–1900', *Journal of Modern History* 77.3 (2005): 523–62.

Bennett, L. 'Colonization in Reverse', http://louisebennett.com/colonization-in-reverse/.

Bentley, E. 'On the Abolition of the African Slave Trade, July 1789'. 1789. Online Archive of California. http://www.oac.cdlib.org/view?docId=kt638nc0hv;NAAN=13030&doc.view=frames&chunk.id=d0e4696&toc.depth=1&toc.id=d0e3939&brand=oac4. 23 July 2014.

Berg, M. *Luxury and Pleasure in Eighteenth-Century Britain*. Oxford: Oxford University Press, 2007.

Berg, M. and E. Eger. 'The Rise and Fall of the Luxury Debates', in M. Berg and E. Eger (eds) *Luxury in the Eighteenth Century: Debates, Desires and Delectable Goods*. Basingstoke: Palgrave Macmillan, 2003. 7–27.

Bergeron, D.M. '"Are We Turned Turks?" English Pageants and the Stuart Court', *Comparative Drama* 44.3 (2010): 255–75.

Bewell, A. *Romanticism and Colonial Disease*. Baltimore and London: Johns Hopkins University Press, 1999.

——'William Jones and Cosmopolitan Natural History', *European Romantic Review* 16.2 (2006): 167–80.

Bhabha, H.K. 'How Newness Enters the World: Postmodern Space, Postcolonial Times and the Trials of Cultural Translation', in *The Location of Culture*. New York and London: Routledge, 2009a [1994]. 303–37.

——'Sly Civility', in *The Location of Culture*. New York and London: Routledge, 2009b [1994]. 132–44.

Bickham, T.O. *Savages within the Empire: Representations of American Indians in Eighteenth-Century Britain*. Oxford: Clarendon, 2005.

Bilston, S. 'A New Reading of the Anglo-Indian Women's Novel, 1880–94: Passages to India, Passages to Womanhood', *English Literature in Transition 1880–1920* 44.3 (2001): 320–41.

Blake, W. *Complete Writings*. Ed. Geoffrey Keynes. London: Oxford University Press, 1973.

Blunt, A. 'Imperial Geographies of Home: British Domesticity in India, 1886–1925', *Transactions of the British Institute of Geographers, New Series* 24.4 (1999): 421–40.

Bollen, K. and R. Ingelbein. 'An Intertext that Counts? *Dracula*, *The Woman in White*, and Victorian Imaginations of the Foreign Other', *English Studies* 90.4 (2009): 403–20.

Boluk, S. and W. Lenz. 'Infection, Media, and Capitalism: From Early Modern Plagues to Postmodern Zombies', *Journal for Early Modern Cultural Studies* 10.2 (2010): 126–47.

Boulukos, G.E. 'The Politics of Silence: *Mansfield Park* and the Amelioration of Slavery', *Novel* (2006): 361–83.

Bowen, H.V. 'Sinews of Trade and Empire: The Supply of Commodity Exports to the East India Company during the Late Eighteenth Century', *The Economic History Review* New Series 55.3 (2002): 466–86.

Brady, J. 'Wish-Fulfillment Fantasies in Dryden's *Aureng-Zebe*', *Philological Quarterly* 83.1 (2004): 41–60.

Brantlinger, P. *Rule of Darkness: British Literature and Imperialism, 1830–1914*. Ithaca, NY: Cornell University Press, 1988.

——*Dark Vanishings: Discourse on the Extinction of Primitive Races, 1800–1930*. Ithaca and London: Cornell University Press, 2003.

——*Victorian Literature and Postcolonial Studies*. Edinburgh: Edinburgh University Press, 2009.

Bristow, J. *Empire Boys: Adventures in a Man's World*. London: HarperCollins, 1991.

Brontë, C. *Villette*. Ed. Herbert Rosengarten and Margaret Smith. Oxford: Clarendon, 1984 [1853].

——*Jane Eyre*. Ed. Richard Dunn. New York: W.W. Norton, 2010 [1847].

Brontë, E. *Wuthering Heights*. Ed. Pauline Nestor. Harmondsworth: Penguin, 2003 [1847].

Brown, B. *A Sense of Things: The Object Matter of American Literature*. Chicago: University of Chicago Press, 2003.

Brown, L. *Ends of Empire: Women and Ideology in Early Eighteenth-Century English Literature*. Ithaca and London: Cornell University Press, 1993.

Brown, T.C. 'Cultural Psychosis on the Frontier: The Work of the Darkness in Joseph Conrad's *Heart of Darkness*', *Studies in the Novel* 32.1 (2000): 14–28.

296 Bibliography

Browning, E. B. 'The Runaway Slave at Pilgrim's Point', in Virginia Blain (ed.) *Victorian Women Poets: An Annotated Anthology*. New York and London: Routledge, 2014. 63–72.

Buettner, E. *Empire Families: Britons and Late Imperial India*. Oxford: Oxford University Press, 2004.

Bunn, J.D. 'The Sleep of the Brave: Graves as Sites and Signs in the Colonial Eastern Cape', in P.S. Landau and D.D. Kaspin (eds) *Images and Empires: Visuality in Colonial and Postcolonial Africa*. Berkeley and London: University of California Press, 2002. 56–89.

Bunn, J.H. 'The Aesthetics of British Mercantilism', *New Literary History* 11.2 (1980): 303–21.

Burgan, M. 'Contagion and Culture: A View from Victorian Studies', *American Literary History* 14.4 (2002): 837–44.

Burke, E. 'On the Genius and Character of the French Revolution as it regards other Nations', *Two Letters Addressed to A Member of the Present Parliament, on the Proposals for Peace with the Regicide Directory of France by the right honourable Edmund Burke*. Rivingtons, 1796. http://www.econlib.org/library/LFBooks/Burke/brkSWv3c2.html. 14 July 2014.

Burnett, M.T. *Constructing Monsters in Shakespearean Drama and Early Modern Culture*. London: Palgrave Macmillan, 2002.

Burns, R. *Poems and Songs*. Ed. James Kinsley. London: Oxford University Press, 1971.

Burton, A. *At the Heart of the Empire: Indians and the Colonial Encounter in Late Victorian Britain*. Berkeley: University of California Press, 1998.

Byron, G.G. *Poetical Works*. Ed. Frederick Page, corrected by John Jump. London: Oxford University Press, 1975.

Campbell, M.B. *The Witness and the Other World: European Exotic Travel Writing, 400–1600*. Ithaca and London: Cornell University Press, 1988.

——'*Anthropometamorphosis*: John Bulwer's Monsters of Cosmetology and the Science of Culture', in J.J. Cohen (ed.) *Monster Theory: Reading Culture*. Minneapolis: University of Minnesota Press, 1996.

——*Wonder and Science: Imagining Worlds in Early Modern Europe*. Ithaca and London: Cornell University Press, 1999.

Campbell, T. *The Pleasures of Hope*. 1799. English Poetry 1579–1830: Spenser and the Tradition. http://spenserians.cath.vt.edu/TextRecord.php?textsid=37917. 23 July 2014.

Card, M.B. 'A Poem on the African Slave Trade'. 1792. http://www.brycchancarey.com/slavery/mbc1.htm. [via http://digital.library.upenn.edu/women/_generate/IRELAND.html]. 23 July 2014.

Carey, D. 'Reading Contrapuntally: *Robinson Crusoe*, Slavery, and Postcolonial Theory', in D. Carey and L. Festa (eds) *The Postcolonial Enlightenment: Eighteenth-Century Colonialism and Postcolonial Theory*. Oxford: Oxford University Press, 2009. 105–36.

Carlyle, T. 'Occasional Discourse on the Nigger Question'. 1849. http://www.efm.bris.ac.uk/het/carlyle/occasion.htm. 18 July 2014.

——*Past and Present*. 1843. http://www.gutenberg.org/files/26159/26159-h/26159-h.htm. 19 November 2014.

Chang, E.H. *Britain's Chinese Eye: Literature, Empire, and Aesthetics in Nineteenth-Century Britain*. Stanford: Stanford University Press, 2010.

Chattopadhyay, S. '"Goods, Chattels and Sundry Items": Constructing 19th-Century Anglo-Indian Domestic Life', *Journal of Material Culture* 7.3 (2002): 243–71.

Chaucer, G. *Complete Works*. Ed. W.W. Skeat. London: Oxford University Press, 1976.

Chaudhury, A. 'Splenetic Ogres and Heroic Cannibals in Jonathan Swift's *A Modest Proposal* (1729)', *English Studies in Canada* 34.2–3 (2008): 131–57.

Chew, E. *Arming the Periphery: The Arms Trade in the Indian Ocean During the Age of Global Empire*. Basingstoke: Palgrave Macmillan, 2012.

Childs, P. *Modernism and the Post-Colonial*. New York: Continuum, 2007.

Christensen, T. 'The "Bestial Mark" of Race in *The Island of Dr. Moreau*', *Criticism* 46.4 (2004): 575–95.

Clarke, R. *The Nabob: Or, Asiatic Plunderers. A Satyrical Poem, in a Dialogue Between a Friend and the Author*. London: Published by the author, 1773.

Clausson, N. 'Degeneration, Fin-de-Siècle Gothic, and the Science of Detection: Arthur Conan Doyle's *The Hound of the Baskervilles* and the Emergence of the Modern Detective Story', *Journal of Narrative Theory* 35.1 (2005): 60–87.

Cohen, D. *Household Gods: The British and their Possessions*. New Haven: Yale University Press, 2006.

Cohen, J.J. 'Monster Culture (Seven Theses)', in J.J. Cohen (ed.) *Monster Theory: Reading Culture*. Minneapolis: University of Minnesota Press, 1996. 3–25.

Cohen, W. 'The Literature of Empire in the Renaissance', *Modern Philology* 102.1 (2004): 1–34.

Coleridge, S.T. *Poetical Works*. Ed. Ernest Hanley Coleridge. London: Oxford University Press, 1973.

Colley, L. *Britons: Forging the Nation, 1701–1837*. New Haven: Yale University Press, 1992.

Collins, W. *The Moonstone*. Ed. Anthea Trodd. Oxford: Oxford University Press, 1982.

Conrad, J. *Heart of Darkness*, in *Youth, Heart of Darkness, The End of the Tether*. London: Dent, 1974. 43–162.

Congreve, W. *The Way of the World*. Ed. Norman Jeffares. London: Edward Arnold, 1966.

Cordery, L. 'The Saracens in Middle English Literature: A Definition of Otherness', *Al-Masaq: Islam & the Medieval Mediterranean* 14.2 (2002): 87–99.

Cosgrove, D. *Apollo's Eye: A Cartographic Genealogy of the Earth in the Western Imagination*. Baltimore and London: Johns Hopkins University Press, 2001.

Cottegnies, L. 'Utopia, Millenarianism, and the Baconian Programme of Margaret Cavendish's *The Blazing World* (1666)', in C. Houston (ed.) *New Worlds Reflected: Travel and Utopia in the Early Modern Period*. London: Ashgate, 2010. 71–91.

Cowley, A. 'To the Royal Society'. 1668. The Abraham Cowley Text and Image Archive, University of Virginia. http://cowley.lib.virginia.edu/works/RoyalSociety.htm. 1 December 2014.

Cowper, W. 'The Negro's Complaint'. 1788. Slavery and Freedom in American History and Memory, Yale University. http://www.yale.edu/glc/aces/cowper2.htm. 17 July 2014.

——'The Task' and Selected Other Poems*. Ed. James Sambrook. London and New York: Longman, 1994.

——'Charity'. 1782. Eighteenth Century Collections Online, University of Michigan. http://quod.lib.umich.edu/e/ecco/004792651.0001.000/1:8?rgn=div1;view=fulltext. 17 July 2014.

Craft, C. '"Kiss Me with those Red Lips": Gender and Inversion in Bram Stoker's *Dracula*', *Representations* 8 (1984): 107–33.

Curtis, M. *Orientalism and Islam: Thinkers on the Muslim Government in the Middle East and India*. Cambridge: Cambridge University Press, 2009.

Daborne, R. *Christian Turn'd Turk*. London: William Barrenger, 1612.

Dacre, C. *Zofloya, or the Moor*. Ed. K.I. Michasiw. Oxford: Oxford University Press, 2008 [1806].

Dadswell, S. 'Jugglers, Fakirs, and Jaduwallahs: Indian Magicians and the British Stage', *New Theatre Quarterly* 23.1 (2007): 3–24.

Daly, K. 'Worlds Beyond England: *Don Juan* and the Legacy of Enlightenment Cosmopolitan', *Romanticism* 4.2 (1998): 189–201.

Daly, S. 'Kashmir Shawls in Mid-Victorian Novels', *Victorian Literature and Culture* 30.1 (2002): 237–56.

——*The Empire Inside: Indian Commodities in Victorian Domestic Novels*. Ann Arbor: University of Michigan Press, 2011.

Davis, D.B. *The Problem of Slavery in the Age of Revolution, 1770–1823*. Oxford: Oxford University Press, 1999.

——*The Problem of Slavery in Western Culture*. Ithaca: Cornell, 1966.

Davison, C.M. 'Getting Their Knickers in a Twist: Contesting the "Female Gothic" in Charlotte Dacre's *Zofloya*', *Gothic Studies* 11.1 (2009): 32–45.

de Certeau, M. *Heterologies: Discourse on the Other*. Trans. Brian Massumi. Minneapolis: University of Minnesota Press, 1986.

298 Bibliography

de Grazia, M., M. Quilligan and P. Stallybrass. *Subject and Object in Renaissance Culture*. Cambridge: Cambridge University Press, 1996.

de Quincey, T. *Confessions of an English Opium Eater and Other Writings*. Ed. Grevel Lindop. Oxford: Oxford University Press, 1985 [1821].

Defoe, D. *A Plan of the English Commerce*. London: Charles Rivington, 1728.

——*The Life, Adventures and Pyracies of the Famous Captain Singleton*. Ed. Shiv K. Kumar. London: Oxford University Press, 1969a [1720].

——*Roxana the Fortunate Mistress*. Ed. Jane Jack. London: Oxford University Press, 1969b [1724].

——*Robinson Crusoe*. Ed. Michael Shinagel. New York: W.W. Norton, 1975 [1719].

——'The Complete English Gentleman', in James Boulton (ed.) *Selected Writings*. Cambridge: Cambridge University Press, 1975. 247–57.

——*Moll Flanders*. Ed. A.J. Rivero. New York: W.W. Norton, 2004.

DeLamotte, E. 'White Terror, Black Dreams: Gothic Constructions of Race in the Nineteenth Century', in Ruth Bienstock Anolik and Douglas L. Howard (eds) *The Gothic Other: Racial and Social Constructions in the Literary Imagination*. Jefferson: McFarland, 2004. 17–31.

Deng, S. '"So Pale, So Lame, So Lean, So Ruinous": The Circulation of Foreign Coins in Early Modern England', in J.G. Singh (ed.) *A Companion to the Global Renaissance: English Literature and Culture in the Era of Expansion*. Malden: Wiley-Blackwell, 2009. 262–78.

Dickens, C. *Dombey and Son*. 1846–8. The University of Adelaide Library. http://ebooks. adelaide.edu.au/d/dickens/charles/d54ds/. 20 July 2014.

——'The Noble Savage'. 1853. Dickens Journals Online. http://www.djo.org.uk/media/ downloads/articles/2204_The%20Noble%20Savage.pdf. 19 November 2014.

——*David Copperfield*. Ware: Wordsworth, 1992 [1849–50].

Dimmock, M. 'Guns and Gawds: Elizabethan England's Infidel Trade', in J.G. Singh (ed.) *A Companion to the Global Renaissance: English Literature and Culture in the Era of Expansion*. Malden: Wiley-Blackwell, 2009. 207–22.

Donne, J. *The Complete Poems*. Ed. A.J. Smith. Harmondsworth: Penguin, 1975.

Doody, M.A. *The True History of the English Novel*. London: Fontana, 1998.

Douglas, A.W. 'Cotton Textiles in England: The East India Company's Attempt to Exploit Developments in Fashion 1660–1721', *Journal of British Studies* 8.2 (1969): 28–43.

Dow, G. 'Translation, Cross-Channel Exchanges and the Novel in the Long Eighteenth Century', *Literature Compass* 11.11 (2014): 691–702.

Doyle, A.C. 'The Adventure of the Speckled Band', in *The Complete Short Stories of Sherlock Holmes*. Bombay: Jaico, 1986a. 97–113.

——'The Adventure of the Empty House', in *The Complete Short Stories of Sherlock Holmes*. Bombay: Jaico, 1986b. 323–35.

——*The Sign of Four*, in *The Complete Long Stories of Sherlock Holmes*. Bombay: Jaico, 1988a. 77–146.

——*The Hound of the Baskervilles*, in *The Complete Long Stories of Sherlock Holmes*. Bombay: Jaico, 1988b. 149–246.

——'A Study in Scarlet', in *The Complete Long Stories of Sherlock Holmes*. Bombay: Jaico, 1988c. 3–74.

Drayton, M. *Poems*. Ed. John Buxton. London: Routledge and Kegan Paul, 1953.

Drayton, R. *Nature's Government: Science, Imperial Britain, and the 'Improvement' of the World*. Hyderabad: Orient Longman, 2005 [2000].

Driver, F. and S. Ashmore. 'The Mobile Museum: Collecting and Circulating Indian Textiles in Victorian Britain', *Victorian Studies* 52.3 (2010): 353–85.

Dryden, J. *Aureng-zebe, A Tragedy*, in *The Works of John Dryden*. Vol. V. London: William Miller, 1808a. 167–284.

——*Amboyna*, in *The Works of John Dryden*. Vol. V. London: William Miller, 1808b. 1–87.

——*The Works. Vol. 1. Poems 1649–1680*. Berkeley: University of California Press, 1956.

——*The Indian Queen*, in *The Works of John Dryden*. Vol. VIII. *Plays*. Berkeley: University of California Press, 1965. 181–232.

DuBois, P. *Slaves and Other Objects*. Chicago and London: University of Chicago Press, 2008.

Dutheil de La Rochère, M.H. 'Body Politics: Conrad's Anatomy of Empire in *Heart of Darkness*', *Conradiana* 36.3 (2004): 185–205.

Eaton, N. 'Nostalgia for the Exotic: Creating an Imperial Art in London, 1750–93', *Eighteenth-Century Studies* 39.2 (2006): 227–50.

Edgeworth, M. 'The Grateful Negro'. 1804. The University of Adelaide Library. http://ebooks.adelaide.edu.au/e/edgeworth/maria/grateful-negro/. 18 July 2014.

Elbarbary, S. '*Heart of Darkness* and Late-Victorian Fascination with the Primitive and the Double', *Twentieth Century Literature* 39.1 (1993): 113–28.

Elfenbein, A. 'Byron: Gender and Sexuality', in D. Bone (ed.) *The Cambridge Companion to Byron*. Cambridge: Cambridge University Press, 2004. 56–73.

Elmer, J. '"Vaulted Over by the Present": Melancholy and Sovereignty in Mary Shelley's *The Last Man*', *Novel* 42.2 (2009): 355–9.

Engmann, R.A.A. 'Under Imperial Eyes, Black Bodies, Buttocks, and Breasts: British Colonial Photography and Asante "Fetish Girls"', *African Arts* 45.2 (2012): 46–57.

Equiano, O. *The Interesting Narrative of the Life of Olaudah Equiano, Or Gustavus Vassa, the African*. 1789. http://www.gutenberg.org/files/15399/15399-h/15399-h.htm

Erdman, D.V. *Blake: Prophet Against Empire*. Princeton: Princeton University Press, 1977. 3rd edition.

Fang, K. 'Empire, Coleridge, and Charles Lamb's Consumer Imagination', *Studies in English Literature* 43.4 (2003): 815–43.

Fanon, F. *Black Skin, White Masks*. Trans. Charles Lam Markmann. London: Pluto, 2008 [1986].

Farnell, G. 'The Gothic and the Thing', *Gothic Studies* 11.1 (2009): 113–23.

Favor, L.J. 'The Foreign and the Female in Arthur Conan Doyle: Beneath the Candy Coating', *English Literature in Transition* 43.4 (2000): 398–409.

Ferguson, M. *Subject to Others: British Women Writers and Colonial Slavery 1670–1834*. London: Routledge, 1992.

Ferguson, M.W. 'Feathers and Flies: Aphra Behn and the Seventeenth-Century Trade in Exotica', in M. de Grazia, M. Quilligan and P. Stallybrass (eds) *Subject and Object in Renaissance Culture*. Cambridge: Cambridge University Press, 1996. 235–60.

Festa, L. *Sentimental Figures of Empire in Eighteenth-Century Britain and France*. Baltimore: Johns Hopkins University Press, 2006.

Field, E.D. '"Excepting Himself": Olaudah Equiano, Native Americans, and the Civilizing Mission', *MELUS* 34.4 (2009): 15–38.

Fletcher, P. 'The Grand Tour on Bond Street: Cosmopolitanism and the Commercial Art Gallery in Victorian London', *Visual Culture in Britain* 12.2 (2011): 139–53.

Fogarty, A. 'Looks that Kill: Violence and Representation in Aphra Behn's *Oroonoko*', in C. Plasa and B.J. Ring (eds) *The Discovery of Slavery: Aphra Behn to Toni Morrison*. London and New York: Routledge, 1994. 1–17.

Forster, E.M. *A Passage to India*. Harmondsworth: Penguin, 1970 [1924].

Franey, L. *Victorian Travel Writing and Imperial Violence: British Writing of Africa 1855–1902*. Basingstoke: Palgrave, 2003.

Franklin, C. '"Some Samples of the Finest Orientalism": Byronic Philhellenism and Proto-Zionism at the Time of the Congress of Vienna', in T. Fulford and P.J. Kitson (eds) *Romanticism and Colonialism: Writing and Empire, 1780–1830*. Cambridge: Cambridge University Press, 2005 [1998]. 221–42.

Free, M. '"Dirty Linen": Legacies of Empire in Wilkie Collins's *The Moonstone*', *Texas Studies in Literature and Language* 48.4 (2006): 340–71.

Freedgood, E. *The Victorian Writing of Risk: Imagining a Safe England in a Dangerous World*. Cambridge: Cambridge University Press, 2000.

——*The Ideas in Things: Fugitive Meaning in the Victorian Novel*. Chicago and London: University of Chicago Press, 2006.

300 Bibliography

Freeman, H.C. 'Opium Use and Romantic Women's Poetry', *South Central Review* 29.1–2 (2012): 1–20.

Freeman, K. '"Eternally Disunited": Gender, Empire, and Epistemology in Sydney Owenson's "*The Missionary*"', *The Wordsworth Circle* 36.1 (2005): 21–8.

Fulford, T. 'Romanticizing the Empire: The Naval Heroes of Southey, Coleridge, Austen and Marryat', *Modern Language Quarterly* 60.2 (1999): 161–96.

——'Blessed Bane: Christianity and Colonial Disease in Southey's *Tale of Paraguay*', *Romanticism on the Net* 24 (2001).

——*Romantic Indians: Native Americans, British Literature, and Transatlantic Culture 1756–1830*. Oxford: Oxford University Press, 2006.

Fullagar, K. '"Savages that are come among us": Mai, Bennelong, and British Imperial Culture, 1774–95', *The Eighteenth Century* 49.3 (2008): 211–37.

Gay, J. *The Poems*. Vol. II. Chiswick: C. Whittingham, 1822.

——*Fables of John Gay*. Ed. W.H. Kearley Wright. London and New York: Frederick Warne, 1889.

Gelder, K. *Reading the Vampire*. London: Routledge, 1994.

George, L. 'The Native and the Fop: Primitivism and Fashion in Romantic Rhetoric', *Nineteenth-Century Contexts* 24.1 (2002): 33–47.

George, R.M. 'Homes in the Empire, Empires in the Home', *Cultural Critique* 26 (1993–4): 95–127.

Ghosh, B. 'On Grafting the Vernacular: The Consequences of Postcolonial Spectrology', *Boundary 2* 31 (2004): 197–218.

Gibson, M.E. 'Henry Martyn and England's Christian Empire: Rereading "Jane Eyre" through Missionary Biography', *Victorian Literature and Culture* 37.2 (1999): 419–42.

Gillies, J. *Shakespeare and the Geography of Difference*. Cambridge: Cambridge University Press, 1994.

Gilmartin, S. 'The Sati, the Bride, and the Widow: Sacrificial Woman in the Nineteenth Century', *Victorian Literature and Culture* 25.1 (1997): 141–58.

Glover, D. *Literature, Immigration, and Diaspora in Fin-de-Siècle England: A Cultural History of the 1905 Aliens Act*. Cambridge: Cambridge University Press, 2012.

Golding, W. *Lord of the Flies*. London: Faber & Faber, 1999 [1954].

Goodman, J. *Tobacco in History: Cultures of Dependence*. London: Routledge, 1993.

Gopinath, P. 'An Orphaned Manliness: The Pukka Sahib and the End of Empire in *A Passage to India* and *Burmese Days*', *Studies in the Novel* 41.2 (2009): 201–23.

Gordon, A.F. *Ghostly Matters: Haunting and the Sociological Imagination*. Minneapolis and London: Minnesota University Press, 1997.

Gorra, M. *After Empire: Scott, Naipaul, Rushdie*. Chicago: University of Chicago Press, 1997.

Grainger, J. *Sugar-Cane: A Poem*. 1764. Early Americas Digital Archive. http://mith.umd.edu/eada/html/display.php?docs=grainger_sugarcane.xml. 20 July 2014.

Grant, K., P. Levine and F. Trentmann. 'Introduction', in K. Grant, P. Levine and F. Trentmann (eds) *Beyond Sovereignty: Britain, Empire and Transnationalism, c. 1880–1950*. London: Palgrave Macmillan, 2007. 1–15.

Gray, T. *Gray and Collins: Poetical Works*. Ed. A.L. Poole. London: Oxford University Press, 1974.

Green, M. *Dreams of Adventure, Deeds of Empire*. London: Routledge and Kegan Paul, 1980.

Greenblatt, S. *Marvelous Possessions*. Oxford: Clarendon, 1992.

——'Learning to Curse: Aspects of Linguistic Colonialism in the Sixteenth Century', in *Learning to Curse: Essays in Early Modern Culture*. New York and London: Routledge, 2013 [1992]. 22–51.

Greene, G. *The Heart of the Matter*. New York: Viking, 1948.

Guest, K. 'Introduction: Cannibalism and the Boundaries of Identity', in K. Guest (ed.) *Eating their Words: Cannibalism and the Boundaries of Cultural Identity*. Albany: State University of New York Press, 2001. 1–10.

Haggard, H.R. *She*. Oxford: Oxford University Press, 2008 [1886–7].

——*King Solomon's Mines*. 1885. The University of Adelaide Library. http://ebooks.adelaide.edu.au/h/haggard/h_rider/king/index.html. 20 July 2014.

——*Allan Quatermain*. 1887. https://ebooks.adelaide.edu.au/h/haggard/h_rider/allan/. 19 November 2014.

Hall, C. *Civilizing Subjects: Metropole and Colony in the English Imagination 1830–1867*. Chicago: University of Chicago Press, 2002.

Hall, C. and S.O. Rose (eds) *At Home with the Empire: Metropolitan Culture and the Imperial World*. Cambridge: Cambridge University Press, 2006.

Hall, K.F. *Things of Darkness: Economies of Race and Gender in Early Modern England*. Ithaca, NY: Cornell University Press, 1995.

Hammack, B.M. 'Florence Marryat's Female Vampire and the Scientizing of Hybridity', *SEL: Studies in English Literature 1500–1900* 48.4 (2008): 885–96.

Hampson, R. '*Heart of Darkness* and the "Speech that cannot be Silenced"', in P. Childs (ed.) *English Literature and Postcolonial Theory: A Reader*. Edinburgh: Edinburgh University Press, 1999. 201–15.

Hardy, T. *The Works of Thomas Hardy*. Hertfordshire: Wordsworth, 1994.

Harpham, G.G. 'Time Running Out: The Edwardian Sense of Cultural Degeneration', *Clio* 5.3 (1976): 283–300.

Harris, J.G. *Foreign Bodies and the Body Politic: Discourses of Social Pathology in Early Modern England*. Cambridge: Cambridge University Press, 1998.

——*Sick Economies: Drama, Mercantilism, and Disease in Shakespeare's England*. Philadelphia: University of Pennsylvania Press, 2004.

——*Untimely Matter in the Time of Shakespeare*. Philadelphia: University of Pennsylvania Press, 2009.

Harris, W. 'The Frontier on which *Heart of Darkness* Stands', in P. Childs (ed.) *English Literature and Postcolonial Theory: A Reader*. Edinburgh: Edinburgh University Press, 1999 [1981]. 227–33.

Haswell, J.E. 'Images of Rape and Buggery: Paul Scott's View of the Dual Evils of Empire', *Studies in the Novel* 33.2 (2001): 202–23.

Hatlen, B. 'The Return of the Repressed/Oppressed in Bram Stoker's *Dracula*', *Minnesota Review* 15 (1980): 80–97.

Hawkes, D. *Idols of the Marketplace: Idolatry and Commodity Fetishism in English Literature, 1580–1680*. London: Palgrave Macmillan, 2001.

Hawlin, S. 'The Savages in the Forest: Decolonising William Golding', *Critical Survey* 7.2 (1995): 125–35.

Hazlitt, W. 'The Indian Jugglers', in *Table Talk: Essays on Men and Manners*. 1828. The University of Adelaide Library. http://ebooks.adelaide.edu.au/h/hazlitt/william/tabletalk/v1.9.html. 19 July 2014.

Hemans, F. *England and Spain*. 1808. Davis British Women Romantic Poets Series. http://digital.lib.ucdavis.edu/projects/bwrp/Works/HemaFEngla.htm.

Heng, G. *Empire of Magic: Medieval Romance and the Politics of Cultural Fantasy*. New York: Columbia University Press, 2003.

Henty, G.A. *The Tiger of Mysore*. 1895. Project Gutenberg. http://www.gutenberg.org/files/18813/18813-h/18813-h.htm. 19 July 2014.

——*Through the Sikh War*. New York: Charles Scribener's, 1902 [1893].

Herbert, G. *The Works of George Herbert*. Ed. F.E. Hutchinson. Oxford: Clarendon, 1972.

Herman, J. 'Men and Women of Feeling: Conventions of Sensibility and Sentimentality in the Sati Debate and Mainwaring's *The Suttee*', *Comparative Literature Studies* 42.2 (2005): 223–63.

Hoeveler, D.L. 'Charlotte Dacre's *Zofloya*: A Case Study in Miscegenation as Sexual and Racial Nausea', *European Romantic Review* 8.2 (1997): 185–99.

Hollings, M. 'Romancing the Turk: Trade, Race, and Nation in Spenser's *The Faerie Queene*', in D. Johanyak and W.S.H. Lim (eds) *The English Renaissance, Orientalism, and the Idea of Asia*. London: Palgrave Macmillan, 2010. 51–76.

302 Bibliography

Hoskins, J. 'Agency, Biography and Objects', in Christopher Tilley, Webb Keane, Susanne Kuchler, Michael Rowlands and Patricia Spyer (eds) *Handbook of Material Culture*. London: SAGE, 2006. 43–59.

Houston, C. 'Utopia, Dystopia or Anti-utopia? *Gulliver's Travels* and the Utopian Mode of Discourse', *Utopian Studies* 18.3 (2007): 425–42.

——'Traveling Nowhere: Global Utopias in the Early Modern Period', in J.G. Singh (ed.) *A Companion to the Global Renaissance: English Literature and Culture in the Era of Expansion.* Malden: Wiley-Blackwell, 2009. 82–98.

——'Introduction', in C. Houston (ed.) *New Worlds Reflected: Travel and Utopia in the Early Modern Period*. London: Ashgate, 2010. 1–14.

Howard, J.E. 'Shakespeare, Geography, and the Work of Genre on the Early Modern Stage', *MLQ* 64.3 (2003): 299–322.

Hughes, W. 'A Singular Invasion: Revisiting the Postcoloniality of Bram Stoker's *Dracula*', in A. Smith and W. Hughes (eds) *Empire and the Gothic: The Politics of Genre*. London: Palgrave Macmillan, 2003. 88–102.

Hulme, P. *Colonial Encounters: Europe and the Native Caribbean, 1492–1797*. London: Routledge, 1992 [1986].

Hunter, P. *Before Novels: The Cultural Contexts of Eighteenth-Century English Fiction*. New York: W.W. Norton, 1990.

Huttenback, R.A. 'G.A. Henty and the Imperial Stereotype', *Huntington Library Quarterly* 29.1 (1965): 63–7.

James, I. *A Counter-blaste to Tobacco*. 1604. http://www.laits.utexas.edu/poltheory/james/blaste/blaste.html. 1 December 2014.

Jardine, L. *Wordly Goods: A New History of the Renaissance*. New York and London: W.W. Norton, 1996.

Jardine, L. and J. Brotton. *Global Interests: Renaissance Art between East and West*. London: Reaktion, 2000.

Jasanoff, M. 'Collectors of Empire: Objects, Conquests and Imperial Self-Fashioning', *Past and Present* 184 (2004): 109–36.

Jenkins, E.Z. 'Introduction: Exoticism, Cosmopolitanism, and Fiction's Aesthetics of Diversity', *Eighteenth-Century Fiction* 25.1 (2012): 1–7.

Johnson, S. *The History of Rasselas, Prince of Abissinia*. Ed. Geoffrey Tillotson and Brian Jenkins. Oxford: Oxford University Press, 1977 [1769].

Jones, E. '"A World of Ground": Terrestrial Space in Marlowe's "Tamburlaine" Plays', *The Yearbook of English Studies* 38.1–2 (2008): 168–82.

Jonson, B. *Bartholomew Fair*. 1614. Ed. E.A. Horsman. London: Methuen, 1968.

——*Every Man in His Humour*. 1598. Ed. G.B. Jackson. New Haven and London: Yale University Press, 1969.

——*The Masque of Blackness*, 1605, in *The Complete Masques*. Ed. Stephen Orgel. New Haven and London: Yale University Press, 1975a. 47–60.

——*The Gypsies Metamorphosed*, 1621, in *The Complete Masques*. Ed. Stephen Orgel. New Haven and London: Yale University Press, 1975b. 316–73.

——*Volpone or the Fox*. 1605–06. Ed. Philip Brockbank. London: Ernest Benn, 1977.

——*The Alchemist*. 1610. Ed. F.H. Mares. Manchester: Manchester University Press, 1979.

——'To Penshurst'. 1616. Poetry Foundation. www.poetryfoundation.org/poem/181031. 19 July 2014.

Jonson, B., G. Chapman and J. Marston. *Eastward Ho!* 1605. Ed. C.G. Petter. London: Ernest Benn, 1973.

Joseph, B. *Reading the East India Company, 1720–1840: Colonial Currencies of Gender*. Chicago: University of Chicago Press, 2004.

Jowitt, C. 'The Uses of "Piracy": Discourses of Mercantilism and Empire in Hakluyt's *The Famous Voyage of Sir Francis Drake*', in C. Houston (ed.) *New Worlds Reflected: Travel and Utopia in the Early Modern Period*. London: Ashgate, 2010. 115–35.

Joyce, J. *Ulysses*. London: Paladin, 1992 [1922].

Kaufman, H. '*King Solomon's Mines*: African Jewry, British Imperialism, and H. Rider Haggard's Diamonds', *Victorian Literature and Culture* 33 (2005): 517–39.

Kaul, S. *Eighteenth-Century British Literature and Postcolonial Studies*. Edinburgh and London: Edinburgh University Press, 2009.

Keats, J. *Poetical Works*. Ed. H.W. Garrod. London: Oxford University Press, 1973.

Keene, H.G. 'The Tomb of the Suttee', in *Under the Rose: Poems Written Chiefly in India*. London: Bell and Daldy, 1868. 131–3.

Keep, C. and D. Randall. 'Addiction, Empire, and Narrative in Arthur Conan Doyle's The Sign of the Four', *Novel* 32.3 (1999): 207–21.

Khader, J. 'Un/Speakability and Radical Otherness: The Ethics of Trauma in Bram Stoker's *Dracula*', *College Literature* 39.2 (2012): 73–97.

Kim, E.S. 'Maria Edgeworth's "A Grateful Negro": A Site for Rewriting Rebellion', *Eighteenth-Century Fiction* 16.1 (2003): 103–26.

Kipling, R. 'The Mark of the Beast', in *Life's Handicap: Being Stories of Mine Own People*. London: Macmillan, 1964 [1891]. 240–59.

——*Kim*. London: Macmillan, 1965 [1901].

——'Wressley of the Foreign Office'. 1888. https://ebooks.adelaide.edu.au/k/kipling/rudyard/plain/chapter33.html. 1 December 2014.

——*A Selection*. Ed. James Cochrane. Harmondsworth: Penguin, 1977.

Knapp, J. 'Elizabethan Tobacco', *Representations* 21 (1988): 26–66.

Knellwolf, C. 'The Exotic Frontier of the Imperial Imagination', *Eighteenth-Century Life* 26.3 (2002): 10–30.

Kowaleski-Wallace, B. 'Tea, Gender, and Domesticity in Eighteenth-Century England', *Studies in Eighteenth-Century Culture* 23 (1994): 131–45.

Kramp, M. 'The Woman, the Gypsies, and England: Harriet Smith's National Role', *College Literature* 31.1 (2004): 147–68.

Krishnan, S. 'Opium and Empire: The Transports of Thomas de Quincey', *Boundary 2* 33.2 (2006): 203–34.

Krishnaswamy, R. *Effeminism: The Economy of Colonial Desire*. Ann Arbor: University of Michigan Press, 1998.

Kunow, R. 'American Studies as Mobility Studies: Some Terms and Constellations', in Winfried Fluck, Donald E. Pease and John Carlos Rowe (eds) *Re-Framing the Transnational Turn in American Studies*. Hanover: Dartmouth College Press, 2011. 245–74.

Lamb, C. 'Old China', https://ebooks.adelaide.edu.au/l/lamb/charles/elia/book2.24.html. unpaginated. Accessed 19 May 2015.

Lamb, J. *Preserving the Self in the South Seas, 1680–1840*. Chicago and London: University of Chicago Press, 2001.

Larkin, P. *Collected Poems*. Ed. Anthony Thwaite. London: Faber & Faber, 2003.

Lauzon, M. 'Welsh Indians and Savage Scots: History, Antiquarianism, and Indian Languages in 18th-Century Britain', *History of European Ideas* 34 (2008): 250–69.

Leask, N. *English Romantic Writers and the East: Anxieties of Empire*. Cambridge: Cambridge University Press, 1993.

——'"Wandering through Eblis": Absorption and Containment in Romantic Exoticism', in T. Fulford and P.J. Kitson (eds) *Romanticism and Colonialism: Writing and Empire, 1780–1830*. Cambridge: Cambridge University Press, 2005 [1998].

Lee, C.H. (ed.). *Western Visions of the Far East in a Transpacific Age, 1522–1657*. London: Ashgate, 2012.

Lee, D. 'Yellow Fever and the Slave Trade: Coleridge's *The Rime of the Ancient Mariner*', *ELH* 65.3 (1998): 675–700.

——*Slavery and the Romantic Imagination*. Philadelphia: University of Pennsylvania Press, 2002.

Lester, A. 'Obtaining the "Due Observance of Justice": The Geographies of Global Humanitarianism', *Environment and Planning D* 20.3 (2000): 277–93.

——'Humanism, Race and the Colonial Frontier', *Transactions of British Geographers* New Series 37 (2012): 132–48.

304 Bibliography

Levine, P. 'States of Undress: Nakedness and the Colonial Imagination', *Victorian Studies* 50.2 (2008): 189–219.

——'Naked Truths: Bodies, Knowledge, and the Erotics of Colonial Power', *Journal of British Studies* 52.1 (2013): 5–25.

Lew, J.W. 'The Plague of Imperial Desire: Montesquieu, Gibbon, Brougham, and Mary Shelley's *The Last Man*', in T. Fulford and P.J. Kitson (eds) *Romanticism and Colonialism: Writing and Empire, 1780–1830*. Cambridge: Cambridge University Press, 2005 [1998]. 261–78.

Lewis, P. '"His Sympathies Were in the Right Place": *Heart of Darkness* and the Discourse of National Character', *Nineteenth-Century Literature* 53.2 (1998): 211–44.

Lewis, R. *Rethinking Orientalism: Women, Travel and the Ottoman Harem*. London: I.B. Tauris, 2004.

Lin, L. 'The Irony of Colonial Humanism: *A Passage to India* and the Politics of Post-humanism', *Ariel* 28.4 (1997): 133–53.

Logan, M.K. *Narrating Africa: George Henty and the Fiction of Empire*. New York: Garland, 1999.

Long, A. 'The Hidden and the Visible in British Orientalism: The Case of Lawrence of Arabia', *Middle East Critique* 18.1 (2009): 21–37.

Lootens, T. 'Victorian Poetry and Patriotism', in J. Bristow (ed.) *The Cambridge Companion to Victorian Poetry*. Cambridge: Cambridge University Press, 2002. 255–79.

Low, G.C.-L. *White Skins, Black Masks: Representation and Colonialism*. London and New York: Routledge, 1996.

Lowe, L. *Critical Terrains: French and British Orientalisms*. Ithaca and London: Cornell University Press, 1991.

Lysack, K. 'Goblin Markets: Victorian Women Shoppers at Liberty's Oriental Bazaar', *Nineteenth-Century Contexts* 27.2 (2005): 139–65.

Mack, M. *The Garden and the City: Retirement and Politics in the Later Poetry of Pope, 1731–1743*. Toronto: University of Toronto Press, 1969.

MacPhee, G. *Postwar British Literature and Postcolonial Studies*. Edinburgh and London: Edinburgh University Press, 2011.

Mahood, M.M. 'Paul Scott's Guardians', *Yearbook of English Studies* 13 (1983): 244–58.

Makdisi, S. *Romantic Imperialism: Universal Empire and the Culture of Modernity*. Cambridge: Cambridge University Press, 1998.

Malchow, H.R. *Gothic Images of Race in Nineteenth-Century Britain*. Stanford: Stanford University Press, 1996.

Mani, L. *Contentious Traditions: The Debate on Sati in Colonial India*. Berkeley: University of California Press, 1998.

Mann, M. 'Dealing with Oriental Despotism: British Jurisdiction in Bengal, 1772–93', in H. Fischer-Tiné and M. Mann (eds) *Colonialism as Civilizing Mission: Cultural Ideology in British India*. London: Anthem, 2004. 29–48.

Mannoni, O. *Prospero and Caliban: The Psychology of Colonization*. Trans. Pamela Powesland. London: Methuen, 1964.

Markley, R. *The Far East and the English Imagination, 1600–1730*. New York: Cambridge University Press, 2006.

Marlowe, C. *The Complete Plays*. Ed. J.B. Steane. Harmondsworth: Penguin, 1975.

Marryat, F. *The Blood of the Vampire*. Ed. Greta Depledge. Brighton: Victorian Secrets, 2010 [1897].

Marvell, A. *The Poems and Letters*. Ed. H.M. Margoliouth. Vol. 1. *Poems*. Revised by Pierre Legouis and E.E. Duncan-Jones. Oxford: Clarendon, 1971.

Massinger, P. *The Renegado*, 1630, in *The Plays of Philip Massinger*. Ed. Francis Cunningham. London: John Camden Hotten, n.d. 133–65.

——*The Plays and Poems of Philip Massinger*. Ed P. Edwards and C. Gibson. Vol. IV. Oxford: Oxford University Press, 2012.

Matthews, J. 'Back where they Belong: Gypsies, Kidnapping and Assimilation in Victorian Children's Literature', *Romani Studies* 5 20.2 (2010): 137–59.

Maturin, C. *Melmoth the Wanderer*. London: Penguin, 2012 [1820].

Maurer, S.L. 'Fathers, Sons, and Lovers: The Transformation of Masculine Authority in Dryden's *Aureng-Zebe*', *The Eighteenth Century* 46.2 (2005): 151–73.

McCants, A.E.C. 'Exotic Goods, Popular Consumption, and the Standard of Living: Thinking about Globalization in the Early Modern World', *Journal of World History* 18.4 (2007): 433–62.

McClintock, A. *Imperial Leather: Race, Gender and Sexuality in the Colonial Contest*. London: Routledge, 1994.

McInelly, B.C. 'Expanding Empires, Expanding Selves: Colonialism, the Novel, and *Robinson Crusoe*', *Studies in the Novel* 35.1 (2003): 1–21.

McLaughlin, J. *Writing the Urban Jungle: Reading Empire in London from Doyle to Eliot*. Charlottesville and London: University Press of Virginia, 2000.

McMahon, D.H. '"Quick, Ethel, Your Rifle!": Portable Britishness and Flexible Gender Roles in G.A. Henty's Books For Boys', *Studies in the Novel* 42.1/2 (2010): 154–72.

Mellor, A.K. 'Embodied Cosmopolitanism and the British Romantic Woman Writer', *European Romantic Review* 17.3 (2006): 289–300.

Merry, R. 'The Wounded Soldier'. 1799. British War Poetry in the Age of Romanticism, 1793–1815. University of Maryland. http://www.rc.umd.edu/editions/warpoetry/1799/1799_12.html.

Mezey, J.H. 'Mourning the Death of the Raj? Melancholia as Historical Engagement in Paul Scott's *Raj Quartet*', *Studies in the Novel* 38.3 (2006): 327–52.

Michasiw, K.I. 'Charlotte Dacre's Postcolonial Moor', in A. Smith and W. Hughes (eds) *Empire and the Gothic: The Politics of Genre*. London: Palgrave Macmillan, 2003. 35–55.

Michie, E. 'From Siminized Irish to Oriental Despots: Heathcliff, Rochester and Racial Difference', *NOVEL: A Forum on Fiction* 25.2 (1992): 1–17.

Middleton, T. *Triumphs of Honour and Industry*, in *The Works of Thomas Middleton*. Ed. A.H. Bullen. Vol. VII. London: John C. Nimmo, 1886.

Mill, J.S. 'On Liberty'. 1859. https://ebooks.adelaide.edu.au/m/mill/john_stuart/m645o/. 1 December 2014.

Milton, J. *Paradise Lost*. 1667. The John Milton Reading Room. Dartmouth College. http://www.dartmouth.edu/~milton/reading_room/pl/book_1/index.shtml. 19 July 2014.

Min, E.K. 'Thomas Percy's *Chinese Miscellanies* and the *Reliques of Ancient English Poetry* (1765)', *Eighteenth-Century Studies* 43.3 (2010): 307–24.

Montagu, M.W. *Letters from Turkey*. 1763. The University of Adelaide Library. http://ebooks.adelaide.edu.au/m/montagu/mary_wortley/letters. 20 July 2014.

Montgomery, J. *The West-Indies and Other Poems*. London: Longman, Hurst, Rees, Orme and Brown, 1823.

Montrose, L.A. 'Spenser's Domestic Domain: Poetry, Property, and the Early Modern Subject', in M. de Grazia, M. Quilligan and P. Stallybrass (ed.) *Subject and Object in Renaissance Culture*. Cambridge: Cambridge University Press, 1996. 83–130.

Moore, T. *Lalla Rookh: An Oriental Romance*. New Delhi: Rupa, 2002 [1817].

More, T. *Utopia*. 1516. Trans. and ed. R.M. Adams. New York and London: W.W. Norton, 2003.

Moreno, B.G. 'Gothic Excess and Aesthetic Ambiguity in Charlotte Dacre's *Zofloya*', *Women's Writing* 14.3 (2007): 419–34.

Morris, J. *Heaven's Command: An Imperial Progress*. Harmondsworth: Penguin, 1984.

Morton, T. 'Blood Sugar', in T. Fulford and P.J. Kitson (eds) *Romanticism and Colonialism: Writing and Empire, 1780–1830*. Cambridge: Cambridge University Press, 2005 [1998]. 87–106.

Motteux, P. *A Poem Upon Tea*. London: J. Johnson, 1712.

Mui, H.-C. and L.H. Mui. 'Smuggling and the British Tea Trade before 1784', *The American Historical Review* 74.1 (1968): 44–73.

Munro, M. 'Wild Thing: Noble Savages, Exoticisms and Postcolonial Space in Jacques-Stephen Alexis's *Les Arbres Musciens*', *French Studies* LVII.1 (2003): 55–67.

Nashe, T. *The Unfortunate Traveller*. Ed. J.B. Steane. Harmondsworth: Penguin, 1978.

306 Bibliography

Nayar, P.K. *English Writing and India, 1600–1920: Colonizing Aesthetics*. London and New York: Routledge, 2008.

——'The "Disorderly Memsahib": Political Domesticity in Alice Perrin's Empire Fiction', *Brno Studies in English* 38.1 (2012): 123–38.

——'The Interracial Sublime: Gender and Race in Charlotte Dacre's *Zofloya*', *Géneros* 2.3 (2013a): 233–54.

——*The English Romantic Poets: An Anthology*. Hyderabad: Orient BlackSwan, 2013b.

Neill, A. 'Buccaneer Ethnography: Nature, Culture, and Nation in the Journals of William Dampier', *Eighteenth-Century Studies* 33 (2000): 165–80.

Nord, D.E. 'Marks of Race: Gypsy Figures and Eccentric Femininity in Nineteenth-Century Women's Writing', *Victorian Studies* 41 (1998): 189–210.

Nordius, J. '"A Kind of Living Death": Gothicizing the Colonial Encounter in Charlotte Smith's *The Old Manor House*', *English Studies* 86.1 (2005): 40–50.

Novak, M. *Economics and the Fiction of Daniel Defoe*. California: University of California Press, 1962.

Nussbaum, F.A. *Torrid Zones: Maternity, Sexuality, and Empire in Eighteenth-Century English Narratives*. Baltimore and London: Johns Hopkins University Press, 1995.

——*The Limits of the Human: Fictions of Anomaly, Race, and Gender in the Long Eighteenth Century*. Cambridge: Cambridge University Press, 2003.

——'Between "Oriental" and "Blacks So Called", 1688–1788', in D. Carey and L. Festa (eds) *The Postcolonial Enlightenment: Eighteenth-Century Colonialism and Postcolonial Theory*. Oxford: Oxford University Press, 2009. 137–66.

O'Brien, K. '"These Nations Newton Made his Own": Poetry, Knowledge, and British Imperial Globalization', in D. Carey and L. Festa (eds) *The Postcolonial Enlightenment: Eighteenth-Century Colonialism and Postcolonial Theory*. Oxford: Oxford University Press, 2009. 281–303.

O'Brien, R.V. 'Cannibalism in Spenser's *Faerie Queene*, Ireland and America', in K. Guest (ed.) *Eating their Words: Cannibalism and the Boundaries of Cultural Identity*. Albany: State University of New York Press, 2001. 35–56.

O'Dell, B.D. 'Performing the Imperial Abject: The Ethics of Cocaine in Arthur Conan Doyle's *The Sign of Four*', *Journal of Popular Culture* 45.5 (2012): 979–99.

O'Quinn, D. 'Who Owns What: Slavery, Property, and Eschatological Compensation in Thomas de Quincey's Opium Writings', *Texas Studies in Literature and Language* 45.3 (2003): 262–92.

Orwell, G. *Burmese Days*. Harmondsworth: Penguin, 1981 [1934].

Overton, M., J. Whittle, D. Dean and A. Hann. *Production and Consumption in English Households, 1600–1750*. London and New York: Routledge, 2004.

Owenson, S. *The Missionary: An Indian Tale*. London: J.J. Stockdale, 1811. 3 vols.

Page, J.W. *Imperfect Sympathies: Jews and Judaism in British Romantic Literature and Culture*. London: Palgrave Macmillan, 2004.

Parker, P. '"Rude Mechanicals"', in M. de Grazia, M. Quilligan and P. Stallybrass (eds) *Subject and Object in Renaissance Culture*. Cambridge: Cambridge University Press, 1996. 43–82.

Parkes, S. '"More Dead than Alive": The Return of Not-Orlando in Charlotte Smith's *The Old Manor House*', *European Romantic Review* 22.6 (2011): 765–84.

Paton, D. 'Punishment, Crime, and the Bodies of Slaves in Eighteenth-Century Jamaica', *Journal of Social History* (2001): 923–54.

Paxton, N.L. 'Mobilising Chivalry: Rape in British Novels about the Indian Uprising of 1857', *Victorian Studies* 36.1 (1992): 5–30.

Peacham, H. *Minerva Brittania*. London: Printed in Shoe-lane at the Signe of the Faulcon by Wa: Dight, n.d. [1612].

Pease, D.E. 'Introduction: Re-Mapping the Transnational Turn', in W. Fluck, D.E. Pease and J.C. Rowe (eds) *Re-Framing the Transnational Turn in American Studies*. Hanover: Dartmouth College Press, 2011. 1–46.

Peck, J. *Maritime Fiction: Sailors and the Sea in British and American Novels, 1719–1917*. Basingstoke: Palgrave, 2001.
Pennell, S. 'Consumption and Consumerism in Early Modern England', *The Historical Journal* 42.2 (1999): 549–64.
Pepys, S. *Diary of Samuel Pepys*. www.gutenberg.org/files/4125/4125-h/4125-h.htm.
Perrin, A. *The Charm*. New York: Desmond Fitzgerald, 1910.
——*The Anglo-Indians*. London: Methuen, 1913 [1912].
——*Government House*. Leipzig: Bernhard Tauchnitz, 1925.
——*The Woman in the Bazaar*. London: Cassell and Co, 1926 [1914].
Peters, L. *Orphan Texts: Victorian Orphans, Culture and Empire*. Manchester: Manchester University Press, 2000.
Phillips, R. *Mapping Men and Empire: A Geography of Adventure*. London: Routledge, 1995.
Pick, D. *Faces of Degeneration*. Cambridge: Cambridge University Press, 1989.
Piper, K.L. 'Inuit Diasporas: *Frankenstein* and the Inuit in England', *Romanticism* 13.1 (2007): 63–75.
Plasa, C. '"Silent Revolt": Slavery and the Politics of Metaphor in *Jane Eyre*', in C. Plasa and B.J. Ring (eds) *The Discovery of Slavery: Aphra Behn to Toni Morrison*. London and New York: Routledge, 1994. 64–93.
Plotz, John (2007) 'The First Strawberries in India: Cultural Portability in Victorian Greater Britain', *Victorian Studies* 49.4 (2007): 659–84.
Poole, W. 'Kepler's *Somnium* and Francis Godwin's *The Man in the Moone*: Births of Science-Fiction 1593–1638', in C. Houston (ed.) *New Worlds Reflected: Travel and Utopia in the Early Modern Period*. London: Ashgate, 2010. 57–70.
Pope, A. *The Poems of Alexander Pope*. Ed. John Butt. New Haven: Yale University Press, 1963.
Porter, D. 'Chinoiserie and the Aesthetics of Illegitimacy', *Studies in Eighteenth-Century Culture* 28 (1999): 27–54.
——'Monstrous Beauty: Eighteenth-Century Fashion and the Aesthetics of the Chinese Taste', *Eighteenth-Century Studies* 35.3 (2002): 395–411.
Pratt, M.L. *Imperial Eyes: Travel Writing and Transculturation*. London and New York: Routledge, 2003 [1992].
Pringle, T. *The Poetical Works*. London: Edward Moxon, 1839.
Punter, D. *The Literature of Terror: A History of Gothic Fictions from 1765 to the Present Day*. London: Longman, 1980.
Quadfleig, H. '"As Mannerly and Civill as any of Europe": Early Modern Travel Writing and the Exploration of the English Self', in G. Hooper and T. Youngs (eds) *Perspectives on Travel Writing*. London: Ashgate, 2004. 27–40.
Quilligan, M. 'Freedom, Service, and the Trade in Slaves: The Problem of Labor in Paradise Lost', in M. de Grazia, M. Quilligan and P. Stallybrass (eds) *Subject and Object in Renaissance Culture*. Cambridge: Cambridge University Press, 1996. 213–34.
——'On the Renaissance Epic: Spenser and Slavery', *South Atlantic Quarterly* 100.1 (2001): 16–39.
Raleigh, W. *The Discovery of the Large, Rich, and Beautiful Empire of Guiana*. https://archive.org/details/discoverylarger00schogoog.
Randel, F. 'The Political Geography of Horror in Mary Shelley's *Frankenstein*', *ELH* 70.2 (2003): 465–91.
Reed, J. 'English Imperialism and the Unacknowledged Crime of *The Moonstone*', *Clio* 2.3 (1973): 281–90.
Richardson, A. 'Darkness Visible? Race and Representation in Bristol Abolitionist Poetry, 1770–1810', in T. Fulford and P.J. Kitson (eds) *Romanticism and Colonialism: Writing and Empire, 1780–1830*. Cambridge: Cambridge University Press, 1998. 129–47.
Richetti, J. *Daniel Defoe*. Woodbridge: Twayne Publishers, 1987.
Ridley, James. 'Sadak and Kalasrade' [Tale IX], in *The Tales of the Genii, or the Delightful Lessons of Horam, the Son of Asmar*. Vol. II. London: C. Cooke, n.d. 57–161.

Riley, D. *'Am I That Name?': Feminism and the Category of 'Women' in History*. Minneapolis: University of Minnesota Press, 1988.

Rivero, A.J. 'Aphra Behn's *Oroonoko* and the "Blank Spaces" of Colonial Fictions', *Studies in English Literature 1500–1900* 39.3 (1999): 443–62.

Roberts, L. 'The "Shivering Sands" of Reality: Narration and Knowledge in Wilkie Collins's *The Moonstone*', *Victorian Review* 23.2 (1997): 165–83.

Robinson, B.S. *Islam and Early Modern English Literature: The Politics of Romance from Spenser to Milton*. London: Palgrave Macmillan, 2007.

Romero, J.S. 'Failed Exorcism: Kurtz's Spectral Status and its Ideological Function In Conrad's "Heart of Darkness"', *Atlantis* 33.2 (2011): 43–60.

Roque, R. 'Stories, Skulls, and Colonial Collections', *Configurations* 19.1 (2011): 1–23.

Roscoe, W. 'The Wrongs of Africa', in *The Poetical Works*. Liverpool: Henry Young, 1853. 25–70.

Rosenthal, L.J. 'The Queen of Sorrow and the Knight of the Indies: Cosmopolitan Possibilities in *The Recess* and *The New Cosmetic*', *Eighteenth-Century Fiction* 25.1 (2012): 9–35.

Rossetti, Christina. *The Complete Poems*. Ed. R.W. Crump. Vol. 1. Baton Rouge: Louisiana State University Press, 1979.

Rousseau, G.S. and R. Porter. 'Introduction', in *Exoticism in the Enlightenment*. Manchester: Manchester University Press, 1990. 1–22.

Roy, A. 'The Fabulous Imperialist Semiotic of Wilkie Collins's *The Moonstone*', *New Literary History* 24.3 (1993): 657–81.

Roy, Anindyo. *Civility, Literature and Culture in British India, 1822–1922*. London and New York: Routledge, 2005.

Roy, P. *Indian Traffic: Identities in Question in Colonial and Postcolonial India*. Berkeley: University of California Press, 1998.

Royle, N. *The Uncanny*. Manchester: Manchester University Press, 2003.

R.T. 'The Worn Soldier'. 1808. British War Poetry in the Age of Romanticism, 1793–1815. University of Maryland. http://www.rc.umd.edu/editions/warpoetry/1808/1808_3.html.

Rubiés, J.-P. 'Oriental Despotism and European Orientalism: Botero to Montesquieu', *Journal of Early Modern History* 9.1–2 (2005): 109–80.

Rudd, A. *Sympathy and India in British Literature, 1770–1830*. London: Palgrave Macmillan, 2011.

Rundle, E. 'Caliban's Legacy: Primate Dramas and the Performance of Species', *The Drama Review* 51.1 (2007): 49–62.

Russell, G. 'The Army, the Navy, and the Napoleonic Wars', in C.L. Johnson and C. Tuite (eds) *A Companion to Jane Austen*. Malden: Wiley-Blackwell, 2009. 261–71.

Ryan, S. 'Inscribing the Emptiness: Cartography, Exploration and the Construction of Australia', in C. Tiffin and A. Lawson (eds) *De-Scribing Empire: Post-Colonialism and Textuality*. London and New York: Routledge, 1994. 115–30.

Sacks, D.H. 'Rebuilding Solomon's Temple: Richard Haklyut's Great Instauration', in C. Houston (ed.) *New Worlds Reflected: Travel and Utopia in the Early Modern Period*. London: Ashgate, 2010. 17–55.

Saglia, D. 'The Exotic Politics of the Domestic: The Alhambra as Symbolic Place in British Romantic Poetry', *Comparative Literature Studies* 34.3 (1997): 197–225.

Said, E. *Orientalism*. New York: Vintage, 1978.

——*Culture and Imperialism*. London: Vintage, 1994 [1993].

Sainsbury, A. 'Married to the Empire: The Anglo-Indian Domestic Novel', in B.J. Moore Gilbert (ed.) *Writing India, 1757–1990: The Literature of British India*. Manchester: Manchester University Press, 1996. 163–87.

——'"Not Yet … Not There": Breaking the Bonds of Marriage in E.M. Forster's *A Passage to India*', *Critical Survey* 21.1 (2009): 59–73.

Sánchez, J.L. 'Byron, Spain, and the Romance of *Childe Harold's Pilgrimage*', *European Romantic Review* 20.4 (2009): 443–64.

Sawday, J. *The Body Emblazoned: Dissection and the Human Body in Renaissance Culture*. London and New York: Routledge, 1996.

Schonhorn, M. *Defoe's Politics: Parliament, Power, Kingship and Robinson Crusoe*. Cambridge: Cambridge University Press, 1977.

Schotland, S.D. 'The Slave's Revenge: The Terror in Charlotte Dacre's *Zofloya*', *Western Journal of Black Studies* 33.2 (2009): 123–31.

Scott, P. *The Jewel in the Crown*. London: Granada, 1978 [1966].

——*The Day of the Scorpion*. New York: Avon, 1979 [1968].

Scott, W. *The Surgeon's Daughter*. 1827. The University of Adelaide Library. http://ebooks.adelaide.edu.au/s/cott/walter/surgeon. 19 July 2014.

Scrivener, M. *Jewish Representation in British Literature, 1780–1840: After Shylock*. London: Palgrave Macmillan, 2011.

Seaton, E. 'Marlowe's Map', *Essays and Studies* 10 (1924): 13–35.

Seidel, M. 'Gulliver's Travels and the Contracts of Fiction', in John Richetti (ed.) *The Cambridge Companion to The Eighteenth-Century Novel*. Cambridge: Cambridge University Press, 1998. 72–89.

Sell, J.P.A. *Rhetoric and Wonder in English Travel Writing, 1560–1613*. London: Ashgate, 2006.

Sen, I. *Woman and Empire: Representations in the Writings of British India (1858–1900)*. Hyderabad: Orient Longman, 2002.

Senf, C. '*Dracula*: The Unseen Face in the Mirror', *Journal of Narrative Technique* 9.3 (1979): 160–70.

Shakespeare, W. *Antony and Cleopatra*, in *The Norton Shakespeare*. Ed. S. Greenblatt, J.E. Howard and K.E. Maus. New York and London: W.W. Norton, 2008. 2633–722.

——*The Comedy of Errors*, in *The Norton Shakespeare*. Ed. S. Greenblatt, J.E. Howard and K.E. Maus. New York and London: W.W. Norton, 2008. 717–65.

——*Hamlet*, in *The Norton Shakespeare*. Ed. S. Greenblatt, J.E. Howard and K.E. Maus. New York and London: W.W. Norton, 2008. 1683–2108.

——*The Merchant of Venice*, in *The Norton Shakespeare*. Ed. S. Greenblatt, J.E. Howard and K.E. Maus. New York and London: W.W. Norton, 2008. 1111–2108.

——*A Midsummer Night's Dream*, in *The Norton Shakespeare*. Ed. S. Greenblatt, J.E. Howard and K.E. Maus. New York and London: W.W. Norton, 2008. 839–96.

——*Othello*, in *The Norton Shakespeare*. Ed. S. Greenblatt, J.E. Howard and K.E. Maus. New York and London: W.W. Norton, 2008. 2109–92.

——*The Tempest*, in *The Norton Shakespeare*. Ed. S. Greenblatt, J.E. Howard and K.E. Maus. New York and London: W.W. Norton, 2008. 3055–116.

——*Titus Andronicus*, in *The Norton Shakespeare*. Ed. S. Greenblatt, J.E. Howard and K.E. Maus. New York and London: W.W. Norton, 2008. 399–464.

Sharpe, J. 'The Unspeakable Limits of Rape: Colonial Violence and Counter-Insurgency', *Genders* 10 (1991): 25–46.

Shelley, M. *Frankenstein*. Ed. J. Paul Hunter. New York and London: W.W. Norton, 1996 [1818].

——*The Last Man*. London: Wordsworth, 2004 [1826].

Shin, H. 'Single Parenting, Homeschooling: Prospero, Caliban, Miranda', *Studies in English Literature* 48.2 (2008): 373–93.

Showalter, E. '*A Passage to India* as "Marriage Fiction": Forster's Sexual Politics', *Women and Literature* 5.2 (1977): 3–16.

Silverman, K. 'White Skin, Brown Masks: The Double Mimesis, or with Lawrence in Arabia', *differences* 1.3 (1989).

Sinha, Mrinalini. *Colonial Masculinity: The 'Manly Englishman' and the 'Effeminate Bengali' in the Late Nineteenth Century*. Manchester: Manchester University Press, 1995.

——'Britishness, Clubbability, and the Colonial Sphere: The Genealogy of the Imperial Institution of Colonial India', *The Journal of British Studies* 40.4 (2001): 489–521

——'Triangular Erotics: The Politics of Masculinity, Imperialism and Big-Game Hunting in Rider Haggard's *She*', *Critical Survey* 20.3 (2008): 27–43.

310 Bibliography

Skinner, S. 'Obscurity, Apophasis, and the Critical Imagination: The Unsayable in *Heart of Darkness*', *Conradiana* 42.1–2 (2010): 93–106.
Smith, C. *The Emigrants*. London: T. Cadell, 1793. British Women Romantic Writers Project. University of California at Davis. http://digital.lib.ucdavis.edu/projects/bwrp/Works/SmitCEmigr.htm. 22 November 2014.
——*The Old Manor House*. Ed. A.H. Ehrenpreis. London: Oxford University Press, 1969 [1793].
Smith, S.D. 'Accounting for Taste: British Coffee Consumption in Historical Perspective', *Journal of Interdisciplinary History* 27.2 (1996): 183–214.
Smollett, T. *The Expedition of Humphrey Clinker*. 1771. The University of Adelaide Library. http://ebooks.adelaide.edu.au/s/smollett/tobias/clinker/complete.html. 18 July 2014.
——*The Adventures of Roderick Random*. Oxford: Oxford University Press, 1979 [1748].
Southey, R. 'Poems on the Slave Trade'. 1797. www.pitt.edu/~ebb8/southey/poemsSlaveTrade.html. 18 July 2014.
——'The Dirge of the American Widow'. 1799. English Poetry 1579–1830: Spenser and the Tradition. http://spenserians.cath.vt.edu/TextRecord.php?action=get&textsid=38644. 18 July 2014.
——*The Minor Poems of Robert Southey*. Vol. 1. London: Longman, Hurst, Rees, Orme, and Brown, 1823.
——*A Tale of Paraguay*. Boston: S.G. Goodrich, 1827.
——*Poems of Robert Southey*. Ed. M.H. Fitzgerald. London: Henry Frowde and Oxford University Press, 1909.
Sparks, T. 'Medical Gothic and the Return of the Contagious Diseases Acts in Stoker and Machen', *Nineteenth-Century Feminisms* 6 (2002): 87–102.
Spenser, E. *The Faerie Queene*. Ed. A.C. Hamilton. London and New York: Longman, 1984.
Spivak, G.C. 'Three Women's Texts and a Critique of Imperialism', in H.L. Gates (ed.) *'Race', Writing, and Difference*. Chicago and London: University of Chicago Press, 1986. 262–80.
Stepan, N.L. *Picturing Tropical Nature*. Ithaca and London: Cornell University Press, 2001.
Stevenson, J.A. 'A Vampire in the Mirror: The Sexuality of *Dracula*', *PMLA* 103 (1988): 139–49.
Stevenson, R.L. *Treasure Island*. 1883. The University of Adelaide Library. http://ebooks.adelaide.edu.au/s/stevenson/robert_louis/s848tr/. 20 July 2014
Stieg, M.F. 'Anglo-Indian Romances: Tracts for the Times', *Journal of Popular Culture* 18.4 (1985): 3–11.
Still, J. 'Hospitable Harems? A European Woman and Oriental Spaces in the Enlightenment', *Paragraph* 32.1 (2009): 87–104.
Stoker, B. *Dracula*. Ed. Nina Auerbach and David J. Skal. New York and London: Norton, 1997.
Suleri, S. *The Rhetoric of English India*. Chicago and London: University of Chicago Press, 1992.
Suranyi, A. 'Virile Turks and Maiden Ireland: Gender and National Identity in Early Modern English Travel Literature', *Gender and History* 21.2 (2009): 241–62.
Sussman, C. *Consuming Anxieties: Consumer Protest, Gender, and British Slavery, 1713–1833*. Redwood City: Stanford University Press, 2000.
Sweeney, C. *From Fetish to Subject: Race, Modernism, and Primitivism, 1919–1935*. Connecticut: Praegar, 2004.
Swift, J. *Gulliver's Travels and Other Writings*. Ed. L.A. Landa. Boston: Houghton Mifflin, 1960a.
——'A Modest Proposal', in *Gulliver's Travels and Other Writings*. Ed. LA. Landa. Boston: Houghton Mifflin, 1960b. 439–46.
——*The Writings of Jonathan Swift*. Ed. R.A. Greenberg and W.B. Piper. New York: W.W. Norton, 1973.
——*Poetical Works*. Ed. Herbert Davis. London: Oxford University Press, 1967.
——'A Proposal that All the Ladies and Women of Ireland should Appear Constantly in Irish Manufactures'. 1729. Jonathan Swift Archive. http://jonathanswiftarchive.org.uk/browse/year/text_10_9_1.html. 1 December 2014.

Taylor, [Philip] Meadows. *Tippoo Sultaun: A Tale of the Mysore War*. New Delhi: Asian Educational Services, 1986 [1840].

Teltscher, K. '"Maidenly and well nigh effeminate": Constructions of Hindu Masculinity and Religion in Seventeenth-Century English Texts', *Postcolonial Studies* 3.2 (2000): 159–70.

Tennyson, A. *The Poems*. Ed. Christopher Ricks. London: Longmans, Green and Co., 1969.

Test, E.M. 'Seeds of Sacrifice: Amaranth, the Gardens of Tenochtitlan and Spenser's *Faerie Queene*', in J.G. Singh (ed.) *A Companion to the Global Renaissance: English Literature and Culture in the Era of Expansion*. Malden: Wiley-Blackwell, 2009. 242–62.

Tidrick, K. *Empire and the English Character*. London: I.B. Tauris, 1990.

Tilley, C. 'Objectification', in C. Tilley, W. Keane, S Küchler, M. Rowlands and P. Spyer (eds) *Handbook of Material Culture*. London: SAGE, 2006. 60–73.

Tobin, B.F. *Colonizing Nature: The Tropics in British Arts and Letters, 1760–1830*. Philadelphia: University of Pennsylvania Press, 1999.

Tomko, M. 'Abolition Poetry, National Identity, and Religion: The Case of Peter Newby's *The Wrongs of Almoona*', *The Eighteenth Century* 48.1 (2007): 25–43.

Trevor, G.H. 'The Suttee of Gorah's Wife', in *Rhymes of Rajputana*. London: Macmillan, 1894. 32–3.

Trumpener, K. 'The Time of the Gypsies: A "People without History" in the Narratives of the West', *Critical Enquiry* 18 (1992): 845–84.

——*Bardic Nationalism: The Romantic Novel and the British Empire*. Princeton: Princeton University Press, 1997.

Urry, J. *Mobilities*. Cambridge: Polity, 2007.

Vazirani, R. 'Indian Jugglers 1820 by James Green', *Literary Review* 41.3 (1998): 368. http://connection.ebscohost.com/tag/INDIAN%2BJugglers%2B1820%2Bby%2BJames%2BGreen%2B%2528Poem%2529. 20 July 2014.

Venturi, F. 'Oriental Despotism', *Journal of the History of Ideas* 24 (1963): 133–42.

Vine, S. '"That Mild Beam": Enlightenment and Enslavement in William Blake's *Visions of the Daughters of Albion*', in C. Plasa and B.J. Ring (eds) *The Discovery of Slavery: Aphra Behn to Toni Morrison*. London and New York: Routledge, 1994. 40–63.

Vint, S. 'Animals and Animality from the Island of Moreau to the Uplift Universe', *Yearbook of English Studies* 37.2 (2007): 85–102.

Viragh, A. 'Can the Vampire Speak? Dracula as Discourse on Cultural Extinction', *English Literature in Transition* 56.2 (2013): 231–45.

Vitkus, D. 'Turning Turk in *Othello*: The Conversion and Damnation of the Moor', *Shakespeare Quarterly* 48.2 (1997): 145–76.

——'Turks and Jews in *The Jew of Malta*', in G.A. Sullivan, Jr., P. Cheney and A. Hadfield (eds) *Early Modern Drama: A Critical Companion*. Oxford: Oxford University Press, 2006. 61–71.

——'Adventuring Heroes in the Mediterranean: Mapping the Boundaries of Anglo-Islamic Exchange on the Early Modern Stage', *Journal of Medieval and Early Modern Studies* 37.1 (2007): 75–95.

——'The New Globalism: Transcultural Commerce, Global Systems Theory, and Spenser's Mammon', in J.G. Singh (ed.) *A Companion to the Global Renaissance: English Literature and Culture in the Era of Expansion*. Malden: Wiley-Blackwell, 2009. 31–49.

Wasson, R. 'The Politics of Dracula', *English Literature in Transition, 1880–1920* 9.1 (1966): 24–7.

Webb, W. Trego. 'The Nautch Girl', in H.K. Kaul (ed.) *Poetry of the Raj*. New Delhi: Arnold-Heinemann, 1984. 36–7.

Wells, H.G. *The Island of Dr. Moreau*. New York: Modern, 2002 [1896].

——*The War of the Worlds*. London: Penguin, 2005 [1898].

Whale, J. 'Indian Jugglers: Hazlitt, Romantic Orientalism, and the Difference of View', in T. Fulford and P.J. Kitson (eds) *Romanticism and Colonialism: Writing and Empire, 1780–1830*. Cambridge: Cambridge University Press, 2005 [1998]. 206–20.

Wheeler, R. '"My Savage," "My Man": Racial Multiplicity in *Robinson Crusoe*', *English Literary History* 62 (1995): 821–61.

312 Bibliography

White, H. 'The Forms of Wildness: Archaeology of an Idea', in E. Dudley and M.E. Novak (eds) *The Wild Man Within: An Image in Western Thought from Renaissance to Romanticism*. Pittsburgh: University of Pittsburgh Press, 1972.

Wiley, M. *Romantic Migrations: Local, National and Transnational Dispositions*. London: Palgrave Macmillan, 2008.

Wilkinson, D. 'The Apartheid of Antiquity', *World Archaeology* 43.1 (2011): 26–39.

Willburn, S. 'The Savage Magnet: Racialization of the Occult Body in Late Victorian Fiction', *Women's Writing* 15.3 (2008): 436–53.

Williams, H.M. 'On the Bill which was Passed in England for Regulating the Slave-trade', *Poems on Various Subjects*. 1823. British Women Romantic Writers Project. University of California, Davis. http://digital.lib.ucdavis.edu/projects/bwrp/Works/WillHPoems.htm#p166.

Willis, M. '"The Invisible Giant," *Dracula*, and Disease', *Studies in the Novel* 39.3 (2007): 301–25.

Wilt, J. 'The Imperial Mouth: Imperialism, the Gothic, and Science Fiction', *Journal of Popular Culture* 14.4 (1981): 618–28.

Wolfson, S.J. '"Their She Condition": Cross-Dressing and the Politics of Gender in *Don Juan*', *ELH* 54.3 (1987): 585–617.

Wordsworth, W. *Poetical Works*. Ed. Thomas Hutchinson. Revised Ed. Ernest de Selincourt. London: Oxford University Press, 1969.

Wright, J.M. 'Devouring the Disinherited: Familial Cannibalism in Maturin's *Melmoth the Wanderer*', in K. Guest (ed.) *Eating their Words: Cannibalism and the Boundaries of Cultural Identity*. Albany: State University of New York Press, 2001. 79–106.

Wu, D. (ed.). *Romantic Women Poets: An Anthology*. Oxford: Blackwell, 1997.

Wycherley, W. *The Country Wife*. 1675. Ed. David Cook and John Swannell. Manchester: Manchester University Press, 1975.

Yang, Chi-ming. 'Asia Out of Place: The Aesthetics of Incorruptibility in Behn's *Oroonoko*', *Eighteenth-Century Studies* 42.2 (2009): 235–53.

Yeğenoğlu, M. *Colonial Fantasies: Towards a Feminist Reading of Orientalism*. Cambridge: Cambridge University Press, 1998.

Young, E. *Love of Fame, The Universal Passion in Seven Characteristical Satires*. London: J. and R. Tonson and S. Draper, 1752. 5th edition.

Young, R.J.C. *Colonial Desire: Hybridity in Theory, Culture and Race*. London and New York: Routledge, 1995.

Zanger, J. 'A Sympathetic Vibration: Dracula and the Jews', *English Literature in Transition* 34.1 (1991): 33–44.

Zonana, J. 'The Sultan and the Slave: Feminist Orientalism and the Structure of *Jane Eyre*', *Signs* 18.3 (1993): 592–617.

Zutshi, C. '"Designed for Eternity": Kashmiri Shawls, Empire, and Cultures of Production and Consumption in Mid-Victorian Britain', *Journal of British Studies* 48.02 (2009): 420–40.

INDEX

abolitionism 160–72; *see also* objectification: ethics (of matter and bodies)

Auden, W.H.: 'Fleet Visit' 287–88

Bacon, F.: 'An Advertisement Touching a Holy War' 248; 'Of Travel' 13, 52; *The Advancement of Learning* 52; *The Great Instauration* 54; *The New Atlantis* 26, 29, 50, 52, 54, 275–76

Baillie, J.: 'Lines to a Teapot' 137–38

Ballantyne, R.M.: *The Coral Island* 24, 57, 83–84, 85, 121, 277; *The Gorilla Hunters* 61, 66–67; *The Young Fur Traders* 22, 25

Barbauld, A.L.: 'Eighteen Hundred and Eleven' 219–20; 'To William Wilberforce, Esq' 200–201

Beckford, W.: *Vathek* 83, 107–8, 112, 122, 250–01, 255

Behn, A.: *Oroonoko* 29, 43, 44, 45–46, 55, 58, 60, 74, 122, 148–49, 156, 249, 260, 276, 283; *The Widow Ranter* 12

Blake, W.: 'London' 28, 248; 'The Little Black Boy' 162; *Vala, or the Four Zoas* 241; *Visions of the Daughters of Albion* 272

Brontë, C.: *Jane Eyre* 63–64, 101, 147, 212–13, 244–46, 256–58, 272–73, 290n9; *Villette* 139–40, 142

Brontë, E.: *Wuthering Heights* 190, 192, 207, 256

Burns, R.: 'The Slave's Lament' 168; 'The Soldier's Return' 216

Byron, G.G.: *Childe Harold's Pilgrimage* 65, 172–73; *Don Juan* 1–2, 115–16, 124, 218–19, 273; *Sardanapalus* 123; *The Bride of Abydos* 129n16; *The Giaour* 113–14, 123; *The Island* 114–15

cannibal 39, 43–44, 57, 73n20, 79–81, 83–85, 90–91, 127n3, 128n6, 222–23

Chaucer, G.: 'The Knight's Tale' 143

chinaware 133, 142–43, 146–47

civilizing (the Other) 238–71; moral imperialism 241–46; amelioration and improvement 246–71; cultural defects 247–58; deculturation and improvement 259–71

Coleridge, S.T.: 'Monody on a Tea-kettle' 137; *The Rime of the Ancient Mariner* 34, 215, 217, 218, 275, 281

Collins, W.: *The Moonstone* 31, 55–56, 187–88, 221–22

Conrad, J.: *Heart of Darkness* 23, 32, 35–36, 49, 52–53, 56–57, 90, 159–60, 174n14, 195–97, 205, 210, 212, 278–81, 285–86

Congreve, W.: *The Way of the World* 134; *The Double Dealer* 184

cosmography 14–25

Cowper, W.: 'Charity' 48, 132, 167–68, 187; 'The Negro's Complaint' 200; 'Sweet Meat has Sour Sauce, or, the Slave Trader in the Dumps' 160–01, 187; 'The Task' 137

314 Index

Dacre, C.: 'The Poor Negro Sadi' 171–72;
Zofloya 108–12
Daborne, R.: *A Christian Turn'd Turk*
104–5, 211
Defoe, D.: *A Plan of the English Commerce*
132; *Captain Singleton* 80, 88, 130; *Moll
Flanders* 60; *Robinson Crusoe* 25, 26, 33,
43–44, 46–47, 48–49, 55, 58–60, 62–63,
73n25, 161–62, 283–84; *Roxana* 92–93;
The Compleat English Gentleman 26
degeneration (of England and Englishness)
see pathologization, discrepant
geographies
discrepant geographies 272–89
Donne, J.: 'A Valediction: Forbidding
Mourning' 27; 'Holy Sonnet VII' 33;
'Hymn to God, My God in My
Sicknesse' 33; 'Love's Progress' 16;
'Obsequies to the Lord Harrington'
15; 'The Bracelet' 182–83; 'The
Good-Morrow' 25; 'The Second
Anniversarie' 16; 'To His Mistress Going
to Bed' 16–17
Doyle, A.C.: 'A Study in Scarlet' 229; 'The
Adventure of the Empty House' 37;
'The Speckled Band' 208–9, 218; *The
Hound of the Baskervilles* 31; *The Sign of
Four* 210, 221, 222–23
Dryden, J.: *Annus Mirabilis* 20; 'To His
Sacred Majesty, A Panegyric on his
Coronation' 47; *Amboyna* 47;
Aureng-zebe 252–55, 290n6; *The Indian
Queen* 47

Edgeworth, M.: 'The Grateful Negro' 146,
157–58, 162–63, 238–39, 248, 250, 259,
266–67
ethnography of the Other 39–62; fantastic
ethnography 39–44; plenitude and
variety 45–51; inquiries 51–62
exoticisation 74–130; savage exotic
78–86; noble savage 87–90; erotic exotic
91–127; femininity (English) 91–99;
houris and harems 99–118; vulnerable
Other (woman) 118–21; masculinity
121–27

Forster, E.M.: *A Passage to India* 39, 76,
116–17, 125–26, 255–56, 271, 286

Golding, W.: *Lord of the Flies* 282–83
Grainger, J.: *Sugar-Cane: A Poem* 146,
156–58, 163
Gray, T.: 'The Progress of Poesy' 89–90

Greene, G.: *The Heart of the Matter* 69,
72n17, 283
gypsies 38, 206, 207–9, 235n15

Haggard, H.R.: *Allan Quatermain* 125, 280;
King Solomon's Mines 29, 36–37, 86, 100,
101, 116, 284; *She* 29–31, 34–35, 42,
101, 124, 209–10, 285
Hardy, T.: 'The Souls of the Slain' 286–87
Hazlitt, W.: 'The Indian Jugglers' 151–54
Hemans, F.: 'England's Dead' 69; *England
and Spain* 112, 114; 'Moorish Bridal
Song' 129n17; 'Spells of Home' 68–69;
'The Indian City' 82, 119–20; 'The
Traveller at the Source of the Nile'
64–65
Henty, G.A.: *A Roving Commission* 259,
291n15; *By Sheer Pluck* 164; *The Tiger of
Mysore* 251, 265; *Through the Sikh War*
265–66

itinerancy 10–17, 20, 22, 25–39, 62; spatial
distancing 26–28; temporal distancing
28–32; somatic geography 32–36

Johnson, S.: *Rasselas* 112–13
Jonson, B.: *Bartholomew Fair* 93, 177–78;
Volpone or the Fox 198; *The Masque of
Blackness* 191; *The Alchemist* 19; *The
Gypsies Metamorphosed* 206; 'To
Penshurst' 157; *Eastward Ho!* 104; *Every
Man in His Humour* 134
jugglers (Indian) 151–54

Kashmiri shawls 142–43
Keats, J.: *Isabella* 199–200; *Lamia* 193–94;
'To Autumn' 200
Kipling, R.: 'Chant-pagan' 274–75;
'Mandalay' 51; 'Recessional' 69; 'The
Mark of the Beast' 210, 214–15; *Kim*
38, 267–68; 'Wressley of the Foreign
Office' 125

Milton, J.: *Paradise Lost* 71n10, 174n10
Marlowe, C.: *The Jew of Malta* 144, 206;
Faustus 144; *Tamburlaine* (Parts One and
Two) 18, 45
Marvell, A.: 'Bermudas' 46, 'On the
Victory Obtained by Blake' 48
Marryat, H.: *The Blood of the Vampire*
213–14, 232
Massinger, P.: 'London's Lamentable
Estate' 180–01; *The Renegado* 91–92,
105, 211

Maturin, C.: *Melmoth the Wanderer* 17, 61, 85–86
Montagu, M.W.: *Turkish Embassy Letters* 74–75, 102–4
More, H.: 'Slavery: A Poem' 165, 187, 243; 'The Sorrows of Yamba', 164, 166
Motteux, P.: *A Poem Upon Tea* 136–37

objectification (of the Other) 130–74; consumption 132–41; matter (as spectacle) 141–54; rhetoric (of objectification) 154–72; labour 155–60; ethics (of matter and bodies) 160–72
Opie, A.: 'The Negro Boy's Tale' 166
Orwell, G.: *Burmese Days* 268, 271, 272, 282, 286, 288

pathologization (of the Other) 175–237; foreign matter 180–88; foreign bodies 188–205; unnameable things 189–97; pathogenic Other 197–205; cultural invasion 205–18; 'going native' 210–12; bloodline contamination 212–15; returning servicemen 215–18; transnational vice networks 218–25; degeneration of England 225–33
Perrin, A. 94–99
Pope, A.: 'Epistle IV: To Richard Boyle Earl of Burlington' 146; *An Essay on Man* 87; *Temple of Fame* 50; *The Rape of the Lock* 106, 135–36, 147; *Windsor Forest* 48, 145, 186

savage exotic 78–86
Scott, P.: *The Raj Quartet* 126–27, 241, 258, 286, 288, 292n21
Scott, W.: *The Surgeon's Daughter* 151
Shakespeare, W.: *A Midsummer Night's Dream* 153, 174n8; *Antony and Cleopatra* 15, 18; *Hamlet* 18–19; *Othello* 26, 39, 128n14; *The Comedy of Errors* 16, 178, 197, 220; *The Merchant of Venice* 18; *The Tempest* 247, 262–64; *Titus Andronicus* 173n6
Shelley, M.: *Frankenstein* 26, 41–42, 189, 193; *The Last Man* 62, 177, 203–4, 215, 220, 225, 229, 277
Smollett, T.: *Humphrey Clinker* 80–81, 210; *Roderick Random* 21, 34

Southey, R.: *A Tale of Paraguay* 202, 264–65, 291n14; antislavery sonnets 198–99; *Madoc* 88; 'The Dirge of the American Widow' 82, 90, 120; 'To the Genius of Africa' 202
Spenser, E.: *The Faerie Queene* 1, 17, 28–29, 45, 78–79, 133, 144, 238, 246
Stoker, B.: *Dracula* 32, 36, 194–95, 210, 223–24, 232, 235n17
Swift, J.: *Gulliver's Travels* 20–21, 26, 33–34, 42–43, 50–51, 61, 276–77; 'A Proposal that All the Ladies and Women of Ireland should Appear Constantly in Irish Manufactures' 106–7; 'A Modest Proposal' 84–85; 'Poetry: A Rhapsody' 21

tea (drinking) 136–41
Tennyson, A.L.: *Locksley Hall* 24; 'Ode on the Death of the Duke of Wellington' 69; 'Opening of the Indian and Colonial Exhibition by the Queen' 67–68; 'The Charge of the Light Brigade' 69; 'The Defence of Lucknow' 68; 'To the Queen' 63
tobacco 133–34
travel *see* itinerancy, cosmography
triumphalist geography 62–69

Williams, H.M.: 'On the Bill which was Passed in England for Regulating the Slave Trade' 167, 201
Wordsworth, W.: 'Emigrant French Clergy' 175; 'Her Eyes Are Wild' 90, 166–67; 'September 1, 1802' 175–76; 'September 1802' 225–26; 'The Complaint of a Forsaken Indian Woman' 120–21; 'The Discharged Soldier' 215; 'The Emigrant Mother' 175; 'The Female Vagrant' [*Guilt and Sorrow, or Incidents Upon Salisbury Plain*] 217–18, 220; *The Prelude* 87–88, 217, 227–29
Wycherley, W.: *The Country Wife* 146–47

Yearsley, A.: *A Poem on the Inhumanity of the Slave Trade* 168–71
Young, E.: *The Love of Fame* 184

eBooks
from Taylor & Francis
Helping you to choose the right eBooks for your Library

Add to your library's digital collection today with Taylor & Francis eBooks. We have over 50,000 eBooks in the Humanities, Social Sciences, Behavioural Sciences, Built Environment and Law, from leading imprints, including Routledge, Focal Press and Psychology Press.

Choose from a range of subject packages or create your own!

Benefits for you
- Free MARC records
- COUNTER-compliant usage statistics
- Flexible purchase and pricing options
- 70% approx of our eBooks are now DRM-free.

Benefits for your user
- Off-site, anytime access via Athens or referring URL
- Print or copy pages or chapters
- Full content search
- Bookmark, highlight and annotate text
- Access to thousands of pages of quality research at the click of a button.

Free Trials Available

We offer free trials to qualifying academic, corporate and government customers.

eCollections
Choose from 20 different subject eCollections, including:
- Asian Studies
- Economics
- Health Studies
- Law
- Middle East Studies

eFocus
We have 16 cutting-edge interdisciplinary collections, including:
- Development Studies
- The Environment
- Islam
- Korea
- Urban Studies

For more information, pricing enquiries or to order a free trial, please contact your local sales team:
UK/Rest of World: online.sales@tandf.co.uk
USA/Canada/Latin America: e-reference@taylorandfrancis.com
East/Southeast Asia: martin.jack@tandf.com.sg
India: journalsales@tandfindia.com

www.tandfebooks.com